*The American
Democratic System*

Under the Advisory Editorship of
DAVID FELLMAN
*Vilas Professor of Political Science
University of Wisconsin*

The American Democratic System

J. KEITH MELVILLE
Brigham Young University

HARPER & ROW, PUBLISHERS
New York   Hagerstown   San Francisco   London

Copyright © 1974, 1975 by Harper & Row, Publishers, Inc.

All rights reserved. Printed in the United States of America. No part of this book may be used or reproduced in any manner whatsoever without written permission except in the case of brief quotations embodied in critical articles and reviews. For information address Harper & Row, Publishers, Inc., 10 East 53rd Street, New York, N.Y. 10022.

Library of Congress Catalog Card Number: 73-15383
ISBN: 0-06-044399-5

Designed by Emily Harste

CONTENTS

PREFACE	vii
PART ONE: THE FOUNDATIONS OF AMERICAN POLITICS	1
1. The Birth of a Constitutional Government	3
2. American Constitutional Principles	18
3. Fundamental Freedoms	45
PART TWO: CITIZEN ROLES IN AMERICAN POLITICS	77
4. Political Participation	79
5. Interest Group Politics	100
6. Political Parties	116
7. Electing the Policy Makers	136
PART THREE: PUBLIC POLICY MAKERS	165
8. The American Executive	167
9. The Legislative Process	192
10. Justice and the Judicial Process	221
PART FOUR: PUBLIC POLICIES IN AMERICA	247
11. Financing Public Functions	249
12. America: The Service State	267
13. America: The Welfare State	282
14. America: War and Peace	297

APPENDIX

The Declaration of Independence	313
Articles of Confederation	316
The Constitution of the United States of America	323

INDEX	341

LIST OF FIGURES

Figure 2.1 Branches of Government	31
Figure 2.2 British Government	32
Figure 2.3 Checks and Balances	33
Figure 2.4 Distribution of Powers	39
Figure 4.1 Core-Periphery Model of Political Participation	95
Figure 4.2 Party-Affiliation Model	96
Figure 6.1 Party Umbrellas	121
Figure 6.2 The Party and the Participants	122
Figure 6.3 Party Organization	131
Figure 8.1 Executive Organization	173
Figure 8.2 Executive and Independent Agencies	182
Figure 8.3 President Nixon's Proposed Reorganization of the Departments	183
Figure 9.1 A Typical Way a Bill Becomes a Law	213
Figure 9.2 Four-Party Structure of Congress	220
Figure 10.1 The Criminal Justice Continuum	224
Figure 10.2 The United States Court System	235
Figure 11.1 Budget Cycle	252
Figure 11.2 Economic Cycles	255
Figure 11.3 Budget Totals Since 1974	258
Figure 11.4 Relation of Budget Authority to Outlays—1976 Budget	259
Figure 11.5 Budget Receipts: 1966–1976	261
Figure 11.6 The Budget Dollar (Fiscal Year 1976 Estimate)	262
Figure 11.7 Changing Priorities	265

LIST OF TABLES

Table 2.1 Similarities Between British and American Constitutions	23
Table 4.1 Vote by Groups in Presidential Elections (Since 1952)	92
Table 6.1 Changing Party Percentages 1940–73	119
Table 11.1 Budget Receipts by Source and Outlays by Function 1966–76 (In Billions of Dollars)	264

PREFACE

1973 will long be remembered as the year in which the American democratic system faced a series of crises unequaled in its history. Basic constitutional principles, especially the principle of separation of powers, were invoked in conflicts over executive privilege to withhold information from Congress and the courts and their need to acquire this information to fulfill their responsibilities; presidential impoundment of congressionally appropriated funds; administrative dismantlement of programs and agencies established by Congress; the war powers of Congress and the President; and court action on these and other constitutional controversies.

Political ethics and public morality were thrust to the forefront of the minds of Americans as Watergate hearings and court action unfolded incredible accounts of political "dirty tricks" and the compromising influence of money in politics; major economic and domestic problems worsened as a beleaguered President, with waning public support, seemed incapable of providing the leadership America needed. And, if this were not enough, criminal charges brought about the resignation of the Vice-President, prompting the selection of his successor under provisions of the Twenty-fifth Amendment.

Probably never in our political history has there been a greater need for citizen understanding of and participation in American politics and government. This book attempts to provide a brief general introduction to the fundamentals of the American political system: its constitutional principles, citizen roles in the electoral process, the institutions of government, and its basic functions. The book was inspired by my many students in American government over the years who demanded a course which was motivating, meaningful, and relevant to the real world of politics. Because of the encouragement and help of colleagues, graduate assistants, and many others too numerous to mention, the book has become a reality. It is greatly improved because of a number of helpful critical reviews of the manuscript—especially those of David Fellman of the University of Wisconsin, Gene R. Urey of Susquehanna University, and the competent editorial staff of Dodd, Mead & Company. And finally, but by no means last, this book is dedicated to my wife Ruth and our children, who understand the necessity of civic involvement.

J. KEITH MELVILLE

*The American
Democratic System*

PART ONE
The Foundations of American Politics

1
THE BIRTH OF A CONSTITUTIONAL GOVERNMENT

An old bellman, so the story goes, waited in the steeple of Pennsylvania's brick state house—later to be known as Independence Hall—for a signal from a boy stationed at the door below. A declaration of liberty was expected from the patriots of the Second Continental Congress, and when the boy clapped his hands and shouted, "Ring! Ring!" the old man resolutely tolled the bell, which was appropriately inscribed with words from Leviticus: "Proclaim liberty throughout all the land unto all the inhabitants thereof." [1]

The formal approval of the Declaration of Independence on July 4, 1776, was not only a fateful political resolution, but the birth certificate of a new nation—a document which contained timeless philosophical principles and a political faith to challenge America's best endeavors.

In fact, the Second Continental Congress had already assumed the responsibilities of a general government for the colonies. It recommended that each colony draft a state constitution, and it established a committee to draft articles of confederation. Following Benjamin Franklin's revised Albany Plan of Union, this committee presented the draft of a federal constitution to the Congress on July 12, 1776. The Articles of Confederation and Perpetual Union contained a long list of general powers which might have been the basis for the development of a viable central government, but the location of sovereignty on the state level prevented this. "The great political mistake made by the supporters of this strictly federal government," Merrill Jensen concludes, "was that any changes in it had to be approved by all the states. Had the Articles of Con-

---

[1] Dumas Malone, *The Story of the Declaration of Independence* (New York: Oxford University Press, 1954), p. 3.

federation been easier to amend, it would have been far more difficult to replace in 1787–1788." [2]

Many problems plagued the infant confederacy in foreign and domestic affairs. Indeed, the economic problems of trade rivalries and public finance deficiencies at home and the need of commercial treaties abroad, plus the related social and political conflicts of the time, prompted the historian John Fiske to refer to these years as the "critical period" of American history. The weakness of the confederacy and the urgency of the times caused a number of leading figures in America to advocate the formation of a stronger central government. Nevertheless, the numerous proposals for a convention—beginning as early as 1780, and made by such men as Alexander Hamilton, George Washington, Thomas Jefferson, John Adams, and James Madison—were thwarted by those who feared the consequences of a stronger central government. The Virginia legislature, however, took the steps that were at last to lead to the Constitutional Convention of 1787.

Delegates from Virginia and Maryland met at Mount Vernon and resolved some of their commercial differences. Then in January of 1786, on the urging of Madison and others, the Virginia legislature invited the other states to send delegates to Annapolis, Maryland, to discuss matters of commerce common to all states. The Annapolis Convention, made up of delegates from only five states, met briefly in September, 1786. Its report to Congress and the states declared that commercial power could not be transferred to the central government without changes in the system which would "render the constitution of the federal government adequate to the exigencies of the union." It called for a convention to meet the next spring for this purpose. Congress and many of the states initially ignored the report of the Annapolis Convention.

The undertow of fear of democracy and the concern over "radical" laws passed in many of the states whose legislatures were controlled by the "new men" were brought to the surface in the fall of 1786, when Daniel Shays led an uprising of backcountry farmers against the judgments of Massachusetts' courts foreclosing farm mortgages and jailing men for debt. The rebellion was stopped when the state sent troops west, but the event solidified the belief among Americans that the central government needed to be strengthened.

When Congress met in January of 1787, the major question in the minds of the delegates was whether or not to call a revising convention. Most in and out of Congress felt that Congress would have to act to make a convention legal. Congress did not act until mid-February when it agreed to call a convention to meet in Philadelphia in May for "the sole and express purpose of revising the Articles of Confederation . . . to render the federal constitution adequate to the exigencies of government and the preservation of the union." The work of the convention was to be approved by Congress and confirmed by the states before

[2] Merrill Jensen, *The Making of the American Constitution* (New York: Van Nostrand Reinhold Co., 1964), p. 28.

any changes became operative. Thus Congress, perhaps unwittingly, advanced the conservative political revolution which was already underway.

THE CONSTITUTIONAL CONVENTION

Men, Myths, and Motives

The winter of 1786-87 was cold, the spring was wet, roads were almost impassable, yet a large number of American notables converged on Philadelphia in May. Of the 74 delegates chosen for the Constitutional Convention, 55 attended, although some arrived late and others left before the Convention ended. Of the 55 who attended, approximately a dozen were key contributors to the Convention, and to the Constitution. James Wilson, Gouverneur Morris, Alexander Hamilton, and James Madison were the outstanding nationalist leaders. In the middle were such men as George Mason, John Dickinson, Oliver Ellsworth, and John Rutledge, who supported the idea of a strong central government, but wanted to continue certain powers of the states in a federal arrangement. Among those who wished to retain the confederal structure of the old government, while acknowledging that the central government needed to be strengthened, were William Paterson, Elbridge Gerry, Roger Sherman, and Luther Martin. Martin was the most vocal opponent of the Constitution in its final form, yet, ironically, he was responsible for the idea which became the supremacy clause of the Constitution, giving a strong nationalist flavor to the new government.

Even though James Madison has been given the title of "Father of the Constitution," because of his constructive work before, during, and after the Convention, George Washington was perhaps the most important single member of the Convention. His presence gave the Convention a "national complexion," and his support of the Constitution probably did more to secure ratification than the many speeches and articles of men of lesser reputations. There is a story which illustrates beautifully the austere dignity of Washington. At a gathering where they were discussing an important question of the day, Gouverneur Morris is said to have related on the following day:

I started up and spoke, stamping, as I walked up and down, with my wooden leg; and, as I was certain I had the best of the argument, as I finished I stalked up to the President, slapped him on the back and said, "Ain't I right, General?" The President did not speak, but the majesty of the American people was before me. Oh, his look! How I wished the floor would open and I could descend to the cellar! You know me, and you know my eye would never quail before any other mortal.[3]

This characterization of Washington was typical of a myth which soon surrounded the Founding Fathers. Thomas Jefferson referred to them as "demi-

---

[3] Max Farrand, *The Fathers of the Constitution* (New Haven: Yale University Press, 1921), p. 113.

gods." For over a century the prevailing imagery of the men who drafted the Constitution pictured them not only as statesmen, but as heroic, classic figures, like the gods of Mount Olympus. In the first decade of the twentieth century, however, beginning with J. Allen Smith's *Spirit of American Government* (1907), scholars began to examine the men behind the masks and an image of the framers of the Constitution as self-interested members of the well-to-do classes began to emerge. A half-century of heated debate has turned on Charles A. Beard's *An Economic Interpretation of the Constitution of the United States* (1913), which portrayed the Founding Fathers as an unrepresentative minority who framed a conservative economic document, through undemocratic means, to protect their personal property by establishing a strong central government under their control and able to block the populistic majorities in the states.[4]

The facts are that the delegates were neither demigods nor demagogues. A composite picture would show that they were young, with the average age of 50 skewed somewhat by Franklin's advanced age of 81 (of the 39 delegates who finally signed the Constitution, 3 were in their twenties, 14 were under forty, and the mean age was only forty-two); well educated—with all but a small minority college-trained; experienced in public affairs—the group included state legislators, judges, and governors—and nearly eighty percent had served in Congress; religious men—only 14 acknowledged no formal religious affiliation; and men of property—including 15 slaveholders, 40 who owned government securities, and 24 who were said to be the chief creditors of their local communities.

The delegates who were selected to attend were successful citizens whose time was precious. The 39 who signed the finished Constitution all made great sacrifices in time and money. They came to Philadelphia because of a variety of personal and public interests, but an overriding reason for their attendance was a sincere concern for America. The delegates, of course, had different views as to the political needs of the system (which would serve best their own interests), as the different plans presented and the conflict in the Convention confirm.

Organization and Procedures

The Convention was called to meet on May 14; but a quorum of seven states did not arrive until May 25, when Washington was unanimously elected president. Major William Jackson (not a delegate) was selected as secretary, on Hamilton's nomination. Almost anyone else would have been a better choice, as his record was sketchy and incomplete. Posterity is fortunate that Madison

---

[4] See Leonard W. Levy, *Essays on the Making of the Constitution* (New York: Oxford University Press, 1969); Forrest McDonald, *We the People: The Economic Origins of the Constitution* (Chicago: University of Chicago Press, 1958).

kept a good record of what went on and that the United States government directed that that record be published in 1840.

Washington appointed a committee to draft rules of procedure. The rules which were adopted included three major procedures. (1) It was agreed that each state should have one vote. (2) No vote was to be taken as final. As much as possible, decisions were to be taken by consensus. Voting on issues was to be avoided until all minor or preliminary points were disposed of. This would allow a delegate to change his mind and not lose face. (3) Everything was to be done in executive (secret) session and mostly in committee of the whole house. This allowed the delegates to speak frankly and freely. They spoke to one another—not to the galleries, the news media, nor their constituents at home.

Constitutional Plans

With the adoption of the rules, the Convention could begin the work for which it was called; and the Virginia delegation was ready with a series of resolutions which, indeed, was a plan for a new government. The Virginians had arrived early and had prepared this set of resolutions in collaboration with the Pennsylvania delegation under the guidance of Madison.

Governor Edmund Randolph opened the main business of the Convention with comments on the difficulty of the crisis of government facing America, and on the necessity of preventing the fulfillment of the prophecies of the American downfall. He declared that any revision of the system must produce a strong government which could secure the nation against foreign invasion, conflicts between the states, and seditions within the states. Its powers, he maintained, ought to be "paramount to the state constitutions."

The Virginia resolutions proposed a revolutionary shift of power from the states to the central government and a radical revision of the structure of government. It called for:

1. A bicameral legislature.
    a. The lower house to be elected by the people.
    b. The upper house to be selected by the lower house from nominations by the individual state legislatures.
2. The national legislature to be supreme.
    a. Veto over state legislation.
    b. Power to use force if a state failed to fulfill its duty.
3. The national executive to be selected by the national legislature.
4. A council of revision, made up of the executive and "a convenient number of judiciary," empowered to examine every state and national act before it was applied and to exercise veto power over both.
5. A national judiciary of supreme and inferior tribunals to be selected by the national legislature.
6. A provision for the admission of new states.
7. The national government to guarantee a republican form of government for each state.

8. Amendment procedures for the Constitution.
9. The Constitution to be ratified by conventions in the states.

The Convention resolved to consider the Virginia Plan in the committee of the whole house the following day.

Mr. Charles Pinckney of South Carolina also submitted the draft of a plan he had prepared which was similar to the Virginia Plan. The Convention also referred this plan to the committee of the whole, but it appears not to have been a significant model followed by the Convention, as the records show the debate centered on the Virginia resolutions for the next two weeks.

Beginning on May 30, the Convention in committee of the whole house considered the Virginia resolutions. Most of the basic ideas and issues which occupied the delegates during the hot summer of 1787 were clearly stated during the first two weeks of debate. The division between those who wanted a strong national government and those who wanted simply to strengthen the existing government was clearly drawn.

Of all of the conflicts between the nationalists and the federalists during the debate over the Virginia resolutions, the most serious threat to the continuance of the Convention was over the question of whether or not the voting in the national legislature should be based on state equality or population. A related issue was whether or not slaves should be counted in the enumeration of the population for representation (and tax) purposes. Compromise was suggested on each issue when Roger Sherman moved that voting in the first branch should be by population and that each state should have one vote in the second branch of the legislature; and when James Wilson proposed that slaves be counted as "three-fifth's of all other persons." The committee agreed that voting in the lower house should be according to some equitable basis of representation. Sherman then moved that the next part of his compromise, that each state have one vote in the upper house, be approved. This was voted down.

The committee of the whole house had completed its work on the Virginia resolutions and was ready to make its report, which now contained nineteen resolutions. It was clearly a victory for the nationalists. But upon the request of William Paterson of New Jersey, the vote on the committee's report was delayed because several of the delegates wished to present a "purely federal" plan. The Convention adjourned that time might be given for this purpose. The nationalists had pushed too hard for their program. "You see," John Dickinson told Madison, "the consequence of pushing things too far."

The intent of the Paterson proposals, or the New Jersey Plan, was to strengthen the central government by amending the Articles of Confederation. The proposed government would be federal in form and the states would retain their equality and sovereignty. Specific powers, however, would be delegated to Congress. The plan proposed:

1. An increase of the powers of Congress over taxation and commerce.
2. That the national government make requisitions first on the states, and if unsuccessful, then on individuals.
3. A plural executive with strong powers.
4. A federal judiciary, appointed by the executive, with original jurisdiction over matters of national concern.
5. That all acts and treaties of the United States shall be the supreme law of the land.
6. A procedure to admit new states.
7. A uniform rule for naturalization.
8. That criminal laws of the states apply to residents and nonresidents alike.

On June 16 the committee of the whole began to consider the comparative merits of the Virginia and New Jersey plans. The two plans were fundamentally different even though they had many similarities. As John Lansing of New York put it, the two systems were "fairly contrasted." He further argued that the Convention did not have the power to create a national government. Paterson called the national plan illegal. The nationalists' answer was that the Convention had the right to propose what the country needed. Randolph said: "When the salvation of the Republic was at stake, it would be treason to our trust, not to propose what we found necessary."

On June 18 Hamilton, who "had been hitherto silent on the business before the Convention" according to Madison, scorned both plans as "too federal." "The great question is," Hamilton asked, "what provision shall we make for the happiness of our country?" The New Jersey Plan was not powerful enough to correct the problems the nation faced under the Articles; and the republican proposal of Virginia, he feared, was also inadequate, though better than the New Jersey Plan. "In his private opinion," Madison records, "he had no scruple in declaring . . . that the British government was the best in the world; and that he doubted much whether anything short of it would do in America." A government which left the states in possession of their sovereignty would fail, thought Hamilton. The central government must "swallow up" the states or be swallowed by them. His plan contained the seeds of monarchy; and he introduced it primarily to amplify his ideas, with little hope it would be accepted.

Conflict and Compromise

On June 19 the Convention rejected the New Jersey Plan and adopted the report of the committee of the whole house, which called for a national government with three branches. The bicameral legislature was to have all powers under the Articles, additional legislative powers to promote harmony in the union, and a veto over state laws. The first chamber was to be elected by the people; the second, chosen by the state legislatures, but with representation in both houses to be based on population including three-fifths of the slaves. A single national executive was to be selected by the national legislature for a single term of seven years, with power to veto acts of the national legislature unless afterwards passed by two-thirds majority in each chamber. The national judiciary was to consist of one supreme tribunal of judges appointed by the second chamber of the national legislature to hold their offices during good behavior. The legislature was to be empowered to appoint inferior judicial tribunals.

The turbulent debate which followed was primarily over the issue of representation. This dispute became so heated that on June 28, Benjamin Franklin made a stirring plea for prayer to invoke divine aid in resolving the controversy. Hamilton and others opposed the motion of Franklin as they were dubious of the tactic of admitting the necessity of an appeal to the Almighty. It is reported, in jest no doubt, that Hamilton was opposed to "foreign aid"! The real reason was simple. The Convention had no funds to pay a minister. Franklin's proposal died without a vote on the motion.

The deadlock over the representation issue was broken in July, beginning with the appointment of a committee on July 2, consisting of one representative from each state. There were more federalists and small-state men on this committee than nationalists. Madison wrote: "That time might be given to the Committee, and to such as chose to attend to the celebration on the anniversary of Independence the Convention adjourned till Thursday." On July 5 the committee proposed: (1) that there be one representative in the first branch of the legislature for every 40,000 inhabitants, counting the whites and three-fifths of the slaves; (2) that money bills originate in this branch of the legislature; and (3) that the states have equal votes in the second branch. The last of these proposals to be agreed to by the Convention, equal votes in the second branch, was finally and barely passed on July 16. As a further concession to the small states, this equality was made unamendable. The Great Compromise, as it is commonly called, thus brought in both equality and population bases of representation in the legislature.

Another plane of conflict developed between the northern and southern states. The North could not see the justification for the slaves to be counted in the apportionment, since they had no voice in public affairs. And if property (slaves) was to be represented, then why not other types of property? The issue was finally resolved by a concession to the South, in that three-fifths of the slaves would be counted for representation purposes; and a concession to the North, in that the slaves would also be counted on a three-fifths basis for direct tax purposes. To further reassure the Southerners, it was agreed that no legislation to prohibit the importation of slaves would be enacted by the central government prior to 1808. This provision was part of an important and conspicuous compromise between the North and the South over commerce powers of the proposed government.

Conflict and compromise persisted throughout the remainder of the Convention, even though the success of the Convention was pretty well assured following the Great Compromise. On July 26 the Convention adjourned until August 6, during which time a committee of detail was to prepare a draft constitution. The committee was weighted on the side of the moderate nationalists and on the side of the South. The draft reflected these facts, which meant new debates on new and old points and more basic compromises. The draft was a forward step, however, as it switched the attention of the delegates from the general principles to the specific details of government organization.

The committee styled the national legislature "the Congress," made up of the House of Representatives and the Senate. The only qualifications mentioned for members of Congress were age, citizenship, and residency. What about wealth, property, and religion? A sticky debate resulted. Quibbling over the organization of Congress also took place, but the only serious argument was over compensation of its members. The delegates were in agreement that the powers of Congress must be strengthened over what had been granted by the Articles, but disputes arose over the first power granted: the tax power. Direct taxes had to be in proportion to population, but what was a direct tax? No one seemed to know. At least Madison noted succinctly that when the question was put to the Convention "no one answered." The power to borrow money and emit bills of credit produced all of the old antagonisms toward paper money which had played such a vital part in calling the Convention in the first place. Discussion of the military powers harrowed up the old fears which were connected with the Revolution; and the power to call up the state militias, to a few of the delegates, was an attack on freedom and the independence of the states.

Debate resulted over the limitations imposed on Congress, restraints upon the states, and whether or not a bill of rights should be included. Relations between the central government and the states prompted more conflict and compromise. Relations between the states were spelled out in a similar fashion to what had existed under the Articles, and admission of new states was a logical outgrowth of the policies of the Congress toward the Northwest Territory, as expressed in the Northwest Ordinance of 1787.

The draft constitution provided that the executive be a single person called the President. A major conflict broke out over the mode of electing him. This issue was one of the last to be worked out and resulted in election by an electoral college. Although the delegates were in essential agreement over duties and powers of the President, some sharp debate ensued over his substantive powers. The model which they drew from most was the New York governor. The New York constitution was established in 1777, a bit later than the other states, and the office of the governor was of the strong rather than the weak executive type. Article II of the Constitution began with a sentence, attributed to Morris, of vast future significance: "The executive Power shall be vested in a President of the United States of America." It does not contain the limitation imposed on the Congress of "herein granted."

Conflict and Compromise—or Consensus?

The differences among the delegates to the Constitutional Convention were indeed intense at times, and many compromises were required to keep the Convention moving toward its goal of a new constitution. To merely stress the traditional attitude that the work of the Convention was a bundle of compromises, however, obscures the fact that the delegates were responding to the political and economic issues of the period and that on many of the basic constitutional principles a high degree of consensus prevailed in Convention Hall.

"On many matters of structure, mechanics, and detail there were angry disagreements," writes Leonard W. Levy, "but agreement prevailed on the essentials." [5] Levy points out that the first substantive vote of the Convention was the adoption of a resolution of the Virginia Plan "that a *national* government ought to be established consisting of a *supreme* Legislative, Executive and Judiciary." Thus the delegates agreed to abandon, rather than to amend, the Articles of Confederation, and to write a new constitution which was to create a national government with direct power over individuals throughout the entire nation—a revolutionary departure from the political system under the Articles.

There were only a few at the Convention who were irreconcilably opposed to a national government. Even the New Jersey Plan had a strong nationalist thrust in comparison to the Articles of Confederation, and it even contained the seed of the national supremacy clause found in Article VI of the finished Constitution!

There was more consensus than conflict over such basic principles as (1) a bicameral legislature; (2) broad national legislative powers, including the power of taxation and regulation of commerce which had been withheld from Congress by the Articles; (3) a strong executive; (4) a national supreme court; and (5) restrictions on the economic powers of the state.

Concluding Days of the Convention

The summer of 1787 had been a long, hot one, and many of the delegates were impatient with further delay. The Convention selected a committee on September 8 to put the agreed points of the draft constitution into final form, which reduced the twenty-three articles of the draft to seven, rearranged many provisions, and revised the language in a lucid and succinct style—reputedly the work of Gouverneur Morris. On September 12 the draft constitution was submitted to the Convention and three days of debate followed. On September 15 further changes in the draft were ended when the Convention unanimously and impatiently voted down a motion by Randolph, supported by George Mason and Elbridge Gerry, calling for a second convention to consider the anticipated amendments coming from the states. These three delegates served notice on the Convention that they could not sign the Constitution in its present form.

---

[5] Levy, ed., *Essays On the Making of the Constitution,* p. xvii.

Most of the delegates had some misgivings about the final document, but the Constitution was ordered to be engrossed and ready for signing on September 17. After the Constitution was read before the Convention on Monday morning, Franklin rose with a conciliatory speech which James Wilson read to the Convention. "I confess that there are several parts of this Constitution which I do not at present approve," Franklin said, "but I am not sure I shall never approve them." He urged all of the delegates to sign the document because he doubted that another convention could produce a better constitution. "Thus I consent, sir, to this Constitution," he said, "because I expect no better, and because I am not sure, that it is not the best."

The Constitution was signed by at least one representative from each of the twelve states in attendance. Governor Randolph refused to sign, because he feared the Constitution in its present form would not be ratified, and he wanted to be free to work for another convention. George Mason, also from Virginia, said he would rather have his right arm cut off than sign the Constitution in its amended, final form, which provided for a government with such "dangerous power . . . that it would end either in monarchy, or a tyrannical aristocracy." Elbridge Gerry also refused to sign the completed Constitution. Where Morris and Hamilton saw anarchy if the Constitution were not adopted, Gerry saw the possibility of civil war in his home state if it were submitted to the people in its present form. There were two parties in Massachusetts, he said, "one devoted to democracy, the worst of all political evils, the other as violent in the opposite extreme." The Constitution might prompt a clash between these two factions.

The last entry in Madison's *Journal* is this little interesting aside:

Whilst the last members were signing, Doctor Franklin, looking towards the President's chair, at the back of which a rising sun happened to be painted, observed to a few members near him, that painters had found it difficult to distinguish in their art, a rising, from a setting, sun. I have, said he, often and often, in the course of the session, and the vicissitudes of my hopes and fears as to its issue, looked at that behind the President, without being able to tell whether it was rising or setting; but now at length, I have the happiness to know, that it is a rising, and not a setting sun.

THE PUBLIC DEBATE

Article VII of the proposed Constitution called for ratification by conventions of nine states; amendment of the Articles called for the consent of all thirteen states! The revolutionary nature of the Convention's work is apparent by this politically motivated violation of the letter of the Articles and departure from the commission that called the Convention. Ratification by conventions instead of state legislatures was purposely proposed to avoid the establishment of state legislatures. Arguments began immediately over the legality of the proceedings.

The promoters of the Constitution knew the support of the Congress was needed. Madison and other convention delegates who also were members of Congress laid the Constitution before Congress three days after the Convention ended, and they urged Congress to send it to the states with its positive approval and an exhortation to ratify as soon as possible.

Richard Henry Lee, who had refused to attend the Convention because he was a member of Congress and would have to act on the Convention's work, led the opposition in Congress. He described the supporters of the Constitution as a "coalition of monarchy men, military men, aristocrats, and drones," who were acting in great haste. Lee argued that Congress could not approve a document which subverted the constitution under which it acted. So effective was the opposition that Congress sent the Constitution to the states without approval or disapproval.

Newspapers and pamphlets carried the arguments for and against ratification throughout the country. The debate, propagandist in tone, touched nearly everyone; and it equaled in intensity the Revolutionary debate. The *Pennsylvania Gazette,* supporting ratification of the Constitution, declared that the former political distinctions of "Whigs and Tories should be lost in the more important distinction of Federal and Anti-federal men. The former are the friends of liberty and independence; the latter are the enemies of liberty, and the secret abettors of the interest of Great Britain." As Merrill Jensen put it,

The supporters of the Constitution thus began their campaign for ratification by mislabelling the opposition and slurring its patriotism. Ever since then the label of Anti-Federalist has been applied to such men as Richard Henry Lee, Patrick Henry, George Mason, George Clinton, and Elbridge Gerry, although in fact they were true "federalists," as both they and the men of the Convention knew.[6]

During the campaigns for the election of delegates to the ratifying conventions, voters and delegates were aligned as friends or foes of the Constitution—and it was a distinct advantage for the promoters of the Constitution to appropriate to themselves the more popular label "Federalists." They also had something positive to propose and took the offensive in the contest; the Anti-Federalists were cast in the negative role, as an "anti" party, and had the responsibility of refuting the "facts" presented by the Federalists.

The Federalists had another distinct advantage over their opposition. Most of the leaders of public opinion were Federalists. The clergy, the lawyers, newspaper publishers, the commercial manufacturing, financial, and creditor interests; and the great planters in the South supported the Federalists. They had more money, they were better organized, and they were united in what they wanted. The Anti-Federalists spoke primarily for the back country farmers. Of course, these generalizations admit of many exceptions.

[6] Jensen, *The Making of the American Constitution,* p. 123.

Basic Issues in Dispute

Jensen maintains that even though there was much quibbling about details of the Constitution, there were three major areas of dispute which stand out above all others. These concerned (1) the nature of the new government itself, (2) the state of the economy and its relationship to the central government, and (3) the question of whether or not a bill of rights should be added to the new Constitution. Richard Henry Lee's *Letters from the Federal Farmer* touches on all three disputed areas in a calm and fair-minded way, which makes it the best critique of the Constitution.

Lee accused the Constitution of being undemocratic. He felt that 65 representatives would be too few to represent the "middle and lower classes," which he classed as the "democracy." He believed that it would result in placing the majority under the control of the minority: "Every man of reflection must see that the change now proposed is a transfer of power from the many to the few."

Lee recognized that the Constitution was a radical change in the form and powers of the government. Samuel Adams expressed similar views after reading the Constitution: "I confess as I enter the building I stumble at the threshold. I meet with a national government instead of a federal union of sovereign states." Lee criticized the Supremacy Clause of Article VI for destroying the federal form of government: "It is to be observed that, when the people shall adopt the proposed Constitution, it will be their last and supreme act." He also feared the powers which the central government could acquire through the Necessary and Proper clause in Article I, Section 8: "It is almost impossible to have a just conception of their powers, or of the extent and number of the laws which may be deemed necessary and proper to carry them into effect, till we shall come to exercise those powers and make the laws."

In regards to the state of economy and its relationship to the central government, Lee was typical of the men of his period. They took it for granted that the government and the economy were interrelated. Federalists and Anti-Federalists differed, however, as to economic conditions at the time and the responsibility of state and central governments for those conditions. They also differed as to which groups should be protected or encouraged by government action. Through legislation the economic future of the nation could be molded, but should the government encourage farming, or commerce, or industry, or some combination of all three? Lee was convinced that the promoters of the Constitution were hurriedly trying to push through this instrument for their own advantage.

Lee was concerned about the omission of a bill of rights. He believed that the individual safeguards, such as the right of *habeas corpus,* and prohibitions on Congress from passing bills of attainder and *ex post facto* laws, should be expanded into a detailed bill of rights. Among those rights which should be included, Lee mentioned freedom of religion, freedom from unwarranted searches and seizures, freedom of the press, and trial by jury. He was fearful that if these rights were not specifically included and the Constitution was left vague concerning them, arbitrary action could result. He said:

> Our countrymen are entitled to an honest and faithful government; to a government of laws and not of men; and also to one of their choosing—as a citizen of the country, I wish to see these objects secured and licentious, assuming and overbearing men restrained; if the Constitution or social compact be vague and unguarded, then we depend wholly upon the prudence, wisdom, and moderation of those who manage the affairs of government.

Thomas Jefferson, who was in France during the drafting of the Constitution, was also concerned with the omission of a bill of rights. He said: "Let me add that a bill of rights is what the people are entitled to against every government on earth, general or particular; and what no just government should refuse or rest on inference." He also objected to the unlimited reeligibility of the President and said that he was "not a friend to a very energetic government." Jefferson, however, approved of most of the Constitution and helped bring about ratification of it.

The Federalist case was a simple one, based on the need of a strong government (1) to maintain internal order (the specter of Daniel Shays and his rebellion was a great ally for the Federalists); (2) to resist any foreign powers, and specifically to get the peace treaty observed and to obtain a commercial treaty with Great Britain; and (3) to promote economic growth for all within the United States.

Contrary to what one might expect from the conflict and debates in the Convention and from the public debate, ratification had a fairly easy time in a majority of the first nine ratifying states. The vote in Delaware, the first state to ratify, was unanimous. In fact, many of the small states were among the first to ratify. More opposition appeared in Pennsylvania, where the Federalists had to have a mob drag enough of the opponents of the Constitution into the legislative hall to provide a quorum to call a convention, but the final ratifying vote was forty-six to twenty-three. In Massachusetts the battle over ratification was touch and go, with the acceptance by the close margin of 187–168. The ninth state to ratify was New Hampshire, on June 21, 1788, meeting the provision of the Constitution to establish the Union. But Virginia, New York, North Carolina, and Rhode Island had not yet ratified the Constitution; and it was inconceivable that Virginia and New York could be left out.

Opinion was closely divided in Virginia, with such able antagonists as Patrick Henry, Richard Henry Lee, and George Mason meeting able proponents of the Constitution of the caliber of James Madison, John Marshall, and George Washington. The action of New Hampshire, no doubt, influenced the Virginia Convention; and after three weeks of discussion and debate Virginia ratified by the close vote of eighty-nine to seventy-nine.

The contest in New York was significant because it turned an Anti-Federalist majority of nearly two-thirds into a slim Federalist majority of thirty to twenty-seven. The campaign also called forth a series of published papers in defense of the Constitution composed by Hamilton, Madison, and John Jay, a series which Jefferson characterized as "the best commentary on the principles of government which ever was written." Known as the *Federalist Papers,* they remain today the best analysis of the Constitution as it came from the Convention (they will be examined in more detail in the following chapter). Essentially they made four major points:

1. The need for a stronger central government to preserve the union.
2. The need for a vigorous executive and judicial branch independent of the legislature.
3. The need for a system of checks and balances within the government structure.
4. The need for a representative republic as against a democracy in a country of large territory and a variety of interests.

It was now possible to establish the new government. Elections were held, and in the spring of 1789 Washington was inaugurated the first President under the new Constitution. Faced with this fact, North Carolina ratified in November, 1789; and Rhode Island in May, 1790, which made the Union of thirteen states complete.

2
AMERICAN CONSTITUTIONAL PRINCIPLES

The principles underlying the Government of the United States are decentralization of power, separation of power and maintaining a balance between freedom and order.

Above all else, the framers of the Constitution were fearful of the concentration of power in either individuals or government. The genius of their solution in this respect is that they were able to maintain a very definite but delicate balance between the Federal Government and the state government, on the one hand, and between the executive, legislative and judicial branches of the Federal Government, on the other hand.

By contrast, in the British system, the Parliament is supreme. In the present French system the primary power resides in the executive, and in some older civilizations the judges were predominant. Throughout American history there have been times when one or the other branches of Government would seem to have gained a dominant position, but the pendulum has always swung back and the balance over the long haul maintained.

The result of these somewhat complex constitutional formulas is greater protection and respect for the rights of the individual citizen. These rights are guaranteed by the Constitution, not only by the first ten Amendments, which specifically refer to them, but even more by the system itself, which is the most effective safeguard against arbitrary power ever devised by man.

These thoughts on the Constitution were written by President Richard M. Nixon in an essay upon his admission to the practice of law in New York State in 1963. One decade later President Nixon was the central figure in one of the most severe constitutional conflicts in the nation's history. The controversy, which turned largely on the principle of separation of powers, had been building for some years; but it flooded the Washington scene following the 1972 reelection of the President, when the Watergate affair broke open and reached the very inner circle of presidential assistants and counselors.

In the criminal trial of the seven defendants charged with breaking into Democratic offices in the Watergate Hotel complex, Chief Judge John J. Sirica expressed marked displeasure that the trial did not get to the bottom of the affair and hoped that the Senate's Select Committee to Investigate 1972 Presidential Campaign Activities would be more successful. The judge contributed to the success of the Watergate Committee's inquiry when he imposed stiff temporary sentences on the seven guilty men, prompting a willingness of witnesses before the committee to talk.

Senator Sam J. Ervin, Jr., a Democrat from North Carolina and considered to be the Senate's leading constitutional scholar, was chosen to head the Watergate Committee because of his reputation for fairness and nonpartisanship. His knowledge about the Constitution results from his having once served as a state judge, his long membership on the Senate Judiciary Committee and as

Copyright 1973 by Herblock in *The Washington Post*

Disaster area

chairman of the Constitutional Rights and Separation of Powers subcommittees. Senator Ervin, who describes himself as a "humble country lawyer" and who delights in making his points by the use of history, scripture, and hard constitutional data, challenged many of the President's constitutional interpretations. At one point in the clash between Ervin's committee and the President over executive privilege (the practice of withholding information from Congress based on the separation of powers principle), Ervin rejected the White House offer to answer questions in writing or permit informal testimony, not under oath. He said: "That is not executive privilege. That is executive poppycock."

Many respected scholars believed the Nixon Administration violated the fundamental principles of the Constitution, some of which Mr. Nixon wrote about in his 1963 essay. Instead of a government of laws, historian Daniel J. Boorstin saw the Watergate scandal as a rise in "the cult of personality." [1] Professor Hans J. Morgenthau believed Watergate was an attempt to disregard the constitutional and statutory restraints vital to the American system of government. "The effectiveness of these restraints," he wrote, "is predicated upon a moral restraint defined by the Founding Fathers as 'republican virtue,' which is as essential to the democratic order as it is rare in the perspective of all recorded history." [2] This ethos Morgenthau referred to is a willingness to play the political game under democratic rules, which are at bottom grounded in the Constitution.

"Watergate and all those attendant usurpations, subversions, and corruptions for which the word has become both a symbol and a short cut," according to the distinguished historian Henry Steele Commager, "is neither a 'deplorable incident'—to use Mr. Nixon's revealing phrase—nor a historical sport. It is a major crisis, constitutional, political, and moral, one that challenges our government system." Commager questioned that the crisis was so imperative that it "require[d] an unconstitutional revolution—require[d], that is, abandoning the separation of powers, discarding limitations on the executive authority, weakening legislative control of the purse, subverting the traditional rule of law, and covering with a fog of secrecy the operations of government." Commager concluded:

The Founding Fathers knew instinctively what Montesquieu proclaimed in his *Spirit of the Laws,* that virtue is the animating principle of a republic. And to the Commonwealth they served—almost always at great personal sacrifice—they paid the tribute of virtue. But this administration which gibbers about "peace with honor" does not exalt virtue, and does not practice it.

But then he turns the accusing finger toward the American citizenry with the question, "But do we?" [3]

Do we understand the virtues of our republican system—indeed, do we un-

[1] *Congressional Quarterly Weekly Report,* July 7, 1973, p. 1795.
[2] "Watergate and the Future of American Politics: The Aborted Nixon Revolution," *The New Republic,* August 11, 1973, pp. 17–19.
[3] "The Shame of the Republic," *The New York Review,* July 19, 1973, p. 10ff.

derstand the whole fabric of constitutional principles fashioned by the Founding Fathers?

THE LIVING CONSTITUTION

There are some Americans who feel that an eighteenth-century document is inadequate to meet the needs of the government of the United States of the twentieth century. The complex problems of modern society, they say, require more efficient political mechanisms. The obvious answer for those who would circumvent or abolish the Constitution is that it has, so far, proved adequate—when it has been followed. It should be understood, however, that the Constitution is not merely the original document of 1787.

The Constitution contains seven basic articles which structure the framework of government, its powers, and its operation. It also contains some restrictions on government designed to protect the people against possible tyranny. But the Founding Fathers did not intend to establish a static system which was incapable of change to meet changing conditions. John Marshall referred to the Constitution as a "living document" which should be changed or interpreted to meet the changing needs of society—and he did just that. Thomas Jefferson advocated that each generation should have the right to set the rules by which the society will be governed.

Article V of the Constitution specifies the procedures to amend the Constitution. These procedures call for two modes of proposing amendments: (1) by two-thirds vote of both houses of Congress, or (2) by a national convention when called by Congress at the request of the legislatures of two-thirds of the states. They also provide for two methods of ratifying proposed amendments: (1) by the legislatures of three-fourths of the states, or (2) by conventions in three-fourths of the states. Congress is given the authority to determine which method of ratification is to be used. Only the Twenty-first Amendment, which repealed prohibition, was ratified by state conventions.

The Constitution has been formally amended only twenty-six times in nearly two centuries—and since the first ten amendments, the Bill of Rights, were proposed by the First Congress and ratification was completed and adoption certified on December 15, 1791, they might properly be considered as part of the basic document. Obviously the formal amendment procedure has proved to be a difficult way to expand or change the Constitution to meet the needs of a changing society. The Constitution, however, has been stretched informally to cover new needs through (1) basic or fundamental laws, (2) judicial interpretations, (3) executive actions, and (4) custom.

One of the best examples of how laws passed by Congress expand and change the scope of the Constitution is the Judiciary Act of 1789. This act not only created and empowered the district and circuit courts, but in creating these courts it established a separate court system on the national level independent of the state courts. This act reinforced the Supremacy Clause of Article VI in making the national government, in fact, supreme.

It is interesting that this act also contained a grant of power to the Supreme Court which Chief Justice John Marshall declared unconstitutional in the famous case of *Marbury* v. *Madison,* a case which helped to establish the principle of judicial review. When the Supreme Court interprets the meaning of the Constitution and declares an act of Congress or the President unconstitutional, it may alter the political system in a substantive way and change the thrust of the Constitution as significantly as a formal amendment would.

An important constitutional issue arose in the trial of Aaron Burr for treason in 1807. The court issued a subpoena to President Jefferson requiring him to appear with certain papers in his possession important to the case. Jefferson refused to appear because doing so, he said, would jeopardize the independence of the executive and interfere with his conduct of executive affairs. President Lincoln on many occasions used the doctrine of separation of powers to support his independent executive actions and to combat congressional policies and committees which he felt encroached on his presidential powers. His controversy with the Committee on the Conduct of the War organized by Congress is a good case in point. Lincoln, relying on the separation-of-powers principle, achieved the greatest concentration of power of any President in our history through his independent actions—with long-lasting impact on the nation's constitutional framework. Contemporary Presidents do not appear before congressional committees, and have cloaked certain members of the White House staff with this executive immunity as well.

Constitutional change has come about through custom or practices over the years. There is no mention of political parties in the Constitution. They developed out of a conflict of policies between Jefferson and Hamilton in Washington's Administration. Now regulated by state and national laws, they are such a vital part of our political system that it is questionable if the system could function without them.

A number of authors have distinguished the American Constitution from the British on the basis that the American Constitution is written, or codified and inflexible, whereas the British constitution is the opposite. In actuality there is more similarity than difference between the two constitutions. Both are made up of basic documents, fundamental statutes, judicial decisions, executive actions, and custom. (See Table 2.1 for examples of the similarities between the British and American constitutions.)

GOALS OF THE CONSTITUTION

Economic Goals

The elimination of the many state trade barriers (taxes and imposts) and the other economic restrictions was one of the primary objectives of the framers of the Constitution. The goal was to free commerce and manufacturing from the

Table 2.1

British Constitution	American Constitution
1. Historic Documents (For example: Magna Charta)	1. The Constitution (The basic Document and Amendments)
2. Basic Statutes (Such as The Act of Union with Scotland)	2. Fundamental Acts (Such as The Judiciary Act of 1789)
3. Judicial Decisions (Such as English Court cases establishing degrees of independence of the judiciary from the Crown)	3. Judicial Decisions (*Marbury v. Madison* is a good case in point wherein the principle of Judicial review was advanced)
4. Executive Actions (The practice of the Crown requesting a Minister to form a Government, for instance)	4. Executive Actions (Presidents claim "executive privilege." Do not appear before congressional committees.)
5. Custom (The resignation of the Prime Minister or the dissolution of Parliament if the government loses a vote of confidence)	5. Custom (The development of political parties)

burdens which stifled it. The national government was given the power to regulate commerce in order to create a common market and a free economy within the whole United States.

Other powers were granted to Congress by the Constitution to promote a free economy. The power to "coin money and regulate the value thereof" is essential in maintaining a uniform and stable currency, which in turn is vital to a free economy. For example, a restriction was placed on the states to avoid the problems of states issuing paper money and having competing or debased currencies. The power to fix the standard of weights and measures is also a great aid to commerce and industry.

The power of the national government to lay duties on imports to raise revenue can also be used to protect the American economy from foreign competition. The tariff has been used to protect domestic industries from the very first Congress, when Hamilton, the Secretary of the Treasury, persuaded the congressmen that a protective tariff was constitutional in his Report on Manufactures. Tariff manipulation, at times lowering or abolishing tariffs, and import quotas or incentives, have been used to achieve economic objectives. Other powers were granted to the national government to promote a national economy. For instance, Congress has the power (1) to enact uniform bankruptcy laws, (2) to establish post offices and post roads, and (3) to grant exclusive patent and copyrights to inventors and authors.

A major economic goal of the framers of the Constitution was to build a strong economic position for the national government and to establish the credit of the United States. To achieve this, they granted the power to lay and collect taxes in order to "pay the debts . . . of the United States," and obligated the government to assume the debts of the Confederation. Hamilton went further and persuaded Congress to assume the states' debts as well. Congress was also given the power to borrow money on the credit of the United States.

Paper money issues of the states, and stay and bankruptcy laws to relieve the debtors of their obligations, were thought to be evil by the Founding Fathers; and a limitation was placed on the states that they should not pass any law which would impair the "obligation of contracts." This "contract clause" was used over and over again by Chief Justice Marshall to support the creditor interests and a conservative economic policy, as he believed with Hamilton that the creditor interests must have a stake in the government to give it a solid economic base.

Social Goals

Even though economic goals were high on the priority list of the Founding Fathers, the protection of the basic individual rights and liberties spoken of in the Declaration of Independence was not overlooked. The major objection to the Constitution—that it did not have a formal bill of rights—was soon corrected with the addition of the first ten amendments. The proponents of the Constitution had argued that the new government was limited to certain specific functions which would not violate the liberties already protected by the state constitutions. They also had included some safeguards of individual liberty in the body of the Constitution, most important of which are the "Privilege of the Writ of Habeas Corpus," thought by many legalists to be the keystone of liberty, and the right of trial by jury. But it must be pointed out that liberty as we think of it today was not protected for all persons by the state constitutions nor by the Constitution, which could have been readily testified to by black Americans of 1787.

Liberty without equality is a hollow word. The Founding Fathers were not strong for democracy; and they had notions about the selfish and evil qualities of men that caused them to feel the need of a constitutional political system which would restrain the vices of men. Nevertheless, the Constitution, in somewhat subdued tones, supports the principles of equality. Article I, Section 9, provides that "no title of nobility shall be granted by the United States" and "no person holding any office of profit or trust under them, shall, without the consent of the Congress, accept of any present, emolument, office, or title, of any kind whatever, from any king, prince, or foreign state." The general American belief in equality was specifically expanded by the Thirteenth, Fourteenth, Fifteenth, Nineteenth and Twenty-sixth Amendments.

The spirit of liberty and equality in America cannot be totally stated with provisions from the Constitution, even as amended. Human dignity, supported by legal safeguards, is yet to be fully achieved. Nevertheless, the Constitution of the United States lays before the American people goals which can challenge our best endeavors. An eloquent statement of purpose and principle is contained in the Preamble:

We the People of the United States, in Order to form a more perfect Union, establish Justice, insure domestic Tranquility, provide for the common defense, promote the general Welfare, and secure the Blessings of Liberty to ourselves and our Posterity, do ordain and establish this Constitution for the United States of America.

Political Goals

As the Preamble suggests, the Founding Fathers were concerned over the need to establish a stronger union to meet the nation's needs in foreign affairs. The independence of the *dis-* United States, made up of thirteen squabbling states with a total population of less than four million people scattered thinly over a large territory, hung precariously in a world of rival and powerful nations. Britain, France, and Spain waited like vultures for new opportunities to gobble up America.

Four numbers of the *Federalist Papers* written by John Jay emphasized the need of a stronger union in the conduct of foreign affairs. Jay maintained that the defense and independence of the United States were directly dependent upon its ability to raise armies, fit out navies, and unitedly resist any military threat from any foreign power.

A strong central government also was considered necessary to prevent conflict and violence from "domestic faction and insurrection." Hamilton wrote that it was impossible to read the history of the small republics of Greece and Italy without "horror and disgust at the rapid succession of revolution by which they were kept in a state of perpetual vibration between the extremes of tyranny and anarchy." He felt the best guarantee against a similar fate for America was the creation of a strong, united nation based broadly on popular consent and republican institutions. To this end Article IV of the Constitution provides that "the United States shall guarantee to every state in this union a republican form of government, and shall protect them against invasion; and on application of the legislature, or of the executive (when the legislature cannot be convened) against domestic violence."

BASIC PRINCIPLES

As the Constitutional Convention came to a close in Philadelphia, so the story goes, Franklin was walking down the steps of Independence Hall when he was stopped by a woman and asked: "Well, Doctor, what have we got, a republic or a monarchy?" "A republic, madam," answered Franklin, "if you can keep it."

Franklin's reply singled out one of a number of fundamental constitutional principles of the American political system. In addition to republicanism, popular sovereignty, limited government, separation of powers, checks and balances, judicial review, and federalism are basic principles found in the Constitution.

Republican Government

James Madison in Number Thirty-nine of the *Federalist Papers* defined a republican form of government as one which derives all its powers directly or indirectly from the people, and is administered by representatives of the people and responsible to them. In Number Fourteen he explained that the large territorial size of the union would not be a handicap under a republican form of government:

As the natural limit of a democracy is that distance from the central point which will just permit the most remote citizens to assemble as often as their public functions demand, and will include no greater number than can join in those functions; so the natural limit of a republic is that distance from the center which will barely allow the representatives of the people to meet as often as may be necessary for the administration of public affairs.

In Number Ten, Madison argues forcefully for a representative system that could cure the "mischiefs of faction," which he defines as a group of citizens "who are united and actuated by some common impulse of passion, or of interest, adverse to the rights of other citizens, or to the permanent and aggregate interests of the community." Madison concluded "that a pure democracy, by which I mean a society consisting of a small number of citizens who assemble and administer the government in person, can admit of no cure for the mischiefs of faction"; but he further concluded that "a republic, by which I mean a government in which the scheme of representation takes place," could—because representatives refine and enlarge the public views. That is, representatives must reflect the views of a variety of different people and the representatives' decisions will tend to be more moderate than those of any given faction or group.

Madison saw safety in a representative system, in which the interests of one group must be mellowed or compromised because of the demands of competing groups. Under such a system, he believed, one group would not be able to control the government and promote its own interests at the expense of all others. Even though some Americans fear the dominance of the industrial-military complex; and there is persuasive data to support elitist theories of governance in America, our representative system operates pretty well along the pluralistic lines Madison predicted.

The representative system is based on geographic or territorial lines. The members of Congress are elected from single-member districts in which the candidate who wins the highest number of votes is elected. This system was attacked in the latter part of the nineteenth century by those who claimed it left the minority without a voice. They wanted multiple-member districts in which the representatives would be designated in proportion to the votes cast for each party. As the nation became industrialized, there was criticism of both territorial and proportional systems of representation. Critics urged a system of representation based on economic or functional interests: that is, teachers should elect their own representatives; factory workers should elect members of Congress to represent them; and so on.

The industrialization of America brought a major shift of population from the rural areas to the metropolitan centers, thus promoting another problem with respect to representation. The legislatures of the states which were dominated by rural representatives were naturally reluctant to redistrict the states and to reduce their own representation. Many of the legislatures also had failed to equitably reapportion the congressional districts.

In 1946 Professor Kenneth Colegrove of Northwestern University brought a suit to the Supreme Court to invalidate the existing scheme of congressional districts in Illinois. The state legislature had not reapportioned since 1901, and glaring disparities had appeared among congressional districts. For example, one district in Chicago had nearly nine times as many people in it as the district with the least population. By a vote of four to three, the Supreme Court in *Colegrove* v. *Green* refused to invalidate the Illinois Apportionment Act of 1901. Three justices ruled the issue was nonjusticiable and the Court should not enter this "political thicket." A fourth justice voted with them as a matter of equity, in view of the "shortness of the time remaining" before the next election. Justices Hugo L. Black, William O. Douglas, and Frank Murphy—in dissent—said that these population disparities denied the constitutional principle of representative government.

It was not until the 1960's that the Court reversed this position and limited the "political questions" doctrine. The Court, in *Baker* v. *Carr* (1962), held by a six-to-two vote that state legislative apportionment was subject to judicial scrutiny and possible remedy under the equal protection clause of the Fourteenth Amendment. Tennessee had not reapportioned its state legislative districts since 1901, even though its own state constitution required reapportionment every ten years! In March, 1963, Justice Douglas, who spoke for a majority of eight, declared in *Gray* v. *Sanders,* that Georgia's county unit system of voting in statewide and congressional primary elections deprived citizens of equal protection of the laws and was therefore unconstitutional. "The conception of political equality from the Declaration of Independence to Lincoln's Gettysburg Address, to the Fifteenth, Seventeenth, and Nineteenth Amendments," he said, "can mean only one thing—one person, one vote."

This case was a voting rights case and not one dealing with legislative apportionment, but it brought forth the rule of "one man, one vote." Two cases in 1964 applied the one man, one vote principle to apportionment of state legislative bodies and congressional districts. *Reynolds* v. *Sims* required that both houses of the state legislature of Alabama be elected from districts of substantially equal populations. Earlier the same year the holding in *Wesberry* v. *Sanders* required that congressional districts within a state must be equal in population, "as nearly as is practicable." And in *Avery* v. *Midland County* (1968), the Court brought county and city governments under similar equality requirements for their legislative bodies.

A conservative reaction demanded that the Warren Court decisions on apportionment be checked, and more than 130 bills were introduced into the House of Representatives to restrict the Court's power in apportionment cases. When these failed to pass, Senator Everett Dirksen introduced a proposed constitutional amendment which in essence would allow one house of a state legislature to be apportioned on other than a strict one man, one vote formula. When he was unable to get this passed by Congress, a national movement was initiated to persuade the state legislatures to call for a convention to nullify the one man, one vote ruling; thirty-three of the required thirty-four legislatures took such action. The proposal is now dead, as the new state legislatures have been filled by persons elected under the one man, one vote formula.

The Court has applied the one man, one vote rule very stringently in cases since 1964. In *Kirkpatrick* v. *Preisler* (1969), the Court ruled that any numerical or population variance, "no matter how small," must be justified by the state or shown to be unavoidable. But on February 21, 1973, in *Mahan* v. *Howell,* the Court approved a Virginia reapportionment plan which contained a discrepancy of 16.4 percent between the largest and smallest state legislative district. In the majority opinion, Justice William H. Rehnquist observed:

Neither courts nor legislatures are furnished with specialized calipers which enable them to extract from the general language of the equal protection clause of the Fourteenth Amendment the mathematical formula which establishes what range of percentage variations are permissible and what are not.

The Court continued: "While the percentage may well approach tolerable limits, we do not believe it exceeds them." The Court reasoned that political boundaries deserve some weight in districting state legislatures, while modifying the strict population factors in the *Kirkpatrick* case.

Not everyone is satisfied with how the American representative democracy or republican system functions. State legislatures and the Congress of the United States cannot please all of the people. Some of the laws they pass are clearly against the public interest and promote special interests of one type or another. But in light of the many difficulties under which it has operated, the American system of representation has worked fairly well for nearly two centuries. In most instances the people's representatives listen to their constituents, measure carefully the arguments pressed upon them from a host of different groups, obtain the best information possible, exercise their best judgment, and place their stamp of approval on legislation before them which seems most likely to serve the public good—allowing of course for exceptions prompted by private, personal, or political interests.

Popular Sovereignty

When the colonists first shot at the British Redcoats and the Declaration of Independence aimed its charges against the King of England, the sovereignty of the English realm was challenged. The Crown in England at the time was sovereign—in theory. With the separation of the colonies from England, a new sovereign state was born. But where were its sovereign powers located? In theory, sovereignty was located in the people.

The theoretical basis for popular sovereignty was ingrained in Americans of the Revolution through the idea of the social contract popularized by John Locke and many others. The social contract theory is grounded on the notion that men created the political system, exchanging their natural freedom for certain benefits that the system was supposed to provide. If government, however, becomes destructive of life, liberty, or property, the people have the right to change it.

The expression "We the People of the United States" of the Preamble is an accidental statement of belief in the principle of popular sovereignty, as the Framers of the Constitution initially intended to list each state by name; but did not do so lest one or more of the states might fail to ratify the Constitution. The Founding Fathers' fear of the masses challenged this idea of popular sovereignty, and a close examination of the Constitution discloses deliberate attempts to restrain the popular will. Acknowledging the sovereignty of the people on one hand, the Constitution attempts to control and refine this power by allowing the people, in some instances, only indirect selection and control of those who govern them. Examples of this are the electoral college method of electing the President and the impeachment procedure for removing him instead of direct election and recall.

Democratic notions have grown significantly in America since the birth of the nation, expanding the seed of popular sovereignty into a generally accepted principle. Even when demonstrations protesting public policies erupt in violence and these acts are censured severely by others in society, they are disparate expressions of popular sovereignty—each group claiming the right to determine what public policies should be. When such polarized expressions of group interest occur, it should be a clarion call to those in governing positions to give heed to another constitutional principle, limited government.

Limited Government

One face of the Constitution describes the government, its powers, and its operation. But there is another face of the Constitution which limits the government in behalf of the people. The argument for constitutional restrictions on government was cogently put by Madison in Number Fifty-one of the *Federalist Papers:*

> In framing a government which is to be administered by men over men, the first great difficulty lies in this: you must first enable the government to control the governed; and in the next place oblige it to control itself. A dependence on the people is, no doubt, the primary control on the government; but experience has taught mankind the necessity of auxiliary precautions.

These auxiliary precautions, to which we give the name "constitutionalism," are the provisions of the Constitution that were purposely contrived to protect the individual from arbitrary government action. "It may be a reflection on human nature that such devices should be necessary to control the abuses of government," Madison wrote, "but what is government itself but the greatest of all reflections on human nature? If men were angels, no government would be necessary." But, alas, they are not! The Framers knew this and placed restrictions on the Congress, the state legislatures, the President, and the state governors—in other words, those primarily involved in policy making.

Limitations on government are found throughout the Constitution but specifically so in Sections 9 and 10 of Article I, which limit, in a variety of ways, the national and state governments respectively; and in the amendments to the Constitution, especially the Bill of Rights and the Fourteenth Amendment. Also, the principles of the American political system which emerge from the Constitution, some of which are the very auxiliary precautions Madison mentioned, stand as sentinels against arbitrary government. Additionally, constitutionalism is advanced and supported by a variety of nongovernmental forces—a national ethos—which help shape the standards and form the norms by which many things are done and others are not done in the society.

Constitutional government attempts to strike that delicate balance between authority and liberty so essential to the best interests of both the society and the individual. Lincoln posed the problem when he asked: "Must a government of necessity be too *strong* for the liberties of its people, or too *weak* to maintain its own existence?" Obviously the American ideal is a balance in which only those powers necessary for the well-being of the society are exercised by the different units of government, and only those restrictions on individual liberties which are necessary to insure the liberties of every other person and preserve the society are imposed on the people. The American Constitution is both an instrument of power and a symbol of restraint.

Separation of Powers

One of the basic principles of the Constitution which serves as a measure of restraint against tyranny in government is that of separation of powers. Nowhere in the Constitution is this discussed; but the very creation of three branches of government, with the organization and powers of each outlined in separate articles, established such a government.

Madison, in Number Forty-seven of the *Federalist Papers,* relied on "the celebrated Montesquieu" to argue for the establishment of three separate branches of government. "When the legislative and executive powers are united in the same person or body," quotes Madison, "there can be no liberty, because apprehensions may arise lest the *same* monarch or senate should *enact* tyrannical laws to *execute* them in a tyrannical manner." Again: "Were the power of judging joined with the legislative, the life and liberty of the subject would be exposed to arbitrary control, for *the judge* would then be *the legislator.* Were it joined to the executive power, *the judge* might behave with all the violence of *an oppressor."*

Legislative and executive functions are to a degree independent of each other, as Congress and the President are elected by separate electoral processes for different terms of office. A Democratic Congress may be at odds with a Republican President, but it cannot remove him from office except through the difficult process of impeachment—and then only for causes of high crimes and misdemeanors, not for political differences. Conversely, the President cannot dissolve Congress, shorten its term, or remove any of its members. The national judiciary, although appointed by the President and confirmed by the Senate, is independent of both in the sense that the judges have life tenure; a fixed salary which cannot be reduced; the power of judicial review of legislative and executive acts; and, once appointed, an independence envied by all elective officers. (See Figure 2.1.)

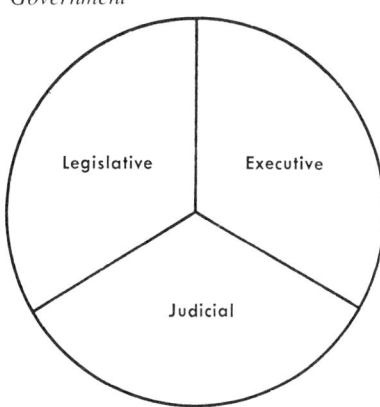

Figure 2.1 Branches of Government

The British constitution stresses fusion more than separation of powers by concentrating the powers of government in the legislature. The executive is actually a cabinet of ministers drawn primarily from the majority party in the House of Commons. The counterpart of the President is the Prime Minister. He is a Member of Parliament and leads his party in the House; but he is also the chief executive, the head of the government, as the executive is called. The government remains in power only so long as it retains the confidence of the House of Commons. Notwithstanding a degree of independence, the English judiciary cannot challenge the acts of Parliament today on the grounds that they are unconstitutional. In fact, the highest court in England is the House of Lords, the upper house of Parliament. Thus the English system is more one of "fusion of powers" and legislative supremacy, than that of separation of powers. (See Figure 2.2.)

Figure 2.2 British Government

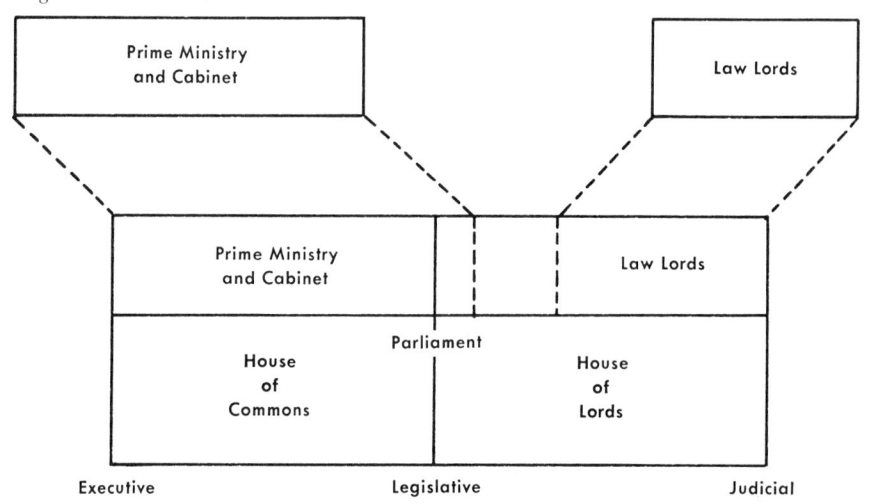

```
┌─────────────────────┐                    ┌─────────────┐
│   Prime Ministry    │                    │  Law Lords  │
│   and Cabinet       │                    │             │
└─────────────────────┘                    └─────────────┘
         ╲         ╲                        ╱         ╱
          ╲         ╲                      ╱         ╱
┌────────────────────────────┬──┬─────────────────────┐
│   Prime Ministry           │  │    Law Lords        │
│   and Cabinet              │  │                     │
├────────────────────────────┤  ├─────────────────────┤
│                    Parliament                       │
│        House         │         House                │
│         of           │          of                  │
│       Commons        │         Lords                │
└──────────────────────┴──────────────────────────────┘
      Executive            Legislative         Judicial
```

Checks and Balances

Each branch of government was not intended, however, to be completely separate and independent of the other branches. Madison pointed this out when he explained that separation of powers "did not mean that these departments ought to have no partial *agency,* in, or no *control* over, the acts of each other." Each branch was granted powers with which it could check the powers of the others. Separation of powers, then, is actually contradicted by a system of checks and balances. It would be more accurate to say that the American Constitution provides for a system of separate branches of government with primary functions, but sharing the power of the other branches as a check upon them.

The Constitution vests the executive power in the President, but one of his most important functions is legislative. The general scope of legislative work is stated in his State of the Union address presented before Congress at the beginning of each session. The most important legislation which Congress considers throughout the year are administration bills. Finally, the President must approve a bill before it becomes a law, or veto it if he is opposed to it. Congress, in turn, can intervene in administrative functions through its powers of legislation, investigation, confirmation, appropriation, and impeachment.

Federal judges are fully independent once their appointments are confirmed; but the appointment comes from the President and the confirmation from the Senate. The President can issue pardons and reprieves; the Congress can change the number of justices of the Supreme Court and also regulate its appellate jurisdiction; the Supreme Court can declare the acts of both the Congess and the President unconstitutional.

It is quite clear that there is not distinct separation of powers in American government. Separation of powers, as modified by the checks and balances, produces a system of three branches of government with overlapping functions. (See Figure 2.3.)

Other check-and-balancing factors are evident in the staggering of elections for the President, senators, and congressmen—each representing different constituencies. The bicameral arrangement in Congress was originally designed to represent the people and the states, and also two different classes in society. Even though the original fears and felt needs for one chamber to check the other have changed, bicameralism still affords another "check and balance" in the system. The constitutional provision that the President, a civilian, be the Commander-in-Chief of the military was intended as an internal check on a possible source of tyranny.

The American governmental system, at times, results in confusion, lack of direction, inaction, frustration, and deadlock. It requires a great deal of cooper-

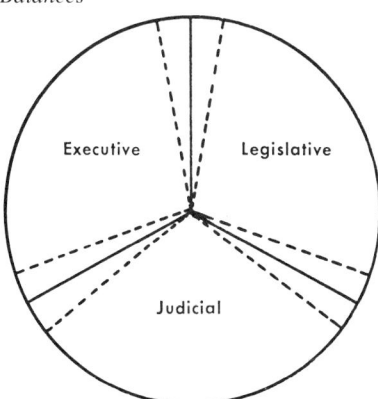

Figure 2.3 Checks and Balances

ation, compromise, and consensus before the engine of government can move. A number of authors during the two decades following World War II believed the "protection" provided by the Founding Fathers in the system of separation of powers and checks and balances was unnecessary—indeed, was a roadblock to effective government. Many maintained that a stronger executive was necessary to meet the demands of the nuclear age. Following the escalation of the Vietnam war, however, there has been a conscious effort to redress the imbalance of power between the President and the Congress.

Many citizens also have been concerned about the path the Warren Court nudged the nation along, and they have agitated for a curb in the Court's powers. Yet the power of the Supreme Court to interpret the Constitution has become a vital agent against arbitrary government and illegal private acts, and is a fundamental constitutional principle of our political system. All in all, more people are satisfied with the balance of our system promoted by separation of powers and checks and balances than are disturbed by the impediments to "progress" prompted by it.

Judicial Review

Judicial review applies to several different processes. It may describe the various courts' role of reviewing the actions of subordinate units of government or their officers to determine if they are acting within their legal powers. It also applies in the federal system, whereby courts are made responsible for enforcing the constitutional division of functions between the national government and the states. In this situation the Supreme Court becomes the umpire of the federal system. Additionally, judicial review is the power of the courts to declare acts of Congress or the President unconstitutional. Does this power deny the Founding Fathers' intent to structure three coordinate branches of government and turn our system into one of "judicial supremacy"?

Although the Constitution does not specifically grant the power of judicial review of legislative and executive acts to the judiciary, concern was registered in the public debate over ratification about the role of the courts. Hamilton, in Number Seventy-eight of the *Federalist Papers,* attempted to persuade the opponents that this power was essential to the system: "There is no position which depends on clearer principles than that every act of a delegated authority, contrary to the tenor of the commission under which it is exercised, is void. No legislative act, therefore, contrary to the Constitution, can be valid." Again: "The interpretation of the laws is the proper and peculiar province of the courts. A constitution is in fact, and must be regarded by the judges as a fundamental law. It therefore belongs to them to ascertain its meaning, as well as the meaning of any particular act proceeding from the legislative body."

If there is no specific grant of the power of judicial review to the judiciary, how did it become so fundamental a principle of the American political system? The significant precedent was established in a rigged case which was brought before the Marshall Court. After the Federalists had lost the election of 1800 to the Jeffersonians, President Adams appointed John Marshall Chief Justice of the Supreme Court while he was also the Secretary of State. The Federalist Congress then passed the Judiciary Act of 1801 and an act pertaining to the District of Columbia which created a number of new judgeships. One week before he was to leave office, President Adams appointed forty-two new justices of the peace for the District of Columbia. Some of the formal commissions of appointment had not been delivered by Secretary of State Marshall when Jefferson took office, and Jefferson ordered his new Secretary of State, James Madison, not to deliver them.

William Marbury, one of these appointees, went directly to the Supreme Court for a writ of *mandamus* under section thirteen of the Judiciary Act of 1789, which authorized such a procedure—to force Madison to deliver Marbury his commission. Chief Justice Marshall professed to believe that section thirteen of the Judiciary Act of 1789 was an unconstitutional enlargement of the Supreme Court's original jurisdiction as listed in Article III of the Constitution. This was absurd, as the provision could be, and had been, interpreted only as a proper remedy in those cases which were properly brought before the Supreme Court under its original jurisdiction. This reasoning would not have served Marshall's purposes, however; otherwise he would have held that the Court did not have jurisdiction and sent Marbury to a lower court for the remedy he sought. Marbury never went to a lower court.

Marshall's primary purpose in the case was to establish the principle of judicial review. In declaring section thirteen of the Judiciary Act of 1789 unconstitutional, Marshall relied heavily on Hamilton's reasoning in Number Seventy-eight of the *Federalist Papers;* and he concluded his arguments by reasoning that it would be immoral if the justices did not uphold the Constitution which they had sworn to support. The reasoning of Marshall is subject to question on a number of grounds, but the principle of judicial review which he helped to fashion has been ratified by time and practice and is an important principle in our federal system.

Federalism

When the colonies made good their bid for independence and organized the United States of America under the Articles of Confederation, the fact that sovereignty was retained in the separate states really left the Congress as little more than an international organization. It performed certain functions for the whole society only so long as one of the states did not object. Each state had ties with the other states as well, but united action was dependent on cooperation from each one of the member states of the league.

The desires of the strong nationalists in the Convention were to create a strong central government which would reduce the states to little more than administrative units of the central government. If they had been successful the new system would have resembled a unitary system similar to that of the United Kingdom today.

As the *Federalist Papers* pointed out in many of its numbers, the final product was a compromise between a federal and a unitary system. In Number Thirty-nine, for example, Madison explained that many federal features of the old government were retained: (1) the Constitution must be ratified by the people of the several states; (2) the Senate derives its powers from the states; (3) the powers of the national government are enumerated by the Constitution; (4) and other powers are left to the states. Madison found certain features of the proposed Constitution to have national features about them, and others to be of a mixed nature. He concluded: "The proposed Constitution, therefore, is, in strictness, neither a national nor a federal constitution, but a composition of both."

The Constitutional Fathers thought they had formed a system in which the functions would be allocated to coordinate units of government, each mutually independent in its sphere of action. In reality a federal system was created which had strong national qualities—if not immediately, then eventually, as confirmed by the supremacy clause of Article VI of the Constitution. The states are autonomous, rather than independent, units enveloped within the larger national system. True, residual powers remain with the states while the national government has constitutionally granted enumerated powers, augmented by the implied powers of the "necessary and proper" clause (Article I, Section 8); but any conflict between the two levels of government is resolved by the Supreme Court, *one of the branches of the national government.*

Alexander Hamilton claimed in his argument over the constitutionality of the Bank of the United States that the national government has two additional powers: inherent and resulting. The inherent power, he explained, derives from the very nature of government. Government has all powers necessary to achieve the purpose for which it is organized, which are not precluded by specific constitutional restrictions. The resulting powers come from the "whole mass of powers of government, and from the nature of political society," he professed, and not as a "consequence of either of the powers specially enumerated." Chief Justice Marshall was influenced by Hamilton's arguments in the case of *McCulloch v. Maryland* (1819), which upheld the constitutionality of the Bank of the United States. Throughout the years Court decisions have greatly enlarged the powers of the national government through a liberal construction of the enumerated and implied powers, and occasionally resorting to inherent and resulting power theories. National powers also have been significantly increased through the President and Congress interpreting their roles broadly.

The Constitution divides the functions between the national government and the states, and it also provides for interstate relations. American federalism requires a great degree of cooperation between the central government and the states, and among the states themselves.

The Constitution provides the ground rules for interstate cooperation in four basic areas: (1) full faith and credit shall be given in each state to the public acts, records, and judicial proceedings of every other state; (2) the same privileges and immunities will be given to citizens in all states; (3) interstate rendition of fugitives from justice; and (4) interstate compacts may be made with the consent of Congress.

Congress was constitutionally empowered to issue uniform regulations in regard to the full faith and credit clause. In 1790 and 1804, Congress provided an uncomplicated method of authentication and commanded that judicial proceedings and public records be given the same effect in every court that they had in the court that issued them. This essentially requires that the civil acts entered into in one state are to be enforced in any other state of the Union. This granting of full faith and credit has become very important in our highly mobile society. Supposing a person entered into a contract to buy a car in Georgia and failed to meet the payments. The creditor then can obtain a court order forcing payment. If the car buyer moves to California thinking he can avoid the payments, the creditor can bring action in a California court, which will issue an enforcing order of its own.

This provision has worked quite well throughout the United States except in divorce cases. Each state has its own requirements for divorce, some of which are very lenient—as in Nevada, Florida, and Idaho. Jurisdiction for divorce in Nevada, for example, calls for only six weeks residence to establish bona fide domicile prior to a divorce decree. The "quickie" divorce in Nevada seems to deny the full faith and credit requirement of marriages contracted in other states where the grounds for divorce are more rigorous. But when Nevada grants a divorce decree according to its requirements, this civil act also deserves full faith and credit.

It has been difficult for the Supreme Court to establish uniform guidelines in this area. Divorce decrees can become exceedingly complex because divorces may involve property settlements, alimony, or the custody of children. The confusion in this area of divorce is one of the prices that must be paid for the luxury of a federal system. Justice Robert H. Jackson expressed his frustration over the inability of the American political system to clearly mark the paths through this divorce thicket in his dissent in *Rice* v. *Rice* (1949): "If there is one thing that the people are entitled to expect from their lawmakers, it is rules of law that will enable individuals to tell whether they are married and, if so, to whom." Without a uniform national law on divorce, about all the Court has been able to tell divorcing couples is that it will uphold a divorce decree if both parties had due notice and came within the state's jurisdiction.

The privileges and immunities clause probably was intended by the Constitutional Fathers to establish a common citizenship and prevent a state from discriminating against citizens of another state. But states do indeed "discriminate" against out-of-state citizens by requiring students to pay a higher tuition; hunters and fishermen to pay higher license fees; professional people to meet certain standards by examination; businessmen and contractors to file bonds, pay different tax rates, and bid more competitively on jobs. The Supreme Court has upheld such requirements if they are reasonable, if the regulatory powers are exercised fairly, and if different treatment does not rest solely on out-of-state citizenship.

As full faith and credit applies to civil acts, "interstate rendition" is the device designed to meet the problems presented by federalism in regard to criminal laws. Article IV, Section 2, of the Constitution provides that:

A person charged in any state with treason, felony, or other crime, who shall flee from justice, and be found in another state, shall on demand of the executive authority of the state from which he fled, be delivered up, to be removed to the state having jurisdiction of the crime.

It is the obligation of the governor of the state where the fugitive is found to return him to the state where he is charged with violating the law, when the governor so requests. The Court has determined that this obligation is a moral one and the national government will not force the rendition. Even though governors occasionally refuse to return a fugitive, orderly rendition is usually followed.

Congress passed a law in 1934, based on its commerce powers, which supports the process of interstate rendition by making it a federal offense to flee across a state line to avoid lawful prosecution. The law requires that the fugitive be tried in the federal district court in the state from which he fled, thus making the prisoner readily available to local authorities.

Interstate compacts were originally applied almost exclusively to boundary problems between states; but today such a compact is a highly useful device to cooperatively solve mutual social, economic, political, and environmental problems. The Port of New York Authority, for instance, is based on a compact between the states of New Jersey and New York. The Authority not only handles the planning and administration needs of the entire port of New York City, but it has expanded its activities to include the rapid transit system between Manhattan and New Jersey and a variety of related functions. The Colorado River Compact allocates the water to the states along the river. Interstate agreements protect the salmon resources of the Columbia River. The migratory fisheries along the Atlantic states are similarly controlled. Interstate compacts dealing with crime, transportation, and oil resources are examples of the expanding role of cooperative federalism among the states.[4]

[4] See C. Herman Pritchett, *The American Constitution* (New York: McGraw-Hill, 1959). Chapter 6.

The federal arrangement proposed by the Constitution (1) enumerates certain powers assigned exclusively to the national government, such as the conduct of foreign affairs; (2) assigns other powers to the national government, powers which are also held concurrently by the states—for example, taxation; (3) denies certain powers to the national government—for example, Congress may not tax exports or give preference to the ports of one state over those of another; (4) denies certain powers to the states—for example, no state may enter into a treaty; and (5) acknowledges that all other powers belong to the states—that is, the states have all residual powers. (See Figure 2.4.)

This neat pattern of federalism is not so tidy in actual practice. Occasionally the American federal system, with its national, state, and local levels of government, is compared to a three-layer cake. "A far more accurate image," according to Morton Grodzins, "is the rainbow or marble cake, characterized by an inseparable mingling of differently colored ingredients, the colors appearing in vertical and diagonal strands and unexpected whirls. As colors are mixed in the marble cake, so functions are mixed in the American federal system." [5] Constitutional lawyers have had much difficulty in drawing a sharp line between the powers of the nation and the states. It is even more difficult as concepts of federalism continue to evolve, and as attitudes of antagonism between levels of government are replaced with notions of "cooperative federalism."

Nation-state cooperation in the nineteenth century included a variety of different internal improvements, such as roads, canals, and railroads; aid to the states in education through land grants for public school use and the establishment of agricultural and mechanical colleges; and many different grants of lands, cash grants, and services to meet the separate needs of the states.

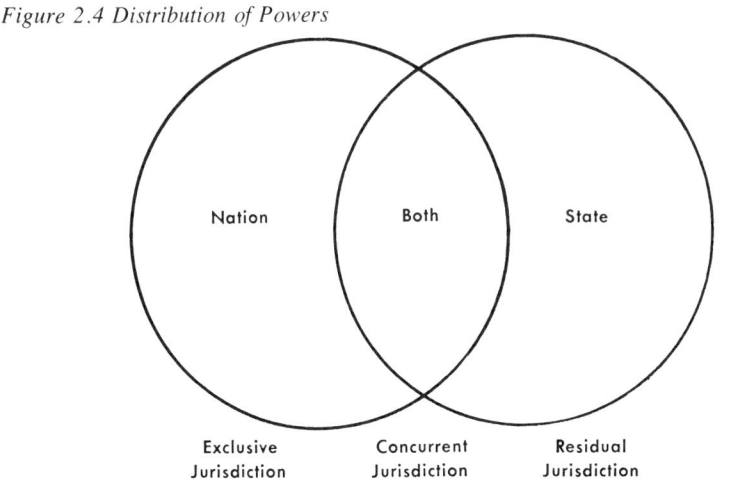

Figure 2.4 Distribution of Powers

[5] Daniel J. Elazar, ed., *The Politics of American Federalism* (Lexington, Mass.: D. C. Heath, 1969), p. 11.

A great increase in national involvement in state affairs accompanied the Great Depression and the New Deal of President Franklin D. Roosevelt. New Deal programs affected agriculture, labor-management relations, transportation, communications, banking and the stock market, and welfare, among others. In many of these areas the Constitution does not grant specific power to the national government. But through the taxing and spending power, the national government became involved in traditional state functions by appropriating money to be used for specific purposes in the states as grants-in-aid. The states were required to pass implementing legislation to receive the money. The states were not forced, but enticed, to participate in the nationally promoted programs.

Prior to the Great Depression, grants-in-aid had been used for highway construction, agricultural and vocational education, and a few other programs; however, the amount was but a small portion of state and national expenditures. The New Deal grants, on the other hand, were massive; and subsequent grants continued to expand in numbers and costs. The programs were still cooperative, but the result of these expanded programs greatly enlarged the role of the national government in the federal arrangement.

The position of the states in the federal system was further minimized beginning in the New Deal period as the growth of the cities brought problems of such magnitude that some cities could not handle them without assistance. The states were unable or unwilling to help solve these urban problems; and the national government, especially following World War II, began to give direct grants to local governments for urban renewal projects, airport aid, rapid transit systems, education, and other programs prompted by metropolitan growth and central-city decay. The states, jealous of their position in the political system, tried to recover their partnership position with the national government by having all national grants to local governments channeled through state agencies.

Presidents Kennedy and Johnson advanced federal grant programs to fight poverty, control pollution, improve local law enforcement, and provide housing, to mention but a few programs which significantly added to the power and control of the national government. Since these federal grants required the state programs to meet specified national standards, national control over state and local policies was greatly augmented. This was so especially in the area of education, where desegregation and busing to achieve racial balance were federally induced; and in the War on Poverty, through which the Office of Economic Opportunity made grants directly to community-based organizations promoting action programs opposed by many of the state and local establishment types—both public officials and private citizens.

During the decade of the 1960's, the number and costs of federal grants increased greatly. Nearly 1,100 grants-in-aid programs, each with its separate requirements, were federally funded in 1969. The federal cost of these programs increased from $7 billion in 1960 to $20.3 billion in 1969. Criticism also grew over these federal programs, but it turned more on the mounting controls than on the expanded programs and costs. A move toward "correcting" this problem of federal control over local policies was made on April 30, 1969, when President Nixon asked Congress for power to consolidate certain related programs into "block grants," allowing more state and local discretion in the use of these funds. This was followed by a broader "no-strings-attached" solution of a proposed revenue-sharing plan in the President's New Federalism speech of August 8, 1969.

Revenue sharing first received serious consideration during the Kennedy years, when Walter Heller was chairman of the Council of Economic Advisers. This was followed by a number of revenue-sharing bills that were introduced and seriously debated in Congress during the Johnson years.

President Nixon, in January, 1971, formally presented his new dimension to the federal arrangement in his budget message to Congress. He called for a "new balance of responsibility and power in America by proposing the sharing of Federal revenues with states and communities—in a way that will both alleviate the paralyzing fiscal crisis of state and local governments and enable citizens to have more of a say in the decisions that directly affect their lives."

Nixon's revenue-sharing program was prompted, he said, by a real financial squeeze on state and local governments. The tax sources (mainly sales and property taxes) available to these units of government were inadequate to meet the demand for services. As a result, combined state and local debt increased by over 600 percent between 1948 and 1971. During this same period the national government helped meet some of this demand through grants-in-aid programs, which accounted for 18 percent of state and local revenues. The President believed that this system of hundreds of separate programs—each with its own policies, its own requirements and procedures, and its own funding—was not only inefficient, but also that it (1) restricted the freedom of state and local governments to spend funds where they were needed most; (2) was unresponsive to the needs of specific local situations; and (3) separated resources and responsibility, because state and local governments had the responsibility for providing services, but lacked the necessary funds.

The President's plan called for $16 billion to be allocated to the states, with a pass-through to localities. Of this amount, $5 billion was requested to be in the form of general revenue sharing, without restrictions. The remaining $11 billion was to be in the form of special revenue sharing, to replace the block grant programs as well as the categorical grants, for six broad subject areas: urban community development, rural community development, education, manpower training, law enforcement, and transportation. The change from block and categorical grants to the six broad areas was to be accompanied by an increase of $709 million in the amounts budgeted for 1972 for federal aid to state and localities.

Even though nearly everyone outwardly agreed with the principle of revenue sharing, hardly anyone could agree on a single version. The liberals wanted the money to go directly to the cities, bypassing the suburban- and rural-controlled state legislatures; the conservatives disagreed. The state governors liked the principle, but wanted to control the allocation of funds within the states and waited to see if federal monies would be more or less than through the grant programs. Republicans and Democrats in the main were in favor, but assessed the political impact of such a measure and how to turn it to partisan advantage. Individual congressmen measured the proposal against their own yardsticks of what was necessary for a victory in their next election.

The President's program was made politically palatable with such phrases as "a stronger voice for the individual taxpayer in how his money will be spent locally," and "it will provide new strength to the federal system by assigning services to the level of government best equipped to perform them." And it was almost assured of passage when Wilbur Mills, the chairman of the House Ways and Means Committee, supported the measure, even though a year earlier he had said that a revenue-sharing bill would be buried so deep in his committee that "it would never see the light of day."

Congress gave the President part of what he requested when it passed HR 14370, establishing a five-year, general revenue-sharing program. It authorized the payments to state and local governments of $30.2 billion for the five-year period, 1972–77. The distribution of these funds was based on one of two formulas. The Senate version, a "three-factor" formula, distributed the funds

Editorial cartoon by Pat Oliphant. Copyright, the *Denver Post*. Reprinted with permission of Los Angeles Times Syndicate.

**"You'd have hated the steaks, so I threw them out—
how about a good old peanut butter and jelly?"**

on the basis of population, tax effort, and per capita income. The House bill was made up of a "five-factor" formula which included two additional factors, urbanized population and state income tax collections. The Senate version provided more money to the smaller, more rural states; the House-passed bill favored the more populous, industrialized states. In a unique compromise, the House and Senate conferees allowed each state to select the distribution formula which maximized its share of the funds. Congress concurred in this compromise, and the President signed this historic measure into law on October 20, 1972.

Within each state, one-third of the funds are allocated to the state government and two-thirds to local governments. Distribution among the local governments is based on the three-factor formula. There are some strings attached, however, to this revenue-sharing measure: (1) local governments must spend their allotments for public safety, environmental protection, public transportation, and other specified "priority" areas; (2) discrimination is not permitted in any programs financed with revenue-sharing funds; (3) funds may not be used as matching money for other federal grant programs; (4) construction workers must be paid at least the prevailing wage in similar construction in the locality; and (5) the state and local governments must account for the use of revenue-sharing funds.

In President Nixon's budget message for fiscal year 1974, which he delivered to Congress on January 29, 1973, he registered marked satisfaction over the passage of the general revenue-sharing measure; and he asked Congress to pass a special revenue-sharing package which was not passed in the Ninety-second Congress. He proposed four programs of broad-purpose grants totaling $6.9 billion for the states to use in the areas of education, law enforcement and criminal justice, manpower training, and urban community development. Calling the existing grant systems inefficient and his proposed special revenue-sharing proposal an urgent priority, he said:

> The federal system is dynamic, not static. To maintain its vitality, we must constantly reform and refine it. No longer will power flow inexorably to Washington. Instead the power to make many major decisions and to help meet local needs will be returned to where it belongs—to state and local officials, men and women accountable to an alert citizenry and responsive to local conditions and opinions.

The problems of nationwide concern—such as deterioration of the environment and pollution, public health needs from drug abuse to the chronic illnesses of the elderly, social security and welfare, mass transit and related transportation pressures, crime, and inadequate housing and urban blight—are today more national than state and local in scope. The meaning of this to our federal system will be an increasing role played by the national government. In spite of the proposals to return more power as well as money to the states and local communities, such programs do not intend to return the American federal system to that conceived by the Founding Fathers. As the people become less provincial and more "American" in their perspectives, and as their representatives in Washington continue to sense this, the federal system will most likely concentrate power on the national level and continue to take on unitary attributes.

3
FUNDAMENTAL FREEDOMS

In the morning mail of January 8, 1962, the Supreme Court of the United States received a large envelope from Clarence Earl Gideon, Prisoner No. 003826, Florida State Prison. Anthony Lewis in *Gideon's Trumpet* explains that standard court procedure requires that all appeals directed to the Supreme Court be printed and a fee paid for docketing the case. Federal statute waives this rule, however, and allows certain individuals "to proceed in any federal court *in forma pauperis,* in the manner of a pauper," without paying the regular costs. The papers which Gideon mailed to the Court were written in pencil on lined prison paper. Prison rules allowed only two letters each week, and Gideon used one of the two letters he was allowed to write in an appeal to the highest court in the land!

Clarence Gideon was one of the most unfortunate of men. He had experienced few successes in his life, had served time for four separate felonies, and expected little from this endeavor. But, like most men in prison, he sincerely believed he had been wronged by being sentenced to five years in the Florida state penitentiary after he had unsuccessfully tried to conduct his own defense in a jury trial on the charge of breaking and entering a poolroom with the intent to commit a misdemeanor. Gideon had asked the Florida court to appoint a lawyer to represent him, but the judge explained that the State of Florida, like a number of other states, provided counsel to indigents only in capital cases.

The Supreme Court granted Gideon a writ of *certiorari* allowing him to file briefs and present arguments before the Court. Justice Hugo L. Black, in a majority opinion, said:

From the very beginning, our state and national constitutions and laws have laid great emphasis on procedural and substantive safeguards designed to assure fair trials before impartial tribunals in which every defendant stands equal before the law. This noble idea cannot be realized if the poor man charged with crime has to face his accusers without a lawyer to assist him.

Considering the technicalities of the legal processes, a judge once said to a defendant who wanted to represent himself: "The person who represents himself is represented by a fool." Gideon was not a fool; he was poor. The Court recognized that "in our adversary system of criminal justice, any person haled into court, who is too poor to hire a lawyer, cannot be assured a fair trial unless counsel is provided for him."

The Supreme Court ruled that a state must furnish counsel to indigent persons accused of noncapital offenses, and in so doing reversed the ruling in *Betts* v. *Brady* (1942). The case of *Gideon* v. *Wainright* (1963) was remanded to the Florida court for retrial with counsel. Gideon was acquitted in the new trial and freed from prison.

The American public received the news of the Gideon case with mixed emotions. Many feared the decision would open the gates of the prisons across the country and free convicted felons to prey upon the law-abiding public. The Court was accused of coddling criminals and not upholding the rights of Americans. Others regarded the landmark decision with optimism, hoping that the poor and the uneducated of America would from now on receive "equal justice" in the procedures of both the national and state court systems.

The Gideon decision was one of a number of cases which gave the Warren Court an "activist" label. Indeed, the post-World War II period in general experienced a revolution in civil rights and civil liberties, in which the Supreme Court responded humanely to social phenomena of the time and promoted new views of fundamental rights.

CIVIL RIGHTS AND CIVIL LIBERTIES

Authority and liberty have lived side by side in America from its first settlement. Personal freedom has been basic to American political life. Colonial charters contained provisions to protect individual liberties. The Declaration of Independence was a plea for human rights, based on a "higher law, a cosmic jurisprudence." The first state constitutions placed restrictions on their governments to protect the people's liberties. Moreover, "auxiliary precautions" were included within the Constitution for this very purpose; and when some maintained that the liberties of the people were inadequately protected, the Bill of Rights, the first ten amendments, was proposed by the first Congress under the new Constitution.

Civil liberties is a term currently applied to those liberties usually spelled out in a bill of rights or a constitution that guarantee the protection of persons, opinions, and property from the arbitrary interference of government officials.

These personal liberties are not absolute, however. Restraints may be placed upon them when they are abused by individuals or groups and when the public welfare requires such restraints.

Civil rights, on the other hand, refer to the positive acts of government to protect persons against discriminatory treatment by government or individuals. Civil rights have taken on special importance since the Civil War, as Congress and state and local legislatures have, with some footdragging, worked to secure equal treatment for blacks, and, more recently, other minority groups subject to discrimination. The recent civil rights laws which require equal opportunity in voting, employment, and the purchase of a home, and those laws which require public transportation, hotels, and restaurants to provide equal facilities, are examples of civil rights legislation. The terms "civil liberties" and "civil rights" are often used interchangeably, however, and it is probably just as meaningful to regard both as "human rights."

The Founding Fathers intended to safeguard human rights by imposing certain restraints on state and national governments, limiting their powers. The Constitution denies Congress the right to pass a bill of attainder, which is a legislative punishment without the benefit of judicial trial; and an *ex post facto* law, which is retroactive, making an act punishable which was legal when it was committed. The Constitution also provides that "the privilege of the writ of habeas corpus shall not be suspended, unless when in cases of rebellion or invasion the public safety may require it." This protection is most basic, as arrest and imprisonment deny a person his civil liberties; the writ of *habeas corpus* is a judicial order to bring the accused before a court where the individual is informed of the reason for his detention. There are countries which hold political prisoners indefinitely without affording the accused this basic protection!

To avoid the imposition of political punishment for unpopular beliefs, the Constitution defined treason specifically and provided that no person would be convicted of treason "unless on the testimony of two witnesses to the same overt act, or on confession in open court." Additionally, Article IV states: "No religious test shall ever be required as a qualification to any office or trust under the United States."

The Bill of Rights was added to the Constitution in 1791 to impose specific restrictions on the national government and to protect human rights. The Fourteenth Amendment was purposefully added in 1868 to protect human rights, specifically the rights of blacks, from infringement by the state governments. Since *Gitlow* v. *New York* (1925), the Supreme Court has selected certain guarantees found in the Bill of Rights and "incorporated" them in the Fourteenth Amendment. The incorporated guarantees include the First Amendment's freedoms of religion, speech, press, assembly, and petition; the Fourth Amendment's protection against unreasonable searches and seizures; the Fifth Amendment's protection against compulsory self-incrimination and double jeopardy;

the Sixth Amendment's guarantee of the right of counsel, the right of a speedy public trial, and the right of confrontation of witnesses against one's self; and the Eighth Amendment's prohibition against cruel and unusual punishment. These guarantees and protections are, in the language of the Court, so "essential to a scheme of ordered liberty" that they are implicit in the word "liberty" of the due process clause of the Fourteenth Amendment. While Justice Hugo L. Black was on the bench he maintained that the entire Bill of Rights applied to the states, as "wholesale incorporation" was intended by the framers of the Fourteenth Amendment.[1]

SUBSTANTIVE AND PROCEDURAL RIGHTS

Obviously, more important than the distinctions between civil liberties and civil rights is the protection of the substance of human rights from either government encroachment or infringement from other individuals. Procedural rights are included in the Bill of Rights to protect these substantive rights or basic freedoms.

Substantive rights are those which define the basic content or substance of individual freedom, such as the First Amendment freedoms of religion, speech, press, petition, and assembly; the Thirteenth Amendment's denial of slavery or involuntary servitude; and the Fifteenth Amendment's insurance that no one shall be denied the right to vote on the basis of race, color, or previous condition of servitude. Procedural rights are those procedures which are designed to make the judicial process fair, such as the Sixth Amendment's guarantee that the accused shall have a speedy and public trial by an impartial jury, as well as assistance of counsel for his defense, and must be confronted with witnesses against him.

The Fifth Amendment's stipulation that no one shall be deprived of life, liberty, or property without due process of law is both substantive and procedural: the substance of life, liberty, and property is not to be denied without the procedural right of due process of law.

FIRST AMENDMENT FREEDOMS

Freedom of Speech, Press, and Assembly

Few liberties are considered more important to democracy than freedom of speech and freedom of the press. John Stuart Mill said in *On Liberty:* "If all mankind minus one, were of one opinion, and only one person were of the contrary opinion, mankind would be no more justified in silencing that one person

[1] See George W. Spicer, *The Supreme Court and Fundamental Freedoms* (New York: Appleton-Century-Crofts, 1967).

than he, if he had the power, would be justified in silencing mankind." Modern precedents with regard to freedom of speech can be traced to the landmark case of *Schenck* v. *United States* (1919). This case involved the federal Espionage Act of 1917, which made it illegal to interfere with military recruitment. Schenck had distributed antiwar pamphlets to potential enlistees. The Court upheld the conviction of Schenck, but Justice Oliver Wendell Holmes developed the famous "clear and present danger" doctrine. This guiderule states that freedom of speech should *not* be curtailed unless it constitutes a clear and present danger to the society.

About two thousand cases involving the Espionage Act arose in the lower federal courts during the war. Unfortunately, in nearly all of them the clear and present danger doctrine was ignored. Any vague statement criticizing the war, the administration, or the American form of government was usually accepted as having a "bad tendency" which was considered sufficient to convict the accused. Under the act, for example, pacifists were convicted for expressing a general opposition to all war; and socialist leader Eugene V. Debs was convicted for merely exhorting an audience to "resist militarism, wherever found."

Even the clear and present danger doctrine must be relative to the needs of the society. The Court speaks with finality on questions concerning the balance of liberty and authority; therefore the inherent rights of the people are what the Court permits, what the political system enforces, and what the people demand. To realize this fact is to awaken to the responsibility of each citizen to be vigilant in keeping the government from unwarranted restriction on these freedoms. Justice Black, a great champion of human rights, insisted that the First Amendment freedoms were absolute and that any abridgment of them is unconstitutional. He argued that no speech or writing should be punished as such, not even slander and libel, and that governments should intervene only when the people do something wrong, not when they say something unacceptable.

The next major free speech case, *Gitlow* v. *New York* (1925), was crucial for two reasons. First, it was the first time the First Amendment of the Bill of Rights was applied to a state statute. In this case the defendants were accused of violating the New York Criminal Anarchy Statute by their public advocacy of socialist revolutionary doctrines. Second, although the majority found that the accused said things which the state legislature thought constituted a clear and present danger, Justices Holmes and Brandeis dissented and claimed the danger was at most only a probability. To the minority, at least, the clear and present danger test was not applied in this case and personal freedom slipped a notch or two while the authority of the state was enhanced.

During time of war or other crisis, freedom of speech and press is severely strained. Unsettled conditions following World War II prompted many state and local governments to pass laws curbing speeches which might disturb the peace. In *Terminiello* v. *Chicago* (1949), the Court by a five-to-four decision applied a clear and present danger solution to a case which pointed up the theoretical conflict between community interest and First Amendment rights. Terminiello, an unfrocked priest who advocated extreme right-wing ideas, had been convicted of disorderly conduct following an incendiary public address in Chicago, in which he attacked his Jewish opponents as "filthy scum" and worse. The speech indeed had produced a riot. Bricks were thrown, a mob of people stormed the doors of the hall, and the peace of the city was disturbed; but the disturbance was on the part of the people outside the hall who were incensed by what Terminiello said and not on the part of his followers. Could a speaker, himself guilty of no disorder, be punished for a breach of the peace on the part of those who objected to his ideas?

Speaking for the majority, Justice William O. Douglas overturned the conviction. The trial judge, interpreting the Illinois statute for the jury, had asserted that it made punishable "speech which stirs the public to anger, invites dispute, brings about a condition of unrest or creates a disturbance." So construed, Douglas said, the law was unconstitutional. The right of free speech, he admitted, was not absolute; but it could not be suppressed unless it prompted a "clear and present danger of serious and substantive evil that rises far above public inconvenience, annoyance and unrest." Douglas thought it intolerable to punish a person merely because his ideas led to violence on the part of those who resented what he said.

On the national level, however, fear of communist subversion prompted Congress and the Court for a period of time to react differently on questions of First Amendment rights and the safety of the society. In 1940, Congress passed the Alien Registration Act, commonly known as the Smith Act, which was intended as a wartime sedition measure. This act had gone virtually unnoticed until the "red scare" of the postwar period. Although it was not aimed at the communists, a section of it made it unlawful to "advocate, abet, advise, or teach . . . overthrowing any government of the United States by force or violence."

In the early 1950's eleven top communist leaders of the United States were indicted for organizing the Communist Party, whose alleged goal was the overthrow of the government of the United States, and for willfully and knowingly conspiring to teach and advocate the overthrow of the government by force. The case, *Dennis* v. *United States,* was heard by the Supreme Court in 1951 at the height of "McCarthyism"; the Vinson Court upheld the Smith Act and the lower court conviction. Nominally the Court accepted the clear and present danger doctrine; in reality, it destroyed the force of this guide rule almost completely. As Douglas and Black pointed out, the Court now had revived the "bad tendency" doctrine of World War I under another name, which in effect held that free speech may be inhibited when there is *probable* danger to the government. To allow the government to forestall probable danger grants it more power to curb freedom of speech than when it is restrained until there is clear and present danger.

The Department of Justice brought more than 150 indictments against communists under the Smith Act during the next six years, which resulted in more than one hundred convictions. In 1957, however, the Supreme Court in *Yates v. United States* overturned the conviction of five "second-string" communists, and held it was advocacy to do something, not mere belief in communism, which the Smith Act denied. This position was modified in *Scales v. United States* (1961), when the Court, with the conservatives in control, ruled that a person having "knowing" membership in a subversive group could not claim protection under the First Amendment. Justice John M. Harlan resorted to the "balancing test," which weighed First Amendment rights against the requirements of public security. Nevertheless, Harlan accepted the all-important distinction, derived from the *Yates* case, between mere advocacy of abstract doctrine and advocacy of specific acts directed to violent overthrow of the political system. This position was upheld in *Brandenburg v. Ohio* (1969).

Freedom of expression confronted national security in the 1970's in a head-on clash over the publishing of the "Pentagon Papers." In this case the government asked for an injunction to restrain the *New York Times* and the *Washington Post*. "Any system of prior restraint of expression comes to this Court bearing a heavy presumption against its constitutional validity," the Court said in *New York Times Co. v. United States* (1971), and it ruled that the publication of the documents could not be restrained because the government did not meet the "heavy burden of showing justification of the enforcement of such restraint." Justice Byron White, with whom Justice Potter Stewart concurred, reasoned that "in the absence of legislation by Congress, based on its own investigations and findings, I am quite unable to agree that the inherent powers of the Executive and the courts reach so far as to authorize remedies having such sweeping potential for inhibiting publications by the press." Justice William J. Brennan thought the nexus between the documents and national security was not close enough. It was Justice Black, however, who eloquently defended the sanctity of freedom of the press:

Now, for the first time in the hundred eighty-two years since the founding of the Republic, the federal courts are asked to hold that the First Amendment does not mean what it says, but rather means that the government can halt the publication of current news of vital importance to the people of this country.

Black concluded:

To find that the President has "inherent power" to halt the publication of news by resort to the courts would wipe out the First Amendment and destroy the fundamental liberty and security of the very people the government hopes to make secure.

First Amendment freedom of the press stood toe-to-toe with political authority in 1972 in a clash over the right of reporters to withhold the identity of their sources of information from grand jury investigations. In *Branzburg* v. *Hayes* (1972) the Court split five to four over the issue, with the four Nixon appointees joining Justice White, who reasoned: "The great weight of authority is that newsmen are not exempt from the normal duty of appearing before a grand jury and answering questions relevant to a criminal investigation." America also divided over the issue, and "shield laws" were introduced into the state legislatures and Congress to protect the newsmen and their sources of information on the theory that the people have a "right to know." Without confidentiality, the news sources, especially "leaks" from within government would dry up.

Another area of First Amendment concern for public officials is the expression of ideas considered to be obscene or indecent through the media of books, magazines, plays, and motion pictures. All levels of government have passed legislation to control the sale of pornographic materials. Even though state and local governments have police powers to protect the "health, safety, morals, and welfare of the people," Congress has prohibited the interstate transportation of obscene printed matter, barred it from the mails, and forbidden its importation under its commerce powers. The Supreme Court has ruled that this control of obscene materials is constitutional, but it has worked hard to define obscenity as a variety of cases came before it. In *Roth* v. *United States* and *Alberts* v. *California* (1957), which upheld federal and state antiobscenity statutes, the Court devised the following test of obscenity: "Whether to the average person, applying contemporary community standards, the dominant theme of the material taken as a whole appeals to prurient interest; and is utterly without redeeming social value."

The *Roth* test served as a guideline for the Court in obscenity cases for several years. The justices, however, were badly divided over this difficult constitutional problem. Even so, none of the Court's decisions sustained a single lower court obscenity conviction between *Roth* and *Jacobellis* v. *Ohio* (1964), suggesting that the justices had for all practical purposes adopted a "hard-core pornography" definition of what was suppressible, consistent with the First Amendment. Justice Potter Stewart in *Jacobellis* commented that the difficulty of the Court in giving content to obscenity was that it was "faced with the task of trying to define what may be indefinable." But in regard to hard-core pornography he firmly declared that "I know it when I see it."

While *Roth* presumed obscenity to be "utterly without redeeming social value," *Memoirs* v. *Massachusetts* (1966) required that to prove obscenity it must be affirmatively established that the material is *"utterly* without redeeming social value." This alteration of the *Roth* test required the prosecution to assume a burden of proof virtually impossible to discharge. This appeared to afford almost any sexually oriented expression protection under the First Amendment. The Court, however, during the same term, upheld the conviction of Ralph Ginzburg for publishing, publicizing, and selling of magazines considered to be obscene, because of the pandering style of marketing, in violation of the federal postal censorship laws.

Chief Justice Warren E. Burger, returning to the *Roth* test, delivered the opinion of the Court in *Miller* v. *California,* one of a group of obscenity cases decided on June 21, 1973, which held that obscene material is not protected by the First Amendment:

A work may be subject to state regulation where that work, taken as a whole, appeals to the prurient interest in sex; portrays, in a patently offensive way, sexual conduct specifically defined by the applicable state law; and taken as a whole, does not have serious literary, artistic, political, or scientific value.

The Court rejected as a constitutional standard the test of *"utterly* without redeeming social value" articulated in *Memoirs.*

The four Nixon appointees, joined by Justice Byron White, also held in *Paris Adult Theater* v. *Slaton* (1973) that there are legitimate state interests at stake in stemming the tide of commercialized obscenity. These include, the Court wrote, "the interest of the public in the quality of life and the total community environment." The Court held that the "zone of privacy" attached to the home as set forth in *Stanley* v. *Georgia* (1969), in which a man may be entitled to read or view obscene materials without intrusions from the state, did not apply in places of public accommodation, including "adult" theaters which excluded minors and gave adequate notice to the public of the nature of the films shown.

These five-to-four decisions of the Court prompted mixed reactions across America. Those who applauded the Court for taking a firmer stand on obscenity and allowing more local control over such matters were matched by others who feared that these decisions would usher in an era of state censorship and an erosion of the First Amendment. Justice William J. Brennan, in his dissent in *Paris Adult Theater* v. *Slaton,* expressed the difficulty the Court has had in reconciling state efforts to suppress sexually oriented expression with the protections of the First Amendment, when he said: "No other aspect of the First Amendment has, in recent years, demanded so substantial a commitment of our time, generated such disharmony of views, and remained so resistant to the formulation of stable and manageable standards."

A new and novel aspect of free speech is the expression of opinions through nonverbal communication, or "symbolic speech." In *United States* v. *O'Brien* (1968), the Supreme Court upheld the district court conviction of David Paul O'Brien for burning his draft card as a protest against the Vietnam war and the draft. Chief Justice Warren said the Court cannot accept the view that any conduct can be labeled "speech" whenever the person engaging in the conduct intends to express an idea. However, the Court, by a narrow five-to-four majority in *Street* v. *New York* (1969), upheld the public burning of the American flag as a symbol of protest over the shooting of civil rights leader James Meredith on the grounds that the constitutional rights of free expression "encompass the freedom to express publicly one's opinions about our flag, including those opinions which are defiant or contemptuous." This line of reasoning was also used to uphold students in wearing armbands as a "symbolic speech" protest of the Vietnam war after they had been suspended from school in *Tinker* v. *Des Moines School District* (1969). In *Street* and *Tinker*, the Court found no strong state interest in suppressing speech, as it purported to find in *O'Brien*, which involved the administration of the selective service laws.

Freedom of Religion

"Congress shall make no law respecting an establishment of religion, or prohibiting the free exercise thereof." The First Amendment, therefore, divides freedom of religion into two specific prohibitions on Congress (and upon the states, through inclusion or absorption by way of the Fourteenth Amendment). (1) Congress shall make no law respecting an establishment of religion—this broad language goes far beyond the establishment of a state religion or the proscription of a given religion. It forbids all laws respecting an establishment of religion. (2) Congress shall not prohibit the free exercise of religion—though laws cannot interfere with religious beliefs or opinions, the action or practices prompted by religious convictions can be controlled.

Establishment of Religion

The First Amendment prohibition against Congress establishing an official religion or actively promoting or proscribing a private system of belief was intended to build "a wall of separation between church and state," according to Thomas Jefferson in a letter he sent to a group of Baptists in 1802. This line of reasoning was used in *Everson* v. *Board of Education* (1947), when the Court was considering the constitutionality of a New Jersey law which reimbursed the parents of pupils attending Catholic schools for transportation costs. The Court upheld the law by a five-to-four decision, but explained the meaning of the establishment of religion clause in the following comprehensive way:

The "establishment of religion" clause of the First Amendment means at least this: Neither a state nor the Federal Government can set up a church. Neither can pass laws which aid one religion, aid all religions, or prefer one religion over another. Neither can force nor influence a person to go to or to remain away from church against his will or force him to profess a belief or disbelief in any religion. No person can be punished for entertaining or professing religious beliefs or disbeliefs, for church attendance or nonattendance. No tax in any amount, large or small, can be levied to support any religious activities or institutions, whatever they may be called, or whatever form they may adopt to teach or practice religion. Neither a state nor the Federal Government can, openly or secretly, participate in the affairs of any religious organizations or groups or vice versa. In the words of Jefferson, the clause against establishment of religion by law was intended to erect "a wall of separation between church and State."

Religion in the public schools has been a most sensitive controversy since the *Everson* decision. The Supreme Court ruled in *McCollum* v. *Board of Education* (1948) that released time for religious instruction violates the establishment clause if held on school premises; but in *Zorach* v. *Clauson* (1952), the Court held it permissible if held off the school premises. A decade later the Court faced the issue of school prayer in *Engel* v. *Vitale* (1962). The New York State Board of Regents, according to state law, composed the following prayer to be said aloud by each class at the beginning of each school day: "Almighty God, we acknowledge our dependence upon Thee, and we beg Thy blessings upon us, our parents, our teachers and our country." Justice Black wrote for a six-to-one Court:

We think that the constitutional prohibition against laws respecting an establishment of religion must at least mean that in this country it is no part of the business of government to compose official prayers for any group of American people to recite as part of a religious program carried on by government.

The Court also struck down a similar Pennsylvania requirement of Bible readings and recitation of the Lord's Prayer in *Abington School District* v. *Schempp* (1963). Justice Tom Clark concluded for the Court:

The place of religion in our society is an exalted one, achieved through a long tradition of reliance on the home, the church and the inviolable citadel of the individual heart and mind. We have come to recognize through bitter experience that it is not within the power of government to invade that citadel, whether its purpose or effect be to aid or oppose, to advance or retard. In the relationship between man and religion, the State is firmly committed to a position of neutrality.

Many Americans did not agree with the Court in the prayer and Bible-reading decisions, and some extreme constitutional conservatives criticized the Court members as being antireligious atheists. But even responsible religious and political leaders spoke out against the decisions. Francis Cardinal Spellman said he was "frightened and shocked" at a decision which strikes at the heart of America's "Godly tradition." Herbert Hoover, then the patriarch of the Republican Party, demanded a constitutional amendment to "correct" these decisions. When an amendment to allow school prayer was before the Ninety-second Congress, Senator Robert C. Byrd of West Virginia warned in support of the amendment that "somebody is tampering with America's soul." Even so, the proposed amendment was defeated in the Senate.

As in the *Everson* decision, the Court has upheld government support of parochial and private schools in providing textbooks, bus transportation, health services, and other benefits, on the "child-benefit" principle. It is on this principle that Congress passed the Elementary and Secondary Education Act of 1965. The public schools receiving the federal funds were expected to share textbooks, library materials, technical facilities, and special services with parochial school children. Following this federal breakthrough, a number of state legislatures passed school aid programs which benefited the children who attend private parochial schools. The Supreme Court does not feel the government's position of neutrality is denied in aid to parochial schools ("parochaid") when the programs benefit students and not schools, and thus does not feel that such aid constitutes state support of religion. The New York parochaid law of 1965 was upheld by the Court in *Board of Education* v. *Allen* (1968) on the grounds that it is secular, and that it "neither advances nor inhibits religion."

However, the Court began to take a more restrictive position on public aid to nonpublic schools in 1971. State laws in Pennsylvania and Rhode Island were held to violate the establishment clause in *Lemon* v. *Kurtzman* (1971). In 1973, the Court in *Committee of Public Education* v. *Nyquist* held that three New York laws, providing (1) financial assistance to nonprofit schools serving low-income families, (2) tuition grants to parents in low-income brackets who send their children to nonpublic schools, and (3) state income tax relief to parents of nonpublic school children who do not qualify for the tuition grants, violated the establishment clause. The majority opinion in *Nyquist* maintained that "the effect of this aid is unmistakably to provide desired financial support for non-public, sectarian institutions," and distinguished the case from *Everson* and *Allen* and other cases which have permitted the states to provide church-related schools with secular, neutral, or nonideological services, facilities, or materials.

Free Exercise of Religion

Limitations on the free exercise of religion develop when religious practices violate the laws and are strongly contrary to the accepted mores of the society. This position was first laid down in *Reynolds* v. *United States* (1879), when the Supreme Court upheld the federal Anti-bigamy Act of 1862 and denied the Mormon practice of polygamy as being protected under the First Amendment. The Court said: "Laws are made for the government of action, and while they cannot interfere with mere religious belief and opinions, they may with practices." In *Davis* v. *Beason* (1890), another Mormon polygamy case, the Court added:

Whilst legislation for the establishment of religion is forbidden, and its free exercise permitted, it does not follow that everything which may be so-called can be tolerated. Crime is not the less odious because sanctioned by what any particular sect may designate as religion.

Since these nineteenth-century cases, the Court has denied a long list of religious practices as not protected by the First Amendment. Religious right to heal by prayer does not permit a person to practice medicine for a fee without a license; but the state can require vaccinations, physical examinations, and even operations by licensed medics contrary to the person's religious beliefs. Laws outlawing religious snake handling have been upheld, and human sacrifices in the name of religion are considered murder. And the list goes on.

The Supreme Court, on the other hand, has upheld the Jehovah's Witnesses in a variety of proselytizing activities which may be in violation of city ordinances. After an initial defeat, school children of the Witnesses were upheld in their refusing to salute the flag and recite the Pledge of Allegiance because it is a "graven image," according to their belief, which they are forbidden to worship. In *West Virginia Board of Education* v. *Barnette* (1943), the Court reasoned: "If there is any fixed star in our constitutional constellation, it is that no official, high or petty, can prescribe what shall be orthodox in politics, nationalism, religion, or other matters of opinion or force citizens to confess by word or act their faith therein."

Wisconsin v. *Yoder* (1972) reached the Supreme Court as a result of members of the Amish church refusing to send their children to school beyond the eighth grade. The State of Wisconsin's compulsory school attendance law requires children to attend school until the age of sixteen. The Amish agree that elementary education is necessary but they object to higher education generally because the values it teaches are contrary to the simple farm values of the Amish way of life. The majority opinion of the Court by Chief Justice Warren E. Burger held the Amish not subject to the statute. The opinion noted that

a State's interest in universal education, however highly we rank it, is not totally free from a balancing process when it impinges on other fundamental rights and interests, such as those specifically protected by the Free Exercise Clause of the First Amendment.

The Court continued: "a way of life that is odd or even erratic but interferes with no rights or interests of others is not to be condemned because it is different." Justice Douglas disagreed with the Court's conclusion in his dissenting opinion: "It is the future of the student, not the future of the parents, that is imperiled in today's decision."

CIVIL RIGHTS AND CIVIL WAR AMENDMENTS

Before the ratification of the Fourteenth Amendment, civil liberties were protected by the Bill of Rights of the United States Constitution only against violations perpetrated by the federal government. As a result, the cases were more routine than interesting, with some noticeable exceptions arising out of the Civil War that concerned the suspension of the writ of *habeas corpus* and military law. With the addition of the Fourteenth Amendment—and particularly the "due process of law" clause as expanded with the selective absorption of many of the safeguards of the Bill of Rights—substantive and procedural rights have been enlarged and protected against all levels of governmental action and against private infringement.

During the immediate post-Civil War period, the comprehensive and explicit federal legislation enacted to protect the civil rights of the newly freed slaves foundered in the Supreme Court, where the legislation was narrowly construed. The High Court clearly had no intention of being a party to any revolution in our constitutional system at that juncture in history.

In the *Civil Rights Cases* (1883), the public accommodations sections of the Civil Rights Act of 1875 were struck down. This Act had been designed to make all public accommodations open to all races. Justice Joseph P. Bradley's opinion for the Court pointed out that the Fourteenth Amendment was "prohibitory upon the states," but not upon private individuals. In effect, this opinion served notice that the federal government could not protect the black against private discrimination and that "white supremacy" in the South would not be federally checked.

Separate But Equal Doctrine

Many states, especially in the South, passed antiblack laws which were prompted by prejudice and the excesses of Reconstruction. Jim Crow laws that segregated the races in public places and facilities were passed throughout the South, and "for white only" signs appeared in many establishments serving the public.

A Louisiana law providing for separate accommodations for whites and blacks in public transportation was challenged in the courts and reached the Supreme Court in *Plessy* v. *Ferguson* (1896). Plessy, who was seven-eighths Caucasian, challenged the Louisiana law on the "equal protection" clause of the Fourteenth Amendment. The Supreme Court, however, upheld the legislation as a reasonable exercise of the state's police powers to promote the common good, peace, and order. The Court held the law did not deprive blacks of equal protection of the laws if they were provided accommodations equal to those for whites.

Justice John M. Harlan registered a vigorous dissent:

> Our Constitution is color-blind, and neither knows nor tolerates classes among its citizens. In respect of civil rights, all citizens are equal before the law. . . . The arbitrary separation of citizens, on the basis of race, while they are on a public highway, is a badge of servitude wholly inconsistent with the civil freedom and the equality before the law established by the Constitution. It cannot be justified upon any legal grounds.

Even so, the "separate but equal" doctrine created by the Court's majority opinion stood for nearly sixty years.[2]

Forces created out of the Great Depression and World War II set in motion a revisionist trend to change the discriminatory practices toward black Americans. The first step in the breakdown of segregation was in the area of higher

---

[2] See Rocco J. Tresolini, *Justice and the Supreme Court* (New York: J. B. Lippincott, 1963), Chapter Three.

education. Beginning with *Missouri ex. rel. Gaines* v. *Canada* (1938), the states were ordered to cease barring qualified blacks from entering their universities for advanced study, and subsequent cases reinforced this decision.

Destruction of segregation in interstate transportation began in *Mitchell* v. *United States* (1941), when the Court held that the denial of a Pullman berth to a black when such facilities were available to whites violated the Interstate Commerce Act. Five years later, in *Morgan* v. *Virginia* (1946), the Court invalidated a Virginia law requiring racial segregation on public buses moving across state lines. In 1950, in *Henderson* v. *United States,* the practice of setting up a curtained-off table in dining cars for blacks was held to violate the Interstate Commerce Act, which forbade railroads "to subject any particular person to any undue or unreasonable prejudice or disadvantage." The ICC, following these decisions, announced in November, 1955, the termination of all racial segregation in trains and buses crossing state lines, and in all auxiliary rail and bus facilities, waiting rooms, restrooms, and restaurants.

Segregation in housing had a significant wedge driven into it by the Court in *Shelley* v. *Kraemer* (1948), when it ruled that judicial enforcement of restrictive covenants (contracts) between private parties, which excluded blacks from owning and occupying real property, constituted state action which violated the Fourteenth Amendment.

The Revolution in Public Education

The revisionist trend reached revolutionary proportions in the landmark civil rights case of *Brown* v. *Board of Education* (1954). The Brown children had been required to attend segregated elementary schools for blacks rather than neighborhood schools in Topeka, Kansas. Chief Justice Earl Warren avoided legal and historical complexities in this case by examining the impact of segregation in the twentieth century on black children. Segregation, said the Chief Justice, generated a feeling of inferiority and damaged their hearts and minds. "We conclude that in the field of public education the doctrine of 'separate but equal' has no place. Separate educational facilities are inherently unequal."

Relying more on sociological and psychological data than judicial or historical precedents, the Supreme Court's decision ushered in a momentous epoch of change and resistance to this change which at times erupted in civil strife. The Brown decision did not issue any enforcement order; instead it asked counsel to re-argue the means of implementing the decision. In May, 1955, the Court handed down its order implementing the earlier case. Utilizing principles of equity law, the Court remanded the cases to the lower courts and ordered them to work out equitable solutions to admit the black children "to the public schools on a racially non-discriminatory basis with all deliberate speed."

The second Brown decision began a protracted legal and political battle of school desegregation throughout the South. Different stratagems were used by the South to resist or delay integration. The South resurrected the dead doctrine of "interposition" which was used by Jefferson and Madison in the Kentucky and Virginia resolutions against the Federalist Alien and Sedition acts, and later by South Carolina when it nullified federal tariff laws. The Georgia legislature adopted a resolution declaring the *Brown* decision "null, void, and of no effect." Other states did likewise. Other evasive laws were passed which added up to the "massive resistance" programs designed to frustrate the *Brown* decision, the most extreme of which was to close the public schools.

The National Association for the Advancement of Colored People (NAACP) countered "massive resistance" with a massive program of lawsuits to force desegregation. Integration orders, sometimes, resulted in rioting and violence. The first dramatic instance of this sort occurred in 1957, in Little Rock, Arkansas, a situation which required President Eisenhower to call out the army to compel submission to federal sovereignty. After more political and court maneuvering, the Supreme Court ruled the Arkansas school closure statutes unconstitutional, in *Faubus* v. *Aaron* (1959); and the Little Rock high schools quietly reopened on an integrated basis.

The interposition and massive resistance legislative devices of Louisiana came to an end without violence in *United States* v. *Louisiana* (1960); but a federal court order requiring the University of Mississippi to admit James Meredith, a black citizen of that state, resulted in a riot. Governor Ross Barnett took over the University, and state police blocked federal attempts to escort Meredith into the school. The governor was issued a contempt citation from a United States Court of Appeals, and President Kennedy issued a proclamation warning the officials and the people of Mississippi to stop resisting federal authority. Reluctantly, the University officials allowed Meredith to register—accompanied by several hundred United States Marshals.

Compliance with *Brown* v. *Board* came slowly. In *Griffin* v. *County School Board of Prince Edward County* (1964), the closure of the county schools was declared to violate equal protection of the Fourteenth Amendment. The Court said: "There has been too much deliberation and not enough speed." The "freedom of choice" plans, which allowed white or black students to attend the schools of their choice within the district and relied on social and economic sanctions to segregate the schools were placed under a constitutional cloud in *Green* v. *County Board of New Kent County* (1968).[3]

The Supreme Court's attempt to destroy the dual school system in the South was resisted from another quarter beginning in 1969. President Nixon's "southern strategy" of wooing the South included the school question. Attorney General John Mitchell favored delay and said "instant desegregation" was unworkable. The Court, with President Nixon's first appointee, Chief Justice Warren Burger, joining the majority, responded in *Alexander* v. *Holmes* (1969) that the "all deliberate speed" formula was no longer "constitutionally permissible"

---

[3] Lucius J. Barker and Twiley W. Barker, Jr., *Freedoms, Courts, Politics: Studies in Civil Liberties* (Englewood Cliffs, N.J.: Prentice-Hall, 1972), Chapter Five.

and instructed the Appellate Court to order the Mississippi school districts involved "to begin immediately to operate as unitary school systems within which no person is to be effectively excluded from any school because of race or color."

With hostility on the part of several federal district and appellate judges in the South toward forcing a unitary school system on the South, reluctance of the Nixon Administration to push energetically for integration, and *de facto* segregation in the larger cities throughout America creating sharp debate over measures such as busing of students to achieve racially balanced schools, it became obvious that the civil rights issue over the public schools was not solved.

The busing issue came before the Supreme Court in *Swann* v. *Charlotte-Mecklenburg Board of Education* (1971). The Court in this case upheld a busing formula designed to achieve racial balance in the schools in line with the racial percentages of the school district. In suggesting that there may be different approaches to meeting the requirements of the *Brown* case, Chief Justice Burger said, in the majority opinion of the Court, that fairness, equity, and "substance, not semantics, must govern." Burger's decision, however, indicated a degree of reluctance on this issue. There are limits to the power of the Court to command compliance, and limits to what public officials and private citizens are willing to do to achieve fully desegregated school systems throughout America.

President Nixon responded with sympathy to busing opponents. In a major address on March 16, 1972, he said the lower courts had gone beyond what the Supreme Court required in busing pupils. "All too often," the President said, "the result has been a classic case of the remedy for one evil creating another evil." The President followed the speech with a two-part legislative proposal to slow, if not stop, the use of busing for desegregation: (1) the Equal Educational Opportunities Act, which would have allowed busing only as a last resort and would have pumped $2.5 billion into poor school areas; and (2) the Student Transportation Moratorium Act, which would have blocked new busing orders until July 1, 1973, or until Congress passed the equal opportunities bill, whichever came sooner.

The President's proposals raised serious constitutional questions over Congressional authority to limit the jurisdiction of the federal courts. The President felt a constitutional amendment would be too slow. Congress responded to the antibusing protests in Michigan and elsewhere across the nation, to presidential pressure, and to antibusing lobbying by amending the higher education bill. The House amendments forbade all use of federal education funds for busing, forbade federal pressure for the use of state or local funds for busing, and postponed the effective date of any court order requiring busing until all appeals of the order were exhausted.[4]

[4] Congressional Quarterly, *Guide to Current American Government, Spring 1973* (Washington, D.C.: Congressional Quarterly, 1973), pp. 78, 79.

Fueling the national fire over busing was a federal district court order to merge the largely black Richmond, Virginia, city school system with the white suburban systems of Henrico and Chesterfield counties. The order required busing approximately 78,000 of the 104,000 pupils in the three systems, an increase of 10,000 bused students. The ruling of Judge Robert Merhige, Jr., was overturned by the Fourth Circuit Court of Appeals, and this judgment was affirmed by an equally divided Supreme Court in *Carolyn Bradley* v. *State Board of Education of Virginia (1973)*.

Keyes v. *School District No. 1* (1973) was the first school desegregation case to reach the Supreme Court which involved a major city outside the South. The school authorities from Denver, Colorado—a city and a state which have not operated public schools under constitutional or statutory provisions which mandated or permitted racial segregation—had created or maintained segregated schools by use of techniques such as manipulation of student attendance zones, school site selection, and a neighborhood school policy. The Court held in its ruling that the "school authorities have been found to have practiced de jure segregation in a meaningful portion of the school system," and remanded the case to the district court to correct the segregation problems in the core city schools if the school authorities could not prove that segregation was not a result or intent of school board policies. The difference to the Court between *de jure* and *de facto* segregation "is purpose or intent to segregate." Justice Lewis F. Powell, in a concurring opinion, maintained that racial imbalance in the schools is a national, not a southern phenomenon, and called for the abandonment of the *de jure-de facto* distinction. Justice Douglas said: "While I join the opinion of the Court, I agree with my Brother Powell that there is, for the purpose of the Equal Protection Clause of the Fourteenth Amendment as applied to the school cases, no difference between *de facto* and *de jure* segregation."

A different type of discrimination in education was discovered by several district courts recently as a result of unequal wealth distribution, resulting in large disparities of taxable income for school purposes among school districts. Developing out of the traditional property-tax method of financing public education, Mexican-American parents in the Edgewood Independent School District of San Antonio, Texas, brought a class action on behalf of school children of poor families who reside in school districts having a low property-tax base, claiming that the Texas system's reliance on local property taxation favors the more affluent districts and hence violates the equal protection requirements of the Fourteenth Amendment. The amount of money available from local, state, and national funds per pupil in the Edgewood district totaled $356; the amount per pupil in Alamo Heights, the most affluent district, totaled $594.

The case reached the Supreme Court in *San Antonio Independent School District* v. *Rodriguez* (1973). The Court majority, the four Nixon appointees joined by Justice Potter Stewart, held:

The Texas system does not violate the Equal Protection Clause of the Fourteenth Amendment. Though concededly imperfect, the system bears a rational relationship to a legitimate state purpose. While assuring basic education for every child in the State, it permits and encourages participation in and significant control of each district's schools at the local level.

The opinion, though, offered a "cautionary postscript" that

the need is apparent for reform in tax systems which may well have relied too long and too heavily on the local property tax. And certainly innovative new thinking as to public education, its methods and its funding, is necessary to assure both a higher level of quality and greater uniformity of opportunity. These matters merit the continued attention of the scholars who already have contributed much by their challenges. But the ultimate solutions must come from the lawmakers and from the democratic pressures of those who elect them.

Justice Thurgood Marshall, one of four who offered dissenting opinions in this case, registered little hope in a "political" solution, as the district court had withheld its decision for two years in the hope that the Texas legislature would remedy the gross disparities in the educational financing scheme, which it did not do. He also scored the majority's holding "as a retreat from our historic commitment to equality of educational opportunity and as unsupportable acquiesence in a system which deprives children in their earliest years of the chance to reach their full potential as citizens."

Other Extensions of Civil Rights

Surprisingly, the *Brown* decision had a much greater impact on other aspects of civil rights than it did on public school education. It seemed to be the signal to apply the pressure generally to abolish the "badges of inferiority" kept alive by the separate but equal doctrine. Lower courts took the cue and held discriminatory practices in public parks, swimming pools, theaters, and the like, to be in violation of the Equal Protection Clause of the Fourteenth Amendment. The Supreme Court confirmed decisions of this kind without opinion.

Significantly, the Court refused to allow application of the "all deliberate speed" rule of the second *Brown* case in these public accommodations cases and demanded immediate integration. The South did not resist these decisions with the same ferocity as it had school integration rulings. Thus *Brown* v. *Board* seemed to have breathed life into the words President Truman spoke in 1948: "We cannot be satisfied until all our people have equal opportunities for jobs, for homes, for education, for health, and for political expression, and until all our people have equal protection under the law."

In a special message to Congress, Mr. Truman had asked for legislation to empower the federal government to protect civil rights in voting, employment, and transportation. He had also asked for an antilynching law, and for other personal protection laws. The first civil rights bill in the twentieth century was

Copyright © 1969 the *Chicago Sun-Times*. Reproduced by courtesy of Wil-Jo Associates, Inc., and Bill Mauldin.

"Hang on, kids—we're decelerating."

passed in 1957. The bill was feeble, but it was a beginning. It created a Civil Rights Commission to study the problems which existed in civil rights and opened the way for additional civil rights legislation in 1960, 1964, 1965, and 1968. The Civil Rights acts can be summarized as follows:

The Civil Rights Act of 1957 prohibited action to prevent persons from voting in federal elections and authorized the Attorney General to bring suit when a person was deprived of his voting rights. It also created a Civil Rights Commission and set up a Civil Rights Division in the Department of Justice.

The Civil Rights Act of 1960 strengthened provisions of the 1957 Act for court enforcement of voting rights and required preservation of voting records. It also contained limited criminal penalty provisions relating to bombing and to obstruction of federal court orders.

The Civil Rights Act of 1964 prohibited discrimination in public accommodations and in programs receiving federal assistance. It also prohibited discrimination by employers and unions and set up an Equal Employment Opportunity Commission. Voting laws and school and public facilities desegregation enforcement were strengthened.

The Voting Rights Act of 1965 authorized the Attorney General to appoint federal examiners to register voters in areas of marked discrimination and strengthened penalties for interference with voter rights.

The Civil Rights Act of 1968 prohibited discrimination in the sale or rental of about eighty percent of all housing. It also protected persons attending school and working, and protected civil rights workers urging others to exercise their rights.[5]

The Civil Rights Act of 1964 was the first to comprehensively meet the major civil rights problems. The heart of this act was Title II, which declared that all persons are entitled to the full and equal enjoyment of the facilities of hotels, motels, and restaurants; motion picture houses and sports arenas; cultural centers such as concert halls and theaters; and other private establishments which affect commerce, or are supported in discriminatory practices by state action.

The public accommodations provisions of Title II came before the Court in *Heart of Atlanta Motel* v. *United States* (1964). Justice Clark, who wrote the majority opinion, held that Congress had sufficient power under the commerce clause to forbid racial discrimination in hotels and motels serving interstate travelers and thus affecting commerce. Clark used similar reasoning in *Katzenbach* v. *McClung* (1964). This case involved a Birmingham restaurant, "Ollie's Barbeque," which did not serve interstate travelers, but did indeed discriminate. To rest the case on the commerce clause, Clark reasoned that a portion of the food served came from outside the state and thus affected interstate commerce. Justice Douglas wrote a separate concurring opinion applicable to both cases in which he argued that the decisions should rest on the equal protection clause of the Fourteenth Amendment. Justice Goldberg also would have preferred the equal protection clause base, as the law in question was for the "vindication of human dignities and not mere economics."

The Voting Rights Act was challenged by South Carolina on the literacy and federal examiners provisions. The Supreme Court agreed to hear the case, *South Carolina* v. *Katzenbach* (1966). South Carolina claimed the Act (1) went beyond the enforcement powers granted to Congress by the Fifteenth Amendment; (2) was not uniformly applied and violated the principle of equality of

---

[5] See Congressional Quarterly, *Civil Rights: Progress Report 1970* (Washington, D.C.: Congressional Quarterly, 1970).

states in the union; and (3) was a bill of attainder, because it barred judicial review of administrative findings.

Chief Justice Warren's opinion for the Court summarily rejected the state's first argument, quoting John Marshall in *McCulloch v. Maryland* on the broad powers of Congress: "Let the end be legitimate, let it be within the scope of the Constitution, and all means which are appropriate, which are plainly adapted to that end, which are not prohibited . . . are constitutional." Dismissing the other arguments with long-standing precedents, Warren concluded the Act was a valid "means for carrying out the commands of the Fifteenth Amendment."

The most important, and controversial, feature of the Civil Rights Act of 1968 is the federal fair housing provision of Title VIII. Although not based on this Act, a housing discrimination case came before the Supreme Court in *Jones v. Mayer Co.* (1969). Justice Stewart, one of the Court's conservatives, delivered the majority opinion based on a portion of the federal code which provided that all citizens shall have the same right to "inherit, purchase, lease, sell, hold, and convey real and personal property." This was originally passed as part of the Civil Rights Act of 1866, based on the enforcement provisions of the Thirteenth Amendment.

Supreme Court support of the federal civil rights acts seemed to say the revolution in civil rights was being won in the 1960's. But ominous developments facing America in the 1970's suggest that such a conclusion would be premature because of the following: (1) the moral force of the Court's earlier decisions was weakened by vigorous dissents in cases coming before it in the early 1970's; (2) the emergence of a white "backlash" threatened to cut the ground from under the Court's position, evidenced by President Nixon's desire to get a "better balance" on the Court in civil rights cases; (3) the Nixon Court became a reality in 1972 with the four appointees of the President often joined by Justice White or Stewart or both [6]; and (4) the solidarity in the black community for a strong national policy on racial integration was weakened by the emergence of an alienated black "left" that professed it was disinterested in reconciliation with the white man's society. The Court's leadership in the civil rights revolution therefore may give way to a judicial retreat, or be repudiated by Congress or the people.

The success of the civil rights movement of black Americans has prompted militance among Indian, Mexican-American, Puerto Rican-American, and other minority groups. These groups have also voiced their demands for equal rights and the end of discrimination. As these groups organized and pressed for socioeconomic and political equality in the late 1960's, the promise of "first-class citizenship" seemed possible in the 1970's.

---

[6] In *Moose Lodge No. 107 v. Irvis* (1972) only Douglas, Marshall, and Brennan dissented when the Court upheld the Lodge, which refused service to Irvis, a black, on the grounds that it was a private club and that this was not changed by the fact that Pennsylvania had issued it a liquor license.

Editorial cartoon by Paul Conrad. Copyright, *Los Angeles Times*. Reprinted with permission.

"When . . . in . . . the . . . course . . . of . . . human . . . events."

In point of numbers, the most important human rights movement—equal rights for women—gained momentum in the early 1970's. Leaders of the Women's Liberation Movement called America's attention to the fact that women were discriminated against in their socioeconomic endeavors just as much or more than America's minority groups. They denied that biology had destined them to a subordinate role, and claimed that discrimination bordering on involuntary servitude was a result of male chauvinism. Their demands prompted the Equal Rights Amendment:

Section 1. Equality of rights under the law shall not be denied or abridged by the United States or by any State on account of sex.

Section 2. The Congress shall have the power to enforce, by appropriate legislation, the provisions of this article.
Section 3. This Amendment shall take effect two years after the date of ratification.

Even though Congress passed the Equal Rights Amendment on March 22, 1972, by a substantial majority, the amendment met stiff opposition in several states when it came before the state legislatures. Opponents of the measure even included some churches, civic organizations, and women's organizations, which feared that the amendment would wipe out the protective laws for women, the family, proper physiological distinctions between the sexes, and other "desirable" attributes of American society. A major objection to the proposal was that it would not exempt women from the selective service laws. During the 1973 legislative sessions, thirteen states rejected the amendment, which means one of these state legislatures must reverse itself for the proposal to pass, as three-fourths (38) of the states are required to ratify an amendment to the Constitution.

More significant, possibly, was the quiet revolution enunciated by Chief Justice Warren Burger, speaking for a unanimous court in *Reed* v. *Reed* (1971), in which a century of precedent was put aside by striking down an Idaho law which gave men mandatory preference over women as administrators of a decedent's estate. Burger interpreted the Fourteenth Amendment guarantee of equal protection as if it had always applied to women. In truth, it never did before. Throughout years of applying that guarantee to blacks, the poor, voters, and even noncitizens, the Supreme Court had never extended the protection to females!

PROCEDURAL RIGHTS

Justice Felix Frankfurter once said: "It is a fair summary of history to say that safeguards of liberty have frequently been forged in controversies involving not very nice people." Often, it is the person who is "obviously guilty," the "hardened criminal," as the public tends to view the accused, whose case the courts decide. However, the procedures followed for the "guilty" are also the protections for the innocent. The fairness of the procedures can only be assured to you and me if they are extended to all. Justice Frankfurter added that the "history of Liberty has largely been the history of observance of procedural guarantees." The Bill of Rights details the procedural guarantees which the federal government is expected to observe. These guarantees include:

Fourth Amendment: "The right of the people . . . against unreasonable searches and seizures," and search warrants must describe "the place to be searched, and the persons or things to be seized."
Fifth Amendment: The accused must (1) be indicted by a grand jury, (2) *not* be tried

twice (double jeopardy) for the same offense, and (3) *not* be compelled to incriminate himself.

Sixth Amendment: In criminal cases the accused shall (1) enjoy the right to a speedy and public trial by an impartial jury, (2) be informed of the nature and cause of the accusation, (3) be confronted with the witnesses against him, (4) have compulsory process for obtaining witnesses in his favor, and (5) have the assistance of counsel for his defense.

Eighth Amendment: The accused shall be protected from (1) excessive bail, (2) excessive fines, and (3) cruel and unusual punishments.

Procedural guarantees in the state courts were largely dependent on state constitutions and state laws until 1961, when the Supreme Court in a series of decisions extended part, but not all, of the guarantees of the Bill of Rights to state criminal proceedings. Actually the inclusion of these guarantees began as early as 1932 in *Powell* v. *Alabama,* when the Court held that the Alabama trial courts failure to give the defendants "reasonable time and opportunity to secure counsel was a clear denial of due process" as guaranteed by the Fourteenth Amendment. Other cases along the way included other Bill of Rights guarantees, but the Court did not speak with a clear and certain sound on this subject until the 1960's.

Unreasonable Searches and Seizures

This constitutional provision was not included to shield criminals, but to require the police to have a third party (a judicial officer) weigh the need to invade the privacy of the home to enforce the law. However, a search without a warrant may be made at the time of an arrest to protect the arresting officer against concealed weapons, to deprive the prisoner of the means of escape, and to prevent the destruction of evidence. In *Chimel* v. *California* (1969), the Court held that searches beyond the arrestee's person and areas within his immediate reach and control "may be made only under the authority of a search warrant."

As early as 1914, in *Weeks* v. *United States,* the Court laid down the rule that evidence obtained in illegal searches must be excluded from federal trials. In *Wolf* v. *Colorado* (1949), the Supreme Court held that the Fourth Amendment had been violated in an illegal search, but due process did not require the evidence thus obtained to be excluded from the state courts. A vacillating Court was evidenced in a series of cases following *Wolf.*

But in *Mapp* v. *Ohio* (1961) the Court acknowledged the inconsistencies of the earlier cases and applied the *Weeks* "exclusionary rule" to state criminal procedure. Justice Clark reasoned:

The ignoble shortcut to conviction left open to the State tends to destroy the entire system of constitutional restraints on which the liberties of the people rest. Having once recognized that the right to privacy embodied in the Fourth Amendment is enforceable against the States, and that the right to be secure against rude invasions of privacy by state officers is, therefore, constitutional in origin, we can no longer permit that right to remain an empty promise. . . . Our decision, founded on reason and truth, gives to the individual no more than that which the Constitution guarantees him, to the police officer no less than that to which honest law enforcement is entitled, and, to the courts, that judicial integrity so necessary in the true administration of justice.

The Nixon Court may bring about a modification of the Mapp position, however, as Chief Justice Burger discussed the problem of excluding illegally obtained evidence in his dissent in *Bivens* v. *Six Unknown Named Agents* (1971). He claimed in his dissent that the exclusionary rule rests on the deterrent rationale—the hope that law enforcement officials would be deterred from unlawful searches and seizures if the evidence so gained was ruled inadmissible often enough.

Some clear demonstration of the benefits and effectiveness of the Exclusionary Rule is required to justify it in view of the high price it extracts from society—the release of countless guilty criminals. But there is no empirical evidence to support the claim that the rule actually deters illegal conduct of law enforcement officials.

Calling for effective substitutes to be formulated by Congress, he concluded:

I believe the time has come to re-examine the scope of the Exclusionary Rule and consider at least some narrowing of its thrust so as to eliminate the anomalies it has produced.

On December 11, 1973, in *United States* v. *Robinson* and *Gustafson* v. *Florida,* Justice Rehnquist, delivering the opinions of the Court, liberalized the rules of search and seizure laid down in *Chimel* and narrowed the exclusionary rule of *Mapp* in upholding convictions on narcotics violations in which the evidence was acquired through searches incident to motor vehicle violations.

Immunity from Self-Incrimination

The Fifth Amendment's guarantee against self-incrimination in federal courts was logically transferred to the states following the *Mapp* decision. This came in *Malloy* v. *Hogan* (1964), a case in which Malloy, a small-time gambler in Hartford, Connecticut, was summoned to appear before a county court that was investigating gambling. Malloy refused to answer the questions put to him on the ground that any response would tend to incriminate him. He was cited for contempt of court and sent to prison until he was willing to answer the questions. His application for a writ of *habeas corpus* was denied by the highest court of the state. Malloy then brought the case to the Supreme Court on a writ of *certiorari*. The Court reversed the state court judgments and held "that the Fifth Amendment's exception from self-incrimination is also protected by the Fourteenth Amendment against abridgment by the states." The Supreme Court also extended the protection of the Fifth Amendment against double jeopardy to apply to the states when it ruled in *Benton* v. *Maryland* (1969) that the states cannot try a man twice for the same crime.

Assistance of Counsel

Closely associated with the protection of the accused against self-incrimination is his right to have legal counsel. But who is obliged to provide counsel, at what stage of the proceedings is it required, and in what types of cases must it be furnished? A person may indeed incriminate himself if he does not have legal assistance at any point in the judicial process.

For a century and a half the Sixth Amendment's provision that "In all criminal prosecutions the accused shall enjoy the right . . . to have the assistance of counsel for his defense" meant simply that a person was free to employ and be represented by an attorney, but not that it was mandatory for the court to furnish counsel if a person could not afford to hire one. During the Depression years, two cases came before the court that began to alter this position. A federal case, *Johnson* v. *Zerbst* (1938), required the court to furnish counsel if the defendant demanded it. The Court held that "the Sixth Amendment withholds from federal courts, in all criminal proceedings, the power and authority to deprive an accused of his life or liberty unless he has or waives the assistance of counsel."

In *Powell* v. *Alabama* (1932), the first of the famous Scottsboro Cases, nine illiterate black boys, ranging in age from twelve to twenty, were charged with the rape of two white girls in an open car of a freight train while it traveled across Alabama. In a hostile setting, eight of the boys were convicted and sentenced to death. A mistrial was declared in the case of the twelve-year-old, when one member of the jury held out for life imprisonment for him. The defendants were not represented by counsel, except by the bar generally, and no effective assistance was received. The Alabama Supreme Court affirmed all of the convictions but one. The case went to the United States Supreme Court on a writ of *certiorari*, and the convictions were set aside as a denial of due process of law clause of the Fourteenth Amendment. Justice George Sutherland ruled

> that in a capital case, where the defendant is unable to employ counsel, and is incapable adequately of making his own defense because of ignorance, feeble-mindedness, illiteracy, or the like, it is the duty of the court, whether requested or not, to assign counsel for him as a necessary requisite of due process of law.

Ten years later, in *Betts* v. *Brady* (1942), the Court declared that due process required the aid of counsel in state felony cases other than capital cases, only if the lack of counsel resulted in grave injustice. The Court concluded that the "appointment of counsel is not a fundamental right essential to a fair trial" in all cases involving felonies. It was another two decades before this position of the Court was overturned in *Gideon* v. *Wainwright* (1963). In a sequel to *Gideon,* the Court specifically extended the right of counsel to "any offense, whether classified as petty, misdemeanor, or felony" involving the possibility of imprisonment of any duration, in *Argersinger* v. *Hamlin* (1972). Justice Douglas opined for a unanimous Court:

Counsel is needed so that the accused may know precisely what he is doing, so that he is fully aware of the prospect of going to jail or prison, and so that he is treated fairly by the prosecution. . . . There is evidence of the prejudice which results to misdemeanor defendants from this "assembly-line justice."

Two cases in 1964 extended the right of counsel established in the *Gideon* case to pretrial police investigations. In *Massiah* v. *United States,* the Court ruled that incriminating statements were not admissible in a federal court against a defendant unless his lawyer had been present at the police interrogations. The state case which came to a similar conclusion was *Escobedo* v. *Illinois.* Prompted by this decision, the Chicago police department admonished the police to:

1. Permit each prisoner to communicate with his attorney and a member of his family.
2. Never use force or coercion in seeking confessions.
3. Respect the right of the accused to refuse to give testimony against himself.
4. Never engage in the use of derogatory terms such as *nigger, boy, spic, wop, kike, chink, shine, dago, polack, bohunk,* etc.

Developing logically out of the *Gideon, Escobedo,* and *Malloy* cases, Chief Justice Warren delivered the opinion in *Miranda* v. *Arizona* (1966), in which he developed what has become known as the "Miranda rules":

Prior to any questioning the suspect must be warned:

1. That he has a right to remain silent;
2. That any statement he does make may be used as evidence against him;
3. That he has a right to the presence of an attorney, either retained or appointed.

A week after the *Miranda* decision, the Court held in *Johnson* v. *New Jersey* that the *Escobedo* and *Miranda* rulings did not apply retroactively, but applied only to cases in which trials began after the opinions of these two cases. The Court said that "retroactive application of *Escobedo* and *Miranda* would seriously disrupt the administration of our criminal laws. It would require the retrial or release of numerous prisoners found guilty by trustworthy evidence in conformity with previously announced constitutional standards."

Even so, bitter controversy raged over the *Miranda* ruling. As crime increased in the nation, strong law and order demands were heard quite clearly, at least by members of Congress. Title II of the Omnibus Crime Control and Safe Streets Act of 1968 purports to "repeal" *Miranda* by allowing "voluntary confessions" in federal prosecutions.

The impact of *Miranda* seems to be that it does not "handcuff" the police, as many of the harbingers of fear claimed, but actually prompts better police techniques in obtaining the evidence necessary to make a solid case in court. Additionally, the *Miranda* ruling brings local police procedures on interrogation, where it is followed, into line with long-standing rules of procedure of the Federal Bureau of Investigation.

Jury Trial

In all criminal proceedings, the right to a jury trial is constitutionally guaranteed by the Sixth Amendment and also by Article III, Section 2, of the Constitution. In the case of *Patton* v. *United States* (1930), this guarantee was said to incorporate the common law requirements of a twelve man jury, a judge, and a unanimous verdict. This standard was made applicable to the states in *Duncan* v. *Louisiana* (1968) by way of the Fourteenth Amendment. However, the Court held in *Williams* v. *Florida* (1971) that the right to a jury trial does not include the requirement of twelve jurors in state cases. In *Baldwin* v. *New York* (1971) the Court ruled that a man should have a jury trial in any case involving a possible sentence of more than six months in prison.

Two noteworthy cases involving jury procedure were decided on the same day by the Court in 1972. In *Johnson* v. *Louisiana* and *Apodaca* v. *Oregon*, with the majority opinion given by Justice White (vote, five to four: Stewart, Marshall, Brennan, and Douglas dissenting), the Court allowed less than unanimous verdicts of the juries to convict defendants in armed robbery and felony cases. Justice Stewart noted that "until today, it has been universally understood that a unanimous verdict is an essential element of a Sixth Amendment jury trial." Justice Thurgood Marshall said that "the doubts of a single juror are in my view evidence that the government has failed to carry its burden of proving guilt beyond a reasonable doubt."

Care must be taken that discriminatory procedures are not involved in the selection of a jury. The Court as early as 1880, in *Strauder* v. *West Virginia*, held that laws barring blacks from jury service were a violation of the equal protection clause and were void. However, the Court also ruled in *Virginia* v. *Rives* (1880) that the mere absence of blacks from a jury did not necessarily mean a denial of right. To prove a denial of due process, an accused black was obliged to prove that blacks were deliberately excluded from the jury trying him. In *Alexander* v. *Louisiana* (1972), the petitioner, a black, challenged the selection of jurors because there were no blacks nor women on the grand jury which indicted him. The Court held that there was no evidence of conscious racial nor sex discrimination in the selection of jurors. An unusual case came from a white accused of burglary who alleged the systematic exclusion of blacks from a grand jury in Georgia. In *Peters* v. *Kiff* (1972), an opinion by Justice Marshall held the jury arrangement void, noting that "whatever his race, a criminal defendant has standing to challenge the system used to select his grand or petit jury, on the ground that it arbitrarily excludes from service the members of any race, and thereby denies him due process of law."

Cruel and Unusual Punishment

The guarantee of the Eighth Amendment against cruel and unusual punishment was almost applied to the states in the case of Willie Francis, a fifteen-year-old black who confessed to the killing of the hometown druggist in St. Martinville.

Sentenced to die in the electric chair, he was subsequently prepared and strapped in the state's portable electric chair; the switch was thrown; but the current was not sufficient to cause death.

A reprieve from an immediate second attempt at execution was granted by the governor; a young Louisiana attorney, Bertrand de Blanc, took the case without pay; and the case was eventually taken to the Supreme Court. Francis' lawyers argued in *Louisiana ex rel. Francis* v. *Resweber* (1947) that a second attempt to electrocute him would be a denial of due process of law under the Fourteenth Amendment, because of the double jeopardy clause of the Fifth Amendment and the cruel and unusual punishment provision of the Eighth. The Court ruled out double jeopardy, assumed the cruel and unusual punishment prohibition was applicable through the Fourteenth Amendment, but concluded the protection is against cruelty inherent in the method of punishment, not in an "unforeseeable accident." Francis was thereafter executed.

In *Trop* v. *Dulles* (1958) the Supreme Court held that depriving a member of the armed forces of his citizenship because he was convicted of wartime desertion was cruel and unusual punishment. In another interesting case, *Robinson* v. *California* (1962), the court ruled that a state law making narcotics addiction a crime to be punished, rather than an illness to be treated, was "cruel and unusual punishment in violation of the Fourteenth Amendment." In *Powell* v. *Texas* (1968), however, the Court denied that criminal conviction for public drunkenness constituted cruel and unusual punishment.

In a long-awaited decision, the Court in *Furman* v. *Georgia* (1972) split five to four over the question of whether the death penalty constituted cruel and unusual punishment, holding that "the imposition and carrying out of the death penalty in these cases constitutes cruel and unusual punishment in violation of the Eighth and Fourteenth Amendments." Separate concurring opinions were filed by Justice Douglas, Brennan, Stewart, White, and Marshall, the alumni from the Warren Court. Separate dissenting opinions were filed by Chief Justice Burger and Justices Blackmun, Powell, and Rehnquist, the Nixon appointees. Only Justices Brennan and Marshall concluded that the Eighth Amendment prohibits capital punishment for all crimes and under all circumstances. The deciding factor ruling out capital punishment was the holding of three justices that the arbitrary, discriminatory, selective application of capital punishment in the three cases (two from Georgia and one from Texas) was the fatal flaw. Thus it appears that the death penalty was not conclusively rejected, and a properly drawn statute would possibly be upheld by the Court. A number of states have rewritten their capital punishment statutes and President Nixon has asked for the death penalty in skyjacking and other heinous crimes.

CONCLUSION

According to a fund-raising leaflet circulated by the Finance Committee for the Reelection of the President in the 1972 campaign, the Nixon-appointed justices "can be expected to give a strict interpretation of the Constitution and protect the interests of the average, law-abiding American." Such a Court was promised by Richard Nixon in the 1968 campaign; was predicted in light of the selection strategies of the President, beginning with the appointment of Chief Justice Burger in 1969; and became a reality in 1972 when Justices Lewis F. Powell and William H. Rehnquist took the oath on January 7. The watershed between the Warren and the Nixon (or Burger) Courts was indicated in the close votes of the 1971–72 term. A transition to a more conservative stance began to unfold in 1972.

The Nixon appointees often persuaded Justice White, the most conservative of the Warren Court alumni, to join them in a number of decisions on the conservative side of the issues before the Court. In criminal law decisions of the full nine-man Court, the Warren Court holdovers usually viewed the earlier decisions as precedents to be adhered to; the Nixon appointees were inclined to view the same decisions as going too far, requiring modifications. Five-to-four decisions were common, with Justice White, and occasionally Justice Stewart, playing the role of "swing man."

Where decisions were political in nature, such as residency requirements for voting, the Nixon Court backed off from *Dunn* v. *Blumstein* (1972), which held

Cartoon by Gene Bassett. © 1973 United Feature Syndicate, Inc.

Precision dancing

a greater-than-thirty-day residency and registration period invalid, and allowed residency requirements of fifty days in *Burns* v. *Fortson* (1973) and *Marston* v. *Lewis* (1973) in state and local elections. The Court threw the Trans-Alaska pipeline controversy into the lap of Congress in *Morton* v. *Wilderness Society* (1973), when it refused to interfere with a lower court decision blocking construction of the pipeline. The Court was involved in a tradeoff between equal protection in education, and local control and legislative policy, in *San Antonio Independent School District* v. *Rodriguez* (1973); it chose judicial restraint instead of activism.

Nevertheless, the Nixon appointees were not always united as a bloc. This was evident in cases that involved equal protection of the laws, political contributions, antitrust suits, and the right of privacy, to mention just a few. In the highly provocative *Roe* and *Doe* abortion cases (*Roe* v. *Wade* and *Doe* v. *Bolton*) decided in 1973, the Court faced a head-on collision between the traditional moral values of the sanctity of life of the unborn with the freedom of the woman to choose her own life style. The Court held that a state could not regulate or prohibit abortions during the first trimester (first three months) of the pregnancy; may pass regulatory laws on abortion procedures to protect the health and life of the pregnant women during the next trimester; and may regulate or prohibit abortions in the last period when the fetus has become viable. It is interesting that Justices White and Rehnquist, the two youngest men on the bench, dissented.

Justices may be appointed by a President to give the Court a certain ideological position; but the justices, once appointed for life, follow their own ideological and legal judgments, which may or may not follow those of the appointing President. Presidents Jefferson and Madison came to realize this with their appointments of Justices William Johnson and Joseph Story, as did President Eisenhower and Kennedy in their appointments of Chief Justice Warren and Justice White. The Nixon Court may indeed become the Burger Court, as the Nixon appointees register their own opinions over the years.

PART TWO
Citizen Roles In American Politics

4
POLITICAL PARTICIPATION

The American sociologist, Talcott Parsons, has called the birth of new generations of children a recurrent barbarian invasion. He, of course, meant this in the sense that the newborn child comes into the world uncultured and unsocialized. These things must be learned and the process of acquisition is called "socialization"—the transmission mechanism of culture from one generation to another.

There are a number of stories of so-called feral children, who have presumably been reared by animals, which illustrate this point. A typical example is the one about Amala and Kamala, two little girls discovered living in a wolf den, who walked about on all fours; lapped milk from a dish; howled and prowled at night; caught and ate chickens raw; and resisted contact with humans—preferring the company of dogs.[1] Whether or not such stories are true, evidence suggests that if a child lived among wolves he would behave as wolves do as far as his biological makeup would permit him to do so. Examples of children locked in an attic or basement, or otherwise kept in virtual isolation from other humans clearly illustrate that cultural growth is dependent upon interaction with other human beings. These incidents demonstrate what sociologist Clarence Leuba meant when he said, "Man is largely a product of the groups to which he belongs." These groups are therefore extremely important determinants of man's customs, beliefs, language, and actions.

Socialization is the process of learning social roles and it occurs in several stages. (1) The infant knows only his own wants and desires. There is for him only gratification or frustration; he cannot substitute or delay. (2) As the infant grows older he learns a language, and, along with the language, rules and du-

---
[1] For accounts of such children see J. A. L. Singh and R. M. Zingg, *Wolf Child and Feral Man* (New York: Harper & Brothers, 1942).

ties, which are imposed upon him. He follows the rules not because they are his point of view, but because he is coerced into obeying. (3) He gradually begins to see the point of view of others, such as his parents, concerning his behavior. He knows before he acts whether they will be pleased or angry about what he wants to do. But there are still no social relations unless they relate to him. (4) The next stage consists of learning what is expected of human beings in certain situations, such as at school or in church. This is when the child realizes that all people are expected to follow rules. He has come to know the meaning of social role. (5) Finally the child perceives that there are behavioral expectations and rules for all human beings. He can see himself, as a human being, in relation to all others and as a member of society.[2]

The child's socialization is important to the development of his political attitudes. If the child's parents are authoritarian and leave little room for self-development or exploration, the child is apt to grow up dependent on others to make decisions for him. He is likely to have little confidence in himself. When he transfers these attitudes to society, he will tend to be passive, submissive, and reliant on external authority. He will be uncomfortable with democratic methods, and he will not work well within a democratic system.

On the other hand, if a child is reared in a democratic home, if he is encouraged to do his own thinking, and if he is given the freedom to make choices, there is greater likelihood that he will grow up to be independent and self-assured. This person will expect to be given reasons for being asked to behave in certain ways. He will expect those in authority to behave rationally. He will expect to share in decision making. He will not be passive or submissive to those in authority if they fail to meet his expectations.[3]

AGENTS OF POLITICAL SOCIALIZATION

Political socialization—the process of acquiring political attitudes, values, and information—is not a simple transfer of attitudes and behavior from one generation to another. If it were, change would never occur. Many young people of today hold different views from their parents. This fact was vividly demonstrated at the Democratic National Convention held at Chicago in 1968. While the "over thirty" generation was ramrodding through the presidential nomination of Hubert H. Humphrey, the younger generation was protesting what they thought Humphrey stood for. A majority of the protesters were from approximately the same socioeconomic groupings as the convention delegates. These protesters were not "inadequately" socialized; they were differently socialized.

---

[2] Deena Weinstein and Michael Weinstein, *The Roles of Man* (Hinsdale, Ill.: The Dryden Press, 1972), pp. 4–10.

[3] James C. Davies, *Human Nature in Politics* (New York: John C. Wiley, 1963).

Different times, different conditions, and different group influences will obviously result in different patterns of socialization.

The Family

Most people inherit their party preference and their initial attitudes about government, politics, and social problems. The preschool child is filled with questions, many of which have direct political significance. He may ask, "Daddy, why can't you park the car here?" The father's response could well be an explanation about law, traffic control, fire protection, or a number of politically related topics. Or the father might reply, "Some stupid cop would give me a ticket." In either situation the child is absorbing attitudes about political life that will influence his subsequent behavior.

Studies in the early 1960's indicate that children of parents who agree on their party preference, as most do, tend to mirror their parents' preference. "All I know," said a little ponytailed girl when questioned by Fred Greenstein about politics "is *we're* not Republicans." Attitudes like these are often retained throughout life. Greenstein observed: "Early impressions tend to coalesce into a natural view of the world. All later experiences then tend to receive their meaning from this original set." [4] If the parents shift parties or fail to vote, the children, as might be expected, tend to identify with no party. Hyman concludes that "foremost among agencies of socialization into politics is the family." [5] David Easton and Robert D. Hess suggest that the "truly formative years of the maturing member of a political system would seem to be the years between the ages of three and thirteen." [6] However, the child has influences other than the family during these years—especially the school.

Recent research has shown that seventy percent of all Americans identify their own party preference as being the same as that of their parents. Since the underlying attitudes that are taught by the parents and other family members are of most importance, the family is the primary agent of political socialization. The attitudes and values that the parents and family instill in an individual are likely to remain and will not be changed unless stronger socializing factors displace or modify the influences of the family.

The School

Recent studies suggest that regarding issues and public policies the elementary schools may be the most important influence in the political socialization process. The family influence reinforces attitudes which are induced by such

---

[4] Fred Greenstein, *Children and Politics* (New Haven, Conn.: Yale University Press, 1963), p. 23.
[5] Herbert Hyman, *Political Socialization* (Glencoe, Ill.: Free Press, 1959).
[6] David Easton and Robert Hess, "The Child's Political World," *The Midwest Journal of Political Science,* VI (1962), p. 236.

school practices as flag ceremonies, the Pledge of Allegiance, patriotic plays on Washington's and Lincoln's birthdays; and other practices which promote loyalty, respect for the symbols of government, patriotism, and the kind of behavior expected of good citizens. However, a significant difference between parents and children has been shown to exist over such political issues or policies as integration or prayers in the schools. Thus the schools play a strong indoctrinating role and often induce political attitudes in the children different from those of their parents.

The political ideas taught by the schools, though, are generally the dominant ideas of that society. American schools successfully teach most children to be loyal, patriotic, law-abiding citizens. Robert D. Hess and Judith V. Torney picture American children as preferring American society to that of other systems, the American flag over flags of other nations. The policeman is viewed as a friendly, helpful person, second only to the child's father. The child believes America offers the good life—especially in a materialistic way. But these conclusions are based on data drawn from urban white children and they picture a "happy, white world." [7]

To the black child living in the ghettos, is the policeman the benevolent friend or the "fuzz"—someone to avoid? What kind of picture of America does the Navajo child in the Four Corners area of Colorado, New Mexico, Arizona, and Utah have, or the Chicano in Los Angeles, or the poor white in Appalachia? Studies of these subcultures come up with quite different conceptualizations of America than the pleasant white world.[8] These studies also show that the nature of the indoctrination varies with the communities. Edgar Litt's study of civic education in three American communities with differing socioeconomic characteristics and differing levels of political activity, concludes that "students in the three communities are being trained to play different political roles":

> In the working-class community, where political involvement is low, the arena of civic education offers training in the basic democratic procedures without stressing political participation or the citizen's view of conflict and disagreement as indigenous to the political system. Politics is conducted by formal government institutions working in harmony for the benefit of citizens.
>
> In the lower middle-class school system—a community with moderately active political life—training in the elements of democratic government is supplemented by an emphasis on the responsibilities of citizenship, not on the dynamics of public decision-making.
>
> Only in the affluent and politically vibrant community are insights into political processes and functions of politics passed on to those who, judging from their socio-

---

[7] Robert Hess and Judith V. Torney, *The Development of Political Attitudes in Children* (Chicago: Aldine Publishing Co., 1967).

[8] For example, see David Schulz, *Coming Up Black: Patterns of Ghetto Socialization* (Englewood Cliffs, N.J.: Prentice-Hall, 1969).

economic and political environment, will likely man those positions that involve them in influencing or making political decisions.[9]

Some high school civics courses have been found to inculcate the notion in black and lower-status students that a good citizen is above all a loyal citizen, rather than an active one. The effect of teaching passive roles to certain deprived classes in America is clearly designed to preserve the status quo. The schools are therefore a vital link in the transmission of traditional values and the perpetuation of existing patterns of political life. Norman Adler and Charles Harrington conclude that "no single institution in society is more responsible for imparting 'mainstream' political knowledge. For lower class children and those from minority cultures, the school takes on paramount importance, almost to the exclusion of other forces." [10] But other forces do influence the attitudes and activities of the maturing and adult citizen.

The Church

Religion and church organizations are no longer as important in the political socialization process as they once were, due to the decline of church membership and attendance. At one time in the earlier history of the United States, religious influence on political attitudes was strong; but today that influence depends on how seriously religion is considered in the family and how much power a particular church has in a given area. Voting patterns in the Baptist "Bible Belt" (northern Texas and southern Oklahoma) since the New Deal, for example, suggest liberal attitudes toward economic programs of government, but a social conservatism in regard to civil rights—attributable in part to religious influences on political behavior.

Religious values are instilled first in the home, and these values are reinforced by the church. It is often an easy transfer to shift these values into the political arena. In addition to influencing church members along partisan or issue lines, the church has had significant impact on public policies. There are still laws on the books that reflect religious doctrines of the predominant church in a given area. In predominantly Catholic populated areas, for example, religious beliefs concerning birth control and abortion have in times past been translated into strict regulatory or prohibitive laws. When court decisions have invalidated such laws, Catholic leadership, if not its membership, has strongly protested and sought political remedies consistent with Catholic doctrinal beliefs. To take another example, the Protestant influence in the Anti-Saloon League's crusade against "demon rum" cannot be denied. Laws regulating the sale and consumption of alcoholic beverages in certain sections of the country reflect to a degree the religious attitudes of the predominant churches. Although

---

[9] Edgar Litt, "Civic Education, Community Norms, and Political Indoctrination," *American Sociological Review* (1963), p. 74.

[10] Norman Adler and Charles Harrington, *The Learning of Political Behavior* (Glenview, Ill.: Scott, Foresman, 1970).

churches are primarily concerned with moral values in society, they influence their members—and public policies as well—in regard to economic, political, and social matters.

The Media

The American press has traditionally functioned on the premise that the government is the servant of the people, and the people have the right to know what the government is doing. But public officials, at times, have interpreted the dissemination of critical news as partisan and propaganda. Former Vice-President Spiro Agnew's attacks on the news media, for example, were based on "mass theory" of communications, the theory that the media has a direct rather than a mediating influence on the individual. This theory is invalid, but is occasionally used as an excuse for government censorship. Two preliminary conclusions appear to be valid as to the effect of the news media on the political socialization process.

First, the media is usually a secondary source of political socialization. Primary agents such as family and peers are constantly modifying the effects of media messages. People generally do not watch television in lonely isolation. Television viewing is a social function and is done in groups, with considerable discussion prompted by the programs. News from all sources is discussed with family and friends, altering its direct effect.

Second, the media is more reflective of society than it is innovative. For instance, television has been accused of displaying too much violence, but is not violence an integral quality of American society? The mythical American hero is a man of action, not thought. If he can't solve a problem immediately, he annihilates it. Violence has long been institutionalized in American life. Any nation that must admit to seven major wars in the first 175 years of its existence, and to the degree of crime and violence existent in America *before* the advent of television, can hardly accuse TV of creating violence and introducing it to American people. Some recent studies do seem to indicate, however, that some types of children are affected by television violence.

A most interesting study was done by Neil Hollander surveying the sources of information high school seniors used. He devised a questionnaire to test several socialization agents in relation to several current issues and problems. The influence of the church was last in every case. Family and peer sources were high most consistently. Interestingly enough, on the issue of war in general and the Vietnam War in particular, the respondents consistently listed the media as their primary source of information. They showed a marked difference from parental attitudes toward war, indicating, among other influences, color television's impact on youth in showing the realities of war.[11]

[11] Neil Hollander, "Adolescence and the War: The Sources of Socialization," *Journalism Quarterly*, XLVIII (Autumn, 1971).

Will Rogers, the great American humorist of the 1930's, used to say, "Well, all I know is what I read in the newspapers." With newspapers, magazines, radio, and television in virtually every contemporary home in the United States, its citizens ought to be better informed on public matters than Will Rogers. It is questionable, though, if the expansion and availability of news sources is producing a better-informed citizenry. Walter Lippmann, one of the foremost columnists and students of politics of the American twentieth century, concluded in the 1920's that democracy was a failure in the United States because it was based on the idea of self-government, which demands an informed public. Intelligent government by the people, he believed, was obstructed by "censorship and privacy at the source, by physical and social barriers at the other end, by

Editorial cartoon by Paul Conrad. Copyright, *Los Angeles Times*. Reprinted with permission.

"All I know is what I read in the newspaper."

"All I don't know is what I don't read in the newspaper."

scanty attention, by the poverty of language, by distraction, by . . . monotony." [12] Recent writings have not substantially altered this view. The news media, government, and the people must all share the responsibility of limiting our democratic system by not promoting a better-informed public.

Political news is often relegated to a secondary position in the newspapers to leave space for the sensational or the trivial. Radio and television carry short news spots or news summaries, but the bulk of their time is devoted to entertainment that will hold audiences, whose attentiveness when measured through surveys, can be used to sell advertising. After all, the media are in business to make money; and news and public service programs (beyond programming that is required by the Federal Communications Commission) must take their place on this economic scale of "values" which sets priorities in programming.

There are notable exceptions to this picture of inadequate news coverage, wherein certain newspapers, radio, and TV stations or networks do an excellent job in bringing vital issues to the attention of the citizenry. The national television networks cover the news well and expend the time, money, and effort necessary for responsible journalism in their documentary and public affairs programs. This coverage is vital to an informed public. The documentaries have dealt with the most pressing problems facing America today: welfare, United States involvement in Southeast Asia, crime, the problems of justice in America, military expenditures, and so on.

The American political system is also weakened by the individual himself, who, for a variety of reasons, does not become better informed. The voter, if he has a choice, will turn on the football game, "I Love Lucy," or some other entertainment rather than the President. When the President speaks to the nation today, it is usually carried on all three national networks. However, President Nixon had competition with one of his telecasts in 1971, as two networks carried their regular programs. On that occasion he had only eleven percent of the listening audience in the New York area, according to a viewers survey! Even though nearly every American home has a newspaper, magazines, and radios, only a small percentage of voters place political news or programs first over other features.

Media news is generally filtered through opinion leaders among the voter's personal associates. The father or mother in the family, a public-spirited friend, an employer or co-worker will most frequently influence political attitudes of the voter, in that order of significance. Much of what finally adds up to people's opinions is acquired by face-to-face transmission of political facts, beliefs, and values from their peers.

Political Information and Propaganda

Nearly all units of government have public relations programs that contribute to the continuing political socialization of adults. The information disseminated is

[12] Walter Lippman, *Public Opinion* (New York: Harcourt and Brace, 1922), p. 76.

supposed to keep the public informed about government activities and policies. Although much data, many documents, and innumerable publications are available to the public, the mainstream of official information about public activities comes from the news releases of public officials who fill the many different public positions in various governmental units. These press releases of the President, congressmen, governors, and administrators contain information; but often the information is what the officials want the public to believe, not necessarily what the public needs to know.

During wartime, governments have found it necessary to withhold information, at times imposing censorship in the interest of national security. Since World War II, the American nation has been involved in cold war or hot, localized wars; and the government continues to classify documents as secret and to withhold information. Some people have questioned the necessity of classifying documents which are not absolutely vital to national security. When the *New York Times* published the "Pentagon Papers"—which documented the mounting involvement of the United States in Vietnam during the Kennedy years, American connivance in the overthrow of Ngo Dinh Diem, and other questionable activities—four problems of public policy became evident: (1) the credibility gap of the Johnson Administration was continued under the Nixon Administration, (2) many documents which the government "stamps" as secret need not be so classified, (3) the public and Congress are not informed adequately about executive action, and (4) there is a continuing need for a probing, but responsible, press to help keep the government itself responsible.

In 1951 Senator Richard M. Nixon insisted that the people had a right to know the full story of the talks between President Harry Truman and General MacArthur which took place on Wake Island on October 15, 1950. "The new test for classifying secret documents," Nixon charged, "now seems to be not whether the publication of a document would affect the security of the nation but whether it would affect the political security of the Administration." The Truman Administration thereupon declassified the documents.

In 1969 President Richard M. Nixon ordered a committee of scientists headed by physicist Richard L. Garwin to prepare a report on the supersonic transport plane (SST). The report advised against government support in developing the SST on grounds of excessive cost, pollution, unprofitability, and unacceptable sonic booms. The report went against Nixon's wishes and he refused to make it known to the public or to Congress. After a year of legal battle, the report was made public on August 21, 1971—sometime after Congress had made a decision against continuing the funding of the SST prototypes. It is difficult to see how the withholding of this information was vital to national security, and how Congress can make wise decisions on public policy without all available information.

It is also difficult to see how the people can make wise decisions at the polls and influence public policies between elections if they are not informed, or are misinformed and unconcerned. Political parties utilize all of the techniques of propaganda from personal testimonials through glittering generalities to card stacking in order to persuade the populace to support their platforms and candidates. The intent of the party is not to inform, but to proselytize; not to educate, but to win votes. Its ultimate goal is to control the powers of government. To achieve this goal, the party may "throw dust in the air" and cloud the issues.

The individual must cut therefore through the political haze in order to clearly see the issues involved and the consequences of the choices he makes. Responsible news media can help the private citizen obtain the necessary political and governmental data to make the decisions democracy demands.

AGGREGATE SOCIALIZING AGENTS

All of the forementioned agents of political socialization combine to produce the fabric of politically relevant stimuli and information that contribute to the development of one's political attitudes, beliefs, and skills. This process is not static; indeed it is a continuous one which only stops at death. Interesting combinations of socialization emerge, which can be best described by a continuum running from a homogeneous socialization process on one extreme to a heterogeneous one on the other.

In a homogeneous socializing experience, a high degree of uniformity exists in the socializing process, wherein all the various agents provide the same type of information and furnish similar experiences. Such a process is characterized by a great deal of consonance and continuity. The person exposed to such an environment acquires a world view of great symmetry and tends to hold to rigid and uncompromising political attitudes.

In contrast, the person exposed to a heterogeneous socializing experience finds himself having to continually integrate the incongruities and conflicts created by disagreement among socializing agents. This disagreement might be in the home, where a liberal mother and a conservative father disagree on the basics of democratic government. It may be in a clash between the values and norms of a person's peer group and those of his family. The result of such a situation is usually a rather flexible attitude toward politics and the capability of integrating many conflicting viewpoints. If the pressure placed upon the individual is too intense, however, he may seek to withdraw and block politically related events from his mind.

In the modern industrial world in which we live, few people are exposed to a homogeneous environment. On the other hand, it is very unlikely that there exists anywhere an environment so fractured that the individual cannot find a tolerable compatibility among socializing agents. Nevertheless, substantial cultural shock can arise when there is an abrupt change in socializing processes, resulting in what may be called "traumatic socialization."

Take, for example, a person who during his impressionable years is living in America during the "golden twenties" of this century. Socialization agents of parents, schools, friends, and so on prompt conservative political attitudes, belief in the work ethic, and positive acceptance of the free enterprise system. But when the Great Depression comes, this person—in spite of his attitudes and efforts—loses his job, his savings, and, with millions of others, is faced with the realities of poverty. Despite the fact that the New Deal program is in contradiction to all that he has been taught, he finds work and is able to support his family once again through one of the government's "make-work" programs. In 1936, he votes for the Democratic President, breaking the long-standing Republican tradition of his family.

Such experiences in life are so shocking that they may generate attitude change even among the most inflexible, those who have been socialized under extremely uniform and homogeneous conditions. On a mass scale, such shocks can shift the political orientation of a nation. The Civil War and the Depression represent such shifts—shifts of such magnitude that the whole political alignment of the United States was restructured.

FACTORS IN POLITICAL SOCIALIZATION

Class Status

Because of the American heritage of equality and individualism and the social and economic mobility of our system, Americans do not have a strong class consciousness. In a recent survey, sixty percent of those polled said they did not think of themselves as belonging to a given class. Yet class status significantly influences political attitudes and activities. Political activity is lowest among the people of the lowest socioeconomic group and it increases as you go up the class scale. This presents a major problem to the Democratic Party, as lower-status people tend to be Democrats.

Attributes of class—social status, occupation, income, and education—influence political preferences. The strongest support for Republican candidates in post-World War II elections came from the professional and managerial class, from other white collar workers, and from farmers. A notable exception to the influence of class and family in political preference is found among the social science faculties across the country. Between seventy and eighty percent of the social scientists prefer the Democratic Party, indicating that the field of study itself and contacts with colleagues have had a strong influence on them.

The more income a person has, the more likely it is that he will be a Republican. This seems to hold true among people from all walks of life and in all areas of the country. There are notable exceptions to these generalizations, of course, as there are many wealthy Democrats. Different influences may overpower the income factor, including the attitude toward wealth. There is a story about the Kennedy brothers sailing in a small boat at Hyannis Port and a friend asked them why they did not have their father buy them a yacht. One of the Kennedy boys replied, "Who do you think we are, the Vanderbilts?"

College graduates vote Republican in higher proportions than high school graduates, who in turn cast more Republican ballots than those with only a

Drawing by Whitney Darrow, Jr.; © 1970 *The New Yorker Magazine*, Inc.

"This year I'm not getting involved in any complicated issues. I'm just voting my straight ethnic prejudices."

grade school education. These similar patterns suggest that the influence of education, occupation, income, and social status are all interrelated as determinants of political preference and voting behavior.

Residence

The traditional patterns of a Democratic, but conservative, South or a Republican Midwest are no longer valid. Regional differences on party politics, created in part because of historical reasons, are giving way to other, more relevant factors. A more consistent pattern of residential differences in political attitudes can be found between communities considered in terms of size, rather than region. The larger cities voted for John F. Kennedy in 1960, which is not surprising since they have been voting Democratic since 1928. The suburbs, on the other hand, are generally Republican, as are small cities and rural areas.

Religion and Ethnic Factors

Protestants, Catholics, and Jews are not found in the two major parties in equal proportions. Northern Protestants tend to be Republicans, and Catholics and Jews tend to be Democrats. This tendency originally was patterned by the waves of immigration to America. The Protestant groups came first and were well established when the Celtic Irish and the southern Europeans, who were predominantly Catholic, came later in the nineteenth century. Some Jews came with the southern Europeans at the end of the nineteenth century and others followed in the twentieth century because of anti-Semitism in eastern Europe. However, those people whose families had been in America first considered themselves to be "natives"; and a virulent outcropping of nativism became manifest in anti-Catholic and antiradical attitudes and activities, and in racial intolerance, directed toward the newcomers. These later immigrants were in the minority; settled in the cities; and were soon numbered among the Democratic Party, which was stronger in the cities. During the Great Depression, Franklin Roosevelt was able to develop a coalition of support which included the minority groups, due largely to the social reforms of the New Deal.

These traditional party-affiliation patterns may be altered by the candidates and the issues in particular elections. Table 4.1, taken from George Gallup's survey research, shows this variation in presidential elections. The Catholic support for John F. Kennedy in the 1960 election suggests that religion was a strong factor in the campaign. It was. But Catholic support for Kennedy was more than offset by Protestant votes against him. The Survey Research Center of the University of Michigan estimated that his religion resulted in a net loss of approximately two million votes.

The political differences found among religious groups are possibly based as much on class status as on religion. A notable exception is the Jewish political preference. The Jews should be Republican, if socioeconomic factors alone were considered; but because of their position as a minority group, their feelings of

Table 4.1 Vote by Groups in Presidential Elections Since 1952
(Based on Gallup Poll survey data)

	1952 Stev.	1952 Ike	1956 Stev.	1956 Ike	1960 JFK	1960 Nixon	1964 LBJ	1964 Gold.	1968 HHH	1968 Nixon	1968 Wallace	1972 McG.	1972 Nixon
	%	%	%	%	%	%	%	%	%	%	%	%	%
NATIONAL	44.6	55.4	42.2	57.8	50.1	49.9	61.3	38.7	43.0	43.4	13.6	38	62
Men	47	53	45	55	52	48	60	40	41	43	16	37	63
Women	42	58	39	61	49	51	62	38	45	43	12	38	62
White	43	57	41	59	49	51	59	41	38	47	15	32	68
Non-white	79	21	61	39	68	32	94	6	85	12	3	87	13
College	34	66	31	69	39	61	52	48	37	54	9	37	63
High School	45	55	42	58	52	48	62	38	42	43	15	34	66
Grade School	52	48	50	50	55	45	66	34	52	33	15	49	51
Prof. & Bus.	36	64	32	68	42	58	54	46	34	56	10	31	69
White Collar	40	60	37	63	48	52	57	43	41	47	12	36	64
Manual	55	45	50	50	60	40	71	29	50	35	15	43	57
Under 30 years	51	49	43	57	54	46	64	36	47	38	15	48	52
30–49 years	47	53	45	55	54	46	63	37	44	41	15	33	67
50 years & older	39	61	39	61	46	54	59	41	41	47	12	36	64
Protestants	37	63	37	63	38	62	55	45	35	49	16	30	70
Catholics	56	44	51	49	78	22	76	24	59	33	8	48	52
Republicans	8	92	4	96	5	95	20	80	9	86	5	5	95
Democrats	77	23	85	15	84	16	87	13	74	12	14	67	33
Independents	35	65	30	70	43	57	56	44	31	44	25	31	69
Members of labor union families	61	39	57	43	65	35	73	27	56	29	15	46	54

SOURCE: American Institute of Public Opinion (The Gallup Poll)

persecution, their location in the larger cities, and their religious beliefs concerning social justice, they are strongly Democratic. They join with many intellectuals from the academic and professional groups to form a leadership elite within the Democratic Party.

There is a strong correlation between religion and ethnic identification or national origins, and political opinion. Like members of any other group, members of an ethnic group are inclined to support the party, the policies, or candidates which will recognize their interests. Ethnic groups have discovered that political power is a way to alter their underprivileged status in the economic and social systems.

Among the many ethnic groups which have suffered discrimination in America, blacks have had fewer opportunities to participate in politics. The Civil War amendments (Thirteenth, Fourteenth, and Fifteenth) were passed to place black Americans on an equal footing with other Americans, but until recently blacks, in large measure, have been denied their political rights. Those who were permitted to vote—in the South during the Reconstruction period and in the North since that time—generally supported the Republican ticket, until the administration of Franklin Roosevelt. From the New Deal period to 1968, blacks voted Democratic in increasing proportions. Over ninety percent of black Americans voted for the Democratic nominee for President in 1964, and George Wallace and Richard Nixon combined polled less than five percent of the black vote in 1968. Only a very slight decline in black voting for Democrat George McGovern was evident in the 1972 election.

Even though H. Rap Brown, a black militant leader, shocked Americans in the late 1960's with the statement that "violence is as American as cherry pie"—which is quite true—most blacks are seeking power within the system. They have joined the Democratic Party and either nominate black candidates or support candidates who are most responsive to their needs. In recent years blacks have won city elections where their numbers are large and their unity is strong. They have also won a significant number of congressional seats, and the Black Caucus is a formidable bloc in Washington. Blacks supported a black man, Channing E. Philips, for President in the 1968 Democratic Convention; Shirley Chisholm, a black congresswoman from New York, was a Democratic candidate for President in 1972; and blacks continue to express interest in the presidency or vice-presidency.

Age

Voters under the age of thirty backed President Nixon by a slight majority in the 1972 election; but they voted Democratic in the previous two decades, with the exception of 1956. Both political parties know that there is a bonanza in votes among this group, and both parties compete for the support of the youth vote. Nevertheless, both parties recognize that younger voters have participated far less than those between the ages of thirty and fifty-five in past elections.

Younger voters also are less motivated by party loyalty and are more attracted to candidates or issues. An attractive candidate with popular issues for youth is likely to win the support of young voters, regardless of party affiliation. This, however, is true with all groups. A person's electoral decision is prompted by what he believes the party or the candidates will be able to do for him and by the constant socialization forces about him.

POLITICAL PARTICIPATION

The Voter—His Associations and Political Activities

Those persons who are organized and unified in their goals, those who understand the system and can manipulate it, and those who have positions of power in society are the people who control the political process and determine the public policies of society. One definition of political power is the ability to turn one's private interests into public policy. The political activity of a person is related to his status in society, what he perceives his role to be, his knowledge about the system, and what he expects from it. (See Figure 4.1, which shows the correlation between education, socioeconomic status, race, and political participation.)

Those persons on the outer edge or periphery of society tend to be alienated or apathetic. They are nonparticipants because they feel that they cannot affect society or the system. Their attitude could be summed up with a statement such as, "Oh well! No one cares what I think. I'm just one person. There's nothing I can do." They lack cohesion with others like themselves. They tend to mistrust groups and the motives of group leaders. They are difficult to organize and motivate. They generally identify with the Democratic Party. Because of their inconsistent voter turnout, however, the Democrats cannot rely upon them. If their vote were reliable, the Democrats would never lose a national election. Students of political behavior believe in the axiom—low voter turnout, Republican victory; high voter turnout, Democratic victory. This is due to the fact that the men who are in the core of society (the first group in the model), and who have the greatest stake in society (it is their system), are consistent in their high voter turnout, election after election. Therefore, the Republican vote is fairly consistent in numbers year after year. It is the Democratic vote that fluctuates widely, depending on the motivation of the peripheral and middle groups.

Parties, Candidates, and Issues

The role of the political party in the political socialization process is one of continuity. The Survey Research Center's study on party identification of

Figure 4.1 Core-Periphery Model of Political Participation

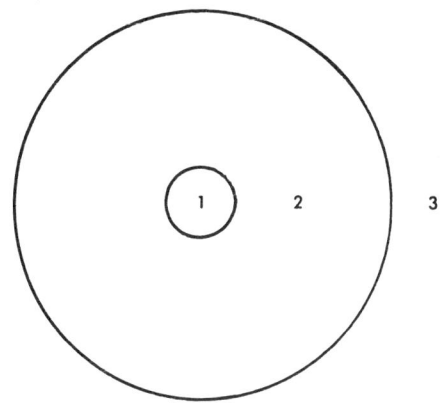

Core of Society	Middle Society	Outer Edge of Society
1	2	3
1. White	1. White	1. Nonwhite
2. Male	2. Male	2. Female
3. Middle-aged	3. Middle-aged	3. Young and old
4. Highly organized socially, as well as in interest groups	4. Organized interest groups	4. Unemployable
	5. Skilled labor	5. Unorganized
5. Professional, managerial, businessmen	6. Farmers	6. Unskilled
	7. Low-middle to middle income	7. Low Income
6. College Educated		8. Uneducated
7. Upper-middle to high income	8. High school education	9. Democrats
8. Republican	9. Majority Democrats	

Americans from 1952 to 1968 reveals a fairly constant pattern of approximately 26 percent Republican and 45 percent Democratic support; 29 percent of the population identify themselves as independents.[13] Elections are won or lost on the support, or lack of support, of this independent group. Even among those who identify themselves as Democrats or Republicans, the voter is much more independent than in times past. It is apparent that the party has lost much of its original meaning for the people and the candidates. The electorate is more inclined to vote for a candidate because of his personal qualities or because of issues, instead of his party label. One of the main reasons for the weakening of party ties is the continual erosion of the patronage jobs once handed out with

---

[13] William H. Flanigan, *The Political Behavior of the American Electorate* (Boston: Allyn & Bacon, 1972), p. 33.

each party victory. At one time, almost everyone could name a relative who held a patronage job because he had worked for the winning party. This was a powerful reason for party loyalty; civil service has destroyed that reason.

Because the independents and weak party-affiliators are not reliable in their voting habits, it has become imperative for the two major parties to become centrist in their appeal to the voters. Neither party promotes radical or extreme policies if it wants to win. Candidates tend to mask their own conservative or liberal views and take moderate stands when campaigning. Both parties have been badly beaten, in recent history, when their presidential candidates departed from the center of the political continuum—in the cases of Barry Goldwater in 1964 and George McGovern in 1972. (See Figure 4.2, which illustrates the fluidity of the American electorate, and the importance of the independent vote.)

The Republican Party has won only two national elections in the last forty years. The first was a postwar, nonpresidential election in 1946, when the Republicans won control of Congress during the Truman Administration. The second was won in 1952, when the popular war hero Dwight Eisenhower won the presidency, his coattail long and broad enough to bring the Republicans into power in Congress. Ike's election in 1952 and his reelection in 1956 were the result of his personal popularity rather than the electorate following party lines.

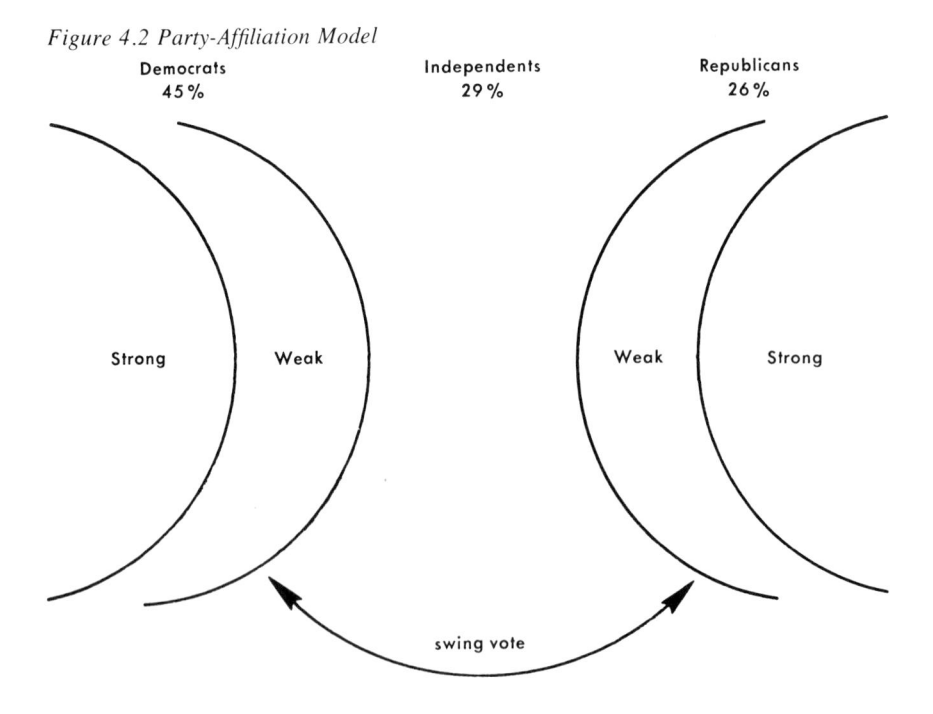

Figure 4.2 Party-Affiliation Model

| Democrats | Independents | Republicans |
| 45% | 29% | 26% |

Strong Weak   Weak Strong

swing vote

What the electorate said, in effect, in 1956 was that they "liked Ike" and also the Democratic Party—or at least the Democratic candidates running for Congress.

In 1964, the voters did not want to rock the prosperous domestic boat, and they feared what Barry Goldwater might do in Vietnam. But, by 1966, they were upset with what Lyndon Johnson had done in Vietnam. The resentment toward the war was a significant factor in the off-year election. The issue was there but it was confusing to both voters and candidates. The voters wanted the war ended, but differed widely on how it should be accomplished. The candidates knew the war was a major issue on the minds of the voters, but were reluctant to take a definite position on it because any stand was the wrong one with many of the voters. The voters, in many instances, registered their displeasure over the war by casting their votes against the Democratic candidates because the Democratic Party was in power.

The war issue had clearly become one of widespread dissatisfaction by 1968. President Johnson, who sincerely wanted a second term, could read it and declined to run for reelection. The normal Democratic majority had enough defectors to elect Richard Nixon, in part at least because he promised to end the war in Vietnam. In the same election, however, the same voters returned a Democratic Congress.

In 1970, the Republicans wanted very badly to win control of Congress. To win a majority in the Senate, they would have to win seven Democratic seats and hold the seats they already had. The strategy focused on certain western Senators in the less populous states, where the cost of a campaign is considerably less than in the larger states. The Republican Party sent all of their "big guns" west on the campaign circuits, including the President and Vice-President. However, the Republicans misread the domestic issues and went down to defeat on the law and order issue. The Democrats charged the administration with ineptness in handling the economic problems of high unemployment and inflation and retained their majorities in both houses of Congress. The war issue had been somewhat defused by the President's "Vietnamization" policy; and bread and butter issues are always near the top of the voter's priority list of domestic issues.

Foreign issues clearly aligned the voters behind President Nixon in the 1972 presidential election. His visits to China and the Soviet Union had reduced international tensions, and his "peace is at hand" in Vietnam claims were hopefully believed by the voters. Although the problems of soaring food prices, inflation, and high unemployment should have helped the Democratic candidate, George McGovern was considered to be too radical on both foreign and domestic issues. Senator McGovern was not playing the game in the center of the political field. President Nixon won reelection; but the Democrats increased their majorities in the United States Senate and in the statehouses, and held onto their majority in the House of Representatives as well.

Public Opinion

James Bryce (1838–1922)—an English observer of American life who wrote the celebrated study *The American Commonwealth*—said that "public opinion is the real ruler of America." Thus, democracy implies government by or for the people as a whole. The concept that the views of the people about social issues influence the policy makers is a tempting one to accept. V. O. Key, however, rather cynically, defines public opinion as "those opinions held by private persons which governments find it prudent to heed." [14] But the notion that public opinion—that is, public opinion as "the aggregate of individual views"—is a real force in setting public policies requires some refinement.

When President Nixon relied on the "silent majority" in support of his programs, was he following public opinion? Unless there is an expressed demand for action on a definable social issue, an intuitive feeling about how the public may feel is hardly based on public opinion. Is silence support, alienation, or apathy? It is an error to assume there is general agreement on any issue, and it is an error to believe that there is one public opinion. It would be more accurate to say that there are different publics in support of, or in opposition to, many different issues.

The different publics in society may be passive or active. The active publics are those groups with expressed demands for action on a social issue. Although the active publics have the most immediate impact on government policies, the passive publics are not unimportant, as they may become active on a given issue and become motivated to make their demands known.

The people as a whole rarely care about most public policies. This low level of opinion simply allows the decision makers to take one of a number of alternatives, including doing nothing, without fearing the next election. It can hardly be said that this level of public opinion rules America!

The passive, supportive role of public opinion continues or maintains the many programs and policies of the government once they have been adopted. This is true also of those programs which were bitterly opposed at the time of adoption. An example of this would be the Social Security Act of 1935. At the time of adoption there was much opposition to the New Deal measure. After thirty years, public opinion, in its supportive role, refused to buy presidential candiate Barry Goldwater's proposal to make social security optional. Goldwater shifted ground and endorsed the system when it became evident that the tide of public opinion was running against him on this issue.

The active, demanding role of public opinion may indeed be directive of government policies. An example of this would be the issue of Vietnam in the 1968 election, which prompted Richard Nixon to promise during the campaign to end the war and to wind down the war with his Vietnamization policy fol-

---

[14] V. O. Key, *Public Opinion and American Democracy* (New York: Knopf, 1961), p. 14.

lowing his election. But, more often, the demanding or directive role of public opinion is played by different publics with different opinions on many different issues. The demands so registered are in addition to the general expressions of public opinion on election days. A continuing fact of political life, they are expressed in an organized way through a number of different pressure groups.

5
INTEREST GROUP POLITICS

As the Ninety-second Congress started its first session in 1971, a major fight was brewing over the continued funding of the supersonic transport prototypes being built by Boeing and General Electric and a host of smaller subcontracting companies. The government's investment had already reached $864 million and the 1971 installment would add another $134 million. The total cost to the government could well exceed $1.3 billion. Government support of technological advances was not new, however: it was an established tradition of the American heritage, going all the way back to the Jefferson Administration when it supported some military inventions of Eli Whitney. What was new was the opposition to certain technological developments because of their possible deleterious effect on the environment.

The Russians had an operational supersonic jetliner and the Concorde, a joint British-French built plane, was approaching its maiden flight. President Nixon considered the building of the SST a matter of national prestige. He told a meeting of Republican legislative leaders: "I am utterly convinced that if we do not go ahead with this dramatic breakthrough, this nation will have lost its feel for greatness." Many Americans in the street, as well as the President, felt strongly that America ought to be "number one," first in all things. Senator William Proxmire and many others, however, believed that national priorities must be redirected toward meeting the pressing social problems. In the transportation area, they felt that more should be done to develop mass transit systems which would serve the people (and the environment) rather than the "jet set" in their intercontinental flights. But to the companies involved and their employees it was a down-to-the-ground matter of company profits and personal income.

Opposition to the SST had already been registered by the Ninety-first

Congress on December 3, 1970, when the Senate turned down a $290 million appropriation to continue the Boeing prototypes. This prompted a team of Boeing executives, led by chairman William Allen and president T. A. Wilson, to meet with President Nixon in January of 1971. The President and a number of his top aides assured the Boeing team of strong administration support for the SST. With this assurance, a well-financed, well-organized campaign to save the SST was directed toward Capitol Hill.

A committee called American Industry and Labor for the SST, headed by a vice-president of one of Boeing's subcontractors and the president of the International Association of Machinists (AFL-CIO), took out full-page ads in all three Washington daily newspapers to promote the plane and announced plans to raise $350,000 to finance a nationwide SST promotion. On Capitol Hill, the National Committee for an American SST, a registered lobbying group, worked hard to offset the arguments of the environmentalists. The SST lobbyists had a suite of offices in Washington and a large staff of workers who put together facts and figures to persuade congressmen to vote for continued support of the project. Many congressmen were impressed with the weight of the convincing arguments of the lobbyists. In Washington, automobiles carried bumper stickers bearing British, Russian, and U.S. flags with the slogan: "SST—Ours or Theirs?" By mid-March, it appeared that the SST pressure group was on the threshold of success.

Senator William Proxmire, an outspoken opponent of the SST, was pictured by the news media as "David among the Goliaths"—a lone antagonist doing battle with strong pressure groups. But the senator was supported by a number of colleagues on the Hill, and by conservation and environmental groups all over the country. The citizen's lobby, Common Cause, headed by John Gardner, former secretary of the Department of Health, Education, and Welfare (HEW), threw its weight behind Senator Proxmire. This group has thousands of members widely distributed across the country. They pay only modest annual dues to finance the organization; but the real strength of Common Cause is in the number and status of its members, and in its dedication to causes which seem to represent the people of America. Private citizens, as well as organized interest groups, became involved in the controversy. Letters came pouring into Washington. Most Congressmen privately admitted that their mail was running heavily against the SST.

In the middle of March, the House defeated the SST bill. A week later the bill came before the Senate. President Nixon threw the weight of his office into the fight to get the bill passed in the Senate. He launched an intensive sales campaign among senators thought to be susceptible to presidential persuasion, by inviting them to the White House. He had his aides work with others. Melvin Laird informed Senator Margaret Chase Smith that the McNamara order to close the Portsmouth Naval Shipyard in 1974 had been rescinded, and the President sent her a "Dear Margaret" letter confirming this action. Secretary of the

Treasury John Connally worked with Senator Lloyd Bentsen, a conservative Democrat from Texas. The President counted heavily on the freshman senators, who supposedly had tipped the ideological balance of the Senate in Nixon's favor after the election of 1970.

Heading into the showdown Senate vote on the SST, the headcount, as best as it could be estimated, showed 49 senators against the plane, 47 for it, two absent, and two wavering: Maine's Margaret Smith and Kentucky's John Sherman Cooper. If Nixon could land these two senators, the plane might yet fly. Vice-President Agnew stood ready to cast a tie-breaking vote for the SST.

When the roll call began, opponents of the SST proceeded slowly in hopes that Senator Birch Bayh could return in time from a skiing trip in Colorado. Slowed by the icy roads, Bayh missed a flight—and the roll call. In the intense, dramatic atmosphere of a close and crucial vote, the Senate was electrified and the President received his first shock when Clinton Anderson from New Mexico voted no. Proxmire smiled with surprise and lifted a closed fist in a "go, team" gesture. Anderson was a close friend of Henry Jackson, the "Senator from Boeing," and had supported the SST in previous votes. He explained his vote on the basis of his current mail running heavily against the aircraft. The galleries murmured again when Texas Democrat Lloyd Bentsen voted no. Proxmire's fist went up again when Senator Cooper voted no. The President's appeal had not influenced him. Hubert Humphrey, still a presidential candidate and deeply indebted to labor for its support, nevertheless cast his vote against the SST. The outcome was clear when the roll call reached the S's. Senator Margaret Smith cast an independent no, indicating she may have been angered at the timing of Nixon's letter. The Proxmire forces were also intent on getting her vote and had asked other senators how to approach her. They were warned to "leave her alone"—which they did—and it paid off.

The Senate vote was close (51–46)—but when it was over the SST was grounded unless private capital could be found to continue the project; the aircraft industry and its lobbyists had suffered a sharp setback; and the President had lost prestige in his efforts to make the SST fly. In the voting President Nixon had lost seventeen Republicans, more than a third of his party's membership in the Senate. The "ideological gain" of the 1970 election did not come across. Only four of the twelve freshmen senators voted for the SST.

The *Los Angeles Times*, which supported the SST, acknowledged that the supersonic plane had become "a symbol to a lot of people—a symbol of resistance to the so-called 'military-industrial complex,' a symbol of resistance to technological spoliation of the environment, even a symbol of distaste for President Nixon." It may well have been a turning point in the American attitude toward technological progress, with a reordering of national priorities. It may also have been a turning point in the American attitude toward having to be first, best, or greatest in all things—an attitude which, at times, may have had detrimental consequences in clouding America's vision.

INTEREST GROUPS AND PUBLIC POLICY

The conflict over the SST reminds us of the concern over "factions" which James Madison wrote about in Number Ten of the *Federalist Papers*. Madison believed that the causes of factions or special interests are "sown in the nature of man," and that people with similar interests will come together and organize their own group at the expense of the public good. He thought factions were essentially economic in nature, resulting from "a landed interest, a manufacturing interest, a mercantile interest, a moneyed interest, with many lesser interests."

Madison creates an image of interest groups, in their attempt to influence public policy, as self-serving and against the public good—and as somewhat immoral in their means and objectives. This has become the stereotype for many Americans. When political interest (pressure) groups are mentioned, this image pops into their minds. The mental caricature of the lobbyist, the person who politically promotes the interests he represents, is of a fat, cigar-smoking, underhanded, immoral type whom honest men avoid! This caricature is generally inaccurate and unfair. Pressure groups and lobbyists may be moral or immoral depending on the standard by which they are measured, on the means they use, or on the objectives they seek. In the main, however, they are amoral—a fact of political life.

Madison recognized that pressure groups are here to stay; and his hope for America was that the size of the country, the opposition of different factions, and the structure of government would prevent any one group from becoming the majority and dominating the whole political process. The fight over the SST seems to uphold Madison's faith in the American system as a pluralistic society with "countervailing forces." [1] However, the SST fight also points out that Madison overstressed the economic factor in his definition of factions. He might have given more weight to other groups which are not primarily economically motivated, such as churches, racial and ethnic groups, cultural and esthetic interests, and civic-minded organizations concerned about a variety of different problems in our society—including our environment.

David Truman defined "interest groups" as those groups that have shared attitudes and make claims upon society. "Political" interest groups are those that make claims upon or work through government.[2] Those interest groups that resort to political action, as nearly all do, to promote their own interests, to protect or regulate their members, and to restrict their opponents can properly be called "pressure groups." A pressure group seeks to influence the policy decisions of government and can be distinguished from a political party, which attempts to win the offices of government in order to exercise the powers of government and to set the policies of the political system.

---

[1] An interesting challenge to this pluralistic concept of American society is found in Theodore J. Lowi, *The Politics of Disorder* (New York: Basic Books, 1971).

[2] David B. Truman, *The Governmental Process* (New York: Knopf, 1951), pp. 33–37.

Pressure groups are usually thought to be private organizations, but the President's role in the SST fight suggests that a branch of government may indeed be a major source of influence on policy decisions. A major portion of the legislation submitted in Congress, as a matter of fact, comes from the administration. The pressures from the inside for this legislation constitute institutional lobbies. Furthermore, the military-industrial complex that President Eisenhower warned about in his farewell address in effect has become a significant semipublic pressure on government policies, when private industrial groups and the military are so closely interlocked in defense contracts.

THE INDIVIDUAL AND POLITICAL ACTION

Occasionally a single individual can influence public policies in an effective way. A recent example is Ralph Nader, who started his crusade for automobile safety in 1964. He wrote a best-selling book, *Unsafe at Any Speed,* which challenged the safety of General Motors' Corvair. Almost single-handedly he was able to get legislation passed to force the automotive industry to add safety devices. Turning his attention then to other problems of American society, Nader was soon joined by young, idealistic college graduates who wanted to help. "Nader's Raiders" became one of the most effective lobbies in the nation's capital—and it all began with a self-appointed lobbyist for the people.

Undertaking a major project of systemic reform of the national government, the Nader forces zeroed in on the Congress, because it most directly represents the people. The Nader *Profiles* on each congressman and senator who was standing for reelection in 1972 were published to give the voters a better understanding of the candidates. The Ralph Nader report on Congress maintained that the people have abdicated their power, their money, and their democratic birthright to Congress, which in turn is dominated by the White House and serves the private rather than the public interest. The report calls the citizens to action to turn "Congress around *for* the people." [3]

Another example of the influence of a single person is that of John Banzhaf, a young attorney in New York who became irritated by the cigarette commercials which periodically interrupted television programs. Banzhaf was aware of the "fairness doctrine" order of the Federal Communication Commission and asked the broadcast media for equal time to counter the cigarette advertising. They laughed him out of their studios. He then filed a complaint with the FCC, which ruled that he was entitled to time under the fairness doctrine, but not equal time. Anticipating the tobacco industry, he appealed the ruling to the federal courts on the grounds that the ruling did not grant equal time. In 1968, the Court upheld the ruling of the FCC and denied Banzhaf equal time; but the

[3] Mark J. Green, James M. Fallows, and David R. Zwick, *Who Runs Congress: The President, Big Business, or You?* (New York: Bantam Books, 1972).

groundwork was well laid for the subsequent developments that removed cigarette advertising from the broadcast media.

Banzhaf became a professor at George Washington University's National Law Center in Washington and also the director of ASH, Action on Smoking and Health, which he created in 1968 to represent the antismoking community. At that time he was under thirty, idealistic, and enjoyed the publicity he received from his public interest law work against the unfair practices of the private corporate interests. Though a legal activist, Banzhaf was not a militant. "I believe there's a great deal that can be done through the system by prodding it and operating on the periphery," he said.[4]

His students, dubbed "Banzhaf's Bandits" by the press, put their teacher's philosophy that "you can often get best results by suing the hell out of people, using all the legal pressure points you can find" into action by identifying unfair trade practices and filing their own complaints with the appropriate court or administrative agencies. SOUP (Students Opposed to Unfair Practices) was able to obtain a cease and desist order from the Federal Trade Commission against Campbell Soup Company's misleading television advertising, which put marbles in televised bowls of soup to make it appear thicker with more solids than it actually contained.

John Gardner, who organized Common Cause, is another example of the influence of a dedicated man on public policies. Because Gardner knew he needed political clout to accomplish his goals of making the American system responsive to the citizen, he enlisted the support of citizens all over the nation. Common Cause had over 200,000 members at the beginning of 1973, when Gardner launched a drive to double the membership. After working for the passage of a new bill to control campaign spending, which was passed in 1971, Common Cause monitored the election in 1972, and brought court action against violators of the new law and the old Federal Corrupt Practices Act. The organization also called for reform of the seniority system in Congress. When the House met in January of 1973, the Republican Conference followed by the Democratic Caucus voted to require each prospective chairman of the standing committees to stand for election by his party's caucus. The Senate also began to move in this direction. Other accomplishments influenced by Common Cause's OUTS (Open Up the System) program included the eighteen-year-old vote, reduction of a number of restrictions on voting, more open and democratic practices at the national nominating conventions, and a variety of "open government" laws on the state level.

These three examples all happened to have public interest goals. Each man used his own methods and selected the pressure points most likely to respond to his approach, but each was joined by others or found it necessary to organize a group to increase his effectiveness. Organization is essential for success when

[4] Robert Paul Wolff, ed., *Styles of Political Action in America* (New York: Random House, 1972), p. 132.

Eric in the *Atlanta Journal*. Reprinted with permission.

"What makes him think he's got a right to do that?"

competing for the benefits governments can dispense. "When all is said and done," Abraham Holtzman has maintained, "organization in politics remains a *sine qua non* for effective action."[5]

THE GROUP BASIS OF POLITICS

The importance of organized pressure groups was brought to the attention of students of politics in 1908, when Arthur F. Bentley published his book *The*

[5] Abraham Holtzman, *Interest Groups and Lobbying* (New York: The Macmillan Co., 1966), p. 5.

Process of Government. Bentley referred to the role of pressure groups as "the stuff of politics." "Groups of people," wrote Bentley, "pushing other groups and being pushed by them in turn—this is the process of government—this is the raw material of politics. . . . When the groups are adequately stated, everything is stated." [6] David Truman, a disciple of Bentley's, applied the latter's theories and concluded that organized interest groups were so important that they constituted the sum and substance of all political behavior.

The "group theory" assumes that groups in open political societies compete with one another for the favors government can bestow. Rival pressure groups check one another so that no one group will dominate the political process to the exclusion and detriment of all others. Out of a system of competing power of checks and balances—blended with the judgment, reflection, deliberation, and debate of policy makers—decisions are made for good or ill which govern America.

TYPES OF PRESSURE GROUPS

Business and Industrial Groups

Business and industrial groups have always been active in influencing public policy. They work through three levels of organized pressure politics: (1) individual company lobbying, (2) trade associations, and (3) general organizations which attempt to represent all business.

The main actors in the political influence business are the individual companies, which are always conscious of the rewards or penalties of government action. They watch each level of government from the national down to the local in order to protect the interests of their company. Some companies are big enough to have lobbyists at each level of government when they are needed. Standard Oil of California retains the services of lobbyists in the capital cities of the states where the company does business, especially during the legislative session; and the company has four registered lobbyists in Washington, D.C. The company usually retains lawyers whose professional work, reputation, and influence with those in government will return dividends to the company.

Standard Oil of California also is a member of two trade associations: the American Petroleum Institute and the Western Oil and Gas Association. This is typical of other companies too, which have their own respective trade associations. The public problems which are common to all of the companies in a given trade association are handled by lobbyists retained by the association. Of the national lobbies, the trade associations are the most noteworthy. They serve as a channel of communication between the government and their industry.

---

[6] Arthur F. Bentley, *The Process of Government,* ed. Peter H. Odegard (Cambridge, Mass.: Harvard University Press, 1967), p. 208.

There are three national general business organizations: the National Association of Manufacturers, the United States Chamber of Commerce, and the Committee for Economic Development. The NAM was organized in 1895 and has member companies and firms all across America. It has been inclined to represent more conservative viewpoints and larger corporations. Its approach has rested heavily on public relations, and the NAM spends considerable sums of money to influence the public—and the representatives of the public.

The Chamber of Commerce was formed in 1912, with numerous state and local branches across the country. Nearly every city has a Chamber of Commerce, which can generate grass-roots pressures on state and national governments when needed. It takes a general stand on issues which are of common concern to business and industry. It has opposed most legislative measures providing for social reforms and benefits for workers.

Fitzpatrick in the *St. Louis Post-Dispatch*. Reprinted with permission.

New national anthem

The Committee for Economic Development was formed by a number of more progressive business leaders during World War II. It plays its role through research and publication of its findings on a number of public questions which are important to the business community.

Labor Organizations

Labor is organized into local unions in the thousands and 130 national craft or industrial unions which make up the 13 million members of the AFL-CIO. Some of these national unions are more powerful than the parent organization. The Steel Workers, Carpenters, and Machinists unions each have nearly a million members; and the influence each of these unions can exercise is considerable. Additionally, there are some fifty national unions not affiliated with the AFL-CIO, such as the United Mine Workers, the railroad brotherhoods, the Teamsters, and the United Automobile Workers. The last two unions formed the Alliance for Labor Action in 1968.

Each union attempts to influence public policy favorable to its membership, with the national organizations giving national clout to the labor movement as a whole. During the New Deal period, the labor organizations won a favored position in their relations with management in the Wagner Act. Other national legislation was passed favorable to the unionized worker. In the post-World War II period that public support for labor was partially withdrawn in the Taft-Hartley Act, which was thought to bring a better balance between labor and management. "Fourteen-B" of the Taft-Hartley Act, which allows state legislatures to pass "right to work" laws not requiring union membership for employment, has been sharply criticized by the unions; and many years of fruitless union effort have been devoted to the repeal of this provision.

The unions, however, are interested in a broad spectrum of public policy, from unemployment compensation to federal aid to education. Many of the programs they support serve the public at large as well as their own interests.

Farm Groups

Beginning in 1867, when the Patrons of Husbandry (the Grange) was organized, the farmer's interests have been represented by a number of farm organizations. The three national organizations are the Grange, the National Farmers' Union (established in 1902), and the American Farm Bureau Federation (organized in 1919).

The Farm Bureau is the largest and the most influential of the farm organizations. The organization tends to be conservative and in recent years has supported the Republican Party. During the Eisenhower years, it worked closely with the Department of Agriculture; and the Farm Bureau's views were publicly supported, especially through many of the agricultural extension agents. During the Kennedy and Johnson administrations, the influence of the Farm Bureau was reduced in the Department of Agriculture. The Farm Bureau represents primarily the corn and cotton farmers, but its membership is spread through all types of farming.

The Grange, which at its beginning was a Midwest cooperative organization with radical public policies, is currently a conservative organization with much of its strength in the Northeast and on the Pacific Coast.

The Farmers' Union is the smallest of the three national farm groups and is geographically strongest in the Great Plains sections of America. The Farmers' Union is a liberal organization even though it represents conservative farmers in the main. Unlike the other two national organizations, it has advocated farm cooperatives, as well as national regulation and support of agriculture; and it has generally supported the Democratic Party and is willing to work with labor organizations.

There are many other farm organizations working to advance the interests of farmers, many of which are organized along commodity lines. Examples include the American Livestock Association, the National Wool Growers Federation, and the National Apple Institute. In addition there are producer associations, for example, the Idaho Potato Growers Association; cooperatives; and marketing groups, such as Sunkist in citrus fruit farming.

The Professions

The two oldest and strongest professional associations active in politics are the American Medical Association and the American Bar Association. A newcomer is the National Education Association. Since the professions are semi-official, self-regulating groups which set their own education standards and administer their own examinations under state supervision, the local organizations tend to be concerned with state politics. However, the national organizations have recently been very active in pressure group politics.

The AMA is one of the best-financed, best-organized pressure groups in the nation, with a membership of approximately seventy-five percent of all practicing physicians and surgeons in America. It has nearly 1,000 staff members in its headquarters in Chicago and maintains a full-time staff of over twenty in Washington. Since it distributes its political literature to every member doctor, nearly every waiting room becomes a library of AMA propaganda. Direct political action is the function of AMPAC (the American Medical Political Action Committee), which is patterned after the AFL-CIO Committee on Political Education (COPE).

The post-World War II political activity of the AMA was prompted by a number of bills providing for government health insurance programs. The AMA labeled these bills as "socialized medicine," and worked diligently to defeat them. With the passage of Medicare, the political activities of the AMA have not diminished, but actually increased. Between $2 and $3 million was spent on congressional races in 1964, and an estimated $4 million was spent similarly in 1968. The AMA boasts that it now has more friends in Congress than ever before; and this is probably the case, as the defeat in 1969 of Dr. John Knowles, a liberal Republican, for the position of assistant secretary of the Department of Health, Education and Welfare attests.

The ABA plays a prominent role in politics, but in a different way from the AMA. Among those elected to public office, a disproportionate number are lawyers. Even though only a third of all lawyers are members of the ABA, the influence of the organization is great. It usually is expressed in such professionally relevant problems as legal aid to the poor, defendants' rights, and selection of judicial personnel. Recently the ABA has played a significant role in the review of prospective federal judges.

The NEA and its local organizations on the state and local levels have become politically powerful in recent years. They have political action committees which are liberally financed and backed by literally millions of teachers. The teachers are primarily concerned with politics on the state and local levels because of the traditional local responsibility in education; but today, with significant national grants-in-aid to education, the NEA has its lobbyists in Washington as well.

Nearly all professions have national associations which promote the professions' interests in Washington. They also have state, and in some cases, local organizations for the same purposes.

Other Pressure Groups

The list of pressure groups is as long and diverse as the varied associational groupings in America—and some significant foreign ones too (the China Lobby). They range across many different types of groupings, from veteran's organizations such as the American Legion, to ethnic pressure groups such as the National Association for the Advancement of Colored People (NAACP), and on to religious interests such as those represented by the National Council of Churches. People long ago discovered that they had better get involved or government would serve some other special interests. And, furthermore, there are some groups which are organized *against* special interests; these attempt to influence government to promote the general interest through good government, for example, the League of Women Voters. Some organizations, such as the American Civil Liberties Union, at first glance appear to be concerned about the welfare of others, rather than their own. However, in these last two cases the philanthropic motives carry personal motives as well; for what promotes the interests of others in the society most likely will advance one's own interests.

PRESSURE POINTS

Pressure may be applied at any stage of the political cycle. Some pressure groups feel their interests are best served by one or the other of the major political parties and cast their support with that party. Members of pressure groups seek offices in the party, run for public office themselves, sponsor and support candidates, and actively work for victory in the elections. But their primary allegiance is to their interest group, not to the party. Labor groups most generally identify with the Democrats, as the Republicans offer little in rewards to merit their support. The AMA, on the other hand, is usually aligned with the Republican Party and openly supports it and its candidates.

Some groups find it expedient to support both parties and their candidates. They look at their financial contributions as "insurance premiums" to open the doors of those elected regardless of who wins. Many banks are found in this category, while other groups consider it best to support neither party. These latter groups feel that money invested in the campaign is money poorly invested. Standard Oil of California maintains this position. United States Steel, in some sections of the country, feels similarly. Of course there are legal restrictions covering direct political participation in a campaign of both companies and unions; but the personal activities of the managers, the public relations and advertising efforts of companies, and the activities of the political arm of the unions are some of the ways political involvement takes place.

Once the elections are over and the decision makers are installed in office, the pressures are first applied where policy is made: on the legislatures and the executives. When a state legislature is in session, it is difficult to tell the legislators from the lobbyists in the halls of the capitol building without a program. The lobbyists are very active. They are always ready to supply the legislator with information, or take him to dinner, or provide some service for him. They are often persuasive. And at times, though rarely, they may walk close to the brink of illegality in their attempts to influence the legislators. A similar pattern, with a little more sophistication and on a larger scale, is found on Capitol Hill in Washington as well.[7]

Since most legislation originates in the administrative branch of government, the lobbyists are frequent visitors to the chief executives of the states and the nation. It would be quite instructive to spend a day in the waiting room of one of the governors and identify the people who come and go. In addition to the heads of departments, other executive or administrative types, tourists, and general visitors, you will find a heavy sprinkling of representatives of pressure groups. This is true the year around. Part of this lobbying is directly connected with the formulation of the program which the executive presents to the legislature and which is intended to influence indirectly the making of public policy. Additionally, the day-to-day execution or administration of laws involves policy-making decisions, rules, or orders which may be vital to the pressure group; and significant pressure may be applied to this aspect of executive law making. The influence of the pressure groups is much more significant on the

---

[7] See Lester W. Milbrath, *The Washington Lobbyist* (Chicago: Rand McNally and Co., 1963), for excellent coverage of lobbying in the nation's capital.

details of legislation or on administration of laws than on the broad policies.

The next application of influence is in the areas where policy is administered: the executive and judicial branches. Even after a policy is established by law, there can be wide latitude in how that law is administered. A final determination in the application of law is rendered by the courts. Interest groups have long used the technique of filing complaints in the administrative agencies or courts to block or force the enforcement of laws, whichever would serve their organization best, just as John Banzhaf did in promoting what he regarded as the public interest.

Pressure groups are very much aware that each stage of government action must be adequately covered. The emphasis on each phase depends upon the nature of the issue and on the most crucial point of pressure for that issue, but most lobbying is done with the legislatures. When the objective is won at one point, attention is given that it is not lost at another point. For example, if a tax break is won in a revision of the tax laws, the companies are not going to lose it by an interpretation of the Internal Revenue Service. If this does occur, the company will undoubtedly challenge the IRS in the courts.

Once the political cycle is run, the pressure group girds itself for a new struggle. Like a prize fight, this struggle has another round to follow; but, unlike a prize fight, it does not end at round fifteen with a final decision.

INGREDIENTS OF PRESSURE GROUP SUCCESS

The successful lobbies usually have a single objective. If this objective has moral overtones, all the better. The Anti-Saloon League, for example, had the single objective of getting rid of "demon rum." To many people in America this was a moral cause which helped the League. When the Eighteenth Amendment was passed, the Anti-Saloon League had no further reason for existence and was disbanded. (It was not reorganized when prohibition was repealed.)

The status and prestige of the organization contributes strongly to its success. Our society places the medical doctor at the top of the social pyramid, and this adds greatly to the political success of the AMA.

Money is an essential to a successful lobbying effort. It is needed for staff, research, printing, advertising and other public relations needs, as well as for the immediate costs of entertainment and direct lobbying expenses. In addition to the AMA, the NEA, labor, and many business groups are financially able to run effective programs.

Good organization adds to the effectiveness of any pressure group. If the group is organized in a unitary way with effective communication from the top down, and the base of the organization reaches out to touch all points of the society, tremendous pressure can be brought to bear on the decision makers.

Able leadership is fundamental to all groups. Those pressure groups that have leaders who are flexible, responsive, informed, and competent strategists are quite apt to achieve the groups' objectives.

Membership which is dedicated, distributed in all areas of the political units (nation, state, or local community), without divisive overlapping membership in other groups adds great strength to a given course. Most people, however, belong to other groups, which weakens the cause. An example of this is a state education association of teachers whose members are widely distributed, reasonably dedicated, and in a position to influence a captive audience of students who are a direct and effective communication line to parents. These parents, when organized, can place great pressures on government; but the teacher may own large amounts of taxable property, resulting in a reluctance on his part to push for the organization's goals.

Interest group techniques are also important for success. The public be damned attitude of some of the powerful industrial giants of former times has given way to following the rules of the game. It is necessary to build public goodwill. Since most lobbying is done with legislators, and both lobbyists and legislators are aware that the desires of the constituency overshadow the pressure group, the smart lobbyist attempts to show the legislator that what the pressure group wants will be "smart politics" for him with his constituents. Both also are aware that bribes and favors are too dangerous. Rarely are they attempted.

LOBBYING: GOOD OR BAD?

Pressure group influence on public policies cannot be denied. Some students of pressure politics, however, estimate that the direct impact of lobbyists on public policies is minimal, while others suggest that nearly every bill which is enacted into law either has its origin with, or has been influenced by, an interest group. Whichever, if you are for a given measure, the influence of pressure is good; if you are against a bill, the pressure applied is bad. Through the years there has been enough concern over the influence of lobbying that Congress has passed a number of laws to regulate it. The first of these was passed as a resolution of the House in 1875, which required lobbyists to register with the Clerk of the House. It had little effect. Another act, the Lobby Registration Act, was passed in 1927; and in 1938 a Foreign Agents Registration law was passed.

Many congressmen believed a more comprehensive law was needed, and the Federal Regulation of Lobbying Act was therefore passed in 1946 (it is Title III of the Legislative Reorganization Act of that year). It provides that lobbyists (those persons who receive money to influence legislation) must register with the Clerk of the House and the Secretary of the Senate. The lobbyist must state his name and address and that of his employer, how much he is paid, how much he receives and spends to influence legislation, and disclose his publications for this purpose. He must disclose the name of any contributor of $500 or more, and account for expenditures of $10 or more. Penalties for failure to comply with the law could be up to $5,000 fine, imprisonment for one year, or both. Anyone so convicted is forbidden to appear before Congress for three years.

The law does not do all that the sponsors had hoped. There are many company representatives, public relations men, lawyers, and organizations engaged in influencing government in one way or another who do not register as lobbyists, as they do not consider themselves to be such. But on occasion the law regulating lobbying can turn the lights on those who would like to operate in the "public dark." At such a time the built-in controls of the system support the legal controls. It should be pointed out finally that public decisions are rarely bought or stolen; the lobbying process is relatively clean; hence it offers little danger to the national system. The states operate about on the same basis. It still seems that the best insurance against corruption is an alert citizenry which elects responsible officials to public office. This can be enhanced by a viable and responsible news media.

It must be recognized also that there are some positive contributions of pressure groups to the American system. The lobbyists are a source of information which congressmen could not do without. In fact, they help Congress (and state legislatures) maintain a degree of independence in face of the strong executive role in America. They are a source of creativity and a source of opinion of at least some segments of the public. Disparate interests need a voice in our system. And in a system which depends on a pluralistic counterbalancing of forces, they contribute stability. The policy-making process is improved because of them. They are a fact of political life; and if they did not exist, it would probably be necessary to invent them in order to improve the functioning of the system.

6
POLITICAL PARTIES

"Young people are asserting themselves politically right now in a manner unprecedented in our country," reported Paul Harvey in an October, 1970, broadcast. "Last summer a bunch of young Democrats in Utah decided to overthrow the Establishment the American way, within the framework of the democratic process." Harvey was looking at one side of a bipartisan student political action program called "Participation 70."

Participation 70 grew out of a climate of student protests and violence which was the result of the United States' invasion of Cambodia and the Kent State tragedy. After some tension on the University of Utah campus, and insistence by a large segment of students that the University be closed, a referendum was held. The students voted to keep the school open and return to class. This did not constitute a vote to do nothing; but, for many at least, it was a vote against what they perceived as a destructive and fruitless means of protest. Instead, they turned to a responsible political action program.

Suzanne Dean, former Vice-President of the College Republicans at the University of Utah, presented a plan in the spring of 1970 to student government officers which would enable the students to work for change through the political party of their choice as an alternative to protest. She urged that a telephone survey be conducted to determine political preferences of university students. The interested students would be encouraged to attend their party's neighborhood mass meetings and run for delegate positions. Later, students could group together in caucuses at county and state conventions of both parties and influence candidates and platforms by voting as a bloc. The plan was approved by student officers, and later by the University regents and the leaders of both political parties.

One of the major tasks was to find quickly the politically motivated out of

22,000 students and give them specific instructions about their particular voting districts in time for the mass meetings in May. At this point the work of Dr. William Viavant, a professor of computer science and an expert in using computers to process voting data, became invaluable. He explained a computer program to the Participation 70 leaders which would match the students from Salt Lake County on the registrar's list with their individual voting districts. After the computer print-out was obtained, the "nuts and bolts" political work began.

From a political "boiler room" in some unused offices on the university campus, Miss Dean and her staff of Participation 70 workers telephoned students and determined their political preference. The most interested student in each voting district was informed about the mass meeting procedure in which the party begins its grass-roots organization, was given a list of other students in his district to call on for help, and was encouraged to run for a delegate position or for other party positions. Over 1,000 students attended mass meetings on May 18, electing approximately 400 students to party offices. More than 200 students won delegate positions to the county and state conventions.

At both the Republican and Democratic county conventions, the student delegates turned the party platforms to more youthful positions on such issues as youth participation in politics, lowering the voting age, environmental politics, civil rights, and a code of ethics for government officials. The Democratic student delegates caucused before the county convention and agreed to support certain candidates. Each student-supported candidate won the largest number of total delegate votes and a place on the primary ballot.

The students went on to the state conventions intending to have a say about their party's platform and the nomination of candidates. They demanded seats on the rules, credentials, resolutions, and platform committees, which were granted. The students fought for and won rules which would give them an equal voice in the convention with the regular state delegates. The platforms and resolutions of both political parties were shaped significantly by student delegates. This was especially true in the Democratic convention, in which student proposals on the Vietnam war, dissent and freedom of speech, civil rights, family planning, and legalized abortion were so shocking to a number of the regular delegates that the convention had to be called to order repeatedly during debate on these proposals. The students stood their ground, exhibited a high degree of political know-how, and won acceptance of their platform proposals and resolutions.

Those at the conventions were quite aware of the student presence. Some believed that they were the most significant bloc at the conventions. The platforms of both parties, as a result, bore an undeniable student stamp. The student delegates took an active role in the nomination contests for the Republican United States Senate candidate, the Democratic candidate for Congress in the First District, and state candidates of both parties. "Phase II" of Participation 70 was directed toward the election of candidates in the primary and general elections which would support their ideas for a better world.

Participation 70 was followed two years later with a similar organization called "Participation 72." Again the students formed a significant bloc in both the Republican and Democratic conventions, and were able to influence the platforms of each party. Democratic students sponsored planks calling for the legalization of abortion and marijuana, which were accepted, only to have them disavowed by the governor and many Democratic candidates. The State Democratic Chairman attempted to have these planks expunged from the platform by polling all of the state delegates after the convention and substituting this poll for the vote in the convention, but this action was not permitted. Even so, the 1972 student effort lacked the vitality of the earlier student involvement and was generally more in line with traditional political participation.

This 1970 Utah example of student political activity appeared to be atypical of students across the nation, who were pictured at that time as being alienated from and critical of the system. Student moods, however, were changing. The 1972 election clearly indicated more of a "politics as usual" attitude by the youth of America—including the students. George McGovern counted heavily on the under-thirty voters, whose ranks were swelled by the newly enfranchised eighteen to twenty-one year old voters. McGovern did win the college student vote across the nation, with notable exceptions in some areas of the South and in some conservative college communities, but the atmosphere on many campuses was one of apathy. There was little exuberance on the part of students. One Yale student told a reporter that "we've moved from crusade to compromise."

No one should think that political action is an easy road, but the Utah experience shows that the political system can be opened up and that those who are willing to work within it can have substantial impact on the political process. Students, especially, should be encouraged to participate in the political system as American politics cannot afford to lose their idealism and crusading zeal. They should be encouraged to formulate goals, develop strategies, and apply programs of action to help solve the urgent problems facing America, for the world they help to build today will be theirs tomorrow.

THE PARTY AND THE PARTICIPANT

Student apathy in the 1972 presidential election was matched by widespread voter apathy among different groupings of Americans. President Nixon's landslide victory was won with fewer than fifty-four percent of the eligible voters—the lowest turnout in twenty-four years. A low turnout has traditionally been thought to hurt the Democrats; but heavy Democratic defections also contributed to the defeat of Senator George McGovern, as Republican cohesiveness aided the reelection of the President.

A key ingredient of McGovern's defeat was a major shift of the independent voter and the old Roosevelt coalition of blacks, Jews, and Catholics toward the Republican Party, with a majority of the Catholics voting Republican. President Nixon also received a majority vote from the blue collar workers. Even so, the Nixon landslide failed to produce a Republican Congress. The Democrats increased their majority in the Senate by two seats, and the Republican net gain of twelve seats in the House still left the Democrats with a majority of 244 to 191. In addition, the Democrats retained their wide margin of control of gubernatorial positions by a net gain of one governor, bringing the total to thirty-one Democrat to nineteen Republican governors.

This widespread shifting of party allegiance and ticket splitting might be attributed to the fact that 1972 was an exceptional presidential election year, with traditional Democratic party patterns holding across the nation, but ticket splitting and party shifting was evident in gubernatorial, Senate, and House elections in all sections of the country. What is evident in this election is a fluidity in politics; a further weakening of party allegiance; a greater independence in voting, with more emphasis on the personality or position of the individual candidate; and a widespread disgust with parties, politics, and government in general. This trend toward less party affiliation and increasing numbers of Americans considering themselves to be independents is indicated in the Gallup poll released in April, 1973. Since 1940, the independents have increased from 20 to 31 percent; the Republicans have gone down from 38 to 27 percent; and the Democrats, though fluctuating over the years, have held at 42 percent. (See Table 6.1.)

Walter Dean Burnham maintains that there has been an onward march of party disintegration since 1900, which was only temporarily interrupted by the appearance of party focus during the New Deal era. "It is clear that the significance of the party as an intermediary link between voters and rulers has again come into serious question," according to Burnham. "More precisely, what

Table 6.1 Changing Party Percentages 1940–73

	Democrats	Independents	Republicans
1940	42%	20%	38%
1950	45%	22%	33%
1960	47%	23%	30%
1970	45%	26%	29%
1973	42%	31%	27%

SOURCE: American Institute of Public Opinion (The Gallup Poll)

need have [Americans] of parties whose structures, processes, and leadership cadres find their origins in a past as remote as it is irrelevant?"[1]

What is the nature of a political party then, and what is its position in the American political system? Edmund Burke, a British statesman of the eighteenth century, defined a political party as "a body of men united, for promoting by their joint endeavours the national interest, upon some particular principle in which they are all agreed." But what particular principle serves to unite such Democratic senators as George McGovern of South Dakota and James Eastland of Mississippi, or such Republican senators as Jacob Javits of New York and J. Strom Thurmond of South Carolina? Actually there is closer alignment on political principles between Thurmond and Eastland, and Javits and McGovern, than their party alignment as Democrats and Republicans would indicate. Clearly, principles vary from one member to another within the same party. The definition of the political party must, therefore, be in broader terms than Burke's "particular principle."

The two major political parties in America play the game of politics in the center of the field, "within the forty yard lines," and only rarely does a Goldwater or a McGovern insist on playing down on the "ten yard line." Each party is like a huge umbrella which allows individuals of disparate ideological views to claim the party label and fuse those disparate views into a measure of ideological agreement for political purposes. Each party attempts to displace the other from the center position, modifying principle for a chance at political power. (See Figure 6.1).

The definition of a political party also must include its particular purpose and its distinguishing method. The "particular purpose" of a political party, simply stated, is to control the government and set the policies for society through winning elections and exercising political power. It is this characteristic that sets off the party from other groups that also seek to influence public policy. Pressure groups, for example, try to influence public policy, but do so by concentrating on *specific* policies rather than on general control of the whole political system.

The "distinguishing method" of a political party, simply stated, is that of mobilizing votes to nominate and elect public officials from among party members. Other groups, including pressure groups, also may try to mobilize votes, but they generally do not themselves offer candidates for office. David Truman, in fact, insists that political parties can be identified exclusively in terms of this distinguishing method.

A political party is thus an organization or group of individuals, with some measure of ideological agreement, which seeks to control the process of government and determine public policies by nominating and electing public officials from its membership and by winning and exercising political power. Of

[1] Walter Dean Burnham, *Critical Elections and the Mainsprings of American Politics* (New York: W. W. Norton, 1970), p. 133.

Figure 6.1 Party Umbrellas

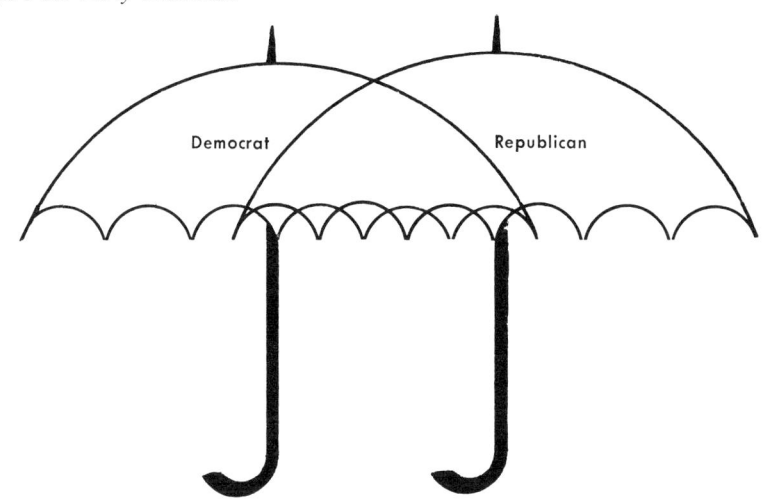

course, as important as winning political power, is *retaining* political power—continuing to win, in other words. Unless a party keeps winning, sometimes at least, it will die. It may be said that the party is primarily an organ for the expression of man's combative instincts, but it serves to sublimate those instincts and to promote a peaceable settlement of differences.

The notion that each party in the United States is a mass organization of "members," however, is at best a polite fiction. The party belongs to those who work at it, and not to the millions who claim the party label or vote for its candidates. The actual party is made up of those who support it financially, those who actively work to elect its candidates, and the leaders and officials who run the party. Among the leaders, officials, and financial supporters, there is an elite group which holds the real power of the party. This situation was classically explained by Robert Michels in 1915 in a chapter of his book *Political Parties,* called "The Iron Law of Oligarchy," which developed the thesis that every political party, regardless of its democratic origins, is ultimately and inevitably controlled by an oligarchy; and the only way the oligarchy can be removed is by a rival oligarchy. Most often the ruling power revolves around someone who holds a position in government, and then usually someone who holds an executive position, such as a mayor, a governor, or the President. (See Figure 6.2.)

The party is often identified as a broker of power, offering candidates for office; and, when elected, setting the policies and controlling the powers of government. Actually, the party is an organization of the politically ambitious to achieve their ends. Thus, the party is a candidate-centered organization that interests and rewards only a few people—the few who hope to win elections and

Figure 6.2 The Party and the Participants

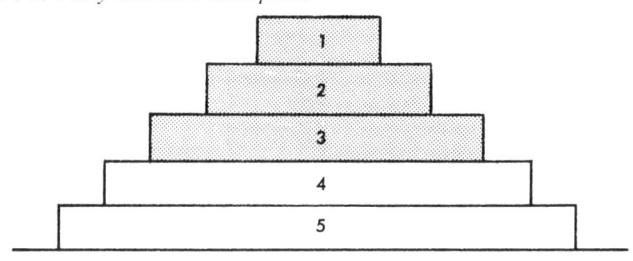

```
        ┌─────┐
        │  1  │
     ┌──┴─────┴──┐
     │     2     │
  ┌──┴───────────┴──┐
  │        3        │
┌─┴─────────────────┴─┐
│          4          │
├─────────────────────┤
│          5          │
└─────────────────────┘
```

1. Leaders and officials
2. Workers (actively for party candidate)
3. Members (dues-paying or financial contributors)
4. Identifiers (when asked on a public opinion poll)
5. Voters

▓▓▓ areas designate real party members

public offices, the few who are manipulators and like the sport of campaigns, the few who enjoy knowing and associating with public officials, the few who are organized into interests that initiate their pressures on government through the party process, the few who get involved because they sense it is a duty of citizenship but a duty that most citizens avoid.

THE AMERICAN TWO-PARTY SYSTEM

The birth of political parties in America was not heralded, as is a newborn child. Indeed, the Founding Fathers seemed to believe the nation would be better off without them and ignored any reference to parties in the Constitution. It was the rivalry between Alexander Hamilton and Thomas Jefferson, secretaries of the departments of Treasury and State respectively in Washington's first administration, which served as midwife to the Federalist and Jeffersonian Republican parties. As these two great men differed, and meddled in each other's affairs, they marshaled partisans for their respective causes. Even the leaders of the Jeffersonian Republicans, Madison and Jefferson, grudgingly referred to parties as "necessary evils which should not be allowed to bring about disunion."

It was with perhaps some wisdom that statesmen made such a strong indictment against the parties, as the initial party conflict found such earlier friends as John Adams and Thomas Jefferson on opposite sides and bitterly opposed to one another. Abigail Adams coaxed long and hard to get Adams to start a correspondence with Jefferson after each had retired from public life.

Party growth from infancy to maturity has witnessed stormy periods, as when the nominating process was really handled through the caucus and Sam Adams and others could control the politics in the community through its application; when the Tweed Ring of New York City operated in the post-Civil War period; when the Plunkitts of Tammany Hall at the turn of the century distinguished between "honest" and "dishonest" graft, the former was expressed by Plunkitt: "I seen my opportunities and I took 'em"; or when the era of political machines and bosses, which Frank Kent described in his book *The Great Game of Politics,* was in full bloom: the heyday of bosses Curley of Boston, Crump of Memphis, and Pendergast of Kansas City. Today the political process is handled by organizations, not machines, and leaders, not bosses; but the struggle for control of political power is strikingly similar. Only the names have changed with the modern sophistication of the "mature" party.

The original party lineup in the United States found the Federalists—the forerunner of the present Republican Party—holding the vision of an industrial, urban society, which they sought to foster by emphasizing the ideas of energetic government, nationalism, centralization, government intervention in the economy, executive rather than legislative power, and a managed public debt. And on the other side were the Jeffersonian Republicans (later to become known as the Democratic Party), holding the agrarian society as the ideal, which ideal they sought to foster by emphasizing the concepts of "least government as the best government," states' rights, decentralization, laissez-faire, legislative rather than executive power, and economy in government.

Notice that the two present-day parties have changed positions on many of these issues. Does this mean that they have abandoned their principles—that the Democrats have rejected Jeffersonian values for Hamiltonian values, while the Republicans have executed the reverse maneuver? Such a conclusion results when one confuses techniques with goals, instrumental values with root values. Jefferson was imbued with faith in the people, and, in a predominantly rural society in which the government was an agency potentially powerful enough to threaten popular freedoms, he was naturally suspicious of government power in almost any form. Hamilton was more impressed with the superiority of the "rich, the educated, and the well-born," and was equally anxious to create a strong government that would reflect that superiority and would control the "unthinking majority." By now the Jeffersonian view has triumphed to such an extent that no politician would reject majority rule as such. But the Democratic Party is still more concerned with the needs of the "underprivileged"; and the Republican Party, like the Federalists, is more attuned to the preservation of greater rewards for the "deserving." The development of an industrialized and urbanized society has simply changed the policies that seem most appropriate for gaining these respective ends.

The first great shift in party doctrines occurred in the 1820's and 1830's, when Jacksonian democracy established the President as the chief spokesman for the popular majorities. The Whigs (formerly called Federalists) rejected the idea of a strong executive and supported instead a strong legislature. So the battle lines formed along the issue of strong executive power versus strong congressional power. The rapid industrialization that took place after the Civil War concentrated private power in the hands of corporations strong enough to constitute a potential threat to majority interests. The Democratic Party looked on this concentration of private power as the chief danger to popular needs, and to the government as the only agent capable of coping with this danger. Republicans, on the other hand, adopted the old Jeffersonian fear of government—looking upon government as, at best, only a "necessary evil."

Late in the nineteenth century, when government began turning to schemes such as income taxes and business regulation, the battle lines between parties became more distinct. But it was not until the Great Depression fell on the country in 1929 that these new orientations were revealed in full. Republicans in Congress voted to curb executive power, to restrict government intervention in the economy, and to prevent extensions of social welfare programs. The Democrats, in turn, strongly favored increased power in foreign relations for the President; government development of power projects; federal action to combat unemployment; and extensions of government aid in such areas as housing, education, health, and social security.

The success with which each party has mobilized its own supporters and enticed those of the opposition camp has varied enough to produce three distinct eras of party dominance. The period from 1800 to 1860 was a time of Democratic supremacy. As the suffrage was gradually extended, the opposition was able to erase the stigma of its original distaste for democracy only twice, and then only by establishing a new party (the Whigs) and by nominating two war heroes for President—William Henry Harrison (1840) and Zachary Taylor (1848).

Overall, the Republicans have enjoyed the longest period of supremacy, from 1860 to 1932. With sectional conflict over slavery disrupting the established competition between parties, the Republicans attained their first success by capturing the mass appeal the Democrats had long enjoyed. Despite its radical origins, the Republican Party emerged from the Civil War with a more "conservative" character. Lincoln's party (1860) had been a farmer-worker party with Declaration of Independence overtones. Grant's party (1868) was farmer-capitalist in nature, with a "declaration" to give the capitalist a free hand in the exploitation of America's natural resources. While the Republicans were appealing to business, they also campaigned for the labor vote. The Democrats were just unable to win the eastern labor vote, and without that they were doomed to play second fiddle. In fact, during the three-quarters of a century from Lincoln to Franklin D. Roosevelt, the Democrats were able to win only four Presidential terms, with Grover Cleveland and Woodrow Wilson. (This picture is modified somewhat if the close congressional contests of the period are examined.)

The third great period of dominance returned the Democrats to power in 1932. With the severe depression that began in 1929 suddenly making the business community unpopular, the Democrats took advantage of the opportunity to label the Republicans as the party of big business. The increased voting strength of immigrants and their children, the high birthrate of lower-income groups, the shift of people from farms to cities, the increasing political awareness of ethnic minorities—all of these gave more votes to Democrats than to Republicans. So the Democratic Party emerged as favoring the "little man," and the Republican Party became the party of "Big Business."

Republicans have scored victories in the period since 1932. Eisenhower's wins in 1952 and 1956, and Nixon's victories in 1968 and 1972, represent personal victories in the midst of a Democratic period rather than the inauguration of a new era of Republican control. It took a Civil War to shatter the first Democratic hold on the country, and a cataclysmic depression to terminate the Republican era. The lack of any such major upheaval in contemporary America, and the inability of the Republican Party to win control of Congress and the statehouses, indicate that the Democratic tide is still running.

To most people in the Anglo-American political tradition, the two-party political system seems to be the most satisfactory system, for the following reasons:

First, it guarantees that both parties will make a wide appeal to the electorate. This sometimes makes the parties so similar that any choice between them is like a choice between Tweedledum and Tweedledee. Since both parties must seek majority support in order to acquire power, they both must please substantially the same people. The fact that both parties resemble each other so closely, then, may mean that both are doing a reasonably good job of interpreting public opinion.

Second, the two-party system encourages compromise within each party before the election, rather than compromise among several parties after the election. Hence, the ultimate coalition in control of the government is chosen by the voters rather than by legislative blocs. Moreover, this method tends to fix responsibility on a continuing and recognizable group.

Third, by making certain that someone will win a majority in nearly every electoral contest, the two-party system increases the chances of coherence and stability in government. Control of the government is fixed by the voters for the entire period between elections. Postelection maneuvers among various blocs is absent.

Fourth, the two-party system insures that the chief executive will represent a general body of opinion. Where only two parties are competing for power, the successful candidate for President, governor, or mayor must inevitably represent the broad base of one of the two parties.

Within the context of the American two-party history, it must be recognized that during the period from 1816 to 1825, the Jeffersonian Republicans became the sole national party; and it is true also that in certain states and counties, one-party systems have existed and presently exist. Often one-party political systems are associated with dictatorships, wherein rival groups are outlawed and political expression and choice are stifled. In America, however, the existence of single-party situations is not necessarily incompatible with democracy. Until recently, the states in the South following the Reconstruction era generally had single-party systems. In the Democratic Party primary, in these states, the voters had a choice between competing personalities or factions. Indeed, the primary for all practical purposes was the election.

Single-party systems, though not necessarily undemocratic, present certain problems in the political process. To the individual, a single-party system offers the citizen no stable reference group or reliable clues for reacting to political stimuli. Such a system tends to lead to relatively low levels of voter turnout. The one-party arrangement often fails to stimulate citizen interest in and information about public affairs. "You can't tell the players without a program," shout the vendors at sporting events. In one-party politics, the citizen not only lacks a "program" to identify the "players"; but his interest also suffers from the fact that, in absence of opposing teams, everyone on the field wears the same uniform.

The single-party system prevents the structuring of political conflict to the extent that the "outs" cannot attack the "ins," as they do not have any collective positions on policy; and it is consequently more difficult to "throw the rascals out." One-party politics also tends toward candidate demagoguery; the lack of effective citizen control of government officials; and favoritism, irresponsibility, and short-term, erratic programs in government.

In the election of 1824, there was a single national party, but there were four presidential candidates. Each candidate represented a different section of the country and the political positions of his section. Thus, what appeared as a single-party situation was more like a multi-party system. The election did not produce a majority of electoral votes for any one candidate, and the House of Representatives selected John Quincy Adams for President, even though Andrew Jackson had a plurality of the electoral votes.

The two major parties have been challenged from time to time by issue-oriented third parties. These third parties, such as the Anti-Masonic Party, the Greenback Party, the Populists, the Progressive Party, and the American Independent Party—to mention some of the major third parties in different periods of American history—flowered locally and had some significance nationally for short periods of time; but they withered and died as their programs were taken over by one or the other of the two major parties.

Multi-party systems are sometimes thought to be undesirable because they usually result in coalition, and at times unstable, governments. Under certain circumstances these conditions may exist, but they are not necessarily undesirable. The positive aspects of multiparty systems include: (1) the possibility of more shades of opinion represented in government; (2) a better chance that all parties will be represented in government, if proportional representation is used in multimember election districts, where each party elects as many members as the percentage of its voting strength calls for; (3) the opportunity for different groups in society to organize and be represented by their own parties, such as a Catholic party, a farmers' party, a labor party, or different ideological parties; and (4) fewer of the Tweedledum-Tweedledee frustrations, as the multiparty arrangements would correspond more closely to the underlying patterns of factional interests in the community. Also, coalitions are a natural process in politics, whether they take place in the party stage, as in the two-party system, or in the governmental process, where two or more parties coalesce to form a majority to run the government.

Where multiparties exist in America, as they currently do in New York City, they are influenced by the realities of politics and the traditional two-party system. Candidates are often backed by more than one party, and a coalition is formed among these parties; or the real contest is between candidates of two of the parties, which reduces the election to virtually a two-candidate election. Thus the two-party system of America has its variations and within it realignments periodically take place.

In addition to the three major periods of party dominance in American political history, there have been certain elections which were fundamental turning points in the electoral process. The elections of 1800, 1828, 1860, 1896, and 1932, according to Burnham, were "critical realignments" of American politics:

Eras of critical realignment are marked by short, sharp reorganizations of the mass coalitional bases of the major parties which occur at periodic intervals on the national level; are often preceded by major third-party revolts which reveal the incapacity of "politics as usual" to integrate, much less aggregate, emergent political demand; are closely associated with abnormal stress in the socioeconomic system; are marked by ideological polarizations and issue-distances between the major parties which are exceptionally large by normal standards; and have durable consequences as constituent acts which determine the outer boundaries of policy in general, though not necessarily of policies in detail.[2]

Burnham's studies presented evidence that the trends of the 1960's suggest the country is in the process of a realignment "en route to a sixth party system." But, he believed there were two things which stood in the way of such a critical realignment: (1) the gross disintegration of the hold of party on the electorate, and (2) the absence of a crystallizing factor. It is evident that the conditions necessary to produce critical elections were in existence in the 1972 elections, but the checking forces Burnham refers to were also in existence. The triggering device necessary to bring about a critical political realignment must be of "scope and brutal force great enough to produce the mobilizations required from a normally passive-participant middle-class electorate." [3] Such a

[2] *Ibid.*, p. 10.
[3] *Ibid.*, p. 170.

detonator was not present prior to the 1972 election, even though significant shifts in voting patterns occurred. Postelection events, however, have produced the possibility of such a trigger in the profound problems of the economy. If sharp, sudden blows occur hard enough to open up a relatively sudden gap between expectations and perceived political, social, and economic realities, a new mobilization of political forces may take place to capture the apparatus of the state in order to alter these situations.

THE STRUCTURE OF AMERICAN PARTIES

Like the overall party system, the internal organization of each party is also shaped by the country's official electoral practices, social customs, legal framework, and so forth. Because the purpose of each party is to gain control of the government by winning elections, party organization is built around the electoral system and within the socioeconomic-political environment. When we begin to identify the points of power within this structure, the neat organization chart is most deceptive.

The Need for Organization

Any group of more than three people setting out to do anything at all must organize. Even a committee of three will normally have a chairman—either formal or informal. In every village or community, there will be clusters of voters who look to the local medical doctor, to the banker, to the postmaster, to a merchant, a preacher, or even a professor, for guidance on how to vote.

Whenever this happens, politicians are at work and a political organization of some kind exists, even though it may be as temporary and as fluid as a passing cloud. Expand the size of the community, increase the number or variety of eligible voters, multiply the number of officials to be elected or of issues to be resolved, and the need for organization grows. For the "average" citizen is too busy, too ill informed, too indifferent, or too lazy to be anxiously engaged in public affairs. He probably knows little about how he is governed, or by whom. Furthermore, he rarely attends meetings, reads official reports, or participates politically unless somebody guides or goads him to do so.

The people who do this essential guiding and goading are the politicians, who in a two-party system usually identify with the Republican or Democratic parties. They are the leaders and workers who make up an oligarchy known to their friends as "the organization" and to their enemies as "the machine." The most energetic and most dedicated of these people are known as "leaders" or "bosses," depending on whether they are friends or foes, or depending on the nature of rewards or inducements offered to get political support.

In a modern democratic state, the election of public officials and, in some cases, the decision of important matters of public policy are made by thousands or even millions of voters. The activation and education (or indoctrination) of these millions of voters is the responsibility of political parties and, more directly, the responsibility of the politicians who make up the party organization or machine. The organization is thus a labor-saving device—it carries on the work of the party so that the rest of us can earn a living, play golf, and watch television. When the election is over, the party collapses like a house of cards, as the voters slip back into their normal routines and television without political ads. Only the core of the party, the basic organization, remains—and it is badly shaken and requires reorganization.

Formal Party Organization

Party organization includes the tiers of party committees that reach from bottom to top of the party hierarchy. It is not the tidy, unified organization suggested by the chart makers, but actually a fragmented, disjointed, localized organization held loosely and periodically together for election purposes. The party reflects the system of government which it serves, with its federal features and even with separation of powers.

The National Committee. The national committee is the continuing organization that heads the national party, at least on paper. The national committee members are chosen in each state by a primary election, by a state party convention, by the state party committee, or by the state delegation to the national convention. The national committee is responsible for the presidential campaign, raising funds, arranging for the next national nominating convention, and filling vacancies on the national party ticket, as the Democratic Party did in 1972 when it named Sargent Shriver to replace Thomas Eagleton as the nominee for the vice-presidency. Actually, the national committee is the point of final authority in the national party in a purely formal sense. The real head of the national party is the national chairman—a man or woman usually selected by the party's nominee for President—and the chairman's executive committee.

The 1972 Democratic convention called for reform of the national committee to make it more representative of grass-roots party people, as well as of certain party leaders. The committee was enlarged to include state party chairmen, members of Congress, and governors. It called for the new national committee to appoint a reform commission to prepare a new party charter and provide for further restructuring of the party along national lines. It was feared that these reforms might be ignored when the McGovern-appointed chairman, Jean Westwood, was replaced by Robert S. Strauss, under pressure from labor and other more conservative and traditional segments of the party. In March, 1973, the Democrats overwhelmingly approved a slate of new members in its biggest show of unity in some time. This slate of twenty-five, at-large delegates was approved by both party regulars and reformers unanimously.

The national chairman acts as the official spokesman of the party. He is officially chosen by the national committee, but in practice he is named by the party's presidential nominee. His primary job is to manage the presidential campaign. In the processes of choosing party candidates for Congress, executing the party program after victory, and even choosing the presidential candidate, the national committee and its chairman normally play only minor roles—and certainly not leadership roles.

Although the national chairman and his committee lack real power over the party's policies and choice of candidates, they can sometimes play a role of some importance. The national committee tends to be as strong or as weak as its chairman. In addition to his usual role as campaign manager, the national chairman serves his party as fiscal leader and as mediator and coordinator for its hundreds of state and local units, as well as for its major factions. An occasional chairman has the qualities to build considerable influence on the basis of these functions, even attempting to coordinate party policy.

Campaign Committees. Alongside the national committee in the party structure are the national congressional and senatorial campaign committees, chosen by each party's representatives in the House and Senate. Their independence of the national committee further suggests the extent to which power in American parties is dispersed. For all intents and purposes, both committees in both houses are autonomous, raise their own campaign chests, remain jealous of their independence, and are quick to resist "encroachment" by any other committee—especially by the national committee and its chairman, who are primarily concerned about the presidential election. The principle of separation of powers, interestingly enough, influences this separate organization.

The four campaign committees function chiefly during campaigns, trying to maintain and increase the seats held by their respective parties in the Senate and the House. Each group keeps a small nucleus staff on a permanent basis. The committees compile voting records of members, analyze political possibilities in the various states, and in other ways prepare for congressional elections.

State Central Committees. On paper, a state central committee oversees all party machinery in its area, directs campaigns for state officers and for United States Senate and House elections, and mobilizes state efforts in behalf of the state and national ticket. In reality, often the state central committee plays about the same role on its level as the national committee plays on the national level. The state chairman is often the governor's, or other high elected official's "man." Every state and national candidate has his own campaign committee and, depending on the state and the candidate, may hardly be aware of the state central committee. Sometimes the central committee is instrumental in fund raising, mediation, and coordination, however. As in the case of the national committee, much of this depends on the vigor and caliber of the state chairman and his assistants. Whether weak or powerful, however, none of the state central committees are subordinate to the national committee. The federal governmental arrangement carries over into the party organization with its "federal" structure of state and national parties.

County and City Committees. At the next level are the county and city committees. They are organized around such subdivisions as townships, precincts, and wards. Their function and structure are similar to the function and structure of the state and national committees, though restricted to a smaller area. Again, seldom are they significant as formal committees; and almost never are they subordinate to the state organization. The chairmen of these committees often possess real power in local politics. Because of their influence over elections to state and national offices, they frequently make their power felt in state and national politics as well. (See Figure 6.3.)

This brief sketch of formal party organization suggests that American parties are little more than loose coalitions of state and local factions, brought together every two years to conduct local, state, congressional and presidential campaigns. Generally, the party achieves at least a surface unity during campaigns. But this unity is loose and voluntary rather than close and disciplined.

Informal Party Organization

The informal organizations of parties often loom large in the political sky. This designation covers a wide range of clubs, associations, ad hoc bodies, and candidates' personal campaign committees—on levels as diverse as neighborhood caucuses and great national campaign committees.

On the national scene, the most influential and the best-financed groups have been those seeking the presidential nomination for a particular aspirant. Such bodies have demonstrated a capacity to secure support and raise money among people who might shun direct party activity. After securing the nomination they often continue activity through the general election campaign.

Figure 6.3 Party Organization

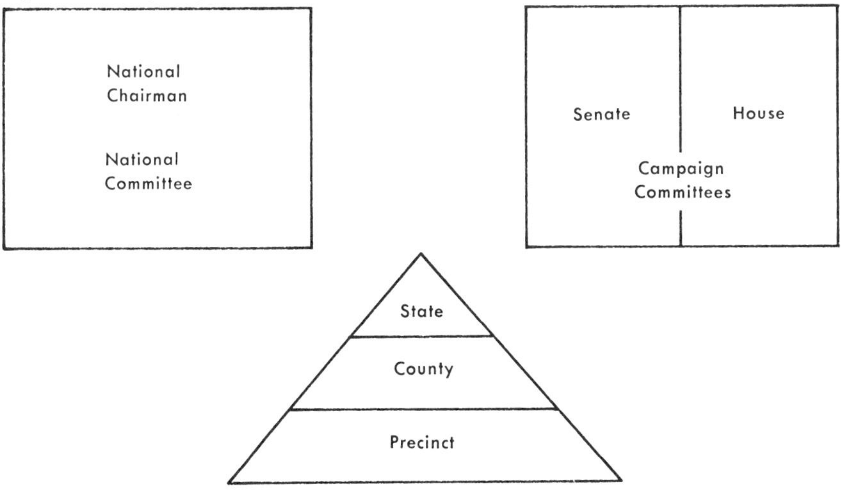

On the state and local level, informal party organizations are assuming more and more importance. Official party bodies are closely regulated by state law, which sometimes denies them the opportunities to mount an effective campaign. Consequently, informal groups often perform the functions from which the formal parties are precluded.

As mentioned above, each candidate has a personal campaign committee. This is usually true whether the candidate is seeking national, state, or local office. The degree of independence, or interdependence, and cooperation between the candidate's committee and the paralleling "official" organization varies greatly from time to time and from place to place. Generally speaking, it would be desirable for the committees to work closely together. But often a candidate must go it alone. Perhaps he may find it expedient to run "apart" from the rest of the party's ticket. From the candidate's point of view his personal committee is almost always the more powerful and the more important. From the voter's point of view, however, perhaps the official, formal committee is of more importance. At least it is permanent and will be available for criticism. In other words, it would appear that it would be more responsible to the voters. Nonetheless, the strategic importance and the dynamic impact of the candidate campaign committees on the American political scene are great indeed. President Nixon's Committee to Re-elect the President is a classic case example of this point.

FUNCTIONS OF POLITICAL PARTIES

Students of political parties have suggested that almost anything essential to the maintenance of democracy must be a consequence of party activities. Perhaps this is because freely competing political parties are not only the hallmark of, but unique to, democracy. Political parties are indispensable to the democratic achievement of choosing leaders and communicating the public interest to them. In the broadest terms, then, the consequences of party activity for the political system as a whole are the public choice of leaders and the open and organized expression of public interests. Political parties can therefore be said to democratize the demand functions of the political system.

In addition to their contribution to the input functions common to all political systems, political parties perform more specific functions for the individual as well as for the political system. First, at the individual level, parties are reference groups which help the citizen organize his opinions. They perform the function of "generalizing" reaction to political stimuli. Once the citizen has decided which party he prefers, he has a cue for reacting to new issues and personalities with a minimum of effort—he need only discover where his party stands or, if he likes real economy of effort, he can support his party on the assumption that it supports the correct position. Second, party activity tends to increase voting turnout, to strengthen party loyalty, and to create more favorable attitudes toward active partisan work among those who are exposed to it. Third, exposure to party activity results in greater interest in and information about public affairs. Those citizens who have been exposed to local party activity are much better informed on national affairs than those not so exposed. The competition of parties for votes thus leaves citizens more politically oriented, more active, more interested in politics, and better informed about public affairs.

At the level of the political system, political parties serve many functions in addition to their basic role of sponsoring candidates for public office. Without political parties, the struggle for power would possibly be less open, less predictable in its outcome, more susceptible to minority manipulation, and more likely to take violent roads to achieve political change. Without parties, countless groups could be expected to pursue extremely different policies, and so many alternatives would be available that choice would be difficult. Each election would present such an overwhelming array of individual candidates that voters could hardly know what policies or even general tendencies they were supporting. Finally, with no party program to help organize their work, official decision makers would presumably rely much more heavily on those interest groups that are organized to promote special interests. These speculations of what political life would be like without political parties make additional functions performed by political parties become more evident.

First, parties structure the conflicts of society. Parties did not create the struggle for power; the struggle for power in the context of a democracy created parties. Thus parties function to control, direct, and stabilize conflict, thereby permitting a peaceable expression of differences. In structuring social conflict, parties develop legitimate opposition to those in control of government and become the functional equivalent of revolutionary movements, but in an evolutionary way. Second, political parties serve to moderate the differences among opposing groups, to stabilize political allegiances, and to bring order to the otherwise chaotic system. In order to win majority support, they must avoid taking extremist positions. Consequently, they must appeal to a wider group than just their own hard core of doctrinaire and dogmatic faithful. Third, political parties organize the decision-making activities of government in such a way as to give ordinary citizens a much better chance of having their interests recognized. And finally, parties tend to lubricate an otherwise complex and complicated system of government. Government in the United States—typified by a distribution of powers between the nation and the states; and by a separation of branches of government into legislative, executive, and judicial—would make decision making extremely difficult, if not impossible, were it not for the coordinating, lubricating function of political parties.

A brief review, then, of the functions served by political parties—both to the individual and to the system—clearly bears out their importance. Hence, the intense interest of students of political affairs in the subject of parties, and the seriousness with which they insist that almost anything essential to the maintenance of democracy must, indeed, be a consequence of party activities. But serious students of politics also may conclude that the party does not do the job well enough—that it may have lost much of its reason for existence.

CRITICISMS OF POLITICAL PARTIES

Popular Complaints

The popular image of politicians and political parties is far from flattering. For those who regard politics as inherently evil, political parties are also evil. This notion has undemocratic origins that are seldom recognized by those who hold it. At their inception, popularly based political parties were naturally opposed by those who resisted democracy and distrusted the masses. Since parties promise to achieve popular control, Americans who still fear "majority tyranny" are logically antiparty. But this bias is a strange one to be entertained by the majority itself, for whom parties provide a voice in public affairs.

A familiar variation on this theme is that, although parties themselves are not inherently evil, the "wrong kind of men" always seem to take over politics. Actual investigation of the kind of people who are active in politics, as bad as some have been from time to time, suggests that they are generally not a whole lot different from the broad cross section of their society. Corrupt individuals are found in all walks of life—but so are honorable people.

A more substantial complaint is that political parties are undemocratic in their organization. Often the 1968 Democratic National Convention in Chicago is pointed out as the blackened example of this complaint. Prompted by charges of undemocratic procedures, the convention established a committee to make the nominating procedure more democratic. Certainly, the mass of Republican and Democratic voters do not maintain an active and continuing control over their parties' procedures, nominations, and policies. Democracy, in theory, is rooted in the responsibility, interest, participation, and vitality of its citizens. So, perhaps the accusing finger should be pointed elsewhere. The active members of political parties probably exercise as much control over their organization as do union members, corporate stockholders, or fraternity brothers do over their respective organizations.

The Basic Criticism: Irresponsibility

The most basic, and perhaps the most valid, criticism of political parties is that they fail to function as the essential mechanism of popular control. Party responsibility demands two things: political parties must bring forth programs to which they commit themselves; and they must possess sufficient internal cohesion to carry out these programs.

The great weakness of American parties lies in their failure to meet the second requirement; that is, to achieve the requisite unity and cohesion to carry out their party programs. Both parties usually attain cohesion during campaigns; but, as pointed out earlier, after the election the parties as such dissolve. What is left to carry out any program, or to pressure their officers into carrying out any party programs? Very little, indeed. This failure of the parties to achieve the postelection unity they need to transform their programs into laws calls forth the criticism of the general public. Hence, much of the public distrust, distaste, and disgust with anything concerning politics, politicians, or parties.

In addition, the concept of "responsibility" demands that we ask the question, "responsible to whom?" Should the elected official be responsible to the party, and the party responsible to its supporters or possibly the people? The argument presented above would hint the answer to the immediately preceding question should be yes. How else could the party carry out its programs? Nevertheless, many would argue that the elected official should be responsible directly to his constituents, to the people of his district and to the political unit as a whole. If this second alternative is the rule, then party responsibility is impossible. The demands of the constituents from District Twenty-two in New York do not always parallel the demands of the national party platform, the state platform, or even the local party leader's views!

In *Toward a More Responsible Two-Party System,* a 1950 report, the Committee on Political Parties of the American Political Science Association recommended certain reforms to bring greater responsibility to the American party system. The reforms suggested were intended to bring about greater party discipline and put the party in a position to hold the elected officials accountable to the party organization. More than two decades have passed since the report and none of the suggested reforms have been implemented. During this same period, many who supported the report have backed away from it.

Demands may occasionally continue to be heard for greater party responsibility, but the majority of the people do not appear to be looking to the party as a source of promoting responsible public policies. The party is gradually losing its significance in the American democratic process. Its traditional roles continue to be performed, but with less and less importance. The party is the agency, initially spawned by the conflicts in the political system and legally entrenched by a host of laws, which is used by the politically ambitious—those who want the power to govern, to fulfill their own ambitions. The party, in other words, is a candidate-centered organization. Candidates control or take over the party apparatus, rather than the party selecting and controlling the candidates. So the party will continue to be the candidate's contrivance, as long as it is needful or useful, to assist in his election to public office.

7
ELECTING THE POLICY MAKERS

The Twenty-sixth Amendment, lowering the voting age from twenty-one to eighteen in all national and state elections, was ratified by the thirty-eighth state, Ohio, on June 30, 1971. However, contrary to what one might expect, the movement to lower the voting age did not begin with the student protests of the 1960's, nor even in the liberal, urban states of the Northeast or the West Coast. The matrix for this movement was in Georgia during World War II, when the state was governed by Eugene Talmadge.

Governor Talmadge ruled Georgia with a strong hand, publicly insulting, intimidating, or threatening anyone who opposed him. When he announced his intention to run for reelection in 1942, the continuation of strong-armed, one-man rule in Georgia seemed certain. A "David" then came forth on the political scene in the person of Ellis Arnall, the Attorney General of Georgia, who challenged Talmadge in the gubernatorial contest. Arnall was a young but seasoned politician who at the age of thirty-five had a number of terms in the state legislature behind him, as well as his current experience as Attorney General. He challenged the "white supremacy, states rights, and the old-time religion" platform of Talmadge with the simple platform that he intended to change the arbitrary policies of the Talmadge administration.

Arnall gained student support by promising to stop the political meddling in university affairs and to lower the voting age in Georgia from twenty-one to eighteen. During this wartime election, when thousands of eighteen-year-olds were being drafted, such campaign slogans as "fight at eighteen, vote at eighteen" were popularly received by the Georgia voters, and Ellis Arnall was elected governor. Arnall pressed for the constitutional change he had promised and in August of 1943, Georgia became the first state in the Union where a citizen could vote at age eighteen.

Also during World War II, proposals to lower the voting age nationwide were promoted by a number of United States senators and congressmen. In 1941, Senator Arthur Vandenberg proposed lowering the voting age from twenty-one. Congress was not ready for such a measure. Then in October of 1943, Congressman Jennings Randolph of West Virginia introduced an amendment to lower the voting age. This was defeated; but Randolph continued to press for lowering the voting age and twenty-eight years later he introduced Senate Joint Resolution 7 on January 25, 1971, which became the Twenty-sixth Amendment.

The pressures which finally built up to the acceptance of the Twenty-sixth Amendment included support from Presidents Eisenhower, Kennedy, and John-

Pierotti in the *New York Post*. Reprinted by permission of Rothco Cartoons, Inc.

"Be careful of these kids—all they do is ask why."

son; such party platforms as the 1968 Democratic pledge to "support a constitutional amendment to lower the voting age"; and student lobby groups such as the New York organization known as CALVA (Consolidated Association to Lower the Voting Age). A noticeable shift in public opinion resulted in arguments from young and old alike that if the eighteen-year-old was old enough to be drafted, pay taxes, and be convicted of crimes, he should have a say in the passing of such laws. The fact that four states had already lowered their voting ages: Georgia and Kentucky to eighteen, Alaska to nineteen, and Hawaii to twenty, and some others were considering doing so, brought precedent on the side of the promoters. In addition, Congress had passed a bill in June, 1970, lowering the voting age to eighteen, with the Supreme Court upholding the law as it applied to national elections, but not for state elections. This meant an expensive dual election system for those states which had not lowered their voting age requirements, if they did not approve the amendment.

Thus the Twenty-sixth Amendment, the most recent of a series of suffrage expansions in the United States, made about eleven million young Americans eligible to vote—and possibly less prone to protest—and increased significantly the "under thirty" group of voters. Using the state of Utah as an example of the potential of new voters as a percentage of total voters, the eighteen to twenty-one-year-olds constituted 13.5 percent of the state's eligible voters in the 1972 presidential election. And in certain university and college counties, the percentage was as high as 17.4 percent.

THE STRUGGLE FOR UNIVERSAL SUFFRAGE

The Founding Fathers left to the states the qualifications for voting in national as well as state elections. Many states had religious, property-holding, or tax-paying prerequisites for voting, as well as the present-day requirements of residence and age. And even though the Founding Fathers allowed slaves to be counted, for representation, on a basis of three-fifths proportion of the total population, none of the states allowed any of them to vote for their representatives. Of course women were not allowed to vote in the man's world of politics.

As new states were added to the Union, the democratic forces of the frontier prompted some of these states to omit the religious and economic requirements for voting in their constitutions. This influenced other states to drop or lower their religious and property-holding requirements. New constitutions were drafted in nearly all of the original states during the 1820's and 1830's extending the suffrage; and by the end of the Civil War, the right to vote was generally enjoyed by all adult, white, male citizens in the United States over the age of twenty-one.

Black Suffrage

Free blacks, if they met the other qualifications for voting, were generally allowed to vote in colonial elections. However, with the expansion of the number of slaves and freed blacks in the nineteenth century and the eruption of the bitter controversy between North and South over slavery, state after state began to erect racial barriers to voting until only New England allowed black voting.

The Emancipation Proclamation, effective on January 1, 1863, did not free any slaves where the Union had jurisdiction, nor did it give any blacks the right to vote. The proclamation was followed by a period of doubt and confusion as to the legal status of the blacks who were actually freed by the Union armies. To eliminate the legal confusion and to make emancipation uniform throughout the states, the Thirteenth Amendment was passed by Congress in January, 1865, and submitted to the states for ratification. The Thirteenth Amendment, however, did not specifically grant the right to vote to male blacks. Although the Radical Republicans in Congress required the reconstructed states to grant the freed blacks the right to vote, many states passed "Black Codes" which relegated the black to an inferior noncitizen status.

Congress attempted once again to bring the newly freed slave into a position of equal rights with other American citizens by passing the Civil Rights Bill of 1866, over President Johnson's veto. This bill was soon followed by the Fourteenth Amendment, which not only defined citizenship and spelled out certain rights that were not to be denied, but included a provision to reduce proportionately the number of representatives of any state which withheld the right to vote from any part of its adult male citizens. Even this did not bring to the blacks the actual right to vote because a number of states evaded the clear intent of this amendment. Congress acted again in a more direct way and passed the Fifteenth Amendment which simply states: "The right of citizens of the United States to vote shall not be denied or abridged by the United States or by any State on account of race, color, or previous condition of servitude." This amendment was ratified in 1870.

The northern leaders in Congress, motivated somewhat by a partisan desire to entrench the Republicans in public office, hypocritically forced the South to allow the blacks to vote while several states in the North rejected amendments to their own state constitutions calling for their enfranchisement. As long as military rule existed in the South, blacks voted and were protected in so doing. Often they were manipulated by the "carpetbaggers" from the North or the "scalawags" of the South, who controlled the political life in the South until Reconstruction was ended.

When the South was "freed" from Reconstruction, the former white leadership regained political control and reacted against black voting with a variety of restrictions. They imposed literacy tests on prospective black voters that required them to "understand and explain the Constitution." They amended their state constitutions to include "grandfather clauses," which freed the descendants of those who were entitled to vote in 1866 from the onerous tests and devices designed to restrict the blacks from voting. They passed poll tax and "white primary" laws, which deterred black voting and denied the right of blacks to participate in a vital stage of the political process. In addition, intimidation of would-be black voters was not uncommon.

The first of these legal restrictions to be declared unconstitutional was the grandfather clause, but this was not until 1915 in *Guinn v. United States*. The next white supremacy rampart to fall was the white primary, which after a series of cases and changing stratagems in Texas was definitively declared unconstitutional in *Smith v. Allwright* (1944). As a result of the black contribution to World War II, the self-image and general position of blacks in American society changed significantly. With the demise of the white primary and stepped-up demands for equal rights, black voting more than doubled during the period from the end of the war to 1960. But there were still restricting devices which made black Americans almost invisible at the voting booths in the South.

The Civil Rights Acts of 1957 and 1960 were feeble attempts to correct a number of the existing inequities of registration and voting rights of blacks through the device of lawsuits. Little change resulted from these laws. Both President Kennedy and the liberal bloc in Congress recognized that further federal legislation was necessary. Their first assault was on the poll tax. An amendment abolishing the poll tax in federal elections was submitted to the states in August, 1962; it was ratified and became the Twenty-fourth Amendment in February, 1964. The Supreme Court followed up with decisions outlawing all poll taxes, both state and national, on equal protection grounds.

President Kennedy in June, 1963, acted to head off an explosive racial crisis with proposals to Congress for a comprehensive civil rights act which would include strengthened provisions to insure voting rights for blacks as well as for other Americans. It called for the end of discrimination at the polls, and placed restrictive controls on the use of literacy tests. Resistance to black voting continued, however, especially in the deep South.

A voting rights confrontation resulted in Selma, Alabama, where hardly any progress had been made in black registration and voting. Early in 1965, Martin Luther King started a series of protest marches directed first against Selma and then against Montgomery, the Alabama state capital, calculated to force an increase in black voting. White officials fought back. At the height of the disorders, two civil rights workers were killed. Liberals in the North were enraged, and thousands went south to participate in a massive new march on Montgomery. Many in the South resented this intrusion. New violence was prevented when President Johnson mobilized the Alabama National Guard.

President Johnson, supported by the liberal bloc in both houses, went before Congress and demanded a strong voting rights bill which would force the South to give voting rights to black Americans. The Voting Rights Act, signed by

President Johnson August 6, 1965, was specifically written to "strike away the last major shackles of those fierce and ancient bonds of slavery," as the President put it. The law automatically suspended literacy tests and similar devices where the Attorney General found them to be in use and where the Director of the Census determined that less than fifty percent of the voting age residents were registered or had voted in the Presidential election of 1964. The law also provided for federal examiners to supervise voter registration and elections in states practicing discrimination in violation of the Fifteenth Amendment, and set stiff penalties for interference with voter rights. The law was upheld in *South Carolina* v. *Katzenbach* (1966).

The impact of the act was remarkable. In 1964 fewer than 1.5 million blacks were registered in the eleven states of the Old Confederacy; by 1969, that figure had risen to over three million. Increased voting of blacks has resulted in a marked upsurge of blacks winning elective offices in the South. In several southern states they hold the balance of power, while the registration drives in the North and in the West have brought black Americans into powerful political positions also in several nonsouthern cities and states. The Black Caucus in Congress is a powerful force on the national scene; it has fought the Nixon Administration's reluctant enforcement of the Voting Rights Act and other policies of the Nixon "southern strategy."

Women's Suffrage

The fight for the rights of women, including that of voting, began before the Civil War when Elizabeth Cady Stanton organized a meeting of friends in 1848, and issued the Declaration of the Rights of Women. The movement gained momentum after the Fifteenth Amendment had been passed, when women advanced the argument that if the uneducated freed slave should have the right to vote, then surely women ought to be granted a similar right.

Mrs. Stanton was joined by the dynamic agitator Susan B. Anthony, and together they toured the United States, organizing militant groups of suffragettes who used all of the techniques of pressure politics to break down the political monopoly of the men.

Wyoming was the first territory to grant women the legal right to vote in 1869. By 1898, only four western states—Wyoming, Colorado, Utah, and Idaho—had granted full voting rights to women. In 1910, a women's suffrage amendment was passed by the State of Washington, and a number of other states were considering the subject. It became an issue in the presidential campaign of 1912. President Woodrow Wilson had conservative views about women in politics. The women, nevertheless, went right on agitating for the right to vote. By 1914, eleven states had granted women the suffrage, but this was too slow to satisfy them. They prepared a huge petition of 404,000 signatures and presented it to Congress, and they opened a lobby in Washington. More male support for the suffragette cause was gained during World War I, and in June, 1919, the amendment giving women the right to vote passed Congress by a narrow margin. Male political chauvinism did not die graciously, but the Nineteenth Amendment was ratified in August, 1920, in time for the women to vote in the presidential election of that year.

> **MODERN REPRESENTATIVE GOVERNMENT**
>
> *Question: If a man represents the women of his household how can he represent himself?*
>
> **IT** is a common notion that men represent women at the polls.
>
> **DID** you ever know a man who asked his wife how she wanted him to vote?
>
> **IF** a man votes as his wife wishes him to do, he doesn't represent himself.
>
> **OR**, if a man votes to please himself, he doesn't represent his wife.
>
> **THE** predicament of a man who attempts to represent a family consisting of a wife, mother and daughters who hold different opinions, is conclusive that it cannot be done.
>
> **IF** there are sons, the idea of a family vote isn't applied; they vote for themselves.
>
> **CAN** you see any sense in the argument that men represent women at the polls? Of course not; there isn't any sense to see.
>
> **VOTE FOR THE SUFFRAGE AMENDMENT IN 1915.**
>
> ---
>
> **EMPIRE STATE CAMPAIGN COMMITTEE**
> **303 FIFTH AVENUE**   **NEW YORK**

The long fight for woman suffrage was basically a campaign for equality for women. In this handbill, however, the suffragists gave the argument a new twist—votes for women would be a boon to hen-pecked husbands and fathers.

Many optimists looked to the women, who more than doubled the potential voters, to improve the moral tone of politics. Many men shuddered over the prospects of women invading their "smoke-filled rooms" and otherwise dabbling in politics. Actually there was no perceptible change in American political life, nor in the lives of women.

The District of Columbia

An irony of American democracy is the "colonial" status of the residents in the nation's capital. Congress jealously controlled the District, and resisted numerous home-rule proposals until late in 1973, when the District of Columbia Home Rule bill was passed by Congress and approved by the President on December 24. This act allows voters to choose a mayor and a thirteen-member city council. Congress, however, still retains the authority to control municipal spending and to veto all actions by the elected city government.

The residents do not elect Senators or Representatives to Congress. They are entitled to elect a delegate to the House as do Guam and the Virgin Islands. Prior to 1964, the residents were not even able to vote for presidential candidates, since the District was not allocated any electoral votes. This was corrected in 1961 by the Twenty-third Amendment, which gives the District of Columbia the same number of electoral votes as the population would provide if it were a state, but in no case more than the least populous state (presently three electoral votes).

Thus universal suffrage has become a legal reality, yet millions of Americans do not vote. Most nonvoting is a result of apathy, alienation, or lack of motivation; but there are certain restrictions which are considered to be legitimate democratic safeguards, such as proper registration requirements.

STATE RESTRICTIONS ON VOTING

A period of residence within a state is required of all voters. Prior to the Supreme Court decision of *Dunn* v. *Blumstein* (1972), millions of Americans were prevented from voting because they did not meet the residency requirement of the states to which they had recently moved. It is estimated that five million people were unable to vote for the President in the 1964 election because of this requirement. In the *Dunn* decision the Court declared the Tennessee law which required residence within the state for one year and within the county for three months by the time of the next election to be a violation of the equal protection clause of the Fourteenth Amendment. "It is sufficient to note here," the Court held, "that thirty days appears to be an ample period of time for the State to complete whatever administrative tasks are necessary to prevent fraud—and a year, or three months, too much." One of the other justifications for such residency requirements—to give the newcomer time to learn about the political needs of his new community—was pointed up by Chief Justice Burger in his dissent: "It is no more a denial of Equal Protection for a State to require newcomers to be exposed to state and local problems for a reasonable period such as one year before voting, than it is to require children to wait eighteen years before voting." In 1973, the Supreme Court lengthened the time period in *Marston* v. *Lewis,* when it held an Arizona residency requirement of fifty days to be valid. The Court ruled: "In the present case, we are confronted with a recent and amply justifiable legislative judgment that fifty days rather than thirty are necessary to promote the State's important interest in accurate voter lists. The Constitution is not so rigid that that determination and others like it may not stand."

All states limit the right to vote to citizens of the United States. This also excludes many people who have chosen America to be their new home. As the suffrage has been expanded in regard to age, sex, and race, it has been narrowed in regard to citizenship, as many states in former times permitted aliens to vote. This was especially true of those immigrants who had taken out their first papers for citizenship.

Most states require the voter to register. This is accomplished prior to the election by satisfying the election officials that he meets the other requirements for voting. This is to prevent fraudulent voter practices, such as voting the "cemetery lists," or casting ballots for people who do not exist and repeating the process. That infamous political figure at the turn of the century, George Washington Plunkitt of Tammany Hall, told of how he handily won an election in his precinct in New York City, when he had his wife iron the ballots for his candidates into stacks of ten (in that day each political party distributed its own ballots for the voters to vote) so they looked like one ballot and then he had his "repeaters" go back again and again to vote his ballots! [1]

Most states have permanent registration arrangements; that is, when a voter is once registered he is continued on the eligible list of voters as long as he continues to live in that voting district and votes in the elections. Some states, however, require periodic re-registration. The Senate of the United States on May 9, 1973, passed a bill to establish a nationwide system for registering voters for federal elections by mail. The bill would authorize the mailing of registration cards to all eligible voters by the Census Department. This is the most significant registration reform proposal among those designed to qualify more Americans to vote.

Age, of course, is still a restriction, even though the voting age is now lowered to eighteen. Most states disqualify people from voting if they are inmates of mental and penal institutions, and some deny the franchise to convicted felons, even after their release from prison. Occasional odd laws, such as one in Florida that restricts a person from voting if he has made a bet on the election, still exist on the statute books of some states—but they are not vigorously enforced.

[1] William L. Riordon, *Plunkitt of Tammany Hall* (New York: E. P. Dutton, 1963).

AMERICAN VOTERS

Every two years, on the even numbered years, the American voter who meets the legal requirements imposed by his state may vote in the general elections held throughout the nation. In light of the struggle to expand the franchise, as a result of which most Americans can now vote, it is incredible how many do not. Of the approximately 122 million Americans who were of voting age in 1968, a presidential election year when significant public issues were at stake, less than sixty-eight percent voted. Utah had the best voting record of 76.1 percent; Minnesota, Hubert Humphrey's home state, was a close second with seventy-six percent of the eligible voters casting ballots.

Among the nonvoting group, over 25 million did not vote because they were away from home or at work and could not leave their jobs; they were ill or disabled; they did not meet the residency requirements; or they had failed to register. It is obvious that many of these nonvoters would have voted if voting was made easier for them. But 15 million eligible voters did not vote because of apathy or other personal reasons. Some European countries hold elections on Sunday and some have compulsory voting, with modest fines for nonvoting.

There is some question if devices to increase the percentage of voting are necessarily beneficial to a democratic system. The nonvoter may feel that his vote will not change things, he may refuse to vote because of alienation from the system, or he may feel there is little real difference between the two slates of candidates and sees no need to vote. It may be too that the nonvoter is not equipped to make judicious decisions and refrains from voting because he is not knowledgeable about the issues and candidates.

One thing is quite certain, however, and that is that every vote counts. This becomes obvious in eyelash victories and defeats. In 1960, John F. Kennedy won the presidency with only a .2 percent margin over Richard Nixon of over 68 million votes cast. This is less than one vote for every voting district throughout the nation. Even narrower margins have decided some state elections. In 1962, the Governor of Minnesota won the election by the slim margin of 91 votes out of 1,240,000. The classic case took place in 1876 when a sick man in Indiana insisted that he be brought to the polls. The congressman he supported won that election by one vote. This congressman, later appointed to a fifteen-man commission to settle the electoral vote dispute between Samuel J. Tilden and Rutherford B. Hayes, voted to award the disputed votes to Hayes. The Commission agreed with him, by a margin of eight to seven. Their decision gave the election to President Hayes by an electoral vote margin of 185 to 184!

THE NOMINATING PROCESS

Winning public office in America requires victory in two contests. The first is winning the nomination, which is a party affair, and the second is winning the general election, which is a public affair. As any candidate painfully knows, he is not in the political ballgame unless he wins his party's nomination. Winning the nomination is always crucial; but in some of the one-party areas of the country, it is tantamount to being elected, as the final election is only "window dressing."

The earliest technique of nominating candidates for public office was the caucus. The caucus was made up of the leading men of the community in each party who decided who would run for office on their ticket. This later gave way to the congressional caucus for the nomination of Presidents and to the legislative caucus for the nomination of candidates for some state offices. The congressional caucus was made up of the members of Congress from each party, who would meet together and select the presidential candidate for their party.

Today, political parties use two basic methods for nominating their candidates: the nominating convention and the primary. The nominating convention is a meeting of selected party members chosen to represent their local party units. The primary is an election open to all party members, and in some states, to all voters. In some states, a combination of both systems is used.

The Nominating Convention

Conventions are used to nominate candidates for public offices at all levels of government. At the county conventions, the candidates for county offices are nominated by delegates to the county conventions who are elected or selected from the voting districts or precincts throughout the county. The delegates to county conventions usually draft a platform and pass resolutions for their level, as do the conventions on the state and national levels.

The state conventions are made up of delegates selected at the county conventions or from the precincts. The state delegates nominate the candidates for state offices and for the United States Senate. State delegates from the congressional districts at the state conventions nominate candidates for the United States House of Representatives, and state convention delegates from regional groupings select state senator or representative candidates to represent those areas. In addition to nominating candidates for the different offices, the state convention approves of the state party platform and passes on various resolutions which may be presented to the convention.

The conventions have gradually lost ground to primary systems for nominating candidates, except for presidential candidates. Party stalwarts prefer the convention system, because they are better able to control its functions. However, because of corruption in the convention system, elections, and other democratic processes, the Progressive Era in the first decade of the twentieth century brought about a number of reforms to correct the ills of democracy, including the direct primary.

The Direct Primary

Introduced in Wisconsin and now used in almost every state, the direct primary was designed to take the nominating power away from the political leaders and place it directly in the hands of the voters. It is really a party election to see who will represent the party for each office in the general election. A candidate will seek a certain office by announcing his candidacy and filing a nominating petition with the county clerk or the secretary of state. Often, more than one candidate will seek the office. The number of signatures on the nominating petition is regulated by law and is designed to indicate a degree of popular support for the candidate. The candidates are then listed on the ballots, and the nomination of those who will represent each party is determined by the voters of each party at the primary election.

The Closed Primary. There are different types of primaries used in the different states. Most states use the closed primary, which requires the voter to declare his party affiliation either at the time of registration or at the polls, so the voter can be given the ballot of the party he indicates. The closed primary is preferred by the politicians over other types of primaries because it identifies the party preference of each voter, and it makes campaigning easier for the candidates and party workers.

The Open Primary. A few states hold open primaries, which allow the voter to make the choice of his party in the privacy of the voting booth. The voter is given a ballot with each party and its candidates listed on it. In the voting booth he selects the candidates of his choice from one party. This portion of the ballot is counted; the voter has made his party choice by his vote on the ballot; and he has not had to divulge his party preference to anyone.

The open primary does invite the possibility of "raiding" by voters of the opposing party. For example, the Democrats may not have any significant party contests, so they cross over and vote for the weaker of two Republican candidates for governor in order that their gubernatorial candidate will have a better chance of winning the general election. This usually does not happen, as generally there is some contest which keeps the partisan voters on their own side of the ballot. Where it occurs most often is in local politics. At times, heated political battles develop for county sheriff, or some other position, in which the personalities of the candidates and the local issues in the campaign are of more importance than the party ticket as a whole.

A variation on the open primary is the "wide-open primary." This does violence to the party idea, as it allows the voter to cross party lines on his ballot and to select candidates from different parties. This system is more like the final election, as the voter is not required to vote for candidates from only one party.

Mixed Convention-Primary Systems

A few states have attempted to get the best of both worlds by combining the convention and the primary into a two-stage nominating process. This mode of nominating candidates usually has a pre-primary convention, which gives the party people the opportunity to narrow the field of candidates to two. The voters then have the opportunity in the primary election to select from between these two candidates. Some states allow a candidate to be nominated directly by the party if he receives a substantial, predetermined percentage of the delegate's votes.

Other Nominating Methods

There are some variations of the above methods of nominating candidates. In addition, there are two other ways to nominate candidates in most states. Independents, who are not aligned with either of the two major parties, can petition to appear on the ballot in November. This usually requires signatures amounting to a certain percentage of the voters in the last election. The percentage required is set by law in each state. Third parties may offer candidates this way or if they continue to win the requisite percentage of the voters, as some do in a few states, they can place candidates in the general elections year after year.

The other way to nominate candidates is to write in the name of the person wanted. Most states allow this by providing space on the ballot for this procedure. This method is not usually successful, but Henry Cabot Lodge won the New Hampshire presidential primary with a write-in vote of 33,007 in 1964.

THE ELECTION PROCESS

The election process is an interesting mixture of candidates, political workers, and ad men; campaigning out on the hustings and in the studios or press rooms of the media; cash outlays, fund raising, and signing notes to borrow more money; corruption and demands for reform; and casting and counting the ballots.

Candidates

America is a nation of many different people. Candidates come from all walks of life and represent this varied populace. The politician or candidate stereotype does not exist. A good rule of thumb is that the candidate is quite representative of the constituency from which he runs—not a great deal better and rarely worse. Candidates may be young or old, but they have to meet the minimum legal age requirements for the office they seek. They may be men or women, since the Nineteenth Amendment, and a sprinkling of interesting women candidates, have broken the monotony of what is still largely a man's world. They come from all religious and ethnic groupings in America, even though white, Protestant, Anglos still dominate the candidate scene.

Candidates for national offices are usually college graduates, and nearly every candidate for public office is a high school graduate. Lawyers contribute more candidates than any other occupation, followed by businessmen, farmers, and teachers in that order. More than half of the members of Congress in 1965 were lawyers (57%); businessmen made up the next largest group (27%). The costs of campaigns have, at times, excluded otherwise qualified candidates, and people of wealth have been candidates in much larger percentages than middle or lower economic-status people. Yet, people from all socioeconomic groupings throw their hats in the ring with considerable success.

Most candidates are honest—but some are not. All are talkers, though some are better in small groups, while others are motivated by a large audience. The successful candidates are always good listeners. They are interested in people, gregarious, and outgoing—although this is a put-on by some. They are most often joiners. They belong to civic clubs and fraternal organizations. They usually have been in the BMOC (big man on campus) group while at school, and leadership qualities are a must. The personal traits of successful candidates seem to be natural and inborn.

Why Candidates Run

The person who becomes a candidate is rarely drafted, regardless of what he tells the public when he announces his candidacy. Most candidates want to run and they work very hard at it. It is true that the candidate must have some support, but when he proclaims, "I have decided to seek this office because of popular demand," it usually means that his wife has agreed—most likely reluctantly. He may believe he is running for public office because of widespread public support, however; for when a person wants to run and is encouraged by two or three friends, it sounds like a chorus in his ears.

In *Politics the American Way* Senator Abraham Ribicoff and Jon Newman asked the following question: "How many applicants would you expect to answer the following want-ad?"

WANTED—male or female for frustrating job. SALARY—less than you presently make. HOURS—long with no payments for overtime. ADVANCEMENT—highly unpredictable. SECURITY—none whatever. WORKING CONDITIONS—subject to constant harassment by members of the public, often at any hour of the day or night.

Not many? Yet this description of elective office attracts thousands of candidates every year, with many thousands more lined up waiting for a chance to apply. Despite the headaches of public office and the heartaches of a losing campaign, the allure of politics grows stronger by the year.[2]

John F. Kennedy answered the want-ad and jokingly commented about politics: "There is no other way that I could move from Lieutenant j. g. to Commander-in-Chief so quickly." The motives of the Kennedys or the Johnsons or the Nixons to run for public office may vary somewhat, and the motives of those who seek the highest political offices in America may be somewhat different from those who seek state and local positions; but all candidates have

---

[2] *Politics the American Way* (Boston: Allyn and Bacon, 1968), p. 39.

motives which include some or all of the following: public service; personal power, glory, fame, or fortune; fun and games; and/or the "political virus."

Some candidates for public office believe they can make a contribution to their society. They want to have a say in how things are being run. Even though each person may improve the quality of life in his community through private, cooperative action, the power of the public official is direct and decisive, as the government has the coercive tools to achieve the ends which may be exasperating and difficult to achieve through other channels. Many citizens, concerned about the actions of others, say: "There ought to be a law!" The candidate takes the next step and campaigns to get elected so he can make or enforce public policies.

Power is an alluring accouterment of politics to many candidates. Others are motivated by a chance for fame or glory. There is a certain glory or fame which accompanies candidacy, even for those who lose. The publicity, the public dinners, the crowds, the pictures, and television and radio coverage bring satisfaction to the glory-motivated candidate; but this is magnified many times by the fame and glory of victory. Even though many public positions are poorly paid, there are always some candidates who seek public office for the money it pays—and the economic advantages they may be able to make out of their positions.

Many politicians find the political process intensely fascinating. In fact it is a big game—chess on the board of real life. This game aspect of politics probably applies more to the political manipulators than to the candidates. Even though candidates may find candidacy exhilarating, exciting, challenging, and fun in some ways, the grueling pace of a campaign, which drains the candidate of everything—time, physical and mental energy, and money—can hardly be added up to "fun" in the general sense of the term. It is more like a disease.

The person who runs for office is often the victim of the "political virus." Once the person has the "bug" and tastes the fruits of victory, there seems to be no cure. Those who win national offices soon acquire a special malady called "Potomac fever." The most effective antidote yet found for the political virus is to lose a primary election.

Campaigns

The strategies used in campaigns vary with the candidates and the offices sought. There is no sure-success formula. A candidate for the town council will use different techniques from those of the candidate for the United States Senate. The geographic size of a communitywide contest may allow the candidate to follow a person-to-person campaign, with little expense in media advertising, staff workers, campaign headquarters, telephones, transportation, and the many other costs of a statewide or national race.

The major expense of a Senate contest, or of any other major race, is media advertising. This usually requires an advertising agency to program a complete advertising package, allocating certain amounts to, and designing ads for, newspapers, radio, and TV. Television is the most costly form of advertising, and audience ratings seem to indicate that it is the most effective. A twenty-second spot on TV during prime time placed with the television station with the highest listener ratings in the less populous areas of the country may cost as much as $250, but it is many times that amount in urban centers such as New York City!

The costliness of major campaigns usually dictates the necessity of having a good political survey prepared early in the campaign, with follow-up surveys done later to determine the major issues of the campaign, and the strengths and weaknesses of the candidate in the eyes of the voting public. The advertising agency and the candidate's staff will work out the strategy to be followed from this survey and how to spend the advertising money.

From the time the candidate for a major office announces he is going to run, he is "running" all of the time until the election day. He cannot keep up with all of the demands on his time and energy without a competent staff. The key staff positions include at least a campaign manager, a fund-raising chairman, a publicity agent, and an appointments secretary. In addition to these key people, the candidate needs researchers, speech writers, and advance men to arrange for his appearances. He also needs the staff to handle his campaign headquarters, and people to serve as regional coordinators, county chairmen, and "foot soldiers" in the field to handle all of the grass-roots chores of a campaign.

Campaign Costs

One of the most important factors in elections is money. A high-ranking official of the Republican Party once said: "There are three important things in winning elections: the first is money, the second is money, and the third is money!" This is why an effective fund-raising chairman is so essential. Nevertheless, the candidate, himself, must go hat in hand to the many interest groups, be the central figure in fund-raising dinners, sign the letters asking for donations, ask his close friends or party people to sign notes to borrow money, put in all of his own money that he possibly can, and even mortgage his earthly possessions. A political campaign is like a wartime budget; the candidate throws in everything he can raise to win.

Many of the major campaigns cost far more than the candidate receives in salary during his term of office. A United States Senator receives $255,000 during his six-year term. The combined expense of senatorial campaigns in the more populous states runs as high as five or six million dollars. Even in such states as Nevada, New Mexico, and North Dakota, the total expenditures of both senatorial candidates will be in the neighborhood of a half million dollars.

During the 1970 campaign, the Republican Party concentrated on three Intermountain Democratic senators who were thought to be vulnerable: Howard Cannon of Nevada, Gale McGee of Wyoming, and Frank E. Moss of Utah. In the Frank Moss-Laurence Burton contest, the Republican Party had a Midwest ad agency handle Burton's advertising campaign; and the Republican Senate Campaign Committee pumped large sums of money into Utah, as did a number of business and professional interest groups, to pick up an "inexpensive" Senate seat for the Republicans. The Democrats, equally intent on holding as many Senate seats as possible, supported Moss financially, as did a variety of national labor unions and other interest groups, with comparable quantities of money. The Moss-Burton race is estimated to have cost $900,000 by those who were close to the campaign.

Due to the ever-increasing expense of campaigns on the order of the Moss-Burton fight, the Utah state legislature fixed a ceiling on the amount which can be spent by each candidate in gubernatorial, congressional, and United States Senate campaigns. Most states, as well as Utah, have corrupt practices acts designed to prevent political parties or candidates from gaining advantage through unfair tactics. In addition to ceilings determining how much money candidates can spend, these laws prohibit forced contributions from officeholders, bar partisan political activity on the part of civil servants, and call for some sort of accounting of expenditures periodically throughout the campaign and at the end of the campaign.

In 1925 Congress enacted the Corrupt Practices Act, designed to regulate campaign financing for presidential and congressional races. The Hatch Act of 1939 prohibits federal civil servants from active involvement in partisan political affairs; a second Hatch Act (1940) restricts state civil servants who are paid from federal funds from such involvement; and each act forbids the solicitation of campaign funds from civil service employees. The Taft-Hartley Act of 1947 bars labor unions from making contributions to federal candidates from the union dues of their members, as the Corrupt Practices Act restricts direct contributions from corporations.

These state and national acts to control campaign contributions and spending were enacted because of the obvious correlation between money in the campaigns and political influence. Campaign gifts are prompted by all sorts of reasons, but the most impelling motive is the expected "return on the investment." In October during the 1972 campaign, for example, according to a *Washington Post* survey, four dairymen's political action committees had $2 million in cash available for the campaigns of presidential, congressional, and state-level candidates, after contributing $192,000 during the preceding months of the campaign. Three of these committees, connected with Associated Milk Producers, had given $322,000 the previous year to fund-raising committees for President Nixon. Fourteen days after refusing to raise supports for milk prices, the Agriculture Department reversed itself, increasing dairymen's milk checks by $500 to $700 million. "The facts of life are that the economic welfare of dairymen does depend a great deal on political action," William A. Powell, President of Mid-America Dairymen said in a letter to a member of his organization. "Whether we like it or not, this is the way the system works." [3] Publicity about the apparent correlation of these campaign contributions and the administration's agricultural policies prompted one more headache for the beleaguered President Nixon and more grist for the investigative mills of the General Accounting Office and the Watergate Committee inquiries into election law irregularities.

Corporations which have governmental contracts are the most faithful contributors to national campaigns. Although they are prohibited by law to contribute directly to campaigns, indirect ways to make contributions seem to be innumerable. Corporate officers contribute as individuals; public relations departments buy all sorts of tickets to a variety of fund-raising functions; printing and other bills of candidates are paid out of corporate funds and entered on the books as "business expenses"; or the company may buy ads in party publications.

In 1964, for example, the Democrats "sold" advertisements in their convention program at $15,000 a page, a device which permitted the corporations to make political contributions and also classify them as tax-deductible "advertising" costs. The Republicans did the same. Some corporations bought "insurance" by buying ads in both programs.

Labor unions also are able to evade the legal restrictions on direct campaign contributions in a myriad of indirect ways. Through "legislative and educational" committees of individual unions and the AFL-CIO Committee on Political Education (COPE), "educational funds" are used to inform union members about candidates and issues, to organize registration and get-out-the-vote drives, and to otherwise further the democratic political system—which usually advances the political fortunes of Democratic candidates. Professional organizations operate in a similar way. The American Medical Association's political action committees and state affiliates were the largest single coordinated block of contributors in 1972 to candidates for Congress and state legislatures. The American Medical Political Action Committee (AMPAC) displayed little bipartisan spirit, as some contributors do, as it over-whelmingly favored Republican legislators. A major unfinished legislative matter for the Ninety-third Congress, elected in 1972, was the consideration of a number of proposals for a national health insurance program.

Even though the base of political contributions has been expanded in recent years through Dollars for Democrats and Republican neighbor-to-neighbor drives geared to large numbers of people contributing small amounts to the party coffers, through mass mail solicitations for five and ten dollar contributions, and through other citizen participation devices, approximately ninety percent of the money in campaigns comes from no more than ten percent of the population. Corporate contributions from business, industry, and banking and financial institutions largely finance both political parties. The "fat cats," how-

[3] *The Washington Post,* October 23, 1972.

ever, returned to the Republican Party in 1968 after a mild flirtation with the Democrats in the 1964 election. The contributions of executives from the largest defense contractors were nearly eight to one for the Republicans—after eight "good" years of defense contracts under the Kennedy and Johnson administrations. Contributions that same election year from the wealthiest families in the nation also ran about eight to one in favor of the Republicans.

In 1971, Congress enacted the Federal Election Campaign Act. It repealed the Corrupt Practices Act of 1925, but it retained the "equal time" requirement of the Communications Act of 1934. The new law strengthened requirements for reporting contributions and campaign costs, regulated media spending, defined more strictly the roles of unions and corporations in political campaigns, and for the first time limited the amount a candidate or his family can contribute to his own campaign. The law became effective April 7, 1972.

The law requires the full name, mailing address, occupation, and principal place of business of any contributors of more than $100, and limits the candidate's communications expenditures to $50,000 (an "escalator clause" raises the limit annually by the same percentage that the Consumer Price Index rises, with 1970 as the base year), or ten cents for each person of voting age in the candidate's district, whichever is greater. The law allows no more than sixty percent of the total to be spent for broadcast media costs. Corporations and labor unions continue to be restricted from making direct contributions from corporate or regular membership funds, but the law sanctions the so-called voluntary political action funds.

Concerned about the fact that no previous campaign financing law had ever been enforced, the citizen's lobby, Common Cause, decided to monitor the new law. Candidates and contributors were found to be ignoring the new law, and this information was released to the news media. A number of candidates found it politically expedient to make full disclosure of the sources and expenditures of their funds. But huge sums of money were raised before the effective date of the law. Common Cause called upon all presidential aspirants to disclose pre-April 7 contributions voluntarily. Some responded and some did not. On June 10, under the new law, political committees had to reveal the amount of money they had on hand as of April 7. It was at this time that it was learned that the Committee to Re-elect the President had over $10 million on hand. Many contributors had made donations early to remain anonymous. Common Cause sued the Committee for violation of the old Corrupt Practices Act and forced release of a partial list of donors. In September, 1973, the Committee to Re-elect the President released the names of secret contributors who gave over $18 million and disclosed that the overall campaign had raised more than $60 million.

Motivated by Watergate and widespread concern over the number of election-financing scandals under the 1971 law, Congress passed the Federal Election Campaign Act Amendments of 1974, designed to limit the influence of big money in elections. It restricts contributions to $1,000 per individual for each primary, runoff, and general election, and a total of no more than $25,000 for all candidates annually. Organizations are limited to $5,000 for each election; and contributions from the candidate or his family are limited to $50,000 for President, $35,000 for Senate, and $25,000 for the House of Representatives. The law repealed the media spending limits of the 1971 law and set the spending limits for presidential primaries at $10 million, general election at $20 million, and convention costs at $2 million; Senate primaries at $100,000 or eight cents per eligible voter, whichever is larger, and general elections at $150,000 or twelve cents per eligible voter; and House primaries and general elections at $70,000 each, plus an additional twenty percent for fund raising expenses.

Full mandatory public financing of presidential general elections was included in the law, with a matching public funds primary formula which required the candidate to raise $100,000 in amounts of at least $5,000 in each of twenty states from contributions of $250 or less. Public funding money would come from the Presidential Election Campaign Fund raised by the dollar check-off on income taxes. Proportional funding was provided for minor candidates.

Significantly, the Second Hatch Act as it applied to political activities of state employees was repealed; a limit was placed on political speakers' honorariums; and government contractors were allowed to have separate political funds raised through voluntary contributions. The law also created a special eight-member bipartisan board to enforce the new law. The House Clerk and the Secretary of the Senate would be ex-officio members. Two members each would be appointed by the House Speaker, President of the Senate, and the President of the United States.

Campaign Corruption

Campaign contributions may compromise candidates, who if elected, may use their political power in ways which are questionable or corrupt. Also parties and candidates for public office, in their desire to win elections and to gain political power, may compromise their principles in campaigns which simply add up to dirty politics. A classic case of mudslinging was the charge in the 1884 campaign that Grover Cleveland was a drunkard and the father of an illegitimate child—a charge which he denied. Cartoons carried such captions as "one more vote for Cleveland," and featured a child going to the polls to vote.

Some campaign literature during the "red scare" of the early 1950's carried implications that a given candidate was a communist sympathizer. A television ad during the 1964 campaign showed a girl pulling petals off a daisy during a countdown that ended in the mushroom-shaped cloud of a nuclear explosion, implying that Barry Goldwater's election would bring nuclear disaster. This ad was taken off the air for being unethical, but it is obvious that during times of public hysteria and anxiety unscrupulous candidates may attempt to capitalize unfairly on these moods.

A Fair Campaign Practices Committee, composed of private citizens and politicians dedicated to clean up campaigns, was organized in 1954 on the national level. This commiittee, which has developed a code of fair campaign practices, attempts to get candidates for national offices to voluntarily abide by this code; and it brings violations of the code to the attention of the candidate involved and the public. There is also an inherent check on dirty politics in campaigns because many of these malpractices have backfired and most candidates are aware of this fact. Probably the most effective restraint on corrupt campaign activities is the press and other news media. This was most noticeable in the infamous Watergate affair, which was not swept under the rug due largely to the dedicated digging of reporters of the *Washington Post*.

Casting and Counting the Ballots

Most Americans who vote today cast a secret printed ballot in an election which is supervised by public election officials and paid for out of tax monies. This has not always been the case in America. The adoption of the Australian (secret) ballot, as it is called, was demanded by reformers at the turn of the century and was adopted with other democratic reforms during the Progressive Era.

The ballot used in a majority of the states is a party-column type which lists all of the candidates for a single party in a column starting with the major offices at the top. This type usually provides a box at the top for those who want to vote a straight-party ticket. Voting machines are also arranged this way, which allows the voter to pull the lever for the ticket as a whole or to vote individually for candidates. The other type of ballot used is the office-block ballot, which lists the candidates for each office in a group. This type of ballot obviously encourages the voter to vote for the man instead of for the party, hence it is not liked by party leaders.

In addition to paper ballots and voting machines, there is a newer voting device which is also secret and can be used with either the party-column or the office-block arrangement. It is a data processing card. The voter arranges this exactly underneath a printed ballot. With a stylus the voter punches the holes in the punch card next to the candidate's name or next to the "yes" or "no" choices in a referendum. The punch-cards are placed in the ballot box, and at the end of the election they are taken to a data processing center where they are tabulated much quicker and more accurately than paper ballots can be counted.

The supervision of this balloting process is conducted by two groups of people: election workers, who are hired and paid for by the government, and party workers, who may or may not be paid out of party funds. The election officials are usually party people who are hired by the county clerk on a legally determined formula from both political parties. This is one of the minor sources of political patronage still left to the parties. The responsibilities of the election officials include arranging the mechanical aspects of the election—such as voting booths, ballots, and ballot boxes—and checking the registration lists, settling minor election disputes, and seeing that the election comes off without fraud.

Both parties have the right to station party workers at the polling place to make sure there are no irregularities. Additionally, they have another significant function in that they keep a record of those who vote throughout the day and keep party headquarters informed of those known party people who have not voted so the party can get them out to vote.

When the polls close, the massive job of counting the ballots begins, though some states allow the votes to be counted throughout the day. Voting machine tabulation is automatic. All that is necessary is to open the back of the machine and read the totals. Each voting district reports its vote totals to a centralized area, usually the county clerk's office, which in turn reports the cumulative totals to the state. The news media check the votes as they come in and have the unofficial totals long before the official totals are available.

It is not surprising to find errors in the tabulations, especially where paper ballots are used. Unless the vote is close, this possibility of error causes little concern. When the vote is close, however, the loser often asks for a recount, which usually involves a court order to impound the paper ballots or seal the voting machines so their totals cannot be changed. Then follows an official recounting of the ballots.

ELECTING THE PRESIDENT

To the candidates or the voters in any unit of government, the election of the mayor, the governor or other executive officers, the state legislators, and the congressional delegation to represent the state in Washington is a significant, exciting process. But all Americans have a special interest in the election of the President of the United States, as he is the one elected official who represents the entire nation. He is the chief executive and spokesman for the United States at home and abroad, causing citizens of foreign lands to be interested in his election with almost the same intensity as that of American citizens.

The Nomination

The nomination of presidential candidates is essentially the same as it has been for over a century. The climax of the nomination still takes place in the nominating convention held in the even years which are divisible by four; in a city selected for its comforts, financial inducements, geographic location, and its political advantage; by delegates chosen by a variety of democratic (and some that are not too democratic) selections beginning at the political grass roots; and in an atmosphere which resembles a three-ring circus but with an undercurrent of intense seriousness befitting the high office of President. Nevertheless, this peculiar American phenomenon, which causes foreigners to wonder, has been changed from time to time as seemed needful.

Until 1916, both political parties sent delegates to their conventions on the ratio of two delegates for each senator and congressman from each state, which made delegate representation roughly proportionate to the population. The Republicans found this gave undeserved weight to the delegates from the solid Democratic South, which never elected Republican presidential electors, and did not reward the states which always elected Republicans and therefore warranted a greater voice in the Republican convention. They consequently changed the system to give bonus delegates to the states which elected Republicans. The Democrats later changed their system to reward the more urbanized states, which were predominantly Democratic. Presently both parties have com-

Roy Justus in the *Minneapolis Star*. Reprinted with permission.

Double feature

plicated bonus systems and have enlarged their total delegations to 1,346 in the Republican and 3,016 in the Democratic conventions in 1972.

Delegates are selected by three basic methods, as determined by state law: (1) elected by state conventions, (2) selected by the state central committees, or (3) elected in presidential primaries. Presidential primaries elect delegates, who may be pledged or unpledged; indicate voter preference among presidential hopefuls; and, in a few states, do both. Prompted by the conflict between different factions of the party that developed in the 1968 convention in Chicago, the Democratic Party initiated a number of reforms in its delegate selection system, as specified by the party's McGovern Commission. Each state party was given guidelines for candidate selection which were designed to bring a better balance of minority group representation; regional representation, in line with the "one man, one vote" principle; and greater representation for women. As a result of these reforms, the 1972 Democratic National Convention was attended by more nonwhites, young people, and women than had ever attended a convention before. Also as a result of this new composition of the convention, George McGovern was able to win the nomination on the first ballot. The Democratic Party's reform commission approved new delegate selection guidelines in a meeting on October 27, 1973, eliminating the mandatory quotas for women, youth, and minorities in state delegations to the national convention. The 1972 Republican convention had a somewhat better balance of delegate representation than it did in 1968, but the change in representation was on a more modest scale than in the Democratic convention.

Presidential primaries also give the candidates the opportunity to test their strength and to build an image of popular support. Presidential aspirants usually enter no more than four or five primaries. They try to pick the ones that they can win, as the primaries can "kill" a candidate. And even if they win, they have no assurance that the convention will follow the primary results. Often the primaries determine who will *not* be nominated. Estes Kefauver won most of the Democratic primaries in 1952 only to have Adlai Stevenson win the nomination. President Harry Truman called the primaries "eyewash." John F. Kennedy, however, won two crucial primary contests in Wisconsin and West Virginia over Hubert Humphrey in 1960 which helped him win the nomination.

Whether the candidate enters the primaries or not, he is active for months or even years before the convention gets under way. Others are also busy in the months preceding the convention in selecting the site, setting the date for the convention, issuing the call to delegates, and doing advance agents work to complete the many physical arrangements for the convention. The heads of committees are selected by the national committee; the state chairmen submit the lists of members to serve on the committees; and one committee, the platform committee, is busy holding hearings while subcommittees are preparing drafts, so that finally a full draft of the platform is prepared in time for the convention.

As the convention begins, there are certain standard preliminaries such as the national party chairman calling the convention to order, the singing of the national anthem, the opening prayer, the welcoming address by a city or state official or both, and the keynote address. The keynote address is like a religious revival sermon, designed to whip up partisan enthusiasm.

In addition to the national chairman, the formal leadership of the convention includes a presiding officer, who is usually the Speaker of the House or someone with comparable experience, a variety of clerks, and four standing committees: credentials, permanent organization, rules, and platform and resolutions. The permanent organization and rules committees generally accomplish their work with little difficulty. This is usually so also with the credentials committee, even though it may have to settle disputes between two delegations from a certain state when both claim to be the official delegation. The Republican convention in 1952 had a dispute between rival delegations supporting Eisenhower and Taft. The decision of the credentials committee helped Eisenhower win the nomination. More recently, the Supreme Court held a special term on July 7, 1972, to hear a challenge of the credentials committee's recommendations regarding the seating of certain delegates to the 1972 Democratic National Convention. The Court would not rule on it and the conflict was settled through compromise at the convention.

The platform committee completes its work at the convention. The platform, which is general and designed to promote unity among the delegates and to appeal to every segment of the populace, is submitted to the convention for its approval. Only occasionally is there a fight over the platform, but a serious conflict occurred in the Republican convention in 1964 when Governor George Romney of Michigan and Governor William Scranton of Pennsylvania tried to give the platform a more liberal tone. Barry Goldwater, the presidential nominee, insisted on the convention approving the conservative platform, which was done.

The main order of business, of course, is the nomination of the presidential candidate. The roll is called by states; and delegations place in nomination their favored aspirants to the accompaniment of much oratory and colorful demonstrations, neither of which has much influence on the delegates. After the nominations the roll is called again by states and the chairman of each delegation announces the votes from his state for presidential candidates.

Once the presidential nominee is selected, attention turns to the selection of a vice-presidential nominee. A major consideration in the choice is to balance the ticket, geographically and ideologically, in order to gain nationwide support and to heal any party differences. The choice of a running mate is really the choice of the presidential nominee, not the delegates. There have been some exceptions to this, however. The most unusual was in the Democratic convention in 1956, when Adlai Stevenson made no recommendation and left the choice of his running mate to the convention delegates. Senator Estes Kefauver narrowly defeated the young Senator from Massachusetts, John F. Kennedy.

The Campaign

The presidential campaign begins with the candidates' acceptance speeches delivered at the conventions. It ends in November after three and a half months of intense activity. The campaign may be characterized in any number of ways: for example, by the skillful handling of major issues important to different sections of the country, as President Truman did in 1948; by the memorable TV debates between Kennedy and Nixon in 1960; by the creation of a public image of the extremism of one of the candidates, as in the case of Goldwater in 1964; by the remarkable efficiency of the Nixon organization and the creation of the "new Nixon" image in 1968; or by the noncampaign of President Nixon in 1972.[4]

It is difficult to determine what motivates the voters to vote for one candidate over another, even with the scientific surveying available today. The deciding

Copyright © 1960 by Burr Shafer. Reprinted with permission.

"Don't bother to outline a program—just criticize the present administration."

[4] Joe McGinniss, *The Selling of the President, 1968* (New York: Trident Press, 1969).

factor might be an issue-oriented campaign, or it might turn more on personalities. But one valid point is quite certain. Each successful candidate will attempt to determine where his greatest vote-getting strength is and concentrate his energies in this direction.

John F. Kennedy started early in his bid for the presidency, as he had to build the entire campaign from the ground up. His try for the vice-presidential nod in the 1956 convention was a beginning block. Then followed the building of a personal party, as the party regulars were not promoting this young senator from Massachusetts. In order to understand better the huge constituency of America, he had some nationwide surveys taken. This gave him a better understanding of which public issues were most important to the people, how to handle these issues in the campaign, what were the partisan proclivities of the people, and where and how to campaign to win the needed majorities in the pivotal states. Knowing that he had enough delegate strength to win the nomination, unless something unforeseen happened, he was ready to go ahead immediately with the campaign and did not have to wait for the lumbering political organization to get moving.

Richard Nixon also had done his political homework well before the 1968 election. For eight years, Nixon had been collecting political IOU's from all parts of the nation with his service to the party in speeches, fund-raisers, and the like. Unlike Kennedy, who built a personal party, Nixon locked in the party leaders and worked through the regular party structure to win the nomination and had immediate party support for the campaign ahead. His strategy at some points was the reverse of his losing campaign in 1960. In the previous campaign he felt obligated to personally visit and campaign in all of the states of the Union. In the 1968 campaign he could almost "sit this one out" because of the tarnished image of the Democrats and their party in-fighting. A "new Nixon" image was created and "sold" to the American public, while the real Nixon could be general in what he did say and sit tight, leaving the burden of vote-winning to Hubert Humphrey.

What is instructive about these two elections is that both candidates used somewhat different approaches to their campaigns, yet both did what was fundamental to success, in building the base from which each could move out to victory. Additionally, both victors won paper-thin pluralities of the popular vote, which really did not matter to them. The crucial vote was the Electoral College vote. Both candidates tailored their campaign strategies to win this vote.

The Electoral College

The Constitution requires each state legislature to set the procedure for the selection of electors equal in number to the senators and representatives from that state entitled to sit in Congress. The Founding Fathers intended the Electoral College to be wise and judicious and exercise an independent vote in the selection of the best man to be President. Resulting from the emergence of political parties during the Washington Administration, however, the electors were chosen on the basis of their party affiliation, and cast their votes for the candidate put forward by their party.

The same holds true today. Each party offers a slate of candidates to be electors. In many states, the short presidential ballot is used, which omits the names of the electors and lists only the names of the presidential candidates to whom they are pledged. Technically, however, the voter is voting for the electors. The slate of electors in a state which wins a plurality of the popular votes wins all of the state's electoral votes. They are not apportioned to the different parties according to the percentage of the votes each received or by districts.

This winner-takes-all system is not constitutionally required, but it has developed out of custom and it usually gives a clear-cut victory to a presidential candidate. All states use the general ticket system, instead of choosing electors by proportional or district systems, because if some states use the general ticket all must do so. For example, if the state of Oklahoma, using the winner-takes-all system, goes Democratic and all the electors of the state are Democrats, then the Republicans in Kansas cannot afford to be nice to their Democrats and share the Kansas electors as determined by a proportional or a district system. The winner-takes-all system also allows a candidate to win the presidency without a popular majority. This results from winning enough states by a very narrow margin to win a majority of the electoral votes, but losing other states by a wide majority, giving the majority or plurality of popular votes to the loser. In 1888, Grover Cleveland won 5,540,309 votes to Benjamin Harrison's 5,439,853 votes, which gave .3 percent more popular votes to Cleveland; but Harrison won 233 electoral votes to Cleveland's 168, or 58 to 42 percent. It is also possible when there are more than two candidates to have a President elected with a majority of the electoral votes, but winning only a plurality, not a majority, of the popular votes. This happened in the three-way contest in 1912, and also in the 1968 election, when only 43.4 percent of the vote was cast for President Nixon.

The 1968 election raised much concern about the Electoral College system of electing the President, and it revived the agitation for constitutional reform. The third-party candidacy of George Wallace threatened to prevent any candidate from receiving a majority of the electoral votes. The paper-thin plurality of Richard Nixon, nevertheless, produced a clear majority of the electoral votes—Nixon, 301; Humphrey, 191; and Wallace, 46. Any bargaining leverage which Wallace may have toyed with in having his electors vote for one or the other of candidates did not develop, as Nixon had an absolute majority of electoral votes over both his opponents. Nor did the possibility of throwing the election into the House of Representatives develop.

What did develop out of this election was a proposed constitutional amendment to abolish the Electoral College and have the President and Vice-President elected directly by popular vote. The proposed amendment set a minimum of forty percent of the popular vote as sufficient to elect them, and it provided for a runoff election between the two top presidential candidates if no one candidate received forty percent. Public opinion polls indicated that the American people favored such an amendment. In 1969, the House of Representatives approved the proposed amendment by an overwhelming majority of 339–70, but southern senators blocked passage in the Senate through a filibuster. The debate over the amendment raised many good questions about its possible impact on the election system. In a close election, what if the loser challenged the accuracy of the votes? It would be virtually impossible to have a recount. Campaign costs, which are astronomically high now, would probably go even higher. It probably would weaken the two-party system in America, and encourage more minor parties. It possibly would force the candidates to campaign in all states, or reach all people through the expensive TV medium, both of which courses of action would be too costly in expending the time, energy, and financial resources of the candidate.

In the face of this controversy over the mode of electing the President which resulted from the election in 1968, a far greater consequence took place on January 20, 1969; Richard Milhous Nixon was inaugurated the President of the United States. Although nearly 57 percent of the voters wanted someone else to be President, the new President, accompanied by the old President, assumed the powers of the most powerful nation of the world without protest. No one rioted. No one attempted to hold on to the powers of government by military force. The torch was voluntarily relinquished; it was graciously received; it was popularly accepted. It is a powerful testament to the success of the American election system and explains why the Electoral College system persists: it produces Presidents with accepted legitimacy.

PART THREE
Public Policy Makers

8
THE AMERICAN EXECUTIVE

The chief executives in America—the President, the governors, and the mayors—have different backgrounds and constitutional bases for their particular roles in the political system; yet, today, the major differences distinguishing one from another are the levels of government each heads, the magnitude of the problems each faces, and the number of people affected by the decisions each makes. All of these officials have the common feature of playing the major role of chief executive for their level of government, as well as a number of supporting roles which place the executive front and center on the public stage. Attention in this chapter will focus on the presidency, but many of the basic features of this office will apply to the other executive offices in the political system.

THE PRESIDENT AND THE PRESIDENCY

The day before he took the oath of office as the thirty-fifth President of the United States, John F. Kennedy called upon President Eisenhower at the White House. "There are no easy matters that will ever come to you as President," Eisenhower told the new President-elect. "If they are easy, they will be settled at a lower level." President Kennedy mentioned Ike's advice almost two years later during a television interview with three newsmen about the dimensions and perspectives of the presidential office. When asked how the job had matched his conception of it, Kennedy said: "Well, I think in the first place the problems are more difficult than I had imagined they were. Secondly, there is a limitation upon the ability of the United States to solve these problems." Although he was speaking of world problems, the same tone was apparent in his remarks about the President's domestic power. "The fact is I think the Congress looks more powerful sitting here than it did when I was there in the Congress. When you are in Congress you are one of a hundred in the Senate or one of 435 in the House, so that the power is divided. But from here I look at Congress, and I look at the collective power of the Congress . . . and it is a substantial power." [1]

In addition, Kennedy learned that he could not snap his fingers and have the bureaucracy immediately respond: "You know, after I met Mr. Khrushchev in Vienna and they gave us an *aide-memoire,* it took me many weeks to get our answer out through the State Department. This is a constant problem in various departments. You can wait while the world collapses."

An American President bears enormous responsibility in the nuclear age, as Kennedy was well aware. In the event of an atomic war, he observed in the interview, "that is the end, because you are talking about Western Europe, the Soviet Union, the United States, of 150 million fatalities in the first eighteen hours. One mistake can make this whole thing blow up." This candid discussion of the presidency suggests both the power and limits of the office. It points up the fact that the President is not simply the symbolic and actual leader of more than 200 million Americans, but also a world leader whose decisions may affect the future of all the inhabitants of the world.

The Office and the Man

The presidency is both an institution and an office held by a man. The institution is the office created by the Constitution, custom, cumulative laws since 1789, and the gradual growth of formal and informal tools of presidential power. The men who have held the office vary greatly—they have been weak, strong, ordinary and extraordinary. Most Presidents have come from the upper middle class; a few, like George Washington, Franklin Roosevelt, and John Kennedy, have been wealthy. Most have been college graduates, and a majority have had legal training. Nearly all Presidents have been Protestant—although Jefferson might better be thought of as a deist, Lincoln had no religious affiliation, and John Kennedy was a Roman Catholic.

"What the presidency is at any particular moment depends in important measure on who is President," records Edward S. Corwin.[2] Any presidency is stamped with the personality of its incumbent—particularly with his style and values.

The Expanding Presidency

In August of 1787, the framers of the Constitution who met at Philadelphia in executive session (that is, the daily activities were not open to the public) felt it

---

[1] "After Two Years—A Conversation with the President," a television interview, December 17, 1962, found in *Public Papers of the Presidents of the United States, John F. Kennedy, 1962* (Washington, D.C.: U.S. Government Printing Office, 1963), pp. 889–904.

[2] Edward S. Corwin, *The President: Office and Powers* (New York: New York University Press, 1957).

was necessary to issue a press release to counteract rumors that were circulating around the country. Printed in the *Pennsylvania Herald,* this press release said: "Tho' we cannot, affirmatively, tell you what we are doing; we can, negatively, tell you what we are not doing—we never once thought of a king." [3]

The difficulties encountered under the Articles of Confederation, however, prompted some to feel the need for executive leadership. The principal advocates for a strong, single, chief executive were James Wilson and Gouverneur Morris, with James Madison eventually adopting the same view. Many of the framers considered legislatures to be dangerous to wealth, private property, and business. A strong executive branch, on the other hand, could protect those areas and check popular government from becoming too radical. The support for a strong, single, independently elected President was by no means unanimous, however. Some delegates to the Convention proposed a plural executive, while others wanted the President to be chosen by Congress.

Out of the debates emerged the basic structure of the presidency as it has been since the Constitutional Convention: a single President heading one of three branches of government, elected independently for a four-year term. The authority given to the President by the framers was limited by the theory of separation of powers, which shared governmental functions among three branches of government; by checks and balances written in the Constitution; by the federal system; and, in time, by other informal controls unforeseen in 1787, such as the rise of political parties and the impact of the mass media.

President James Polk wrote in his diary in 1848: "I prefer to supervise the whole operations of the government myself . . . and this makes my duties very great." [4] Those duties have become so awesome in the twentieth century that the President, who now heads the executive branch with some 2.5 million civilian employees, would not even dream of attempting to do what Polk had done. What has caused the change?

Since 1789, strong Presidents have contributed to the growth of the presidency. George Washington, Woodrow Wilson, and Franklin Roosevelt all enlarged the presidency in their own ways. Certain emergencies and crises also have combined to create a powerful Chief Executive.

The United States and the Soviet Union each possesses the capability to destroy the other country with nuclear missiles in minutes. As a result, the constitutional power of Congress to declare war has given way to the power of the Commander-in-Chief to use nuclear weapons, to commit United States military forces to meet sudden crises, and to fight so-called limited wars.

The position of the United States in world affairs since World War II has thrust upon the President a paramount, if not indeed a dominant, responsibility in foreign affairs. President Truman was not exaggerating much when he told an informal gathering of the Jewish War Veterans in 1948: "I make American

---

[3] Carl Van Doren, *The Great Rehearsal* (New York: Viking Press, 1948), p. 145.

[4] Richard F. Fenno, *The President's Cabinet* (Cambridge, Mass.: Harvard University Press, 1959), p. 217.

foreign policy." Even though some of President Nixon's diplomatic and military initiatives have been challenged by Congress, the President's strong powers in foreign affairs remain virtually unchanged.

In addition to the increase of presidential power in foreign affairs, there has been a great increase in presidential power in domestic affairs. President Roosevelt's New Deal programs brought social acceptance of the idea that government should be active and reformist, rather than simply protective of the established order of things. With the steady growth of government-as-manager, the President directs a large bureaucracy concerned with domestic affairs. The government is often expected to solve social problems, from racial discrimination to health care; and the President is expected to be the chief problem solver.

Television and the other mass news media have helped to magnify the person and the institution of the presidency. All the major broadcasting networks, newspapers, magazines, and wire services have correspondents assigned to cover the President's activities wherever he goes. When a President wants to talk to the people, the networks make prime time available for him to make his announcements. The people identify with a President they see so often in magazines, newspapers, or on television; and this popular support strengthens his paramount roles in our political system.

PRESIDENTIAL ROLES

President Kennedy was having breakfast in the White House on October 16, 1962, when McGeorge Bundy, his national security adviser, informed him that U-2 reconnaissance photographs had disclosed the existence of medium-range Soviet missiles in Cuba. For the next seven days, the President and his most trusted top-level advisers debated in utmost secrecy how the United States should respond. At the same time, President Kennedy went about his routine duties to maintain an air of normalcy. He gave a luncheon for Crown Prince Hasan al-Rida al-Sanusi of Libya; observed National Cultural Center Week; signed a bill to establish a National Institute of Child Health; flew to Connecticut, Cleveland, and Chicago to campaign for Democratic congressional candidates; presented the Harmon International Trophies to a group of outstanding aviators; and took astronaut Walter Schirra and his family out on the White House lawn to see his daughter Caroline's pony. Then, on October 22, he went on television and revealed that the United States and the Soviet Union stood face-to-face in a nuclear confrontation, and announced the naval quarantine of Cuba.

President Kennedy's public activities during the first week of the Cuban missile crisis, and the decisions he made in private with his assistants, demonstrate the astonishing scope of the presidency. The President is one man but he wears many different hats: Chief of State, Chief Executive, Commander-in-Chief, Chief Diplomat, and Chief Legislator, all of which are required of him by the Constitution. He also fills five extraconstitutional roles, according to Clinton Rossiter, as Chief of Party, Voice of the People, Protector of the Peace, Manager of Prosperity, and World Leader.[5] This classification of presidential responsibilities may result in an incorrect assumption, however: that each presidential duty can be neatly classified into one specific category and that the President is constantly taking off one "hat" and putting on another as he performs the duties of his office. To the contrary, most presidential decisions and actions may relate to functions in several areas. Seldom, if ever, does the President conceive of himself as the Chief of State, as the Chief Executive, or as the Commander-in-Chief. Instead, he thinks of himself as the President.

Chief of State

As Chief of State, the President performs many of the same functions as monarchs perform in such countries as Great Britain, Holland, and Sweden, and as the ceremonial presidents perform in other European countries. The President, like a monarch, serves as a symbol of the unity, continuity, and purpose of the country. As the ceremonial head of the nation, the President is expected to engage in a variety of activities. He greets and entertains visiting dignitaries from other countries. He receives delegations of businessmen, labor leaders, farmers, educators, and representatives of many other groups. He decorates astronauts, military servicemen, and government employees. He addresses such groups as the Chamber of Commerce, the American Legion, and the student bodies of colleges or universities. He throws out the first ball of the baseball season, buys the first Christmas seal, serves as the honorary president of the Boy Scouts, reviews parades, and proclaims national holidays.

In personally performing most of these activities (sometimes these responsibilities are delegated to the Vice-President, Cabinet members, or leaders of Congress) he adds to his own stature, prestige, and influence, thereby enhancing all of his roles and powers; for he is seen as the representative of the entire nation, the symbol of the country. But these ceremonial functions consume time and abilities of the President that could better be devoted to his executive and other vital roles. A good case can be made for a separate ceremonial head of state, as the symbol of the nation to whom the patriotism and emotional attachments of the citizens could be directed; but with another person—on the order of a prime minister, premier, or chancellor, who could be held accountable to effectively administer governmental policies—holding the real executive powers. Criticism of presidential policies, which may be vitally necessary to keep the ship of state on an even keel, is frequently challenged as being unpatriotic. Actually criticism of presidential acts may be more patriotic than si-

[5] Clinton Rossiter, *The American Presidency* (New York: Harcourt Brace Jovanovich, 1960), pp. 16–41.

lence. Separating these roles therefore could well reduce the confusion in the mind of the citizen concerning his feelings of patriotism and his rational responsibilities toward the government.

Chief Executive

"The executive power shall be vested in a President of the United States of America" as the Constitution so states; and the President-elect takes the following constitutionally prescribed oath: "I do solemnly swear (or affirm) that I will faithfully execute the Office of President of the United States, and will to the best of my ability, preserve, protect, and defend the Constitution of the United States." The Constitution also adds, "He shall take care that the laws be faithfully executed." He is authorized to appoint public officials, and through constitutional and statutory authority, to make them responsible to him. Ultimately, the President is responsible for the execution of all national public policies.

The responsibility for running the huge national government with its many foreign and domestic programs falls heavily upon the President. When it is realized that the national government expenditures are nearly a quarter of the gross national product of America, it becomes obvious that no executive in private industry has responsibilities that match the President's.

The Chief Executive, of course, has help in discharging his executive responsibilities. Congress created three departments—State, Treasury, and War—in 1789 and has expanded (and contracted) the number of executive departments as conditions seemed to demand. Presidents also have had personal advisers, such as Jackson's "Kitchen Cabinet" or FDR's "Brain Trust." Recognizing that the President needed official advisers and staff to assist him, an act of Congress authorized the Executive Office of the President in 1939, which has been changed since its initial creation as need has dictated. (See Figure 8.1)

Though the line organizations of the departments and the executive agencies, and the staff organizations of the Executive Office of the President can be neatly drawn on an organizational chart, the President in actuality is the head of an executive two-headed Hydra, which is often working at cross-purposes. In addition to his official line and staff organizations, a President always has an unofficial inner circle of advisers—usually drawn from his principal subordinates, Cabinet, or White House Office, such as Kennedy's "Ivy-league Mafia" or Nixon's "Krauts"—who will have a primary role in policy decisions.

Additionally, the bureaucratic monster usually moves at its own speed and often in its own direction. President Truman knew the difficulties a President faces in controlling the executive branch and having the bureaucracy carry out his decisions when he said of his successor, President Eisenhower: "He'll sit here, and he'll say, 'Do this! Do that!' *And nothing will happen.* Poor Ike—it won't be a bit like the Army. He'll find it very frustrating." President Franklin D. Roosevelt found the whole administrative apparatus exasperatingly difficult to move, but especially difficult was the Navy. He said it was like a punching

Figure 8.1 Executive Organization

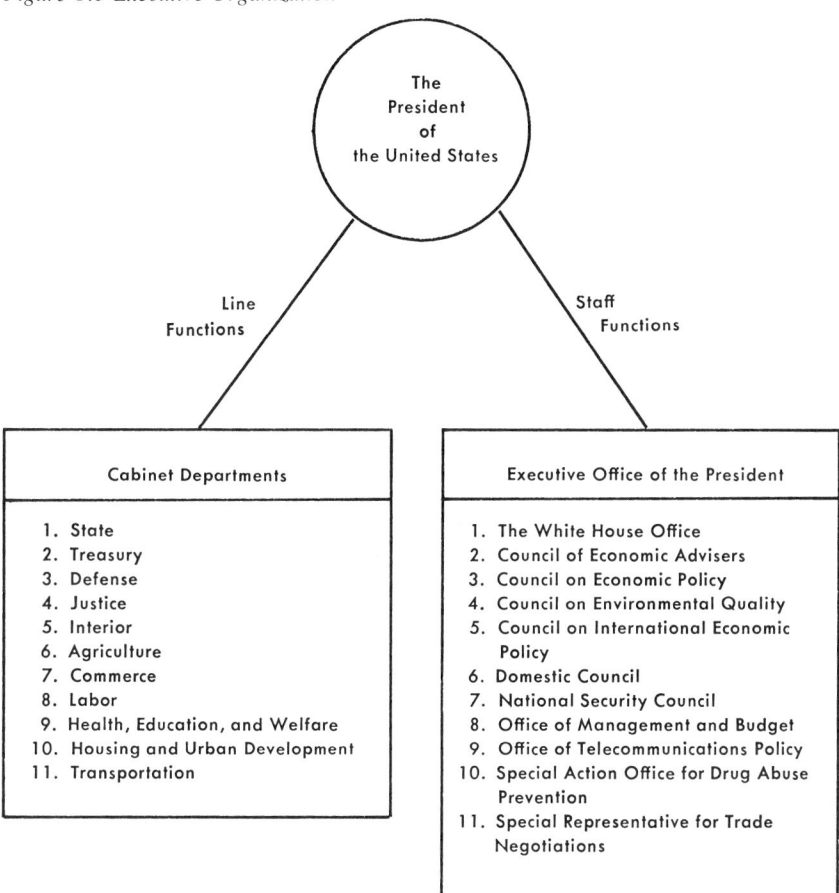

```
                    The
                 President
                    of
              the United States

        Line                    Staff
     Functions                Functions
```

Cabinet Departments	Executive Office of the President
1. State	1. The White House Office
2. Treasury	2. Council of Economic Advisers
3. Defense	3. Council on Economic Policy
4. Justice	4. Council on Environmental Quality
5. Interior	5. Council on International Economic Policy
6. Agriculture	6. Domestic Council
7. Commerce	7. National Security Council
8. Labor	8. Office of Management and Budget
9. Health, Education, and Welfare	9. Office of Telecommunications Policy
10. Housing and Urban Development	10. Special Action Office for Drug Abuse Prevention
11. Transportation	11. Special Representative for Trade Negotiations

President Nixon proposed in 1973 to eliminate the following staff offices:

National Aeronautics and Space Council
Office of Economic Opportunity
Office of Emergency Preparedness
Office of Science and Technology
Office of Consumer Affairs
Office of Intergovernmental Relations

From *The Herblock Gallery* (Simon & Schuster, 1968)

Bicycle built for two

bag—you could hit it again and again and it would still remain the same. Despite his vast constitutional and extraconstitutional powers, the President is often as much a victim of bureaucratic inaction as anyone else. Richard Neustadt, in *Presidential Power,* reports President Truman's assessment of his powers: "I sit here all day trying to persuade people to do the things they ought to have sense enough to do without my persuading them. That's all the powers of the President amount to." [6]

In his effort to persuade people, the President can draw upon a formidable array of tools, not the least of which is his power to appoint and remove of-

---

[6] Richard E. Neustadt, *Presidential Power: The Politics of Leadership* (New York: Wiley & Sons, 1960), pp. 9, 10.

ficials from their positions. Under the Constitution, the President "with the advice and consent of the Senate" appoints Cabinet members, Supreme Court judges, and about 2,000 upper-level federal officials. The Constitution leaves it up to Congress to decide whether the President, the courts, or the department heads should appoint "inferior" officers of the government. The great bulk of the federal employees are appointed through the civil service system.

The Constitution does not specifically give the President the power to remove governmental officials; but the Supreme Court ruled in *Myers* v. *United States* (1926) that the President has the right to remove purely executive officials whom he has appointed, such as postmasters. During Franklin Roosevelt's Administration, however, the Court held in *Humphrey's Executor* v. *United States* (1935) that, except for statutory reasons, the President did not have the right to remove officials serving in administratively independent "quasi-legislative or quasi-judicial agencies," such as members of the Federal Trade Commission. Even though commissioners of regulatory agencies are thus by law and judicial decision theoretically immune from removal by the President, in practice, they may not be. In 1958, Richard A. Mack "voluntarily" resigned from the Federal Communications Commission (FCC) when a House investigating subcommittee disclosed that he had voted to award a Miami television channel to an applicant whose attorney had paid him several thousand dollars. The White House did not deny that it had asked for Mack's resignation, and President Eisenhower called the commissioner's decision "wise."

To the role of Chief Executive, therefore, the President brings powers of persuasion that go beyond his formal, constitutional, and legal authority. By the nature of his job, he is the final decision maker in the executive branch. As the sign on Harry Truman's desk said: "The buck stops here."

Commander-in-Chief
Regardless of his other duties, the President is at all times Commander-in-Chief of the armed forces of the United States, as he is so designated by the Constitution. This fact is dramatically demonstrated by the fact that the President has immediate access to "a national security portfolio of cryptographic orders" that he would use to authorize nuclear retaliation in the event of a nuclear attack on the United States.

Normally, a President delegates most of this authority to his generals and admirals; but he is not required to do so. During the Whisky Rebellion of 1794, George Washington personally led his troops into Pennsylvania. During the Civil War, Abraham Lincoln often visited the Army of the Potomac to instruct his generals. Franklin Roosevelt and Winston Churchill conferred on the major strategic decisions of the Second World War. Harry Truman made the decisions to drop the atomic bomb on Japan in 1945 and to intervene in Korea in 1950. John Kennedy authorized the invasion of Cuba at the Bay of Pigs. Lyndon Johnson personally approved bombing targets in Vietnam. Richard Nixon made

Editorial cartoon by Pat Oliphant. Copyright, the *Denver Post*. Reprinted with permission of Los Angeles Times Syndicate.

"Hey, wake up—where are we?"

the decision to send American troops into Cambodia in 1970 and to resume the bombing of North Vietnam in December, 1972, when the peace negotiations were stalled; and he ordered the bombing of Cambodia in 1973.

While only Congress can declare war, it has not done so since December, 1941, against Japan and Germany. Since then the President has made the decision to go to war—Truman in Korea, and Kennedy and Johnson in Vietnam. Since 1970, however, Congress has been trying to regain some of its control over the war power. Congress repealed the Gulf of Tonkin Resolution, which it had passed in 1964 to support President Johnson's Vietnam policy; it passed an amendment originated by Senator John Sherman Cooper of Kentucky and Senator Frank Church of Idaho restricting President Nixon's future use of American troops in Cambodia; and it ordered a halt to the bombing in Cambodia as of August 15, 1973.

The way a President plays the role of Commander-in-Chief can also have a significant impact on domestic affairs. A decision to fight an undeclared war can change a President's popularity at home, and destroy or enhance his ability to get through Congress the programs and measures he desires. Even lesser decisions, such as hiring and firing professional soldiers, can affect a President's standing with Congress or the people, as Lincoln found out when he changed generals during the Civil War and Truman when he relieved General Douglas MacArthur of his command during the Korean conflict.

On November 7, 1973, Congress overrode the President's veto of a bill that spelled out for the first time in history the war-making powers of Congress and the President. The measure provided that the President would be required to report to Congress in writing within forty-eight hours after the commitment of the armed forces to foreign hostilities; and the action would have to terminate in sixty days unless Congress authorized the commitment, but this deadline could be extended for an additional thirty days.

As Commander-in-Chief, the President may make a different kind of impact on domestic affairs by utilizing the regular armed forces and the National Guard to suppress riots and internal disorders. President Eisenhower ordered troops to Little Rock, Arkansas, to enforce federal court decisions ordering desegregation of educational facilities. Also, upon the request of state officials, the President may direct units of the armed forces to assist state and local police in maintaining law and order, as President Johnson did in 1967 when, upon the request of Governor George Romney of Michigan, he sent troops to help control riots in Detroit.

Chief Diplomat

In the role of Chief Diplomat, the President makes foreign policy. He directs the relations of the United States with the other nations of the world. The Con-

Editorial cartoon by Lou Grant of the *Oakland Tribune*. Reprinted with permission of Los Angeles Times Syndicate.

A little something from Congress

stitution confers this power on the President indirectly. It authorizes him to receive foreign ambassadors, to appoint ambassadors, and to make treaties with the consent of two-thirds of the Senate. Because it requires the President to share some foreign policy powers with Congress, the Constitution has been called by Edward S. Corwin, "an invitation to struggle for the privilege of directing American foreign policy." In this struggle the President usually has the advantage, because the State Department, the Pentagon, and the Central Intelligence Agency (CIA) report to him as head of the executive branch. Thus the President has more information about foreign affairs available to him than do members of Congress.

The President has sole power to negotiate and sign treaties. Any doubt regarding this point was answered when the Supreme Court ruled in *U.S. v. Curtiss-Wright Export Corporation* (1936) that the President has "exclusive power . . . as the sole organ of the Federal Government in the field of international relations." Neither members of Congress nor private citizens may legally negotiate with foreign governments. The conduct of foreign affairs requires unified action, occasionally a considerable degree of secrecy, and sometimes swift decisions—all of which are lacking in Congress.

Because a President can sign an executive agreement with another nation without the necessity of going to the Senate, the use of this device has increased enormously. This has been particularly true since the Second World War, as the United States' role in international relations has expanded.

The President also has sole power to recognize or not to recognize foreign governments. The United States did not recognize the Soviet Union until November, 1933, sixteen years after the Bolshevik Revolution, and had no formal diplomatic relations with the People's Republic of China (Red China) for over twenty years. Since Woodrow Wilson, who refused to recognize the revolutionary government of Mexico, Presidents have used diplomatic recognition as an instrument of foreign policy.

The major crises that Presidents have had to face in the last half-century have been in foreign affairs (two world wars, the Korean and Vietnam conflicts, problems in the Middle East, and the Cuban missile crisis). As spokesman and leader of one of the most powerful nations in the world, the President is expected to develop, articulate, and execute policies that will strengthen other countries and encourage them to support efforts toward expanding freedom and seeking peaceful solutions to international problems. In essence, the people of the entire world are deeply affected by the judgment of the President of the United States.

Chief Legislator

Article II of the Constitution clothes the President with legislative powers: "He shall from time to time give to the Congress information of the State of the Union, and recommend to their consideration such measures as he shall judge necessary and expedient." Based on this statement, Presidents often use their "State of the Union" address, delivered to a joint session of Congress in January, as a public platform to announce their annual legislative program. In the succeeding months, the details of proposed legislation are sent to Congress through a series of special presidential messages.

Since Theodore Roosevelt, major legislative programs have been identified with the President and not with Congress. For example, Franklin Roosevelt, not the Seventy-third Congress, is given credit for the New Deal, which was made up of many laws designed to alleviate the conditions of the Great Depression; and Lyndon Johnson, not the Eighty-ninth Congress, is credited with civil rights and antipoverty legislation. Several Presidents have sought to arouse attention and public support for their legislative programs by giving them descriptive titles such as Theodore Roosevelt's "Square Deal," Wilson's "New Freedom," Truman's "Fair Deal," Kennedy's "New Frontier," Johnson's "Great Society," and Nixon's "New American Revolution." In fact, a President is primarily judged by his legislative successes, which points out the significant policy-making role of the President.

The President participates directly in the legislative process after a bill has passed both houses of Congress and is sent to him for his approval or veto. He has several constitutional options. He can sign the bill, which is the final act necessary to make it into law. He can let it become law without his signature, which automatically takes place after ten working days while Congress is still in session. If Congress adjourns within the ten-day period, and the President does not sign the bill, the bill dies. This is called a "pocket veto." Finally, the President can veto the bill by sending it back to Congress, stating his objections to the bill in a veto message. A two-thirds vote majority in both houses of Congress is then required to override the vetoed bill, in order for it to become law.

The President has an important constitutional weapon in the veto. The advantage of the veto is that it is difficult for each house of Congress to obtain the two-thirds vote required to override it, while the major defect of the veto is that it is total. Unlike some state governors, the President lacks the item veto, whereby he can reject particular parts of a bill and approve the rest. Instead, the President must accept or reject a bill as a whole. The threat of veto, known as the "soft veto," is an effective lever of legislative persuasion, however. When President Nixon selectively impounded funds appropriated by Congress for specific programs, he essentially was exercising an "item veto."

The President is not limited to constitutional authority in trying to get his legislative measures passed. In his effort to put together a legislative majority, he may have his staff assistants in charge of legislative liaison pressure Congress to pass his program, or he may confer personally with legislators to solicit their support or to work out compromises. Woodrow Wilson conferred frequently with congressional leaders or sent his "political ambassador," Postmaster General Albert S. Burleson, in his place. John Kennedy was the first President to meet with every major committee in Congress. Lyndon Johnson's experience and skill as Senate Majority Leader helped him immensely after he became President.

The President's real ability to persuade Congress to support his legislative program often rests on his personal popularity. A President's capacity to enlist public support for his programs will directly influence the extent of his prestige with both houses of Congress. His influence on Congress also is directly related to the degree of his control over his own party members.

Chief of Party and Other Roles

When a candidate for the presidency receives the nomination, he in fact, if not formally, becomes head of his party. He can neither be elected nor effectively perform his duties without his party's support. He is literally the "Chief Democrat" or "Chief Republican," and he must put his hand firmly to the plow of politics. The national committee reports to him; he selects the national chairman; he carries out the party platform, which he has helped to write; and while in office he usually develops his own program, which then becomes the party's program.

As Chief of Party, the President is expected to help raise campaign funds, to select most of his appointees from his party, and to campaign for congressional candidates in off-year elections. But he also is the voice of the people; and if he overplays the role of Chief of Party, it weakens his position as the spokesman for the people. In addition, if his administration is to be successful, he must have the support of members of both parties. In short, the President is expected to be both a partisan and nonpartisan political leader.

The President, it must be reemphasized, fills all presidential roles at once. His duties and powers are not divisible; and consequently his roles may overlap and complement each other, or they may come into conflict. The presidential office requires someone with great political skill to keep things operating in proper balance, or as Richard Neustadt has said, "The Presidency is no place for amateurs."

As well as these six roles, the President is also expected to fulfill many other roles. As the manager of the economy he is expected to prevent a recession, ensure prosperity, and hold down the cost of living. When a major civil disturbance occurs, he is expected to act as a policeman and restore law and order. And, as if this were not enough, the President is somehow expected to speak for all the people of the country and to arouse their deepest aspirations and ideals. He is expected to inspire confidence in the people. Scandals such as the Tea Pot Dome oil scandal of the Harding Administration and the Watergate affair of the Nixon Administration not only tarnish the image of the President, but they also weaken the morale of the citizens. Franklin Roosevelt once said,

"The Presidency is not merely an administrative office. That is the least of it. It is pre-eminently a place of moral leadership."

GETTING THE JOB DONE

In the exercise of his executive power, the President of the United States relies on the 2.5 million civilian employees of the executive branch. The executive branch includes the whole administrative structure, comprised of the Cabinet; the personnel of the eleven departments; the agencies, boards, the commissions; the Executive Office of the President; and the Vice-President. (See Figure 8.2.)

The Cabinet

The Cabinet consists of the President, the Vice-President, the secretaries that head the executive departments of the government, and may include executives specified by the President. The Constitution mentions "the principal officers in each of the executive Departments" and the "heads of Departments," but the Cabinet is not specifically provided for by the Constitution or by law. The Twenty-fifth Amendment, however, does provide for the possibility of the department heads to act as a group in case of disability of the President.

The President is not required by law to form a Cabinet, to use one, or to keep one. The Cabinet has become institutionalized by usage alone. Each President makes use of the Cabinet in whatever way he chooses. Theodore Roosevelt and Woodrow Wilson both regarded their Cabinet members as administrators rather than as policy advisers. Franklin Roosevelt made little use of the Cabinet as an advisory group, and sometimes even bypassed Cabinet members to talk directly to lower-level officials. President Truman tried to make the Cabinet meetings more useful by having the agenda distributed in advance and a record made of the points agreed upon after discussion. President Eisenhower extended this approach by creating a Cabinet Secretary to make up the agenda of what would be included for discussion. President Kennedy took an opposite view to Eisenhower's and minimized the importance of Cabinet meetings. President Johnson stood somewhere between the Eisenhower and Kennedy positions, holding Cabinet meetings frequently; and members even offered advice on matters outside their departmental responsibilities. When Richard Nixon became President, he decided to meet with his Cabinet about once a month or less, preferring smaller Cabinet-level advisory groups on specific problems.

President Nixon proposed a major restructuring of the executive branch in his 1971 State of the Union address. This restructuring was one of the six major goals of the "New American Revolution." Nixon wanted to reduce the number of executive departments to eight. The Departments of State, Treasury, Defense, and Justice were to remain; but all other departments were to be consoli-

Figure 8.2 Executive and Independent Agencies

EXECUTIVE AND INDEPENDENT AGENCIES

THE PRESIDENT

EXECUTIVE OFFICE OF THE PRESIDENT

The White House Office
Council of Economic Advisers
Council on Economic Policy
Council on Environmental Quality
Council on International Economic Policy
Domestic Council
National Aeronautics and Space Council [1]
National Security Council

Office of Economic Opportunity [2]
Office of Emergency Preparedness [3]
Office of Management and Budget
Office of Science and Technology [3]
Office of Telecommunications Policy
Special Action Office for Drug Abuse Prevention
Special Representative for Trade Negotiations

DEPARTMENT OF STATE
DEPARTMENT OF AGRICULTURE
DEPARTMENT OF COMMERCE
DEPARTMENT OF THE TREASURY
DEPARTMENT OF LABOR
DEPARTMENT OF DEFENSE
DEPARTMENT OF HEALTH, EDUCATION, AND WELFARE
DEPARTMENT OF JUSTICE
DEPARTMENT OF HOUSING AND URBAN DEVELOPMENT
DEPARTMENT OF THE INTERIOR
DEPARTMENT OF TRANSPORTATION

SELECTED AGENCIES, BOARDS AND COMMISSIONS

ACTION
Administrative Conference of the United States
Advisory Commission on Intergovernmental Relations
American Battle Monuments Commission
Appalachian Regional Commission
Atomic Energy Commission
Canal Zone Government
Central Intelligence Agency
Civil Aeronautics Board
Commission on Fine Arts
Commission on Civil Rights
Consumer Product Safety Commission
Cost of Living Council
District of Columbia
Environmental Protection Agency
Equal Employment Opportunity Commission
Export-Import Bank of the United States
Farm Credit Administration
Federal Communications Commission
Federal Deposit Insurance Corporation
Federal Home Loan Bank Board
Federal Maritime Commission
Federal Mediation and Conciliation Service
Federal Power Commission
Board of Governors of the Federal Reserve System
Federal Trade Commission
Foreign Claims Settlement Commission
General Services Administration
Indian Claims Commission
Interstate Commerce Commission
National Aeronautics and Space Administration
National Capital Housing Authority
National Capital Planning Commission
National Credit Union Administration
National Foundation on the Arts and Humanities
National Labor Relations Board
National Mediation Board
National Science Foundation
Panama Canal Company
Railroad Retirement Board
Renegotiation Board
Securities and Exchange Commission
Selective Service System
Small Business Administration
Smithsonian Institution
Subversive Activities Control Board
Tennessee Valley Authority
U.S. Arms Control and Disarmament Agency
U.S. Civil Service Commission
United States Information Agency
United States Postal Service
United States Tariff Commission
Veterans Administration
Water Resources Council

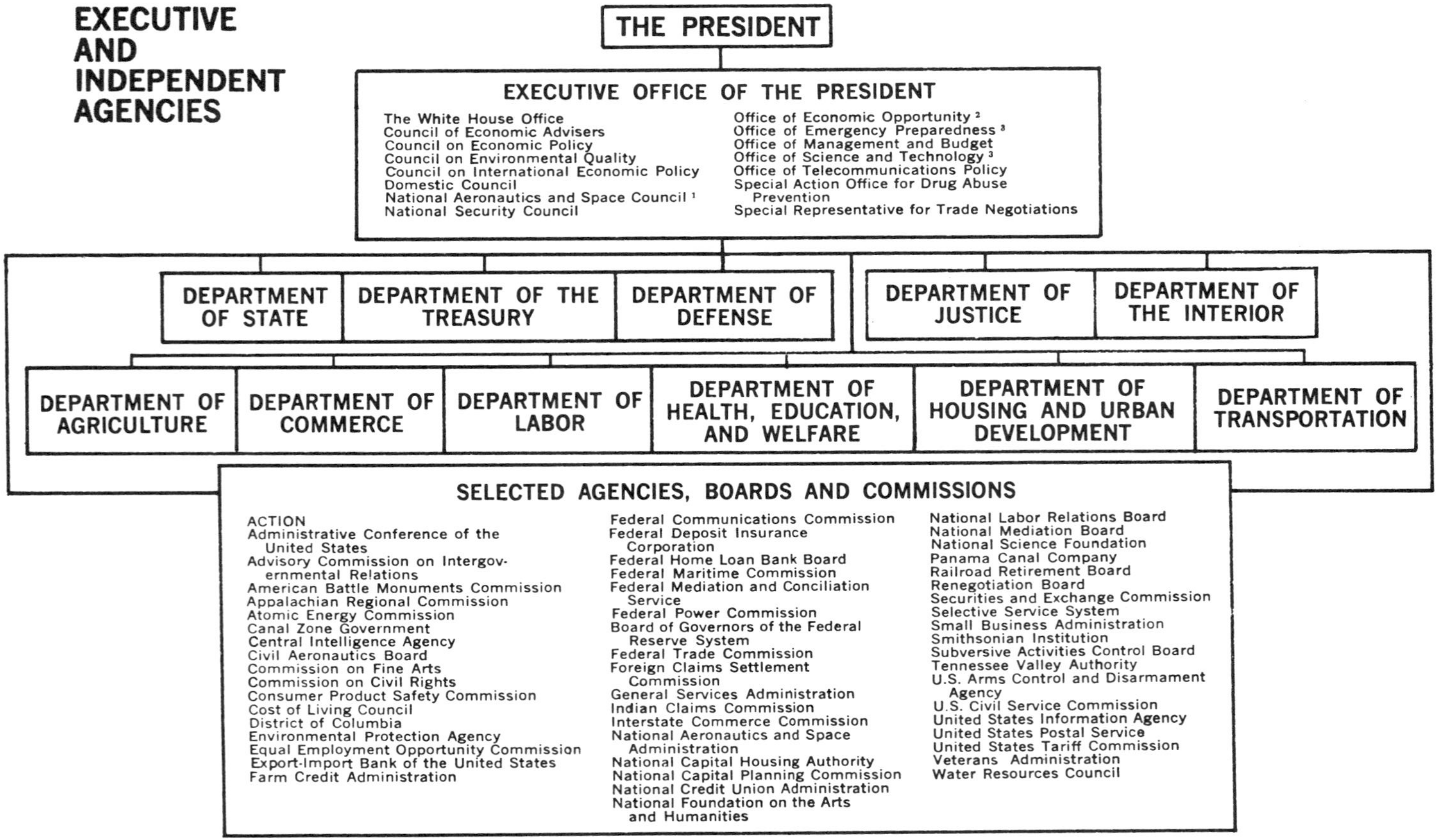

[1] Abolition proposed by Reorganization plan.
[2] Office to be discontinued, functions to be distributed to other agencies.
[3] Abolition proposed by Reorganization plan, functions to be transferred to other agencies.

SOURCE: Office of Management and Budget, *The U.S. Budget in Brief, Fiscal Year 1974* (Washington, D.C.: U.S. Government Printing Office, 1973).

dated into four new departments: Human Resources, Community Development, Natural Resources, and Economic Development. (See Figure 8.3.)

The Ninety-second Congress did not act on the President's reorganization plans. Stymied by a reluctant Congress and by what he considered an unresponsive bureaucracy, President Nixon, on January 5, 1973, ordered one of the most sweeping executive reorganizations in history, purportedly to make the government work more efficiently. The reorganization program called for the establishment of a "super Cabinet" and "super assistants" to assist the President in administering the government, streamlining the Executive Office of the President, and decentralizing the functions of the national government.

Figure 8.3 President Nixon's Proposed Reorganization of the Departments

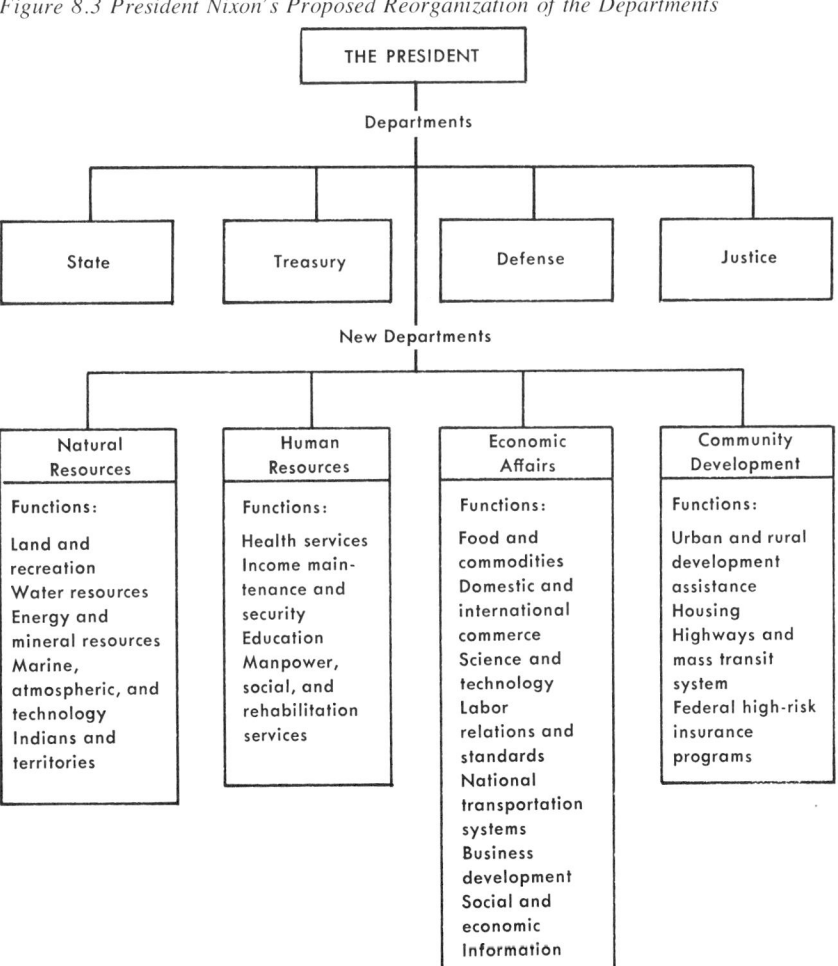

THE PRESIDENT

Departments

| State | Treasury | Defense | Justice |

New Departments

Natural Resources	Human Resources	Economic Affairs	Community Development
Functions:	Functions:	Functions:	Functions:
Land and recreation	Health services	Food and commodities	Urban and rural development assistance
Water resources	Income maintenance and security	Domestic and international commerce	Housing
Energy and mineral resources	Education	Science and technology	Highways and mass transit system
Marine, atmospheric, and technology	Manpower, social, and rehabilitation services	Labor relations and standards	Federal high-risk insurance programs
Indians and territories		National transportation systems	
		Business development	
		Social and economic Information	

184 *Public Policy Makers*

The President elevated three Cabinet officers to the level of White House counselors to be responsible for three broad areas of domestic responsibility in addition to their departmental duties. Earl L. Butz, Secretary of Agriculture, was placed in charge of natural resources policy—with responsibilities which fell largely within the Departments of Agriculture and Interior. Caspar W. Weinberger, Secretary of Health, Education, and Welfare (HEW), was given overall responsibility for human resources policy—administrative functions which were scattered throughout the federal establishment. James T. Lynn, Secretary of Housing and Urban Development (HUD), was placed in charge of community development policy—functions which were centered largely in HUD and the Transportation Department.

These three "super Cabinet" positions were placed under five presidential assistants: H. R. Haldeman, for administration of the White House; John D. Ehrlichman, for domestic affairs; Dr. Henry A. Kissinger, for foreign affairs; Roy L. Ash, the new head of the Office of Management and Budget, for executive management; and George P. Shultz, Secretary of the Treasury, for economic affairs. The three counselors were to report to the President through the domestic affairs assistant, John D. Ehrlichman.

The new arrangement was what the President had asked Congress for in 1971. What Congress did not approve legislatively, the President did adminis-

Copyright © 1960 by Burr Shafer. Reprinted with permission.

"Oh, Washington himself is all right. It's the men around him like Jefferson and Adams and . . ."

tratively. He said the reorganization was a result of the message of the 1972 election: "Americans are fed up with wasteful, musclebound government in Washington and are anxious for a change that works." Some of the members of Congress, however, saw in this move a greater concentration of power in the President. The question of executive privilege is a sore spot in congressional-presidential relations. By making this move, the President could restrict the four secretaries of Cabinet departments—as counselors and assistant to the President—from testifying before congressional committees; whereas department heads have in the past been available for testimony, reducing further the powers of Congress in overseeing the administration of governmental policies.

In the wake of Watergate, as investigations and testimony implicated top White House officials, President Nixon was forced to reshuffle his top staff on June 6, 1973—the third reshuffling in only five months. With the appointment of Melvin R. Laird, former Secretary of Defense, as counselor to the President for domestic affairs, the President took a more conciliatory stance toward Congress and backpedaled on his reorganization objectives in order to keep his administration afloat.

Cabinets may be useful to some degree to a President seeking advice, but the President can never forget that each department has its own interests, its own relations with Congress and with powerful interest groups, and its own clientele. Usually the secretaries as leaders of their departments will reflect some degree of bureaucratic bias in their advice to the President. This is one reason why there is a tendency for Presidents to rely more heavily on their special assistants in the White House Office and on other staff assistants in the Executive Office of the President.

The Executive Office of the President

In 1939, after a committee of scholars reported to President Roosevelt that "the President needs help," the Executive Office of the President was established by executive order, as authorized by an act of Congress. Since that time the Executive Office has become an institutionalized growing body of staff support for budgeting, economic policy, national security, and domestic policy. Operating in the Executive Office Building just west of the White House, these policy staffs constitute a powerful component of the presidential advisory system. The most significant of the offices in advising the President on policy matters is the White House Office.

The White House Office. All modern Presidents have relied on personal advisers. Wilson had his Colonel House, Franklin Roosevelt his Harry Hopkins, Eisenhower his Sherman Adams, Johnson his Bill Moyers, and Nixon his Henry Kissinger. Those advisers who have the ear of the President become powerful extensions of presidential power. The size of the White House Office varies with each President.

In recent administrations, the President's adviser for national security affairs has taken a major role in the formulation of foreign policy. With access to the President and the White House "Situation Room"—the office into which all military, intelligence, and diplomatic information flows—he has emerged as a powerful rival to the Secretary of State. This rivalry was temporarily checked in the Nixon Administration when Henry Kissinger was appointed Secretary of State and held both positions.

The President needs a personal staff to fill a variety of functions. Some try to schedule the best use of the President's time. Some work only with Congress, while others serve as links with the executive departments and agencies, channeling problems and conflicts among the departments to the President. Others advise the President on political questions, patronage, and appointments, or write his speeches. Twice daily, the press secretary holds press briefings and issues presidential announcements on matters large and small.

A major criticism of the President's staff is that, inevitably, his vision is filtered through the eyes of these assistants. Someone like an Eisenhower or a Nixon, with a rigid staff system, may become isolated in the White House. A Lyndon Johnson, with an overpowering, demanding personality, may hear an echo of his own views instead of the candid thoughts of his assistants. In short, the President's staff may not let him hear enough, or it may tell him only what he wants to hear.

The National Security Council. The National Security Council (NSC) has the responsibility for advising the President "with respect to the integration of domestic, foreign, and military policies relating to national security." The NSC is composed of the President, who serves as the chairman; the Vice-President; the Secretary of State; the Secretary of Defense; the Director of the Office of Emergency Preparedness; and the Director of the NSC itself. The President also invites other persons to attend meetings whose advice he may want on particular issues or problems, including the U.S. Ambassador to the United Nations, the Chairman of the Joint Chiefs of Staff, the Director of the Central Intelligence Agency, and members of the White House staff.

The principal purposes of the NSC are to bring together the top officials who have responsibilities for national security and foreign policies, and to provide them with information that will permit a thorough analysis of all aspects of such policies. Information and analysis of relevant factors are provided by the staff of the NSC; by governmental units represented on the NSC; and by the Central Intelligence Agency, which operates under the direction of the council. Thus NSC serves as a planning and coordinating agency.

The Domestic Council. In 1970, President Nixon created a Domestic Council to advise him "on the total range of domestic policy." In the area of domestic affairs, the council occupies a functional position equivalent to that of the NSC in the field of national security. The council is composed of the President, who serves as chairman; the Vice-President; members of the Cabinet, except the Secretaries of State and Defense; two counselors to the President; the Director and Deputy Director of the Office of Management and Budget; and the Chairman of the Council of Economic Advisers.

The Domestic Council's chief functions are to assess national needs, to identify alternative ways to achieve national goals, to respond rapidly on urgent domestic problems, to help establish national priorities for the allocation of available resources, and to maintain a check on existing programs.

The Office of Management and Budget. The Office of Management and Budget (OMB) was also created under the same reorganization plan that established the Domestic Council. The OMB, which succeeded the Bureau of the Budget, was designed to tighten presidential control over the bureaucracy and to improve its efficiency.

The OMB has two overlapping functions: to prepare the federal budget and to serve as the President's principal arm for the exercise of his managerial functions. The director of the office advises the President on the allocation of federal funds, and he attempts to resolve the competing claims of the departments and agencies for a larger share of the budget. Because of OMB's supervision of federal spending, it serves as a valuable instrument of presidential control over the executive branch.

In its second function as a managerial tool, OMB has responsibility for evaluating the efficiency of federal agencies to ascertain which programs are achieving their intended results. OMB is also responsible for improving government organization, developing information and management systems, creating programs for the recruitment and training of federal career executives, reviewing legislation for its potential impact on the budget, and supervising all federal statistical information.

The Council of Economic Advisers. Congress acknowledged in 1946 the responsibility of the federal government for promoting prosperity and economic stability by passing the Employment Act, which created the Council of Economic Advisers (CEA) and established it as a unit of the Executive Office of the President. The CEA consists of three professional economists, usually selected from leading universitites, who are appointed by the President with Senate confirmation. The CEA, and its staff of economists and statisticians, continually analyze national economic trends and developments, appraise the economic programs and policies of the government, and advise the President regarding policies that will encourage economic growth and stability. The CEA also prepares for the President an annual report on the national economy that the President sends to Congress.

The Council on Environmental Quality. The Council on Environmental Quality (CEQ) was established by the National Environmental Policy Act of 1969 to formulate and recommend national policies to promote the improvement of the quality of the environment. The Council consists of three members appointed by the President by and with the advice and consent of the Senate. One of the members is designated by the President as Chairman.

Other Executive Office Units. There are several other important units inside the Executive Office of the President: the Office of Telecommunications, which is responsible for overall supervision of national communications matters; the Council on International Economic Policy, which is responsible for achieving consistency between domestic and foreign economic policy; the Special Action Office for Drug Abuse Prevention, which is responsible for planning and policy, and establishes objectives and priorities for all federal drug abuse prevention functions; and the Special Representative for Trade Negotiations. The President's reorganization plans of 1973, however, proposed to discontinue the Office of Emergency Preparedness, the Office of Science and Technology, the Office of Consumer Affairs, the National Aeronautics and Space Council, the Office of Intergovernmental Relations, and the Office of Economic Opportunity. Most of the functions of these staff offices were to be transferred to other agencies. The dismantling of the Office of Economic Opportunity, the largest office in the Executive Office of the President, brought about sharp criticism from a number of liberal members of Congress and court action to block the President's actions. This controversy also raises questions about presidential style and his relations with the other branches of government.

THE VICE-PRESIDENT

Under the Constitution, the only duties the Vice-President has to perform are to preside over the Senate; to vote in that body in case of a tie; and (under the Twenty-fifth Amendment) to help decide whether the President is disabled, and, if so, to serve as Acting President. However, if the President dies, resigns, or is removed from office, the Vice-President becomes President.

Because of the situation Harry Truman found himself in when he became President after Roosevelt's death, succeeding Presidents have attempted to keep their Vice-Presidents informed and to utilize their services. In particular, President Eisenhower encouraged his Vice-President to engage in a variety of activities. While he was Vice-President, Richard Nixon traveled to fifty-four countries, addressed various organized groups, campaigned for political candidates, met with party leaders, and attended meetings of the Cabinet and the National Security Council. Under Presidents Kennedy, Johnson, and Nixon, the Vice-Presidents have engaged in similar activities, although less extensively than under Eisenhower.

When Vice-President Spiro T. Agnew resigned from office on October 10, 1973, and pleaded nolo contendere—no contest—to a 1967 tax fraud charge, the Twenty-fifth Amendment was invoked for the first time. Section 2 of the Amendment provides: "Whenever there is a vacancy in the office of Vice President, the President shall nominate a Vice President who shall take office upon confirmation by a majority vote of both Houses of Congress." On October 12,

President Nixon nominated House Republican Leader Gerald R. Ford from Michigan to replace Agnew, and on December 6, the House followed the Senate's action and overwhelmingly confirmed the nomination. Nine months later Mr. Ford became "Mr. President" on August 9, 1974—the first nonelected American President in history—climaxing two years of Watergate and a week of unprecedented events. Four months later, Nelson A. Rockefeller was sworn in as Vice-President on December 19, after Congress confirmed his nomination.

Faced by a hostile Congress where impeachment was certain in the House and conviction was likely in the Senate and an adverse decision of the Supreme Court (*U.S. v. Nixon,* July 24) over his right to withhold the White House tapes subpoenaed by Special Prosecutor Leon Jaworski, President Nixon released transcripts of conversations of July 23, 1972, only six days after the Watergate break-in, which clearly involved him in the coverup. Immediately, his former supporters began to join the pro-impeachment forces. On the evening of August 7, House Minority Leader, John J. Rhodes, Senate Minority Leader, Hugh Scott, and Senator Barry Goldwater met with the President. The agonizing decision to resign followed this meeting. On the evening of August 8, President Nixon announced his resignation—another historic first—in a televised speech to the world. The morning of August 9, President Nixon and his family emotionally bade farewell to the Cabinet and the White House staff and enplaned for San Clemente; Secretary of State Kissinger received Nixon's letter of resignation about 11:30 a.m.; and Ford was sworn in as the thirty-eighth President minutes before by Chief Justice Warren E. Burger. An "active-negative" President's term had ended; the country was ready for a change; and President Ford, though ideologically similar to Nixon, offered America the prospect of a more positive presidential personality and style.

PERSONALITY AND STYLE IN THE WHITE HOUSE

The personality, style, and concept of the office that each President brings to the White House affect the nature of his presidency.[7] Thomas Jefferson thought of the presidency as "a splendid misery." Some Presidents, such as Franklin Roosevelt and John Kennedy, brought great vigor and vitality to the job; they seemed to enjoy being President. Theodore Roosevelt saw the Chief Executive as "a steward of the people" and believed that it was not only his right but his duty to do anything that the needs of the nation demanded, unless such action was forbidden by the Constitution or by the laws.[8] Abraham Lincoln and Franklin Roosevelt went even further, contending that in great emergencies the President could exercise almost unlimited power to preserve the nation.

---

[7] See James David Barber, *The Presidential Character: Predicting Performance in the White House* (Englewood Cliffs, N.J.: Prentice-Hall, 1972).

[8] Arthur Bernon Tourtellot, *The Presidents on the Presidency* (Garden City, N.Y.: Doubleday, 1964), pp. 55, 56.

Cartoon by Pierotti. Reprinted by permission of *New York Post.* © 1973, New York Post Corporation.

Louis W. Koenig classifies Presidents as "literalist" (Madison, Buchanan, Taft, and Eisenhower) and "strong" (Washington, Jackson, Lincoln, Wilson, and the Roosevelts), adding that many Presidents fall somewhere in the middle. A literalist President closely obeys the letter of the Constitution; while a strong President, who generally excels in times of crisis and change, interprets his constitutional powers as liberally as needed.[9]

James MacGregor Burns develops three basic models of presidential government. He retains the literalist classification and labels it the "Madisonian model." But he divides the strong President classification into two models: the Hamiltonian and the Jeffersonian. The Hamiltonian model utilizes all of the powers granted by the Constitution and adds those which can be "implied" from the Constitution. To these powers is added "inherent" powers which include all of the old prerogatives of the king or those powers inherent in being

[9] Louis W. Koenig, *The Chief Executive* (New York: Harcourt, Brace & World, 1968), pp. 10–12.

a sovereign state. Hamilton added even another power, which results from a combination of all the foregoing powers. The "resulting" powers of the Hamiltonian model thus build upon the others and augment them. The Hamiltonian model calls for strong, personal leadership. Its weakness, according to Burns, is not only its dependence on the personal leadership factor, but also its short-range goals.

The Jeffersonian model is based on majority rule and strong presidential leadership. Although the President, shares his powers with party leaders in this model, his base of power is larger and his influence with Congress is greater. The model, according to Burns, includes long-range goals, which, along with the broad base of democratic support, makes it potentially the most powerful model. Burns suggested to President Kennedy that he fashion his presidency after the Jeffersonian model.[10]

A President's personality and approach to the office may leave a more lasting impression than his substantive accomplishments or failures. Eisenhower's golf, Kennedy's youth and glamour, Johnson's cowpuncher image all say something about how they occupied the office of President. President Nixon may be remembered more for the way he reacted to the Watergate scandal than for his positive initiatives in foreign affairs.

A prerequisite to achievement in the presidency is style. "For style is a crucial element in the Presidency: without the ability to lead, to inspire, to release potential energies and create a sense of hope, a President seems lacking in something vital to the office." [11] Given the problems that face the nation today, a President must also act. The President, along with the Vice-President, is the only official of the American government elected by all of the people, the only person who represents the people as a whole and who can symbolize their aspirations. He can be the greatest force for national unity—or disunity. He can recognize the demands of minorities for social justice or he can repress their rights. He can lead the nation into war or preserve the peace. Such is his power that he leaves his indelible mark on the times, with the result that the triumph or tragedy of each presidency is, in some measure at least, the triumph or tragedy of America.

[10] James MacGregor Burns, *Presidential Government: The Crucible of Leadership* (New York: Avon Books, 1967).
[11] "The Kennedy Years: What Endures?" *Newsweek*, February 1, 1971.

9
THE LEGISLATIVE PROCESS

"Morris (Mo) Udall arrived in Congress from Arizona's horse latitudes in 1961, replacing his brother, Stewart, who had become Secretary of the Interior for John F. Kennedy. The Udalls are an old political family, furnishing Arizona with legislators and judges, and before Mo was out of grammar school in St. Johns village he was thinking of the law and Congress."[1]

Morris Udall, likeable, competent, a former basketball star and student body president at the University of Arizona, became involved in liberal causes shortly after his arrival in Washington, and began to attack some of the anachronisms of the American political system—especially the seniority system in Congress. Seniority places Congressmen in positions of power, not because of their competence but because of the length of time served continuously on one of the congressional committees or in party leadership positions. Udall believed that system no longer served the interests of the nation.

Following the Democratic conflicts and problems of the Chicago convention in 1968, the Democratic Party was flat on its back and not particularly helped by the old Speaker of the House, John McCormack. But the House has never been noted for "killing its kings." However, Morris Udall believed the issues facing the nation were of such importance that the system in Congress should be changed and the Speaker challenged. Udall informed McCormack that he would run against him in the Democratic caucus. Udall did as he said he would, and was defeated by the thumping margin of 178 to 58, even though he had eighty-one "firm" pledges and afterward upwards of a hundred colleagues whispered they had voted for him! (The inexplicable mystery to every losing

---

[1] Larry King, "The Road to Power in Congress: The Education of Mo Udall—And What it Cost," *Harpers Magazine,* June, 1971. The quotes and much of the substance about this struggle for power involving House leadership positions are from Mr. King's interesting article.

candidate is how he could have lost in light of the many people who offer the following condolence: "Sorry you lost. I voted for you!")

When the scandals of influence peddling by members of the Speaker's staff caused the "old man" to step aside and not seek reelection in 1970, it became apparent that Udall had won a "moral victory." Some of Udall's fiery liberal followers urged him to challenge Carl Albert, the former Majority Leader and heir apparent for the vacated Speaker's position. But Udall replied: "Carl's in line, he's respected, and I think he'll do a good job."

Udall turned instead to win the seat Albert would be leaving, that of Majority Leader. His chief opponent was the late Hale Boggs from Louisiana, who had been Majority Whip for nine years and had patiently been inching up the ladder of in-House politics—and power. Knowing Boggs would be a formidable foe, Udall studied previous leadership fights, developed a "good guy" image, maintained "extensive personal contact," circulating in all of the social gatherings, and collected around him loyal supporters who would actively campaign for him.

Both of the major contenders had weaknesses which could be turned against them, but Udall had challenged tradition and had "ruined old John McCormack." Another Udall minus developed when James O'Hara, a serious-minded liberal from Michigan, announced his candidacy. But this was offset when a small group of Southerners, who distrusted Boggs, persuaded Bernie Sisk from California, a moderate liberal grown conservative over the years, to seek the position. A fifth candidate, the vitriolic Wayne Hays from Ohio, also announced. With five candidates in the race, the balance seemed to be tipped in favor of Udall.

The political strategies and maneuvering involved in such a contest are exceedingly complex. How do you deal with the members of the House who represent different regions from all over America, who have different interests, and who hold different ideas on nearly every issue—with only the label "Democrat" in common? What about the freshman Democrats? And the "old bulls" of the House? How do you play the press, especially the *New York Times* and the *Washington Post,* which influence congressmen even about their own organizational matters? What about the lobbyists for labor and other powerful interest groups? What favors does a candidate have to distribute? Who should give the nominating and seconding speeches?

The Tuesday morning of the balloting for Majority Leader the marble hall dividing the Speaker's rooms from the House chamber was alive with all sorts of people. In the chamber, the candidates greeted colleagues, consulted their loyalists, and tried to avoid each other. On the first ballot Boggs had ninety-five votes, Udall sixty-nine, Sisk thirty-one, Hays twenty-eight, and O'Hara twenty-five. Hays and O'Hara withdrew, and Udall's thought, "I've had it," was confirmed as the second ballot was reported: Boggs one-hundred and forty, Udall eighty-eight, and Sisk seventeen.

The Library of Congress

The Capitol in 1861. Abraham Lincoln, guarded by sharpshooters stationed around the unfinished dome, delivers his first inaugural address.

Monkmeyer Press Photo Service

The Capitol today.

Among the postmortems, Gary Hymel, assistant to Boggs, remarked: "Many of Udall's people were amateurs when it came to in-house politics. They didn't count very well. Hale Boggs has spent many years counting votes. He's been on the inside, with the leadership and part of the leadership, and that helps you develop a sensitive feel for internal matters. You don't learn this place overnight." Congressman Boggs and his staff worked hard and touched all bases to win the votes. Being on the leadership ladder was important, and the traditional patterns of power worked to Boggs's advantage.

With the twenty-twenty vision that hindsight brings, Udall saw clearly what had defeated him:

I was defeated by a combination of defecting freshmen, labor, and liberals, with ten to fifteen years in the House. Labor hurt me badly, though Ive been with them much more than not. I could just never bring myself to jump like labor commands. The leadership ladder bit—tradition, promotion, seniority—was stronger medicine than I originally thought. This House apparently just insists on people getting in line, serving time. Boggs played the freshmen like a virtuoso: he could pass out more goodies than I. He had people all over Washington—lawyers and lobbyists and bureaucrats—dating back to the New Deal, and almost all of them knew somebody to pressure for him.

Udall was denied any of the "goodies" which were given to the "deserving." He campaigned for a seat on the party Ethics Committee, where he thought he could work for reforms in the political process. One afternoon he received a call from the Ways and Means Committee: "Aspinall and Hébert are not quitting. There is no vacancy." "I got the message," Udall told a friend. "There's nothing here for ole Mo. I'm catching on."

Udall and his wife took a short vacation home to Arizona to sit in the sun, play in the sand, and heal his political wounds. He had learned that he could not change the power structure of Congress quickly. His zeal for reform within the system in order that Congress might play a more effective part in meeting the crises of society, however, was not a lost cause. His challenge of the power structure of the House was a part of a larger force for systemic reform of Congress. Pressures in the late 1960's and early 1970's from outside and within Congress slowly began to bring about the reforms for which Udall had fought the battle to become the Majority Leader of the House of Representatives.

ORGANIZATION AND POWER IN CONGRESS

The Congress of the United States is a bicameral body made up of 435 members of the House of Representatives and 100 Senators. It has important functions to fulfill in the American democratic system. The Founding Fathers knew it would be impossible for all Americans, or even for the natural leaders of all communities, to assemble to enact the laws to govern the country, so they provided for a representative system. These representatives of the people determine the policies which govern society through their law-making or legislative powers. In determining what laws or policies are needed for the nation, Congress performs a deliberative function in debating and deliberating on the problems and issues before it. In addition, the Constitution establishes separate branches of government, with shared powers based somewhat on Montesquieu's theory of separation of powers. This system has resulted in each branch of government being able to check the others. Congress therefore has a natural interest in overseeing the executive branch to make certain the laws it enacts are "faithfully executed." In addition to the representative, legislative, deliberative, and executive oversight functions, the Constitution charges Congress with a number of minor roles to perform. Over the years, Congress has developed a system of party leadership, functional standing committees, norms and rules of procedure, and informal situations of power to carry out these functions.

Party Leadership

In his book on congressional government, first published in 1885, Woodrow Wilson maintained that the power of Congress is scattered among committee chairmen or "petty barons," who "exercise an almost despotic sway within their own shires, and sometimes threaten to convulse the realm itself." Although this shot in locating power in Congress is still fairly close to the mark, the position of Majority Leader, which Morris Udall sought, might today be thought of as a "prince of the realm" and the Speaker of the House as a "king" among the "barons, counts, and dukes" of the House of Representatives.

The Constitution states that "The House of Representatives shall choose their Speaker and other officers." The Speaker of the House has always been a powerful officer of the House, even though his power has fluctuated throughout the years. The power of the Speaker reached an apex with the Speakership of Joseph Cannon (1903–10), which was followed by a revolt of the members of the House in 1910–11. The Speaker was stripped of his key power, notably his control over chairmanships and committee assignments and his seat on the powerful Rules Committee. The modern Speaker's power, however, is considerable. He is the presiding officer of the House and, as such, he exercises the power of recognition of speakers on the floor, has some control over the course and timing of debate, with the advice of the parliamentarian, and determines the procedures of floor action. He may assign bills to committees, assist in the scheduling of legislation, and appoint House members to conference committees. In short, the Speaker has the responsibility to see that the House functions smoothly to perform its duties.

Although the Speaker is formally elected by the House, he actually is the choice of the majority party. Each party nominates a candidate in its caucus or conference, which takes place at the beginning of a new Congress following the national election. The majority party candidate is almost always elected Speaker, and the minority party candidate—the losing candidate—becomes the Minority Leader. The majority party also selects the Majority Leader, Majority Whip, assistant or regional whips, and the standing committee chairmen; the minority party's candidate for Speaker becomes the Minority Leader and the party selects minority counterparts of the majority leadership.

The constitutionally designated presiding officer in the Senate is the Vice-President, who occasionally functions in this capacity and can cast a tie-breaking vote. But the majority party selects a President *pro tempore* and the other leaders of the Senate—a Majority Leader, a Majority Whip, assistant whips, and the standing committee chairman. The minority party selects a Minority Leader, a Minority Whip, assistant whips, and ranking minority members of the standing committees.

The power of the party leadership is largely a power of persuasion. The leaders in both parties can count on a core of loyal partisan support on most measures; but the lack of party discipline allows the maverick to stray from party lines, when constituent, committee, or lobbyist pressures or ideological beliefs dictate a different vote. Another limitation on the power of the House leadership is the independent influence on legislative scheduling of the powerful Rules Committee. This committee is often referred to as the "traffic cop" of legislation, but "mortician" might be a better appellation because of the number of bills it "buries." Probably the most significant limitation on the power of the party leadership in both houses is the existence of other leaders, especially the standing committee chairmen.

The Committees

Woodrow Wilson is often quoted as saying that "it is not far from the truth to say that Congress in session is Congress on public exhibition, while Congress in its committee rooms is Congress at work." The committee system is the way Congress divides the huge volume of legislative work which comes before it. The committee members are assigned to each of the twenty-one standing committees in the House and to the seventeen standing committees in the Senate by each party's committee on committees. The majority and minority members of each committee are in proportion to the number of members of each party in each chamber of Congress. The committees vary in power and prestige, with the House Committees of Rules, Ways and Means, Appropriations—the Big Three—and Armed Services and Public Works among those considered most desirable by members. Among the most prestigious committees of the Senate are Foreign Relations, Finance, Judiciary, and Appropriations. The Post Office and Civil Service, and the District of Columbia committees in both chambers are usually considered to be the least desirable committee assignments by members. Congressmen seek assignments to different committees, however, for a variety of different reasons. The Westerner, for example often prefers the Interior Committee; some congressmen may prefer to work for a prestigious committee, while others prefer the quicker route up the seniority ladder in, say, the Veterans Affairs Committee; but all congressmen work hard for committee assignments which will increase their chances of reelection.

"Once a man is assigned to a committee as a freshman," Senator Fred Harris concluded, "he has only to remain alive and get reelected in order to insure that he will one day chair that committee." This process of selection of the powerful chairmen of the standing committees on seniority rather than on competence has prompted much criticism. Those who have benefited most from the seniority system are those politicians who come from safe districts. In times past the safest, no-contest areas have been in the South. When the Democrats are in the majority in Congress, as they have been with only two exceptions since 1932, the committee leadership is dominated by congressmen from the South. In the Ninety-third Congress, nine of seventeen Senate chairmen and twelve of twenty-one House chairmen were from the South. These southern chairmen were all nominally Democrats; but on certain issues, such as civil rights and other liberal issues, many of them voted with the conservative Republican opposition.

According to Barbara Hinckley, the criticism of the seniority system on the grounds that it rewards politicians with the safest seats—the safest seats being from the South—is not quite accurate. "Safeness is not an exclusively southern or rural phenomenon," she maintains. "It is enjoyed by approximately fifty percent of congressmen from all regions and population densities." Based on a comparison of the membership and the leadership positions in Congress during a twenty-year span (1947–66), she concludes that "leadership posts are distributed quite equitably for the Republican party and less so, yet approximately proportionately, for the Democratic party." She admits that there is a slight imbalance of southern Democratic chairmen in both the House and the Senate. On the charge of wide ideological variance from party positions, she adds: "While some conservative bias is observable for the Democrats, basically the seniority system distributes leadership posts in accord with *traditional party strength*." [2]

Hinckley believes that the critics have overstated their case, feels that the seniority system is a practical system that works, and wonders if there is an alternative that would be better. Her position is held by many Congressmen, who repeat the old joke: "The longer I'm here the more I like the seniority system." Critics claim that even one or two chairmen like Howard Smith, the Representative from Virginia who chaired the Rules Committee, would justify a change in the system. Any time Smith did not want to consider a piece of legislation he would go "inspect his barn" on his Virginia farm and the committee would not

---

[2] Barbara Hinckley, *Stability and Change in Congress* (New York: Harper & Row, 1971), pp. 75–79.

meet; Congress could not act on that bill; and the legislative mill ground to a halt.

Among the numerous critics of the seniority system, Robert Sherrill points out that it is a tradition that is not very old. "Seniority is treated with far more hallowed respect as a custom than it deserves," he maintains. "Although the rule of seniority has been almost ironclad since the Second World War, before then it was violated a great deal." [3]

Winds of change have been blowing against this "hallowed custom." The ironclad quality of the seniority system and the ironclad rule of the chairmen have prompted such citizen lobbies as Common Cause and Nader's Raiders to demand a change in the seniority system. Help from the inside brought about a crack in the system in 1971, when the Republicans adopted the policy in the House of Representatives of requiring the ranking minority members to stand for reelection at the beginning of a new Congress. The Democratic Party required prospective chairmen to stand for election beginning with the Ninety-third Congress (1973–74). In the Senate, both parties moved a step closer to electing their chairmen on merit; again, the Republicans took the lead.

In January, 1975, as the Ninety-fourth Congress was organized, three southern House chairmen were replaced by the Democratic caucus: Henry S. Reuss of Wisconsin became the chairman of the Banking and Currency Committee in place of Wright Patman of Texas; Thomas S. Foley of Washington replaced W. R. Poage of Texas as chairman of the Agricultural Committee; and Melvin Price from Illinois succeeded F. Edward Hebert of Louisiana, chairman of Armed Services. Senate Democrats on January 17, 1975, voted to select committee chairmen by secret ballot whenever one-fifth of the caucus requested it. Senator Dick Clark of Iowa, a sponsor of the reform measure, said he did not expect "removal of sitting chairmen next time, but there's a message there."

Another aspect of committee work which reformers have worked hard at changing is the amount of secrecy that has shrouded the public's business. The Legislative Reorganization Act of 1970 was aimed in part at opening committee meetings. Senate and House Committees were to be open unless closed by a majority vote of the committee members. Secrecy continued. Forty percent of all committee meetings in 1972 were held in secret. During the Ninety-second Congress, the House Appropriations Committee held ninety-two percent of its meetings in secret.[4] Rules changes in 1973 in both the House and the Senate encouraged open mark-up sessions—where members work through the details of bills to be presented to the full chamber—and in 1973–74, the House closed only eight percent and the Senate closed twenty-five percent of their committee sessions.

[3] Robert Sherrill, *Why They Call It Politics: A Guide to American Government* (New York: Harcourt Brace Jovanovich, 1972), pp. 91, 92.

[4] Congressional Quarterly, *Current American Government, Spring 1973* (Washington, D.C.: Congressional Quarterly, 1973), pp. 84–86.

The conference committees have been the most secretive of all in recent sessions of Congress. In 1974, however, twelve open conferences were held; the most important and controversial was on S425 to regulate strip mining. The experiment apparently worked well, and the House Democratic caucus approved a proposal by Dante B. Fascell of Florida to open all conferences except when either the House or Senate conferees voted in open session to close them. An identical resolution was offered successfully in the Senate Democratic caucus and in the Republican conference.

Norms and Power in Congress

Congress is a system of its own wherein certain patterns of action have developed and certain norms have evolved governing the conduct of its members. One of the norms already discussed is that of seniority. Freshmen representatives and senators are expected to be "seen and not heard," like chilren in the family; to do their homework, take their cues from the more seasoned members, and start as an apprentice—or possibly as a protégé—and unobtrusively move up in seniority.

Congressmen cannot know everything about the congressional system. Even senior members are sometimes woefully ignorant of practices, rules, or procedures outside of their own committee assignments. This is of no great concern to the leadership, as senators and representatives are expected to specialize and stay out of other areas. Seniority and specialization complement each other. Wilbur Mills, the former Chairman of the House Ways and Means Committee, spoke with authority on tax legislation not only because of his seniority and chairmanship; because of his long service in this area, he knew more about taxes than anyone else in Congress.

Seniority and specialization result in another norm which is commonly called "log rolling." This is a matter of reciprocity, in which members support each other's specialty interests. In the private exchanges between congressmen, a typical comment along this line might be: "I'll support your shrub research center, if you will vote for my cranberry bill." Loyalty is expected among committee members in support of programs in Congress, and many congressmen vote as their committee decides. Loyalty to the House or Senate leadership may conflict with a member's political views or his loyalty to his constituency. The usual road to power, however, is by playing the game. Sanctions may be applied to the uncooperative. The individualist may be isolated, refused recognition on the floor, denied a desired committee seat, and even censored.

There are some, however, who violate these norms of Congress and still rise to positions of power. Senator William Proxmire from Wisconsin is a classic example. Senator Proxmire simply could not be unobtrusive and run with the herd. He talked on all subjects, offered amendments to bills out of his committee areas, filibustered on measures he did not like, and participated in a variety of "unacceptable" activities during his first year in the Senate. He is a self-admitted maverick, but one with power. True, the opportunity for individualism is more likely in the Senate than in the House, but there are also certain nonconformists in the House who have built positions of power. Obviously, there are factors of powers in both chambers that are not strictly based on the norms.

Nevertheless, seniority is unquestionably the surest stepping-stone to power in Congress. Another source of power is found in the connections a member has with the "Congressional Establishment"—the powerful in Congress. The power of personality may push those who are so endowed up the power hierarchy. Some congressmen are far more intellectually capable than others and are able to gain more influence because of their wits. Some have Machiavellian instincts which make the quest for power natural for them. The most powerful members of Congress often have a combination of part or all of these factors.

A committee chairmanship may enhance the power of an individual, but the power of the person also may increase the power of the committee. The Ways and Means Committee is significantly more powerful since the chairmanship of Wilbur Mills. Of course, the power of Mills with Presidents, pressure groups, party leaders, and even foreign governments is legendary. "He has consolidated his clout by skilled Machiavellian maneuvering," reports the Nader Congress Project. "When he became chairman in 1958, he abolished all subcommittees and concentrated all the power in his own hands. He keeps junior committee members starved for information. They sometimes learn about hearings—such as those on tax treatment of single and married people, for only one example—by reading about them in the morning newspapers." [5]

In theory, the rest of the House could repudiate Mills's bills; but because of the closed rule on any tax matter reported out of his committee, the members must either accept a bill without amendments or reject it. In 1971, during the lunch hour with few representatives on the floor, Mills pushed through by a voice vote a revenue act which reduced corporate taxes by $7.5 billion, an action which is illustrative of his power, his techniques, and the importance of the public matters he and his committee handle. When Mills was bitten by the "Presidential bug," a colleague questioned: "Why do you want to be President when you already run the country from Capitol Hill?"

A changing cycle may alter the position of an "isolated" Senator into one of power. Senator Edmund S. Muskie, for example, was assigned to the Air and Water Pollution subcommittee of the Public Works Committee. When environmental issues turned up at the top of the nation's priority list, Muskie was at the top with them. Another example is the case of Senator Sam Ervin, Jr., of North Carolina. He had been pecking away on the Separation of Powers subcommittee of the Judiciary Committee, developing an enviable expertise on constitutional principles, when the presidential-congressional controversy which flared up in 1972–73 over presidential impoundment of funds versus the "power of

[5] Mark J. Green, James M. Fallows, and David R. Zwick, *Who Runs Congress? The President, Big Business, or You?* (New York: Bantam Books, 1972), p. 73.

the purse" of Congress, the question of executive privilege versus the power of Congress to obtain testimony in its hearings, and the Watergate affair all came to the forefront of national concern. Ervin came to the forefront too.

Representative Richard Bolling of Missouri was quickly marked for a position of power in the House because of his keen intellect—buttressed by other power-producing qualities. In the Ninety-third Congress, he served as the Chairman of the Select Committee on Committees, and was a powerful member of the powerful Rules Committee. He is the author of *House Out of Order* and *Power in the House,* each a study of the House of Representatives. Senator Robert C. Byrd from West Virginia, the Senate Democratic Whip, won this position when he challenged Senator Edward Kennedy in the Democratic caucus because the other senators recognized his competence, his hard work, and his influential manner. Congressman John McFall from California, the Majority Whip of the Ninety-third Congress, was selected in part because of his intellectual abilities.

Subcommittee chairmen, at times, develop more power than their committee chairmen or than chairmen of other committees with similar functional responsibilities. One of the best examples of this situation is found in the House Appropriations Committee with Representative Jamie Whitten of Mississippi, who chairs the Agriculture–Environmental and Consumer Protection subcommittee. That his power surpasses that of Congressman W. R. Poage of Texas, who is the chairman of the Agriculture Committee, is best illustrated by the statement of former Secretary of Agriculture Orville Freeman: "I have two bosses—Lyndon Johnson and Jamie Whitten." The Nader Congress Project assesses Whitten's power as follows:

Jamie Whitten, to the American consumer, environmentalist, and farmer is the most powerful subcommittee chairman in Congress. A courtly Southern Democrat from the hill country of northern Mississippi, Whitten has parlayed his thirty-two-year seniority in the House into an astonishing array of key committee posts on the House Appropriations Committee. . . . He is the chairman of the Appropriations subcommittee which has financial control over the $7 billion farm budget, the Environmental Protection Agency, the Food and Drug Administration, the Council on Environmental Quality, and the consumer protection programs of the Federal Trade Commission. "Everyone is terrified of Whitten," reports one leader of a conservation group. . . . When EPA chief William Ruckelshaus came before Whitten's subcommittee last year, the congressman observed, "Mr. Ruckelshaus, I feel sorry for you. Congress has given you far more power than a good man would want or a bad man should have or that any ten men could handle." Ruckelshaus could have said the same of Mr. Whitten, but didn't.[6]

An interesting test over who really runs the House of Representatives took place in October, 1972, over the bill to increase the public debt limit which had a provision to grant President Nixon authority to limit spending to $250 billion.

[6] *Who Runs Congress,* pp. 79–81.

The Speaker of the House, Carl Albert from Oklahoma, and the Chairman of the Appropriations Committee, George Mahon of Texas, were opposed to the bill and favored an amendment offered by Mahon which would grant the spending limit, but would require the President to submit his proposed spending cuts to Congress for approval. Wilbur Mills, from Arkansas, Chairman of the Ways and Means Committee, opposed the Mahon Amendment and favored passage of the bill. The Republicans essentially sat back and watched the fight. Mills referred to the Mahon Amendment as nothing more than "cotton candy"—without substance—and stressed the problems of inflation and other economic problems. Mahon considered the bill without his amendment an abdication of the constitutional powers of Congress over revenue matters. Albert relinquished the Speaker's chair, came down on the floor, and made an impassioned plea for the Mahon Amendment. At the end of his last speech, Mills shifted from his economic arguments to his real motive:

I am not exaggerating the situation, Mr. Chairman, I am trying to be brutally frank with my colleagues. I just say, as others have said, the political part of this worries me greatly. I have been fighting to do everything I can to keep Carl Albert, the Speaker of the House, in that chair where you sit in the next Congress.

If we abdicate here any willingness to join in controlling spending and thereby reducing the inflationary pressures, all in the world that the President has to do is to go before the American people on television and ask for a Congress as a result of the vote on November 7, a Congress that will cooperate with him in getting control of spending and in doing something about inflation.

I tell you—you are playing with your own political lives and destinies when you vote for the Mahon amendment. I hope it will be voted down.[7]

A teller vote was called for on the Mahon Amendment. Mills turned so he could see each member who voted for the amendment. The amendment lost 216 to 167. Among these power barons—all senior members from the South—it is obvious who ruled the House of Representatives before the "Tidal basin episode" with Fanny Foxe began to erode Mills's power.

THE REPRESENTATIVE FUNCTION

When populations are large, it is clear that not all citizens can gather to deliberate issues important to them all and collectively make decisions for their welfare. The public is forced to delegate its power to a smaller, more functional group of citizens who will represent their interests. The smaller group, in this case the Congress, assumes the public trust; and each congressman theoretically should act on behalf of that segment of the public who elected him.

The taxpayers of America pay a handsome price for this representation. True, the $42,500 salary paid to representatives and senators is not exorbi-

---

[7] *Congressional Record*, 92nd Congress, 2nd Session, October 10, 1972, pp. H9359–9400.

tant—probably low compared to comparable positions in business and industry—but the operational costs of the legislative branch of the national government are estimated to total $607 million in 1974. Each congressman is provided with office space in Washington, D.C., and up to two offices in his home district; an allowance to cover the salaries of his staff members; an allowance for stationery, office equipment, telephone and telegraph service, and stamps (free mailing privileges are known as the "franking privilege"); a designated number of publicly paid trips to his home district; use of folding rooms for packaging mail (and nearly anything else), printing shops, and recording studios; and use of the Library of Congress, with its invaluable legislative reference service, to assist the congressman in fulfilling his representative and other responsibilities.

In addition, there are numerous fringe benefits such as dining halls, underground tram service to the Capitol building from the office buildings, swimming pools, gymnasiums, steam baths, health service, ice and carbonated water, flowers and plants from the National Botanical Gardens, and a variety of other services to make the congressman's work in Washington more pleasant. There is a pension plan to which the congressman contributes that can return as much as $31,875 a year to the thirty-year man upon his retirement.

Now how does the congressman serve his constituents and the taxpayers? The relationship between the trustee (the legislator) and the trustor (the constituent) is not clearly understood by both parties. Four fundamental views exist which suggest the nature of the legislator-constituent relationship. The first view, espoused by Edmund Burke, says the legislator is a free agent who makes his decisions on the basis of his own convictions. The role of legislator is interpreted in terms of what the congressman or senator feels or "knows" is best for his constituents. Burke called this view "virtual representation." The second view differs significantly by suggesting that the legislator reflects the opinions of the constituents, irrespective of his own convictions. This view requires, of course, that the legislator knows the *will* of his constituency. The third view is considerably more flexible. It suggests the legislator changes the manner in which he executes his responsibilities as the issues change. On one issue he may solely reflect the views of the people and on another issue he will act on the basis of his own convictions. A fourth view is that of the legislator as partisan, in which he does the bidding of his partisan supporters.

Theoretically, representation by members of Congress is an extremely important political principle. But here again some profound changes have taken place through the years. Perhaps the most significant among these changes is the ever-increasing problem the elected official has of knowing the "will" or interest of his constituency. On the majority of issues pending before Congress, the public's apathy is huge, while its information level is low. Many of these issues are foreign to the daily experiences of the citizen and fall outside of even his casual interest. Other issues are emotion-laden. Here, interest is high, information varies, and the debate is heated. Still other issues do not arouse general public interest but ignite serious conflicts among private interest groups. Under these conditions, the member of Congress is at a loss to know what his constituency wants, and he is left to his own devices.

Since reading the public's mind is such a difficult task, frequently the mail received by congressmen and senators is the only key they have to the constituency's feelings. However, a close examination of the patterns in constituency mail reveals the idiosyncratic nature of it. There are the "regulars" who write every week on every issue, the solicited writers who send letters because their boss or union leaders require it, the uninformed mailers, and the crackpot mailers. These sources of mail are not representative of the constituency and therefore yield little if any valuable information. Even the letters that are motivated by sincere concern over public issues do not represent the true feelings of a congressman's constituency, and there is no way to balance or weigh all letters and come out with the people's will. Irrespective of the mail's quality, a future-oriented member of Congress answers all the letters dutifully, indicating his thanks for the constituent's interest and for his "valuable" suggestion or opinion, and concluding by saying he will take it under advisement (which is probably a "safe" response).

The greatest single importance of the exchange of mail between legislator and constituent is the use to which the legislator puts his response. He *uses* his reply to gain favor with the constituent. He wants to impress the citizen with his openness and responsiveness, with his familiarity with the subject, his dedication to the job, and his commitment to taking the constituent's suggestions under advisement. Thus, the return mail has high political payoff possibilities for the public official. But, there are a few members of Congress who have returned year after year to the Capitol who never take the mail seriously. On one occasion, a senior senator, Stephen M. Young of Ohio, related his policy toward crackpot mail. He would simply return the letter to its sender with the comment that he thought the sender should know some "crackpot" was using his name and address to send out absolutely foolish mail.

In representing his constituents, the member of Congress often feels he knows the desires of his district without any formal communication, because the district is his home; he goes home as often as possible and talks to people; he is interested in and visits projects in his district; and he studies the needs of his district. As one congressman said, "I would have been defeated in the last election, if I didn't know the desires of my district." This notion of an intuitive "feel" for the district has defeated many congressmen, however, when they were really out of touch with the home people and did not realize it.

The congressman deals daily and directly with public problems. His constituents are largely passive—the attentive ones are probably organized and have a lobbyist knocking on his door—and may not have any views, or any sound ones, about many public issues. The congressman, on the other hand, may have differing, but better, positions from his constituents as a result of his studying the issues. This raises another view concerning the representative function—that of its educational responsibility. This educational, or informational, responsibility goes far beyond routine letters of response to constituent mail. Some congressmen perform this educational role quite effectively in their newsletters, editorials and news releases, media broadcasts, tapes, messages on recorded telephone services, and in personal and staff participation in meetings, forums, and other educational settings. Congressman Morris Udall's newsletters are classic and penetrating analyses of the public issues facing America, and they are designed to help satisfy this educational approach to the representative function.

Numerous communications with congressmen request service. People seek advice, favors, information, government publications, and help with problems they have with the governmental agencies. Much of the time of a congressman's staff is spent in fulfilling this service role. One of the most important members of the congressman's staff is a competent, effective caseworker, who knows the intricacies of the bureaucratic process and can get help for the constituent. The problem might come from the mayor of a small town needing assistance to get his grant for the city water system from the regional office of the Department of Housing and Urban Development. It might be from a rancher who has a problem with the Bureau of Land Management over grazing permits. It might be a student who did not receive his GI Bill check for the month.

Most congressmen want to perform such chores for their constituents. The problem is how to divide their time between legislation and running errands. Representative F. Edward Hébert from Louisiana has this philosophy, developed over his long years in office:

I was elected to legislate, but I'm lucky to spend ten percent of my time at it. I spend the other ninety percent giving services to my constituents. The Congressman is a doorman to the big government bureaucracies in Washington. He opens the door to let in the constituent who has a perfect right to get in by himself but is often kept out by the bureaucrats. The big tycoon pays up to $100,000 a year to have someone here looking after his interests. The little guy pays only his taxes. Yet the high-salaried lobbyist can't accomplish for the tycoon what one lowly Congressman can do for his petitioners.[8]

THE LEGISLATIVE PROCESS

The major responsibility of a member of Congress, as Representative Hébert indicated, is to determine the public policies of the country through lawmaking—the legislative process. Legislation is probably the supreme act of representation. The idea of a bill may come from a constituent, the congressman, a

[8] Jack Anderson and Carl Kalvelage, *American Government . . . Like It Is* (Morristown, N.J.: General Learning Corporation, 1972), pp. 12, 13.

pressure group, or the executive branch of the government; the bill may propose to increase social security benefits, to provide a national health insurance program, to exclude billboards from the freeways, to regulate strip mining, to establish an all-volunteer army, to send men to the moon, or to create innumerable other special programs; the sum total of all measures enacted into law by the 535 members of Congress constitutes American national policy.

Sources and Introduction of Bills

Drafts of bills, and ideas for possible legislation, come from many different sources. The major sources of legislation are as follows:

First, and perhaps most obvious, is the representative or senator himself. A member of Congress may develop ideas for legislation during the course of his own campaign for election or reelection. Also, a member may originate a proposal out of recognition of the need for action regarding a public problem, or for amendment or repeal of outdated laws.

A second general source of legislation is the member's constituents, and other interested voters. This category may include individuals and small groups acting on their own accord; but more often it includes the activities of large, formal organizations which seek to influence congressional decision making in a manner favorable to their own interests. Economic interests (e.g., labor unions, business and manufacturer's associations, and agricultural organizations); professional groups (law, medical, and educational groups); religious and humanitarian groups; ideologically-oriented groups; veterans' organizations; and ethnic and minority groups pressure members of Congress to sponsor bills which they frequently have all drafted to be introduced. All of these groups, and many others, avail themselves of the right to transmit legislative proposals to their elected representatives. Since the members of Congress cannot be expected to know all of the details regarding every problem or proposal, they often depend upon interest groups such as these to furnish important information and statistical data.

It may be said that any subject upon which Congress legislates is a subject upon which a segment of the public may organize to express itself, since most congressional actions affect favorably or unfavorably a significant number of citizens or groups. That this is so is indicated by the third major source of legislation: the executive branch of government. The President is a major initiator of legislation. In his State of the Union address and in other oral and written communications, the President sets forth a general program of legislation which he desires Congress to enact. The President's cabinet members, or the independent regulatory agencies and bureaus, may also initiate legislation regarding issues which fall within their jurisdiction. The most important specific communication from the executive branch is the President's annual budget message to Congress. The budget message is the blueprint for the President's legislative program. The legislative proposals contained in the budget message will be sponsored by the President's congressional party and will be followed up by the congressional liaison officers in the White House and departments or agencies.

With the increasing complexity of relationships between the national government and the state and local governments, many legislative proposals also come from the state or local level. The mayors of large cities, for instance, have on occasion organized to express their desires regarding federal financial grants to urban areas.

Proposals introduced into Congress may be categorized into four principal forms: the bill, the joint resolution, the concurrent resolution, and the simple resolution. The bill is by far the most common form of legislation. Bills may originate in either house of Congress—with the exception of revenue bills which, as provided by Article I, Section 7, of the Constitution, must originate in the House of Representatives. A bill originating in the House of Representatives is designated by the initials "H. R." followed by a number. A bill originating in the Senate is designated by the letter "S" plus its number.

Joint resolutions may also originate in either house of Congress, and they become law in the same manner as bills. Legislation may originate as a bill and later be amended by way of joint resolutions. Such a resolution originating in the House of Representatives is designated by "H. J. Res." followed by a number; one beginning in the Senate is designated "S. J. Res." plus a number. These resolutions are not as numerous as bills, and usually deal with more temporary matters; but they have the same legal force once enacted into law.

A concurrent resolution usually concerns a matter affecting the operations of both houses of Congress. These resolutions are not normally legislative in character, and are not the equivalent of a bill or a joint resolution. They are used merely for expressing facts, principles, opinions, or purposes of the two houses, and are not transmitted to the President for action. They are designated "H. Con. Res." or "S. Con. Res." plus a number, according to where they originated.

Simple resolutions, finally, are addressed only to matters affecting the operations of either chamber alone. They are designated "H. Res." or "S. Res." plus a number, and are considered only by the chamber in which they originate. The House of Representatives, for example, provided for electronic voting in its chamber by passing H. Res. 1123 on October 13, 1972; and a committee amendment made electronic voting effective on January 3, 1973.

Any member of Congress may introduce a legislative proposal. In the House of Representatives, this is done by placing the proposal in the "hopper," a box at the side of the clerk's desk in the House Chamber. In the Senate, a Senator gains the recognition of the presiding officer, states that he is offering a bill for introduction, and then presents it to the Secretary of the Senate.

Committee Action

The most intensive consideration of a proposal takes place in the appropriate committee, to which it is assigned after being introduced. The Parliamentarian of the House, or the President of the Senate, refers a bill to the committee,

210 *Public Policy Makers*

which has jurisdiction over the bill's subject matter. In addition to twenty-one standing (permanent) committees in the House of Representatives and eighteen in the Senate, there are standing joint committees of both chambers, as well as several select or special committees.

The chairman of the committee to which a bill is referred may, in turn, refer it to one of his subcommittees (most committees contain two or more subcommittees). If a bill is significantly important or controversial, the committee may hold public hearings at which representatives of interested organizations or government agencies are invited to testify. Committee sessions are open to the public unless closed by a majority vote of the committee. The committee has virtual life-or-death power over bills which are sent its way. It may "pigeonhole" a bill, failing to report it to the chamber floor for further action; it may

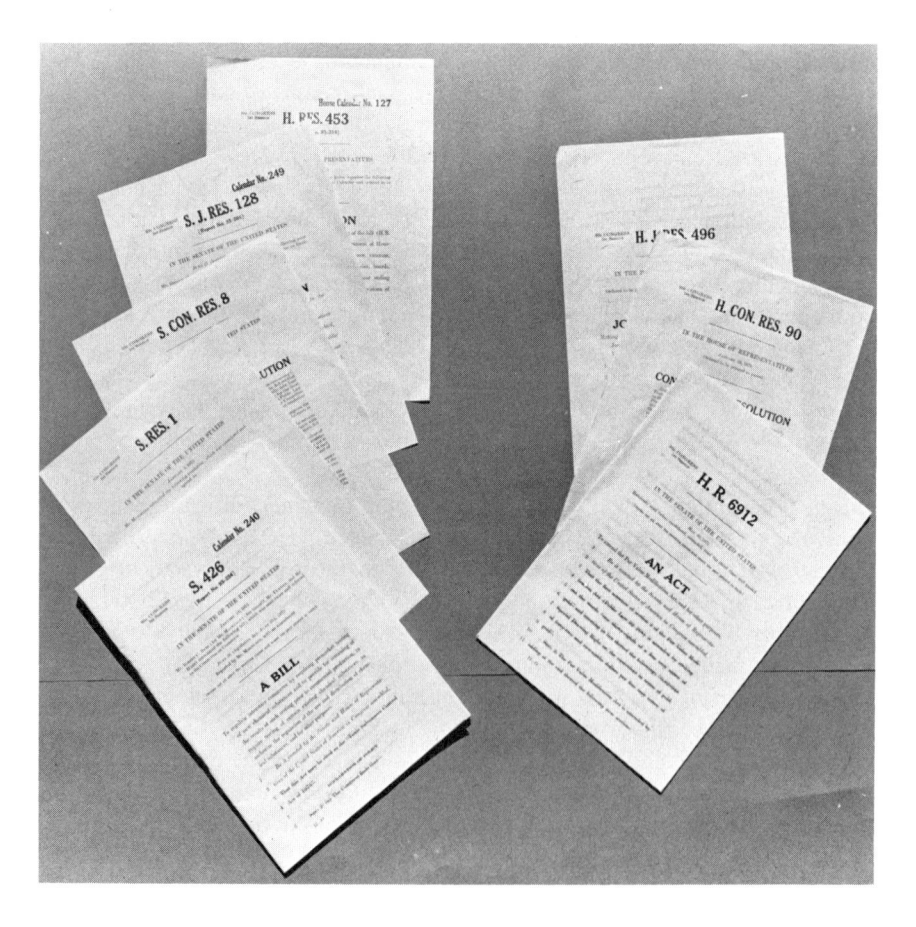

A group of different types of bills showing S. and H. R. numbering

amend or revise the bill; or it may vote to report the bill to the floor without any substantial changes. Because committees kill or pigeon-hole most bills that come before them, and because Congress usually accepts without major change those bills which are reported out to the floor, it is evident that committee work is the key part of the legislative process. It is also evident why interest groups pay particular attention to influencing the committee's decisions.

The Bill Goes to the Floor

A bill may reach the floor of either house if the majority of the committee votes to report it favorably. In this case, it is transmitted together with a report describing its purpose and the reasons for its suggested approval. A bill may also be brought to the floor, in the House of Representatives, if a majority of the members sign a discharge petition. This method, seldom used, is possible only when a committee refuses to report a bill.

In the Senate, the committee phase is over as soon as the majority of a committee votes to report a bill to the floor. In the House, however, the Rules Committee must decide whether, when, and under what conditions a bill, except money bills, may come to the floor. This great power of the Rules Committee is a frequent subject of criticism—at least by those who are ideologically opposed to the Republican-Southern Democratic majority which usually controls this committee. Few bills are held up arbitrarily in this committee, however, and the discharge petition may be used against this committee as well as the others.

Floor Action

Once a committee reports a bill to the floor of the chamber in which it originated, the bill is placed on a "calendar" or a list of pending bills. In the Senate, the policy committee of the majority party—often with the aid of the Minority Leader—establishes the order in which bills will be debated. In the House of Representatives, departures from the calendar are made under the direction of the Rules Committee.

The two main calendars of business in the House of Representatives are the Union Calendar and the House Calendar. The Union Calendar designates the dates for action on public bills, particularly revenue and appropriations bills. The House Calendar pertains to public, nonrevenue, and nonappropriation bills. In addition, there is the Consent Calendar, on which noncontroversial bills may be placed. There is, finally, a Private Calendar, to which bills dealing with private claims and other such private-type legislative matters are referred.

The House of Representatives may transform itself into a Committee of the Whole House on the State of the Union (Committee of the Whole), which enables it to function more informally as one big committee, with a quorum of 100 members instead of the regular majority of 218. This device is usually used for appropriations bills.

Debate on a bill in the House of Representatives is strictly limited because of the large numbers in the House. In the Senate, a tradition exists of unlimited, relatively unregulated debate. This permits use of the filibuster, a device to literally "talk a bill to death" by preventing it from reaching a vote. Liberals and conservatives have both used this technique; and it is defended as a method of protecting minority rights, as well as attacked for being cumbersome and outmoded. Debate in the Senate may be limited somewhat by the "two-speech rule," which allows a member to speak no more than twice on the same subject in one legislative day. Debate on relatively noncontroversial bills may be closed by unanimous consent. Closure on significant legislation, under Rule XXII, required a two-thirds vote of those present. This rule was amended on March 7, 1975, allowing closure by an affirmative vote of three-fifths of all senators.

Reconciliation of Differences: Conferee Action

After the voting in each chamber takes place on a bill, it is seldom that important legislation passes each house in identical form. Where differences are relatively inconsequential, the differences are settled by one or the other of the chambers simply accepting the work of the other. But if differences are more important, or if one or both chambers refuse to compromise, then differences must be settled by a special committee of conferees appointed from both chambers to work out the differences of the bill. The members of this conference committee are appointed by the presiding officers of each chamber from among the senior members of the committees which originally considered the bill. When a conference committee reports a compromise bill, each chamber must accept or reject it as it stands with no further amendment. However, either chamber may send a bill back to conference a second time, making it clear which changes are desired before it will accept the bill.

Presidential Action

Once a proposal clears both congressional houses, and goes through the conference committee stage if such is necessary, the only further action is for the President to sign it into law. The President may approve the bill by signing it; allow it to become law (automatic after ten working days) without his signature; "pocket veto" the bill by not acting on the measure if Congress adjourns within the ten-day period; or veto it and return it to the house in which it originated with a message explaining the reasons for his disapproval. A presidential veto usually dooms a bill to failure, since it is difficult to get the two-thirds majority of those present in each chamber to override the President.

A bill becomes law on the date of the President's approval, or on the date of passage over his veto, unless it expressly provides for a different date of effect. Following enactment into law, the legislation is printed and made public by the General Services Administration, and added to the *Statutes At Large*. (See Figure 9.1.)

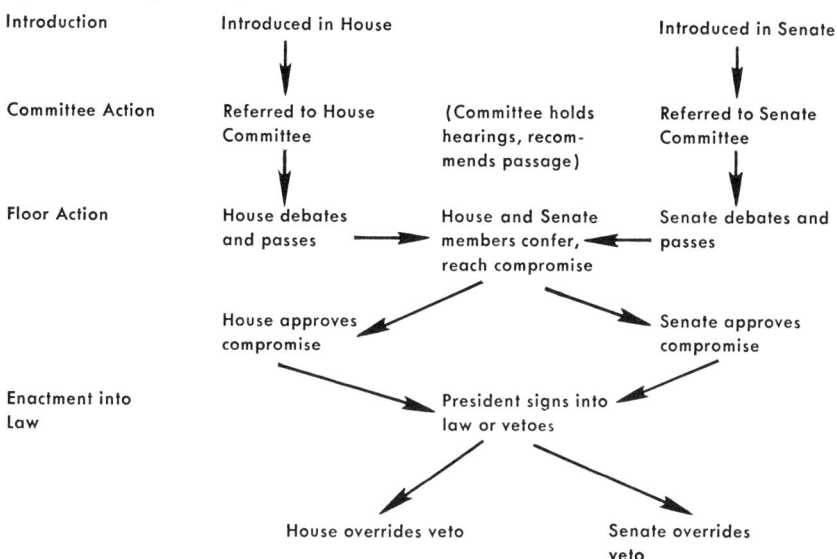

Figure 9.1 A Typical Way a Bill Becomes a Law

Introduction	Introduced in House			Introduced in Senate
Committee Action	Referred to House Committee	(Committee holds hearings, recommends passage)		Referred to Senate Committee
Floor Action	House debates and passes	House and Senate members confer, reach compromise		Senate debates and passes
	House approves compromise			Senate approves compromise
Enactment into Law		President signs into law or vetoes		
	House overrides veto		Senate overrides veto	

THE DELIBERATIVE FUNCTION

Congress is not only a representative and legislative body, it is also a deliberative assembly in which important issues of public policy are discussed, debated, and deliberated. The intensive examination of public problems given in the public forum of the Congress can be a source of enlightenment for the whole nation. News coverage of these congressional deliberations is the source of information most generally available to the populace; but the serious student, who knows what information to look for, can listen to key floor debates, attend critical committee hearings, read bills and committee reports, selectively use the *Congressional Record*—"that compendium of American wisdom, wit, and witlessness"—and gain deep insights into the important public issues which should be the concern of all Americans.

The Founding Fathers intended the legislative process to include rational deliberation and debate. Over the years the Congress has produced some great orators, such as Daniel Webster; some men of keen intellect, the likes of John C. Calhoun, whose steel-trap mind wrestled with the most difficult problem of minority rights in a democratic system of majority rule; senators sensitive to international understanding, foremost among some greats of his period being J. W. Fulbright; outstanding environmental protectionists, among whom Edmund Muskie would rank high. Given just these examples, one must conclude that Congress has not failed in its deliberative function.

Robert Sherrill, however, raises some doubts about the quality of this deliberation in his chapter entitled: "Congress: The Most Deliberative Body, and a Swamp." He writes:

In some respects Congress can claim to be the most deliberative body in the world. But it is not always clear whether this means thoughtful or plodding. In 1969, for example, while legislation for electoral reform, equitable taxation, crime control, and appropriations piled up awaiting action, the Senate spent twenty-nine days—the sixth longest debate in a quarter century—discussing the merits and demerits of the Sentinel antiballistic missile complex (ABM). When the Senate wishes to ponder and talk, it ponders and talks; and no force in the world seems capable of rushing it. The House, even without the protracting influence of the filibuster (it was outlawed in the House in 1841), sometimes talks through the night.[9]

The great national forum for deliberation is the Senate of the United States, which allows unlimited debate. Discussion does not have to be relevant or germane to the issue, as required in the House. However, the Senate does fix in advance by unanimous consent the time at which debate will stop and voting begin. This is done to expedite the legislative process on noncontroversial matters. The filibuster, nevertheless, continues to be the sacred parliamentary maneuver in the Senate to stall, alter, or kill unwanted legislation. The filibuster is used by one or more senators, by both liberals and conservatives, and by northern and southern senators. The key to the use of the filibuster is whose "ox is being gored."

Southern senators have used the filibuster to delay or kill civil rights legislation; liberal senators have used it to block legislation favoring corporate interests. Twelve senators filibustered against President Woodrow Wilson's proposal to arm American merchant ships at the end of the session in the spring of 1917. Wayne Morse from Oregon spoke over twenty-two hours against a bill to give offshore oil resources to the states in 1953; Paul Douglas from Illinois spoke for three days against a bill to relax controls over natural gas.

Some of the best southern cooking recipes have been given during a filibuster, and at times entire telephone directories have been read. To be effective, the filibuster usually requires group action, and then it must be performed near the end of the session when the pressure to enact vital legislation before adjournment will cause the promoters of the bill to drop it until the next session.

The Senate first provided for cloture, a provision to limit debate to not more than one hour for each senator, in 1917, by amending the Senate's rules of procedure. The most recent amendment, S. Res. 4, modestly liberalized cloture by requiring an affirmative vote of "three-fifths of the senators duly chosen and sworn," only after Senator James B. Allen of Alabama exhausted every conceivable parliamentary maneuver to block it. The advocates of unlimited debate

---

[9] Sherrill (above, n. 3), p. 102.

cite Jefferson's *Manual of Parliamentary Procedure,* the basic guideline of procedure in Congress, which states: "The rules of the Senate which allows full freedom of debate are designed for the protection of the minority, and this design is part of the ways and work of our Constitution." Contemporary proponents have argued that the filibuster may serve as a check on unwise action which popular pressures may demand. The arguments of the opponents of the filibuster can be reduced to the proposition that a handful of willful men should not be able to block the will of the majority.

There is a popular saying in Washington that "the House kills the good bills, the Senate kills the bad ones." The record of the Senate with the filibuster is as good, if not better, than the House without it. Anyway, the Senate can afford the luxury of free and unlimited debate because of its size, and still keep up with the workload of the House. The House, in contrast, must limit debate to accomplish its work. The Senate continues to be the world's freest forum where deliberation and debate of great public issues can and do take place. There may come a time when the pressures of legislative business demand a further relaxation of the rules of cloture in order to more readily restrict debate in the Senate, but for the immediate future the senators prize their powers of unlimited speech on the affairs of state.

LEGISLATIVE OVERSIGHT

House members as well as senators have been very vocal about the rights and powers of Congress to oversee the enforcement and adjudication of the laws Congress passes. Congressmen have complained about the trend toward strong executive government, which has been going on since 1789, and the atrophy of congressional power. Even so, a *Washington Post* editorial on October 13, 1972, chastised the House of Representatives for its continued capitulation to the President: "The House of Representatives is a legislative body composed of people who complain 364 days a year about the erosion of congressional power. And then, on the 365th day, they vote by a large majority to give the President the remnants of their control over spending." The issue before the House was the spending ceiling of $250 billion which the President requested. The House-passed measure, in substance, granted the President an item veto—something the Constitution does not grant. The Senate, however, refused to accept Congressman Mills's "view that the Democrats ought now to sign away Congress' constitutional responsibilities in order to preserve their majorities and their committee chairmanships," and did not pass the bill. On his own authority President Nixon went ahead and impounded funds and dismantled programs. This action raised the temper of congressmen and brought about court action as well.

Editorial cartoon by Pat Oliphant. Copyright, the *Denver Post*. Reprinted with permission of Los Angeles Times Syndicate.

"Charge!"

If legislation is the supreme act of a representative of the people, the power to see that the laws are properly executed and adjudicated is not far behind. There are a number of tools at the disposal of Congress to accomplish this oversight function. These powers include (1) impeachment, (2) organization of the administrative structure, (3) advice and consent, (4) appropriations, (5) congressional access to information from administrative officers, (6) concurrent and simple resolutions, (7) the inclusion of oversight power in laws, (8) the establishment of legislative procedures institutionalizing oversight, and (9) oversight of the judiciary.

Impeachment is the constitutional authority of the House of Representatives to impeach (bring charges against) "all civil officers of the United States" for "treason, bribery, or other high crimes and misdemeanors," whereupon they are to be tried before the Senate. Conviction of impeachment requires a two-thirds vote of those senators present and voting. If the President of the United States is impeached, the Constitution calls for the Chief Justice of the Supreme Court to preside over the trial in the Senate—this was done in the impeachment trial of President Andrew Johnson. The House has impeached only twelve persons, and the Senate has convicted only four of these throughout the history of the United States. Impeachment is the "heavy artillery" of legislative oversight; indeed, it is so heavy that it rarely is used. Only the most serious situation would activate Congress to use this "big gun."

The basis of legislative oversight is the actual creation and organization of administrative departments, agencies, commissions, corporations, and authorities. Although these are organized to assist the President in executing the policies enacted into law by Congress, the power of Congress to oversee the activities of its creations is obvious. Congress at times, however, has defaulted in the exercise of this power. Closely coupled with the organization of government is the staffing of these offices. The President has the constitutional authority to appoint the principal officers of the national government, but these appointments must be confirmed by the Senate. The Senate may examine the nominations very carefully to determine the acceptability of the nominee to fulfill the responsibilities of the particular office. The Senate's investigation of L. Patrick Gray III in 1973, President Nixon's nominee for the position of Director of the Federal Bureau of Investigation, brought to light a close connection of Gray to the White House in the government's investigation of the Watergate caper, causing many senators to register concern over the political overtones of Gray's actions. As criticism of his actions mounted, Gray withdrew as a nominee for this position and resigned as the acting director of the FBI.

Congress has the constitutional authority to raise revenue, grant spending authority, and appropriate funds for the operation of government and its programs. The President has the responsibility to carry out the programs. President Jefferson delayed spending money authorized for gunboats; President Lincoln spent unappropriated funds; and President Nixon refused to spend the funds which Congress did appropriate. Congress periodically has enacted laws governing the appropriation process as a tool of legislative oversight, but in most instances Congress has failed to use these tools effectively. The Budget and Accounting Act of 1921 virtually granted the President control over the budget and management of the spending process. Concern over President Nixon's impoundment of funds prompted Congress to pass the Congressional Budget and Impoundment Control Act of 1974 (PL 93-344). The law establishes an institutional and procedural counterforce to the executive Office of Management and Budget, giving Congress a better control over federal spending and fiscal policy.

Congressional committees call department heads and other executive officers before them to testify on bills being considered in order to obtain the information necessary to enact needed legislation. Frequently the executive officers are there voluntarily as "in-house lobbyists" testifying to the urgency of certain legislation, making requests for more funding, and so on. There are times, however, when the committees are attempting to gain information contrary to the wishes of the President. At times the President has refused to divulge information which he considers to be a violation of confidentiality between himself and his subordinates, or to divulge information which he considers to be vital to national interests; and at times subordinates have been cloaked with this "executive privilege." Precedent for this action begins with George Washington. Andrew Jackson took a firm stand on the confidentiality of his "Heads of Departments acting as a Cabinet Council" in a controversy with the Senate. When William P. Rogers was Attorney General in 1958, under President Eisenhower, he testified before the Constitutional Rights subcommittee that the President has the exclusive right to determine what information should be released, but "non-disclosure can never be justified as a means of covering mistakes, avoiding embarrassment, or for political, personal or pecuniary reasons." No President has exercised the right of executive privilege as extensively as President Nixon, which has provoked a strengthening of the congressional spine to keep the channels of information open to Congress in the performance of its oversight function.

Congress may apply checks on administrative action through the use of concurrent or simple resolutions. These may terminate programs, enable or require the executive to perform certain functions, or constitute a legislative veto in the case of reorganization plans submitted to Congress. Under the Reorganization Acts of 1939, 1945, and 1949, the President is granted the authority to reorga-

Editorial cartoon by Paul Conrad. Copyright, *Los Angeles Times*. Reprinted with permission.

"First of all, Mr. President, we want our dome back!"

nize the executive offices of government, but he must submit the plan to Congress. If either chamber "vetoes" the plan within sixty days, it does not go into effect.

Congress may draft bills in such a way that legislative oversight becomes part of the law. For instance, the law may require prior consent from Congress or from certain committees before executive action can take place. If the Mahon Amendment had passed, which required the President to submit proposed cuts in spending for fiscal year 1973, it would have been an example of the process of oversight through legislative enactment. Also, Congress could institutionalize its oversight function by establishing an additional "calendar" which would set aside certain days each month when oversight matters would be considered, as it now does for District business.

Oversight of the judiciary is another function of Congress. The Senate's confirmation of judicial appointees carries an oversight impact on the judiciary. Also, Congress may reverse decisions of the Court by proposing a constitutional amendment. This was done after the Supreme Court declared the income tax provision of the Wilson-Gorman Tariff act of 1894 unconstitutional in *Pollock* v. *Farmers' Loan and Trust Co.* (1895). The Sixteenth Amendment, which allows the income tax, was ratified and became effective in 1913. Congress can circumscribe the appellate jurisdiction of the Supreme Court, as was done during the Reconstruction period in *Ex parte McCardle* (1868). In this case Congress had passed an act that repealed the Court's jurisdiction in all cases arising under the Habeas Corpus Act of 1867. Finally, Congress may pass legislation which will alter, stay, or reverse particular decisions of the Court. The controversy over *Swann* v. *Charlotte-Mecklenburg Board of Education* (1971), which required busing to achieve racial balance in the school district, prompted Congress to amend the Higher Education Act Amendments of 1972, to delay the effect of the Court's decision.

The purpose of legislative oversight is not to "control" the other branches, nor to bludgeon them into a subservient position. History has demonstrated that Congress does not have the power, nor the nerve, to do so. Legislative oversight is not intended to achieve congressional dominance, but rather to achieve balance and promote coordination between the branches. Indeed, legislative oversight can strengthen the other two branches, and it can be a strength to the American system of government.[10]

THE LEGISLATIVE BRANCH: A BROKEN TWIG?

Congress, in spite of its impressive functions and powers provided for by the Constitution, has not been a match for the power of the President. It is the first

---

[10] See the chapter on "Legislative Oversight" in Cornelius P. Cotter, *et al., Twelve Studies of the Organization of Congress* (Washington, D.C.: The American Enterprise Institute for Public Policy Research, 1966).

pressure point of the big interest groups—and their efforts are well rewarded. It has systemic troubles which seem to defy rapid reform. It refuses to establish an ethical code of conduct for its members and conflicts of interests are legion among its members. It is guilty of the practice of "boodle," or pork barrel, whereby each congressman loads his district with as many public works as he can get passed—dams, military installations, federal buildings, and on and on. Congress is slow to meet the needs of minorities, but rushes with the majorities—at times unwisely. Generally it is a conservative body, which infuriates the liberal reformer. Deadlock can exist between Congress and the President; it also can set in within Congress itself because of its "four party" arrangement of liberal and conservative Republicans, and Democrats and Southern Democrats. (See Figure 9.2.)

The case for or against Congress is dependent upon the political values and interests of each individual. With its weaknesses and faults, many of which are crying for correction, the Congress of the United States is probably the most powerful national assembly found in political life. Its patterns and processes are duplicated, with variations, in the fifty state legislatures. Some similarities exist between Congress and the legislative councils, boards, and commissions of local governments. Congress and the legislative bodies on the state and local levels represent inattentive publics in the main, and, considering this fact, it is surprising that the legislative process in America serves democracy as well as it does.

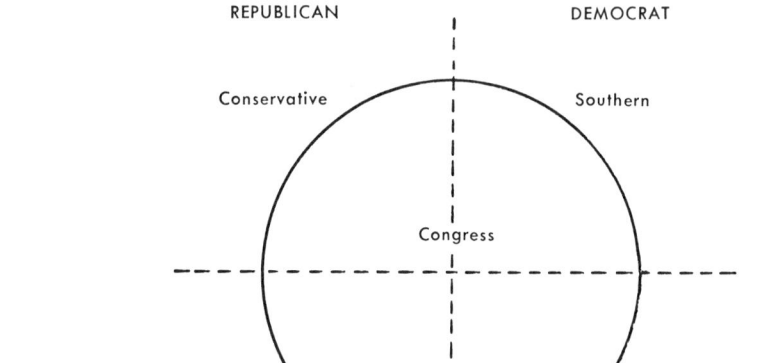

Figure 9.2 Four-Party Structure of Congress

10
JUSTICE AND THE JUDICIAL PROCESS

It was a warm day in May. Miss Dollree Mapp had just finished washing the dinner dishes when a firm knock came upon the front door. "Who's there," she called. "Police," came the crisp reply; "open up this door!"

Three Cleveland police officers had made this impromptu visit pursuant to information that a person wanted for questioning in connection with a recent bombing was hiding out in Miss Mapp's home. After telephoning her attorney, and upon his advice, she refused to admit the officers without a search warrant. The officers did not have a warrant, so they advised their headquarters of the "complications." Headquarters ordered them to keep close surveillance of the house and not let anyone out.

Three hours later additional officers arrived. Again, there was a knock on the door. "Open up," blurted an officer. And when Miss Mapp did not immediately come to the door, the door was broken down and the officers entered the house with guns drawn. They found Miss Mapp, clothed only in her nightgown, halfway down the stairs from her upper floor bedroom, on her way to answer the front door. She demanded to see a search warrant to justify such a crude and high-handed entry into her home. One officer held up a piece of paper which he claimed was a search warrant. Miss Mapp grabbed the paper and placed it in her bosom. A struggle ensued between the woman and the eight police officers, in which the officers recovered the "warrant," threw her to the floor, and handcuffed her.

The officers thoroughly searched the woman's home, including chests and closets in her bedroom, personal papers and a photo album, and even a trunk in the basement. While these intrusions were occurring, Miss Mapp's attorney arrived on the scene. The officers, however, would not permit him to see his client. Neither would they allow him to enter the house. No person was discovered in the search. What was found, though, were certain lewd and lascivious books, pictures, and photographs.

Several days following the search, Miss Mapp was charged with a violation of Section 2905.34 of the Ohio Revised Code for willingly and unlawfully having in her possession and under her control certain obscene materials. What had started as a search for a person, had led to the forceful entry by the police into a private home, the illegal search and seizure of personal documents, and now the use of those documents as evidence to convict the occupant of a crime.

Months later, Miss Mapp received a summons to appear before the Cleveland Municipal Court for a hearing on her case. She approached the place named in the summons down a street lined with signs advertising bailbond brokers, attorneys, and notaries public. She entered a battered building, passed a police booking desk and a barred door, through which escaped the fetid odor of a city jail, and climbed the stairs to the courtroom.

Sometime between 10:20 and 10:40 the bailiff called the court to order; the judge whisked out of his private door to the bench; and court commenced. The first thirty cases were all drunkenness charges. Most of the defendants were "repeaters." The judge greeted several by their first names. They were disposed of in fifteen minutes—all guilty, some freed on suspended sentences, some sent to the workhouse. It was "justice" at the rate of two cases per minute. Other cases were quickly handled. Gradually, the crowd thinned. At five minutes to twelve, the court adjourned until Monday morning and the Mapp case was carried over.

When the day did come for Miss Mapp's day in court, her trial was conducted in much the same manner as everyone else's. The actual time elapsed for the entire trial—including opening arguments, presentation of evidence, argumentation by the lawyers, and deliberation of the judge—was twenty-two minutes. She was found "guilty as charged!" Thereupon she was reprimanded by the judge for her "unwholesomeness and immorality," and given a fine. Miss Mapp had had her day in court.

And, for the vast majority of Americans, the judge's decision would have been final. Indeed, for most Americans, such would have been their first, last, and only contact with the American system of criminal justice. Few and far between are citizens who are financially able to challenge such "justice" through appeals to higher courts. However, the Mapp case was ultimately heard by the federal Supreme Court, which applied the "exclusionary rule," prohibiting the admission of evidence obtained through illicit searches and seizures, to state criminal trials. Thus *Mapp* v. *Ohio* (1961) made such police practices unfruitful, and added another protection for all Americans in criminal cases.

Untypical as the *Mapp* case may be, it does call attention to the fact that problems do exist in the American system of criminal justice. Miscarriages of justice may surface anywhere in the country for a variety of reasons. Though some statistics show that rural communities are more conservative, as well as that their police forces are more punitive and have a higher percentage of arrests, the total problems of rural criminal justice are not as pressing as in the urban areas, partially as a result of unofficial solutions of these problems through an interaction of social forces made up of churches, schools, families, neighbors, and so on, which reduces the caseload of the official agencies. Problems of the cities, on the other hand, add to the number of cases which overload the urban systems to a point where there is great temptation to take the easy and quick rather than the just solution. Instead of dispensing justice, the overloaded judicial system disposes of cases.

Possibly the symbol of justice, the blindfolded lady with the balance scales in her hand, needs to take off the blindfold and see what is happening, which means, in the final analysis, that the people of America must demand reform of the judicial system to meet the challenges of our times. The quality of justice in America, however, must be measured at each stage of the criminal justice system. Success at one stage may be offset by failure at another; the system must therefore be considered as an interrelated and interdependent unit.

THE CRIMINAL JUSTICE CONTINUUM

The continuum of criminal justice is made up of legislatures (and executives) which enact laws that relate to crimes and justice; the law enforcement agencies which are charged with law enforcement and maintenance of order; the prosecutor (district attorney) whose responsibility is to investigate, to secure indictments, and to prosecute accused persons (the defense counsel, or in some jurisdictions, the public defender, is the counterpart of the prosecutor in our adversary system of justice); the court system, which has the responsibility of determining the innocence or guilt of the accused; and corrections, which is charged with supervision, custody and/or rehabilitation of the guilty.[1] (See Figure 10.1.)

The legislative or policy-making bodies in all three levels of government are not only involved in defining the crimes of society, but also in passing the legislation which affects the criminal justice system in such areas as organization, jurisdiction, operations, personnel, and funding of the criminal justice agencies. It is obvious that the quality of justice is largely dependent upon the policies that are enacted into law. The legislative process, however, has been treated above, and the bulk of this chapter will be devoted to the judicial process; so this section will briefly discuss the law enforcement agencies, the prosecutor, and the system of corrections.

Law Enforcement Agencies

Police protection and law enforcement in the American federal system have been exercised primarily by state and local governments. Federal law-enforcing

---

[1] See Paul B. Weston and Kenneth M. Wells, *The Administration of Justice* (Englewood Cliffs, N.J.: Prentice-Hall, 1973).

Figure 10.1 The Criminal Justice Continuum

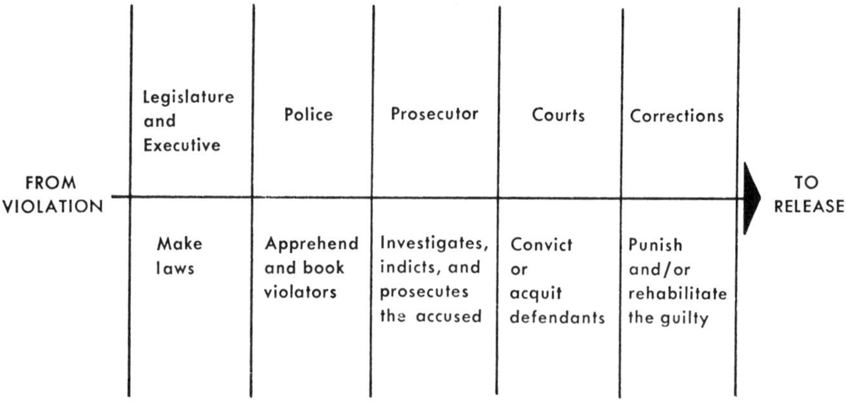

	Legislature and Executive	Police	Prosecutor	Courts	Corrections	
FROM VIOLATION						TO RELEASE
	Make laws	Apprehend and book violators	Investigates, indicts, and prosecutes the accused	Convict or acquit defendants	Punish and/or rehabilitate the guilty	

agencies are concerned only with federal crimes. There is, nevertheless, a cooperative relationship between the law enforcement bodies of the three levels of government.

The national government does not have a national police force, as such, but does have investigating and policing roles performed by different agencies and officials. Federal law-enforcing activities are performed principally by the Federal Bureau of Investigation (FBI) of the Department of Justice, the Secret Service of the Treasury Department, postal inspectors, narcotics agents, treasury inspectors, and border patrol and immigration officials. It should be noted as well that the federal marshal of TV-westerns fame actually does exist in the real world. He is an officer of the Department of Justice attached to each federal district court. His duties correspond to those of the sheriff in county government. He makes arrests in federal criminal cases, keeps accused persons in custody, maintains order in the courtroom, and executes orders and decisions of the court. The United States marshals have played a prominent role in the enforcement of desegregation orders of the federal courts.

All states now have some type of state police force. The majority of the state police systems resulted from the advent of the automobile and are primarily concerned with matters of highway patrol. The oldest state police organization, the Texas Rangers, established in 1835, was founded to supplement the military and patrol the border.

The sheriff is the primary police officer in the counties. He is responsible for the enforcement of state laws as well as the local laws adopted by the county governing boards. Customarily, the sheriff and his deputies exercise jurisdiction only in the unincorporated areas of the counties; the municipalities are the responsibility of the city police. The sheriff is generally elected by the voters, rarely well trained in police science, and often poorly paid.

The municipal police may consist of only a few patrolmen in the small cities, ranging up to a department of well-trained and highly specialized police personnel in the larger cities. The larger departments are organized in a semimilitary fashion, with divisions that handle different functions of police work. The professionalism that exists in the police departments of Los Angeles, New York City, and many other larger cities, with their police academies, scientific laboratories, communications systems, computers, and so on, make these police departments the finest in the world.[2]

Regardless of the quality of the police force, not all laws of the community are enforced. "The laws which are selected for enforcement," according to Dan Dodson, the Director of the Center for Human Relations and Community Studies at New York University, "are those which the power structure of the community wants enforced. The police official's job is dependent upon his having radar-like equipment to sense what is the power structure and what it wants enforced as law."[3] And according to Patricia M. Wald, in an article written for the President's Commission on Law Enforcement and the Administration of Justice (1967), the great majority of those accused of crime are the poor: "High crime and low income inhabit the same quarters. As a result, saturation patrols designed to deter major crime produce increased surveillance of slum residents, and a greater likelihood that they will be picked up for minor offences."[4] The poor frequently are black, or from one of the ethnic groups, and live in the city slums—which means that the poor and the minorities who live in the ghettos feel the lash of the law more heavily than others in society.

If the drunk is poor, he is picked up and put in the drunk tank to sober up. The next morning he is herded quickly through the police court, where he is charged; asked how he pleads (usually "guilty"); and is sentenced. The more affluent drunk with money in his pocket is often put in a taxi and sent home instead of being arrested.

Case studies show that there is discriminatory treatment all along the criminal justice continuum. Those people who are part of the power structure of any community and those who are in the mainstream of the society are treated differently than those who are not. Patricia Wald concludes: "The poor are arrested more often, convicted more frequently, sentenced more harshly, rehabilitated less successfully than the rest of society."

The Prosecutor

The Attorney General of the United States, along with the Department of Justice which he heads, is responsible for the enforcement of federal laws, furnishes legal counsel in federal cases, and construes the laws under which other

---

[2] Henry A. Turner, *American Democracy: State and Local Government* (New York: Harper and Row, 1968). This source covers state and local functions and services in Chapter Five.

[3] Arthur Niederhoffer, *Behind the Shield: The Police in Urban Society* (Garden City, N.Y.: Doubleday, 1967), p. 12.

[4] Article reprinted in Gene L. Mason and Fred Vetter, eds., *The Politics of Exploitation* (New York: Random House, 1973), pp. 93, 94.

departments act. The Department of Justice is responsible for the prosecution of all suits in the Supreme Court in which the United States is concerned; supervises the federal penal institutions; investigates and detects violations against federal laws; and represents the federal government in legal matters generally, rendering legal advice and opinions upon request to the President and to the heads of the executive departments. The Attorney General also supervises and directs the activities of the United States attorneys and marshals in the various judicial districts.

Each state has an attorney general who, along with the governor, is responsible for the enforcement of state laws. In some states the attorney general is authorized to supervise the work of local law enforcement officials. Most of the prosecution of suspected lawbreakers is handled by the county or district attorney, who, in some states, may be designated differently—such as "prosecuting attorney" or "county solicitor." These officials are usually elected, though some states have systems of appointment, for a term of two to four years. It is the prosecutor who decides whether or not to prosecute, to negotiate for a plea of guilty to a lesser charge (commonly called "plea bargaining") with the defense attorney, or to drop the case for lack of evidence. The prosecutor exercises discretion over which cases are taken to court; the decision rests heavily on how carefully the police have done their work in the case.

Prosecutors, like the police, develop an enthusiasm for the chase and a hunter's instinct. Political ambition often motivates the prosecutor, and prestige is associated with a high percentage of convictions. The prosecutor thus tends to try those cases in which there is a good chance of a conviction. Yet, the primary duty of prosecutors is to see that justice is done. The role of the defense attorney, or public defender, helps in approaching the ideal of justice.

Corrections

The corrections stage of criminal justice consists of two tracks: (1) probation, and (2) custody and parole. The court sentence, depending upon the requirements of the law in a particular case, may place the offender on probation or it may send him to a correctional institution.

The probation officer, who is normally recruited from college graduates in the social sciences, is a member of the court system to which he is attached, and the supervisor of the convicted defendants assigned to him who are placed on probation. As a member of the court's staff, he normally will conduct a presentence investigation of the criminal offender and the circumstances related to the crime. His report includes discussions of such topics as the motives for the crime and a judgment as to whether or not the offender can be rehabilitated without a prison term. As a supervisor of the probationer, this sociolegal officer assumes a semiparental role in guiding the offender back into the mainstream of society. The success of the probation officer can be measured by the recidivism rate (the number of offenders who return to crime) of his probationers. The maturity and skill of the probation officers, the nature of the offense, the attitude of the offenders placed on probation, and the environment in which the rehabilitation process takes place are all factors in the success rate of offenders placed on the probation track—which is markedly better than those who move along the prison and parole route.

Prisons and other correctional institutions have a threefold purpose: (1) they enforce the prison sentence ordered by the court, which is punishment to the offender; (2) they protect society by restraining the criminal from committing more crimes by keeping him in custody; and (3) they are supposed to rehabilitate the offender. Even though the emphasis of prisons has shifted from the penal to the rehabilitation role, the stretch in prison too frequently is a criminal "graduate school," rather than a schooling in resocialization. Prisons, by and large, do not attract the most qualified personnel; are often faced with defiant inmates; are governed by an unofficial inmate organization, which compromises the effectiveness of the warden and other officials; and have built-in brutalization and dehumanization factors which seriously challenge the best of rehabilitation programs.[5]

The role of the parole officer is similar to that of a probation officer, but the former has a more police-related function. His role of supervision of the offender begins after the parolee has served part of his sentence in prison. Unlike their probation counterparts, parole officers work with the poorer risks of law enforcement. The parolees have been exposed to the "socialization" of prison life, with all of its attendant conflicts and hostilities. In spite of the high caliber of most parole officers, this officer's chances of successful rehabilitation of his charges are significantly poorer than the probation officer's.

CRIME IN THE UNITED STATES

The Federal Bureau of Investigation's *Uniform Crime Reports for the United States, 1970* reveals the following information on crime: The crime rate (number of offenses per 100,000 population) increased 144 percent from 1960 through 1970. Murder increased 56 percent. Crimes against property increased 147 percent. In 1970 alone, Americans lost in excess of $2.1 billion dollars to burglary, larceny, and auto theft. One person was murdered every thirty-three minutes. Eleven major crimes were committed every minute. Part of this increase is due to improved reporting methods and the creation of state data centers. Crime statistics during the ten-year period were most complete for the last year, 1970.

The President's Commission on Law Enforcement and Administration of Justice has stated that "America's best hope for reducing crime is to reduce ju-

---

[5] See Chapter Three of Ramsey Clark, *Crime in America: Observations on Its Nature, Causes, Prevention and Control* (New York: Simon and Schuster, 1971).

From *The Herblock Gallery* (Simon & Schuster, 1968)

"It's a shame the way they coddle criminals—I mean the unincorporated ones."

venile delinquency and youth crime." If such is the case, a look at juvenile crime statistics might prove interesting. Between 1960 and 1969, while the total juvenile population increased only 26 percent, the rate of arrest in this same group increased 94 percent. And, even more startling, the rate for the "most serious crimes"—criminal homicide, forcible rape, aggravated assault, and robbery—increased by an unprecedented 148 percent. Two trends are evident. First, there is more youth crime. Second, youth crime is becoming more violent and more serious. So if America's best hope for reducing crime generally is to reduce youth crime, America faces a serious challenge.

These "most serious" crimes are those that concern Americans the most because they affect their personal safety—at home, at work, or in the streets.

Threatening and widespread though they are, they represent only a minute part of the total crime picture in the United States.

White-Collar Crime

The term "white-collar" crime was first popularized by Edwin H. Sutherland.[6] He defined white-collar crime as "crime committed by a person of respectability and high social status in the course of his occupation." As compared to the offenders described above, white-collar offenders have enjoyed a variety of social and economic advantages. They have received better educations and are better equipped to earn their livings legitimately. They do not define themselves as criminals, and are not defined as such by their peers.

Few reliable statistics are available regarding the incidence of white-collar crime. There are, for example, no consolidated statistics comparable to the FBI's *Uniform Crime Reports* in the area of "traditional" crime. Such information as is available, however, indicates that white-collar crime pervades our entire society and causes enormous economic and social harm.

Types of white-collar crimes include embezzlement, financial fraud, building code violations, price fixing, violations of health laws, graft, conflicts of interests, charging for services not rendered, and tax fraud. These crimes also represent serious economic and social losses. For while losses from much-publicized robberies and burglaries are expressed in terms of millions of dollars, losses from white-collar crime must be expressed in terms of billions of dollars.

Organized Crime

Organized crime is a "subsociety" that operates illegally within the larger society. It involves thousands of criminals, working within structures as complex as those of any large corporation, subject to "laws" more rigidly enforced than those of legitimate governments. Its actions are not impulsive but are rather the result of intricate planning, carried on over many years, and aimed at gaining control over whole fields of activity in order to amass huge profits.

The core of organized crime activity is the supplying of illegal goods and services—gambling, loan sharking, narcotics, and other forms of vice—to countless numbers of citizen customers. Organized crime penetrates legitimate business, professions, labor unions, and governments. Here it employs illegitimate methods—monopolization, terrorism, extortion, tax evasion, political favors, and protection—to exact illegal profits from the public.

Conclusion

The crime picture in the United States, then, is a big picture. There are more than 2,800 federal crimes and a much larger number of state and local ones. Some involve serious bodily harm; some stealing; some, public morals or

---
[6] *White Collar Crime* (New York: Holt, Rinehart and Winston, 1949).

public order; some, governmental revenues; some, the creation of hazardous conditions; some, the regulation of the economy. Some are perpetrated ruthlessly and systematically; others are spontaneous derelictions. Gambling and prostitution are willingly undertaken by both buyer and seller; murder and rape are violently imposed upon their victims. Vandalism is predominantly a crime of the young; driving while intoxicated, a crime of the adult.

The court system of the United States, with all its imperfections and inefficiencies, is called upon not only to deal with this vast crime picture, but to handle the thousands of civil cases as well. Small wonder, then, that the courts that play such an important part in American life have such a complex structure. Indeed, they have a structure far more complex than the judicial systems of most nations of the world.

STRUCTURE OF THE COURTS

Throughout the United States there are two judicial systems. One is that of the state and local courts, established in each state under the authority of the state government. The other is that of the United States courts, set up under the authority of the Constitution by the Congress of the United States.

The state courts have general plenary power to decide almost every type of case, subject only to the limitations of state law. The great bulk of legal business is handled by these courts. The federal courts, on the other hand, have power to decide only those cases in which the Constitution gives them authority.

Structure of the Federal Courts

Constitutional Courts. Article III of the Constitution begins: "The judicial power of the United States shall be vested in one Supreme Court, and in such inferior courts as the Congress may from time to time ordain and establish." Through the years, Congress has created a number of these inferior courts. Included among them are the ninety-three United States district courts and eleven courts of appeals. In addition, Congress has established tribunals having specialized jurisdictions. The Court of Claims, for example, hears the claims of private persons against their government, such as suits for breach of contract and for injuries caused by the negligent or wrongful behavior of a federal employee. The Customs Court hears cases arising from the decisions made by customs officials concerning imported goods. And the Court of Customs and Patent Appeals hears appeals from decisions of the Customs Court and the Patent Office.

All of these tribunals, including both those of general jurisdiction and those of specialized jurisdiction, are classified as constitutional courts, because these courts are created by Congress pursuant to authority contained in Article III of the Constitution; that is, they are governed by the same provisions which govern the Supreme Court. Their judges, for example, are appointed for life terms, and receive compensation that cannot be diminished during their terms of office. Above all, their jurisdiction is limited to "cases or controversies"; and thus they do not perform functions regarded as nonjudicial, such as giving advisory opinions to the President or Congress.

Legislative Courts. The legislative courts are also authorized by the Constitution and created by Congress. Unlike the constitutional courts, however, they are not created pursuant to authority granted in Article III. Rather, they are created under the implied-powers clause as "necessary and proper" instruments for carrying out specific authority delegated to Congress under Article I. Under its power to provide for the organization of the armed forces, for instance, Congress has created a Court of Military Appeals, which reviews the decisions of courts-martial. Likewise, the power to govern territories led Congress to establish courts for these areas.

The provisions of Article III concerning jurisdiction, terms, pay, and removal apply to judges of constitutional courts only; Congress has a free hand in providing for judges of legislative courts. It is interesting to note, however, that despite Congress' greater control over legislative courts, their number has steadily diminished during recent years. Indeed, Congress has purposefully removed courts from the legislative-court status. Thus, the Court of Claims, the Customs Court, and the Court of Customs and Patent Appeals, one by one, have been changed from legislative to constitutional courts by statute.

The Supreme Court. Although legislative courts and courts of special jurisdiction are a major factor in the dispensation of justice in the United States, it is the hierarchy of the Supreme Court, the courts of appeals, and the district courts that ordinarily comes to mind when the term "federal court system" is used.

The highest tribunal, the court of last resort, the apex of the judicial pyramid of the United States, is the Supreme Court. It is composed of eight associate justices and a Chief Justice, all of whom are appointed by the President and confirmed by the Senate for life terms. The salary of an associate justice is $60,000 annually, and the Chief Justice receives an annual salary of $62,500. Any of the justices may retire at age seventy after serving ten continuous years, or at sixty-five after serving fifteen continuous years, at full salary.

The Supreme Court has original and appellate jurisdiction. This means that some cases start, or originate, before the Supreme Court, whereas others get there by way of appeal from lower federal and state courts. The Supreme Court has original jurisdiction in two types of cases: (1) those affecting ambassadors, other public ministers, and consuls; and (2) those in which states are parties to an action. For example, the High Court settled a border dispute between Texas and Oklahoma by determining which branch of the Red River formed the boundary between the two states.

All other cases that do not originate in the Supreme Court come to it by three

The Justices of the United States Supreme Court. Back row, left to right: Justices Lewis F. Powell, Thurgood Marshall, Harry A. Blackmun, and William H. Rehnquist; front row, left to right: Justices Potter Stewart, William O. Douglas, Chief Justice Warren Earl Burger, Justices William J. Brennan, Jr., and Byron R. White.

methods today: (1) a writ of *certiorari,* (2) appeal, or (3) certification. On petitions for *certiorari,* the Court has the option of granting or denying review. If granted, as comparatively few are, lower federal or state courts are directed to send up the entire record of the proceedings for review. About eighty percent of the Supreme Court's business arises from petitions for *certiorari,* and about ninety percent of the petitions for *certiorari* are denied.

Appeals come to the Supreme Court either from state courts or from lower federal courts. The Supreme Court must review cases from state courts in the following two instances: (1) where the state court has held invalid a treaty or statute of the United States; (2) where a state law has been challenged on the ground that it contravenes the Constitution, treaties, or laws of the United States, and the state court upholds its validity. Also, appeal is available if a federal court stops the machinery of state government by declaring a state law invalid as repugnant to the Constitution, treaties, or laws of the United States. Actually, since 1902, the Supreme Court has exercised the power of dismissing appeals if they do not involve substantial federal questions. The Court has almost complete control of its dockets, or in other words, it hears only those cases it wants to hear.

The method of certification is seldom used. It results when a lower court requests that the Supreme Court answer certain questions of law so that a correct decision may be made.

A few cases come directly from federal district courts, but most of them are sent up from the courts of appeals. Congress, in 1925, gave the Supreme Court broad powers to decide what cases it will hear. Of the 4,533 cases on the dockets during the 1971–72 term, the Supreme Court disposed of 3,645 cases, heard oral arguments in 177 cases, and delivered written opinions in 129 cases.

Courts of Appeals. Immediately below the Supreme Court stand the courts of appeals, created in 1891 to facilitate the disposition of cases and ease the burden on the Supreme Court. They operate in the District of Columbia and in ten circuits, or regions, into which the nation and its territories have been divided.

United States courts of appeals have between three and fifteen judges, depending upon the number of cases heard in the circuit. The senior judge who has not yet reached his seventieth birthday is designated the Chief Judge. Members of the courts of appeals are appointed for life by the President at an annual salary of $42,500.

The courts of appeals have no original jurisdiction; they are exclusively appellate courts. With few exceptions, cases decided in the district courts, legislative courts, and quasi-judicial boards and commissions go next to the courts of appeals. Only the Supreme Court reviews the decisions of the courts of appeals.

District Courts. The great majority of all cases heard in federal courts originate in the ninety-three United States district courts located in the fifty states, the District of Columbia, and the territories. Each state has at least one federal district court; and New York, Texas, and California have four each. The volume of business transacted determines the number of judges assigned to each district court, with the number varying from one to twenty-seven. These judges are appointed by the President, with the consent of the Senate, for life terms at an annual salary of $40,000.

Each district court has a clerk, one or more referees in bankruptcy, probation officers, court reporters, and a magistrate. The United States magistrate, who is selected by the judges of the district, holds preliminary hearings and determines whether accused persons are to be held for action by the grand jury, grants bail, signs arrest and search warrants, and so on.

The Department of Justice is represented in each federal judicial district by a United States marshal and a United States attorney. The attorney serves as government counsel and as prosecutor in criminal trials. He is responsible for federal law enforcement in the area to which he is assigned. He conducts investigations of lawbreaking, often in conjunction with the FBI, and submits evidence to the grand jury summoned by the court to ask for indictments when he believes that a trial is warranted.

United States district courts heard approximately 87,300 civil cases, 38,100 criminal cases, and 194,400 cases in bankruptcy in 1970. The caseload has increased at about six percent per year since then. Of the civil cases in which the United States is a party, a large number concern violations of the Food and Drug Act, the payment of federal taxes, the collection of money due on promissory notes, or breach of contract. Of the cases involving private parties living in different states, a large number arise from automobile accidents. Most of the criminal cases heard in district courts involve fraud, theft, violation of the immigration laws, the transportation of stolen vehicles, and the violation of liquor tax laws. (See Figure 10.2.)

Structure of the State Courts

The judicial systems of most states are characterized by decentralization. Organized on a district or county basis with elective judges, as most of them are, each court is nearly autonomous. Some uniformity is provided by constitutional provisions, acts of the legislature, and rules of procedure established by higher courts. By and large, however, when compared with the federal judicial system, the court organization of most states seems complicated.

Trial Courts. At first glance, the judicial system of a particular state may seem to lack any definite structure at all. On closer examination, however, three levels of courts are recognizable. At the lowest level are the trial courts, composed of two divisions: courts of minor jurisdiction and major trial courts. Courts of minor jurisdiction are restricted as to the types of cases that come before them. These courts have a variety of names. Justice of the peace courts are principally found in rural areas. They hear minor criminal cases such as disturbance of the peace, disorderly conduct, petty theft, and traffic violations. In

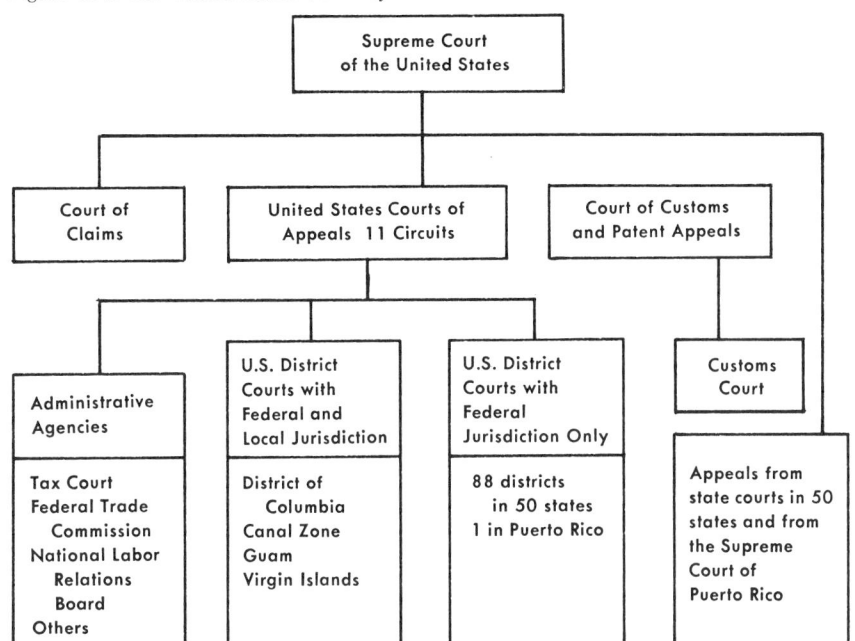

Figure 10.2 The United States Court System

```
                        ┌─────────────────────┐
                        │   Supreme Court     │
                        │ of the United States│
                        └─────────────────────┘
```

Court of Claims	United States Courts of Appeals 11 Circuits	Court of Customs and Patent Appeals

Administrative Agencies	U.S. District Courts with Federal and Local Jurisdiction	U.S. District Courts with Federal Jurisdiction Only	Customs Court
Tax Court Federal Trade Commission National Labor Relations Board Others	District of Columbia Canal Zone Guam Virgin Islands	88 districts in 50 states 1 in Puerto Rico	Appeals from state courts in 50 states and from the Supreme Court of Puerto Rico

urban areas lower criminal courts are usually called municipal, magistrate, or police courts. Like justice of the peace courts, these urban tribunals hear the lesser criminal cases. Some of them hear minor civil cases as well, such as small claims suits. This is the level of the American court structure that most citizens see.

Above the minor courts stand the major trial courts, which handle the great majority of serious cases litigated throughout the country. These courts most often try cases of murder, burglary, assault and battery, rape, and suits for damages. Their districts are outlined by state legislatures and usually include one or more counties.

The names of such courts vary. In Idaho they are known as district courts; in California, as superior courts; elsewhere, as county or circuit courts. Some cases reach these courts on appeal from lower courts, such as those of justices of the peace, in which case it is customary to rehear the entire case.

Courts of Appeal. Some of the most populous states have a court of appeals above the trial courts and below the state supreme court. They review cases on points of law which come up to them from the trial courts. The decisions of these courts are reached by majority vote; and the facts, reasoning, the legal ruling, and disposal of the case are written by one of the judges.

State Supreme Courts. The state supreme courts hear cases of appeal from the lower state courts and in a few instances have original jurisdiction. As is evident, state courts differ from federal courts in organization, in name, and in jurisdiction. The selection of judges also differs at the state and federal levels. As previously noted, all federal judges are appointed by the President, subject to approval of the Senate. In thirty-eight states, judges are elected by the voters for terms varying from two years to life. In five states, judges are chosen by the legislature. And in the remaining seven states, they are named by the governor and confirmed by the legislature.[7]

JUVENILE JUSTICE

Juvenile courts hold a special place in the American court system. They are organized on the theory that the state has a protective responsibility for children. Juvenile courts have a greater interest in rehabilitating than in punishing the offender—the state does not stand as an adversary—and all of the procedures followed in the regular courts in criminal cases are not applied in juvenile cases. Juvenile records are separated from criminal records; trials are informal and not open to the public, nor must there be a jury except in felony cases; and the juvenile's name usually is withheld from the public.

The advantages of a sociological over a legal approach in juvenile cases, however, may result in injustice. To deny the juvenile certain rights guaranteed by the Constitution may result in such unjust penalties as happened in the *Gault* case, in which a fifteen-year-old boy was sentenced to a state industrial school for making an obscene telephone call, with the possibility of remaining there until he was twenty-one. The penalty for an adult on this charge would have been a fine of fifty dollars and two months in jail. When the Supreme Court heard the case, *In re Gault* (1967), it held that certain constitutional rights must be provided in juvenile cases: notice of charges, right to remain silent and have counsel, and confrontation of witnesses. Not all of the procedural safeguards of the Bill of Rights have been extended to juveniles, however, as the Court held in *McKeiver v. Pennsylvania* (1971) that a jury trial was not required.

PROCEDURE IN THE COURTS

The procedure followed in the American court system is intricate, detailed, and complicated. Not even the most competent attorneys ever master all the facets of judicial procedure followed by the different types of courts. Indeed, like doctors in the field of medicine, lawyers must specialize in a particular field of law. Entire books, indeed, complete libraries, are devoted to the subject of

[7] See Henry Robert Glick and Kenneth N. Vines, *State Court Systems* (Englewood Cliffs, N.J.: Prentice-Hall, 1973).

judicial procedure. What is presented here are certain selected areas from the vast array of subject matter concerning judicial procedure.

The Trial Court

The trial court on the federal level is called the United States district court. On the state level, the names vary, but generally it is called the district or superior court. The procedure in the major trial court, whether state or federal, is basically the same. There is a difference of procedure, however, according to whether the case involves a criminal action or a civil action.

Civil Actions. Civil actions involve two or more parties. Generally, the aggrieved party seeks compliance with the terms of a contract or seeks money damages for an alleged injury. In such cases, the complaining party, or plaintiff, initiates a lawsuit against the defendant. The state acts merely as referee and is not a party to the dispute. It furnishes the judicial machinery through which the case is adjudged, though; and when the court hands down a judgment, the state will enforce it.

The first step in a civil lawsuit is the filing of "pleadings" with the clerk of the court. The plaintiff files a "complaint" which briefly states the injury and names the defendant. He further requests the court to issue a "writ of summons," to be delivered by the sheriff, which orders the defendant to appear in court to face the alleged charge. Through his attorney, the defendant files an "answer." Elaborations of the pleadings are submitted later, usually on demand of the opposing party; these are often known as "bills of particulars." There are many devices for clarifying issues prior to the actual trial, which lawyers are expected to know thoroughly.

The next stage is that of preparation for a court trial. While attorneys for both the plaintiff and the defendant are busily preparing themselves to argue the case in court, the court itself is making certain preparations. Principal among these is the selection of a jury. Attorneys participate, often actively, in the selection of the jury. Depending on the court and the amount in question, the jury may consist of from six to twelve men and women chosen at random from voter lists.

Finally comes the day in court. The plaintiff's attorney first presents an "opening statement," in which he sets forth what he intends to prove before the court. He then calls witnesses and presents other evidence. The defendant follows the same pattern to present another side of the case. Witnesses may be cross-examined. Evidence or testimony introduced in court can be, and often is, objected to. If the judge rules with the objecting party, then that evidence or testimony cannot be considered by the jury, and the jury is so instructed. When all evidence has been presented, each party to the dispute gives a "closing argument," the plaintiff first—leaving the last say to the defendant.

At this point the judge and jury take over. The judge first instructs the jury concerning the various points of law involved in the case. He then retires the jury to a private room adjoining the courtroom where it considers the facts presented by both sides, and tries to apply these facts to the points of law as explained by the judge. When the jury reaches a decision, it returns to the courtroom and a foreman chosen by the jurors themselves delivers the jury's decision.

Lastly, "awards" of the court are made. These awards may include money, property, orders to cease and desist, and so on. These awards may be ordered by a jury or by the judge, depending on the particular court. They are final, subject only to review by a higher court on appeal, and will be enforced by the state.

Criminal Actions. Criminal actions are those in which the state itself is the aggrieved party, and is the initiator of the action. In the *Mapp* case, the City of Cleveland was the plaintiff, and Miss Mapp was the defendant.

In criminal actions, the detection of a criminal act and the apprehension (or arrest) of a person suspected of committing that act represent the first stage. If the violation is committed in the presence of an officer, he may arrest the person "on the spot," or if the violation is a felony the policeman may arrest a suspect for probable cause. In other situations, the officer cannot make an arrest unless he has first secured a "warrant" from a court magistrate.

The second stage in a criminal case is that of the "preliminary hearing." This is the stage at which a formal accusation is made. The state must first prove that a crime has been committed; and, secondly, that there is evidence which links that crime to the person charged. The judge then decides whether or not there are sufficient grounds to bind the defendant over to the court for a trial.

The third stage involves the issuance of a formal "complaint." Depending on the jurisdiction, this is done with a filing by the grand jury of an "indictment," or with a filing by the prosecuting attorney of an "information." In either case, the charges are clearly detailed; evidence that has been collected is itemized; and witnesses are named.

The fourth stage in a criminal action is what is called an "arraignment." Here, the defendant appears before the trial judge. The formal complaint, by indictment or by information, is read to him, and he enters a plea of guilty or not guilty. If the plea is guilty, the judge immediately sets the penalty. If the plea is one of not guilty, the judge sets a date for the trial.

The trial stage of a criminal case is very similar to that of a civil case. The jury is selected similarly, and the presentation of arguments, evidence, and witnesses is conducted in like fashion—always with the state (the plaintiff) initiating, and the defendant concluding each part. Finally the judge "charges" the jury as to the points of law and the jury retires to consider a verdict, just as in civil actions. As the plaintiff has the burden of proof in a civil suit, the state has the burden of proof in a criminal case. The defendant is considered innocent until proven guilty beyond reasonable doubt. If the jury returns a verdict of guilty, the judge, in behalf of the state, sentences the person according to the requirements of the law in the case.

Appellate Court

The proceedings in appellate courts differ quite radically from those of trial courts. Appellate courts are generally much more matter-of-fact and much less dramatic. A panel of judges, usually from three to nine in number, presides. No witnesses are called. The judges rely upon briefs submitted by the prosecuting attorney and by counsel for the defense, and upon the record of the proceedings in the lower court, for their prior knowledge of the case. Appellate courts decide disputed "questions of law," not "questions of fact," which presumably have been determined by the lower court. The hearing itself consists of a presentation of the state's case and the case for the defense by the respective attorneys, and the questioning of the lawyers by the judges. When the hearing ends, the judges return to their chambers to prepare their decision.

Supreme Court of the United States

It has been noted that trial courts, whether state or federal, operate somewhat similarly. Likewise, state and federal levels of appellate courts follow the same basic procedures. Undoubtedly, too, procedural features of state supreme courts and the Supreme Court of the United States resemble one another in many areas. On the other hand, there are significant differences between these two levels of high court. Therefore, rather than generalize for all supreme courts, the discussion that follows is limited specifically to the Supreme Court of the United States.

The Supreme Court term begins annually on the first Monday in October and usually ends the following June. Special terms may be called by the Chief Justice when the controversy is of unusual importance and urgency. A special term was called on July 7, 1972, just prior to the Democratic National Convention. The controversy was over the recommendations of the Credentials Committee of the 1972 Democratic National Convention regarding the seating of certain delegates. The Court concluded, in *O'Brien* v. *Brown,* that the limited time did not allow due consideration of the case. Such problems in the past had been handled by the parties themselves, and the Court left the solution of this problem to the Democratic National Convention. All sessions are held in the Court's beautiful and spacious white-marble building in Washington, D.C.

The Chief Justice is the executive officer of the Court; he presides at all sessions and announces its orders. Legally, however, his votes have no greater weight than those of the other justices. Associate justices have precedence according to the date of appointment, or if appointed at the same time, then according to their age. In the absence of the Chief Justice, the associate justice first in precedence performs the duties of the Chief Justice. The Court divides

240 *Public Policy Makers*

its time about equally between listening to oral argument and intervening recesses for study and writing of opinions.

The justices listen attentively to the arguments presented by each side. From time to time, they interrupt the counsel, ask him to clarify a point, or question his statements. The proceedings are informal, almost conversational; but the questions asked are penetrating, and the answers are expected to be direct and uncompromising.

On Fridays, and some Saturdays, the nine justices meet in strict privacy in the conference room of the Supreme Court building. The cases heard during the previous oral argument period are discussed, and a preliminary vote is taken, with the most recently appointed justice indicating his position first and the Chief Justice giving his opinion last. When the Chief Justice belongs to the majority, he writes the opinion himself or assigns the responsibility to one of the

Drawing by Whitney Darrow, Jr.; © 1965, *The New Yorker Magazine,* Inc.

"Well, we lost the appeal, but you'll be delighted to learn there was a brilliant dissenting opinion in your favor."

justices on the majority side; if the Chief Justice votes with the minority, the senior justice of the majority faction writes the opinion or asks another member of the group to prepare it. If there are dissenting justices, they generally agree among themselves which one will write the minority opinion, though each justice may write a concurring or dissenting opinion of his own, if he desires. In the recent capital punishment case, *Furman* v. *Georgia* (1972), the vote was five to four, but each justice wrote a separate opinion.

The writing of an opinion usually takes weeks, for major decisions are well researched. When the first draft of the decision is complete, it is printed and circulated among the justices. Their oral and written comment on the decision may lead the writer to revise it. Justice William J. Brennan once circulated ten printed drafts before one was finally acceptable to the Court. Justices are swayed by the views of their fellows, particularly when they are expressed in a brilliantly written opinion. As a result, those who were in a minority when the preliminary vote on a case was taken may find themselves in the majority as one or more justices shift position. No one but the justices, their clerks, and the printers, who are sworn to secrecy, know the decision of the Court until it is announced by some justice, usually the one who writes the opinion. Opinions are customarily delivered by the justices on Mondays, but may be delivered on any day the Court is in session.

THE FUNCTIONS OF COURTS

Settling Disputes
Settling disputes is one of the oldest functions of courts. Some of these disputes are civil, in which two or more parties are involved; others are criminal, in which the state accuses someone of breaking one of its laws. Although settling disputes is a very important function of the courts, the courts do not initiate cases. A case or controversy must be brought before the courts. Lawlessness may exist in the community, but unless the police and prosecutors bring the offenders into court, no judge can pronounce sentence. Likewise, while courts can decide cases, they must rely on the executives to enforce their decisions. In the American system, settling disputes is a cooperative action—indeed, it is a community function.

Administering Justice
Of all public offices, the courts generally enjoy a position of esteem in the community, because they are professionally responsible for the "administration of justice." The trial courts, comprising the level that touches most citizens directly, carry most of the burden and responsibility for the administration of justice in the community.

The ideal of justice falls from its lofty pedestal, though, when unjust practices occur at any point in the judicial process, or when unjust or corrupt men administer "justice." Legally, justice is what the courts say it is, but Americans today demand a justice based on a higher, more absolute standard, though this is difficult to define.

Law enforcement activities in the local communities at times reflect parochial prejudices and predilections, and even the personal likes and dislikes of the judges. The efforts of the Warren Court to develop and impose a national norm of justice met with some resistance, as evidenced by the citizen who affixed twin stickers on his car bumper: "IMPEACH THE SUPREME COURT," and "SUPPORT YOUR LOCAL POLICE." The concern of the justices for maintaining the constitutional rights of all defendants is sometimes regarded as "coddling criminals" or "handcuffing the police." When the Court protects the "known criminal" on some constitutionally guaranteed principle, such as the right of counsel in the *Gideon* case, or the right to remain silent in the *Miranda* case, or the protection against unreasonable search and seizure in the *Mapp* case, it is in reality protecting all Americans against such unjust procedures. Such cases might be entitled: *Americans* v. *Unjust Criminal Justice Proceedings!*

Most American courts do accept "equal justice for all" as their norm of professional behavior. As with all norms, there are bound to be deviations. But America does not have concentration camps, even though the relocation camps for Japanese-Americans during World War II stand as an exception; the writ of *habeas corpus* is a constitutional guarantee available to all. America does not have a gestapo, even though gestapo-like tactics are, at times, used; when law enforcement officers act too brashly or brutally, their cases fail in court—even if appeal all the way to the Supreme Court is what it takes to do it. Due process of law is written into the supreme law of the land. Every man accused is entitled to a speedy, public, and impartial trial, though sometimes these stipulations are not fulfilled. And every man accused is entitled to "due process of law" at every stage in the proceedings against him.

Interpreting the Law

All courts are involved in interpreting the laws within their jurisdictions. This also may involve the courts in determining the constitutionality of laws. On the national level this activity has brought important review functions under the jurisdiction of the United States Supreme Court. As *Marbury* v. *Madison* (1803) and other cases developed the principle of judicial review, the Supreme Court's review functions have brought to it two important responsibilities: the determination of (1) the constitutionality of congressional legislation and presidential acts, and (2) the constitutionality of state acts.

Thus the Court serves an important role in the policies of the nation. It not only checks or sustains Congress when its legislation is challenged as being unconstitutional, but it also may determine the constitutionality of the acts of the President. The conservative Court during the 1930's declared a number of laws passed by Congress unconstitutional, and in so doing, it cut the heart out of President Roosevelt's New Deal program. Later, in *Youngstown Sheet and Tube Co.* v. *Sawyer* (1952), the Court held that President Truman's seizure of the steel industry to avert a strike was an unconstitutional usurpation of legislative power. The Court rejected the President's justification for his action, his authority "under the Constitution and laws of the United States" and as Commander-in-Chief. Justice Hugo L. Black's majority opinion rested on the principle of separation of powers and denied the theory of executive prerogative. This case suggests another role of the Court: that of umpire between the President and Congress when the powers and policies of each come into conflict, as recently demonstrated in President Nixon's impounding of funds appropriated by Congress to be spent for specific programs.

The Court also serves as an umpire of the federal system through its power to review executive, legislative, and judicial acts of the states involving federal questions. Of the many cases which have come to the Supreme Court based on the guarantees of the Fourteenth Amendment, *Argersinger* v. *Hamlin* (1972), a sequel to *Gideon* v. *Wainwright* (1963) involving the right of counsel, is a good example of the power of the Court to review state and local acts in order to define the requirements that must be observed to meet the demands of the Constitution and to bring uniformity in the application of procedures throughout the nation. In this case the Court held that the right of counsel extends to "any offense, whether classified as petty, misdemeanor, or felony," involving the possibility of imprisonment.

Another umpire function that the Court serves is its settlement of disputes between the states, as it did in *Arizona* v. *California* (1963), when it ruled in favor of Arizona in the long, heated dispute over water rights of the Colorado River. The Court also resolves problems between the states and the nation. A recent example of this arose over the constitutionality of a local tax on airline tickets to help defray the costs of airport construction and maintenance. The question was whether a charge by a state or municipality of one dollar per commercial airline passenger was in conflict with the constitutional powers of Congress to regulate commerce. The Court held in *Evansville-Vanderburgh Airport Authority District* v. *Delta Air Lines* (1972) that the tax was not an unconstitutional burden on interstate commerce, in the absence of contrary federal legislation, and that it was a legitimate use of the state's taxing powers. But soon afterwards, Congress passed a law, under its commerce power, which outlawed such taxes.

Communication. The written opinions of the courts explaining the rational bases of their decisions provide us with knowledge about the major political, economic, and social issues in every era of our nation's history. Courts take very seriously what they regard as the judicial function of communication. The decisions of the Marshall Court (1801–34) were communications on judicial nationalism directed to the President, Congress, the states, and the American people of that day. The decisions of the Taney Court in the pre-Civil War period were instructions on balanced federal-state relations, emerging democratic processes, and the divisive controversy over slavery. The post-Civil War Court's rulings gave aid and comfort to the industrial giants of the period. The opinions of the Court during the depression years of the 1930's were often cries of protest against Franklin D. Roosevelt's New Deal measures. The Warren Court's communications, through a number of the cases brought before it, were actually instructions to Americans on civil rights and social justice.

Policy Making and Judicial Review. Theoretically any court can, and does, exercise the function of policy making and judicial review. It must be recognized that judicial decisions are not the routine mechanical exercises that they were once thought to be by a few people. All courts, in all cases, make policy to some degree. Indeed, activist courts are often condemned for being a "third branch of the legislature" when their decisions become "legislative" in nature in the eyes of the public.

Policy making through judicial review at the Supreme Court level is the ultimate function of the judiciary in the American political system. As long as the High Court performs the task of judicial review, it must function to some extent and in some ways as one of the major policy-making organs of the nation. The Court participates in public policy whether it invalidates (checks) or validates (legitimizes) the political actions of government. The people rely on the Court not only to nullify what is unconstitutional, but also to uphold what is constitutional. Even if the first Congress had exercised its option not to establish inferior courts, this ultimate power would still have been vested in the Supreme Court.

Criticism of the activism of the Supreme Court in making policy decisions is not new, as the complaints of Jefferson against the Marshall Court confirm. Some of the most responsible criticisms of activism on the bench have come from members of the Court. Justice Oliver Wendell Holmes told his fellow justices during the Progressive Era that they should not substitute their own social and economic philosophies for those of the state legislatures; and Justice Harlan F. Stone reminded the Court in 1936 that it must exercise self-restraint. From time to time other justices have offered similar cautions to their colleagues against making policy judgments, as did Justice John M. Harlan when the Warren Court became involved in the apportionment cases of the 1960's.[8]

There are also checks on the Court beyond the self-restraint of the justices. For instance, the Court is amenable to the influence of the President through his appointments, his pronouncements, and his enforcement of its orders. An observer of the changing position of the Court in its battle with President Roose-

---

[8] See David F. Forte, ed. *The Supreme Court in American Politics: Judicial Activism vs. Judicial Restraint* (Lexington, Mass.: D.C. Heath, 1972).

velt following the 1936 election observed: "A switch in time saves nine." Congress, in addition to the powers of the Senate to approve or reject Court nominations, can pass legislation which alters the decisions of the Court, as it did on the busing issue; propose constitutional amendments to undo Court decisions; "pack" the Court through increasing or reducing the number of justices; and, if angry enough, abolish the Court's appellate jurisdiction. Public attitudes even influence the Court, as the delightful satirist Finley Peter Dunne expressed in his essay on the Supreme Court's decisions when he wrote in 1901: "th' supreme coort follows th' iliction returns."

The most important function of the courts, and especially of the Supreme Court, is to interpret the Constitution so as to maintain the stability and continuity of our fundamental principles and at the same time to permit necessary flexibility for changing times and new ideas.

REFORM IN THE COURTS

The judiciary, though the weakest of the three great departments of government—"it has no influence over either the sword or the purse," to quote Hamilton—is the most important of all to the citizen in distress who is looking for a fair trial. The right to a fair trial is the most fundamental of all rights, for without it all other rights are mere words, empty and meaningless. Everything that is necessary to accord the citizen a fair trial is an essential of a sound judicial system.

Some people believe that the essentials of a sound judicial system are relatively few in number, are constitutionally guaranteed, and are well known to the legal profession from centuries of experience. But there must be reforms to meet the problems which crop out at any point in the judicial process, from the making of the laws through the corrections stage.

Some needed reforms include legislation reducing the burden on those involved in the enforcement of the laws, legislation expunging needless laws from the statute books and/or enlarging, training, equipping, and financially supporting the enforcement officers. The selection and training of police and prosecutors need careful study to insure the best performance of these officers in the best interests of the accused and the society.

Overloaded court dockets, which cause delays, might be corrected by the employment of two sets of court personnel, possibly on a part-time basis—one set starting early in the morning, the other running into the evening, resulting in more efficiency and more convenience for those who must go to court. Selection of judges, especially on the state level where popular election is common, possibly could be improved by executive appointments based on judicial qualifications. Impaneling juries on bases which insure competent, intelligent, and fair jurors is a difficult process, but this must be attempted.

Corrections policies which protect society from the criminal and rehabilitate him to resume a responsible place in society must be carefully, and continuously, reexamined. Punishment, rehabilitation, pardons, parole, and probation policies must emphasize the well-being of both the offender and the society.

There are specialists who are working to improve the system at all levels, at each stage in the criminal justice process, and in the settlement of civil disputes. A number of innovations have been initiated as suggested by Chief Justice Warren E. Burger in his "Report on the Problems of the Judiciary" to the American Bar Association on August 14, 1972:

> The need for better methods and modern concepts of administration has long been recognized. The States, notably New Jersey, New York, Colorado, and California, pioneered the use of court executive officers. The Association, working with the American Judicature Society, the Institute of Judicial Administration and others, took the leadership in creating the Institute for Court Management at the University of Denver Law School and in persuading Congress to create the position of court executive for each of the eleven Circuits. These two forward steps were closely related. Without the institute there was no source of trained personnel, and without court executives we could not bring modern concepts of private business and public administration into the federal courts.

Constructive improvements are to be observed also in the policing, prosecuting, and corrections stages—even though the bloody riots in the prisons across the country, such as the tragedy at the New York State Correctional Facility at Attica in 1971, demand more and faster action. The details of reform are difficult to come by and must be left to those who are specialists in the subject, but a concerned citizenry is necessary for overall improvement.

PART FOUR
Public Policies in America

THE BUDGET DOLLAR
Fiscal Year 1975 Estimate

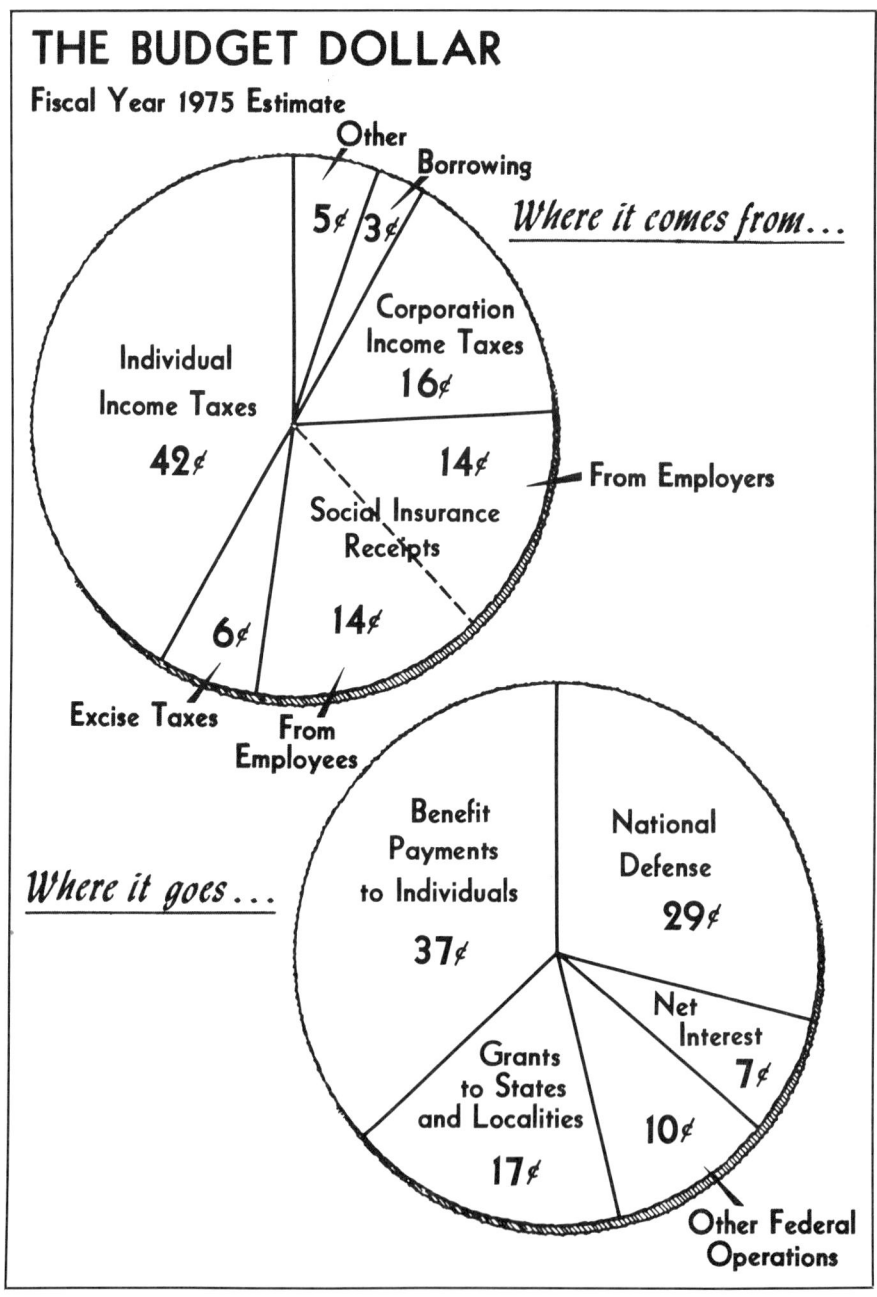

Where it comes from...

- Other 5¢
- Borrowing 3¢
- Individual Income Taxes 42¢
- Corporation Income Taxes 16¢
- Social Insurance Receipts 14¢ — From Employers
- 14¢ From Employees
- Excise Taxes 6¢

Where it goes...

- Benefit Payments to Individuals 37¢
- National Defense 29¢
- Grants to States and Localities 17¢
- Net Interest 7¢
- Other Federal Operations 10¢

SOURCE: Office of Management and Budget, *The U.S. Budget in Brief, Fiscal Year 1975* (Washington, D.C.: U.S. Government Printing Office, 1974).

Compare this 1975 estimated budget with the 1974 budget on page 264.

11
FINANCING PUBLIC FUNCTIONS

President Richard Nixon cast himself in the role of the leader of the "New American Revolution" in January, 1971, when he delivered his State of the Union address before a joint session of the Ninety-second Congress. The Congress was controlled by Democrats and not significantly different from its predecessor, which had dragged its feet on many administration programs and had infuriated the President.

Using rhetoric normally attributed to the radical left, President Nixon's reform proposals were couched in revolutionary terms. His State of the Union address was a wide-sweeping declaration intended as a modern-day parallel to that of 1776—to chart a new course for America. He outlined "six great goals" through which America could bring about this new domestic revolution: (1) to reform the welfare system, (2) to achieve full prosperity in peacetime, (3) to restore and enhance the natural environment, (4) to improve health care and make it available to all Americans, (5) to strengthen and to renew state and local governments, and (6) to reform the federal government itself. The President had expressed his revolutionary ambitions a week earlier in a cabinet meeting: "We want to be the Administration that, in 1971, presented the most imaginative, innovative approach ever seen—and when adopted it will carry the country for the next hundred years."

In his budget address the President proclaimed: "The budget expresses our fiscal program for the New American Revolution—a peaceful revolution in which power will be turned back to the people—in which government at all levels will be refreshed, renewed, and made truly responsive. This can be a revolution as profound, as far reaching, as exciting, as that first revolution almost two hundred years ago." The Nixon Administration claimed that the 1972 budget had an historic, revolutionary identity of its own because of the following innovative features:

(1) *It provides a new balance of responsibility and power in America* by proposing the sharing of Federal revenues with States and communities—in a way that will both alleviate the paralyzing fiscal crisis of State and local governments and enable citizens to have more of a say in the decisions that directly affect their life.

(2) *It introduces a new fairness in American life*, with the development by the Federal Government of national strategies to improve health care and to assure, with work incentives and requirements, an income floor for every family in this Nation.

(3) *It adopts the idea of a "full employment budget,"* in which spending does not exceed the revenues the economy could generate under the existing tax system at a time of full employment. The full employment budget is in the nature of a self-fulfilling prophecy: By operating as if we were at full employment, we will help to bring about that full employment.[1]

The President was not able to achieve his revolutionary goals in 1971–72. Congress enacted some legislation touching on part of his proposals, but it did not enact in full any one of his "six great goals." A general revenue-sharing measure—a revolutionary beginning in one goal area—was enacted by Congress; but the President's budget request for special revenue sharing was not passed. Significant legislation was enacted in the environmental and health care fields, but they were basically programs of Congress, not the President.

The President's budget message, however, contained a "revolutionary" idea in the proposal of the "full employment budget." This proposal portrayed the budget as being balanced; that is, the requests for spending would not exceed the revenues—if America was at full employment. But many Americans were unemployed when the budget for fiscal year 1972 was proposed, therefore reducing the taxable income necessary to produce a balanced budget, which resulted in a deficit budget. The 1973 and 1974 budgets also were shrouded in the "full employment" garb, but the naked deficits were obvious when close examination pushed the shroud aside.

Was the full employment budget principle simply throwing dust into the air to cloud the budgetary perspectives of Congressmen and the public? Was it designed to make the President look more responsible in fiscal matters than he actually was?

During the election year of 1972, President Nixon charged Congress with inflationary program authorizations and appropriations, and asked Congress to set a $250 billion ceiling on spending for fiscal year 1973. Congress refused to set such a ceiling. Some Congressmen pointed out that the President's charge was untenable and politically motivated because his budget and supplementary requests went beyond the $250 billion mark. These Congressmen also claimed

---

[1] Office of Management and Budget, *The U.S. Budget in Brief, Fiscal Year 1972* (Washington, D.C.: U.S. Government Printing Office, 1971), p. 5.

the President was largely responsible for the nation's deficits during his first four years in office, which they said would reach approximately $110 billion—more than the deficits of his four predecessors combined. (The actual deficits of President Nixon's first term did go over $100 billion, excluding the trust fund surpluses which were included with the general revenues.) The President impounded nearly $12 billion of certain congressionally appropriated funds; that is, on a selective basis he refused to spend these monies, resulting in a "line item veto" which the Constitution does not grant to the President. These presidential policies were challenged by certain interested parties in the courts and by Congress verbally and legislatively in an effort to get the President to "faithfully execute the laws."

Even so, Congress was partially responsible for this clash over the control of federal spending. For over a hundred years, Congress had assumed the economic powers granted to it by the Constitution and carried out its fiscal assignment unaided by the President. But as the functions of government expanded in the twentieth century, Congress conceded that it was not able to control the budgetary needs of the sprawling national government and passed the Budget and Accounting Act of 1921, which provided that the President prepare and present an annual budget to Congress. This executive budget is the blueprint which spells out the costs of the programs to achieve the goals outlined in the State of the Union address and to continue the ongoing programs.

Editorial cartoon by Pat Oliphant. Copyright, the *Denver Post*. Reprinted with permission of Los Angeles Times Syndicate.

"Stop worrying—we'll call it protective reaction!"

BUDGETING AND ACCOUNTING

The Budget and Accounting Act of 1921 established the Bureau of the Budget, changed to the Office of Management and Budget (OMB) in 1970, to assist the President in fulfilling his budget responsibilities; and the General Accounting Office (GAO), an independent agency to assist the Congress in providing legislative control over public expenditures. Even though the fiscal responsibilities of the nation were shared by the act, the initiative in fiscal affairs was clearly transferred to the President, with Congress now simply reacting to his proposals.

The budget and accounting process has four identifiable phases: (1) executive formulation and submission; (2) congressional authorization and appropriation; (3) budget execution and control; and (4) review and audit. (See Figure 11.1.)

When the President presents his budget message to Congress, it is actually the climax of about ten months of planning and analysis throughout the executive branch. In the spring of the previous year, each agency evaluates its programs, examines its continuing or new needs, and makes budgetary projections. These budget estimates are reviewed in each agency and by the OMB, and preliminary plans are presented to the President. The President also receives projections of the economic outlook and revenue estimates prepared jointly by the Treasury Department, the Council of Economic Advisers, and the OMB.

Following a review of both sets of projections, the agencies are given guidelines for the preparation of their budgets. Agency budgets are prepared and reviewed in detail by the OMB throughout the fall and early winter and then

Figure 11.1 Budget Cycle

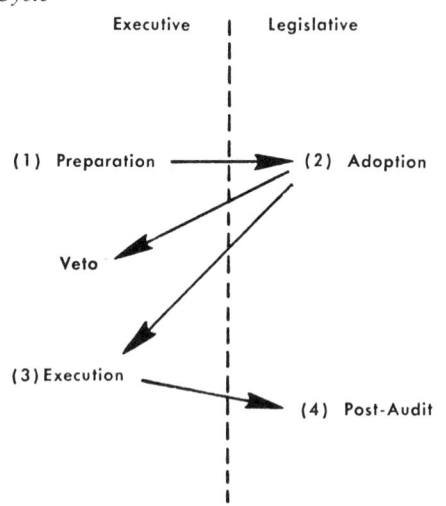

presented to the President. Overall fiscal policy problems are reviewed again in relation to the individual program requests, and the budget submitted to Congress reflects both of these considerations.

Congressional review starts when the President sends his budget to Congress. Congress can change programs, eliminate them, or add new ones. Until the conflict over control of spending erupted between Congress and the President in 1972-73, the usual course for Congress was to adopt the President's budget with only minor adjustments. In April, 1973, however, leaders of a special Senate and House study committee proposed major reforms in the congressional budget process. The Congressional Budget and Impoundment Act of 1974 requires Congress to adopt a budget resolution setting target figures for total appropriations, total spending, and appropriate tax and debt limits before acting on appropriations and spending measures. The law provided for the creation of new House and Senate committees to analyze alternatives and prepare the budget resolution. A Congressional Budget Office (CBO), with needed experts and computers, was provided for in the law to assist the budget committees in their functions.

The law imposes on Congress a budget timetable from March until October, following the submission of the President's budget, which requires a well-orchestrated effort by committees, the new Congressional Budget Office, and the new budget committees with the traditional authorization, appropriations, and tax legislative processes. Final action on appropriations bills, on a second budget resolution, and on a budget reconciliation measure takes place in September, and the new fiscal year begins October 1. The change from July 1, is to enable Congress to complete its budget role before the fiscal year begins and avoid the traditional practice of passing "continuing resolutions" authorizing agencies to continue operations until the appropriations are passed.

Once the budget is approved by Congress, it becomes the basis for the program operations of each agency. Central control is provided by the OMB, which apportions the appropriations and other budget authority to each agency by time periods (usually quarterly), or by activities. The agencies are not permitted to incur obligations in excess of the amounts apportioned. Since OMB is the President's agency and is responsive to his directives, it exercises its powers to insure flexibility in program administration as conditions in each agency change or as required by the values of the President.

Review and audit are the final steps in the budget process. The agencies are responsible for assuring that the obligations they incur and the resulting outlays are in accordance with the provisions of the authorizing and appropriating legislation. The OMB also reviews agency program objectives. In addition, the GAO conducts a continuing program of auditing, examination, and evaluation of administrative action. Its findings and recommendations for corrective action are made to Congress, to the OMB, and to the agencies concerned.

THE BUDGET AND THE ECONOMY

"In the 1972 budget, the federal government accepts responsibility for creating the climate that will lead to steady economic growth with improving productivity and job stability." The Nixon budget policy statement acknowledged, however, that "the object of prosperity without inflation" also required the monetary policy of the independent Federal Reserve System to provide fully for the growing needs of the economy, and that the wage and price decisions of labor and business must be characterized by increased restraint. "Only through a combination of fiscal policy, monetary policy, and private common sense can orderly economic growth be achieved."

The 1972 budget, with its full employment principle, committed the government to an activist role in promoting the nation's prosperity. The deficit spending was to be a stimulus to the economy, but the spending was to be held within the guidelines of the full employment budget principle. This policy was supposed to help bring about full employment without injurious inflation. The 1974 budget continued to postulate the federal government's responsibility to "help create and maintain—through sound monetary and fiscal policies—the conditions in which the national economy will prosper and new job opportunities will be developed. However, instead of operating primarily as a stimulus, the budget must now guard against inflation." President Nixon claimed that the surest way to avoid inflation or higher taxes or both was for Congress to join him in a concerted effort to control federal spending, and he asked Congress to establish a ceiling on spending at his budget request figure of $268.7 billion before any appropriation bills were passed.

These two budgets, with their attempts to stimulate the economy on one hand and to dampen the inflationary pressures on the other hand, reveal the theoretical justification for the full employment budget concept—to stabilize the economy from the periodic inflationary-depressionary swings of economic cycles. The full employment budget then is not so much a deceptive device to cloak the real government deficits, as it is an artful acceptance of government responsibility in the nation's economy.

The theory behind government programs to influence the economy is that the periodic, natural cycles of "boom and bust" can be flattened out, approximating an optimum level of full employment, steady economic growth, and real purchasing power which is not robbed by inflation. The theory requires government programs to stimulate the economy, using built-in stabilizing economic factors—such as tax incentives, public works programs, lower interest rates, more money in the income stream—to turn the economy up during depressions or recessions; and other stabilizing factors—such as increased taxes, and restrictive credit and monetary policies—to do the reverse during boom or inflationary periods. It also requires men in government positions with sufficient economic understanding to do the right thing at the right time. (See Figure 11.2.)

Figure 11.2 Economic Cycles

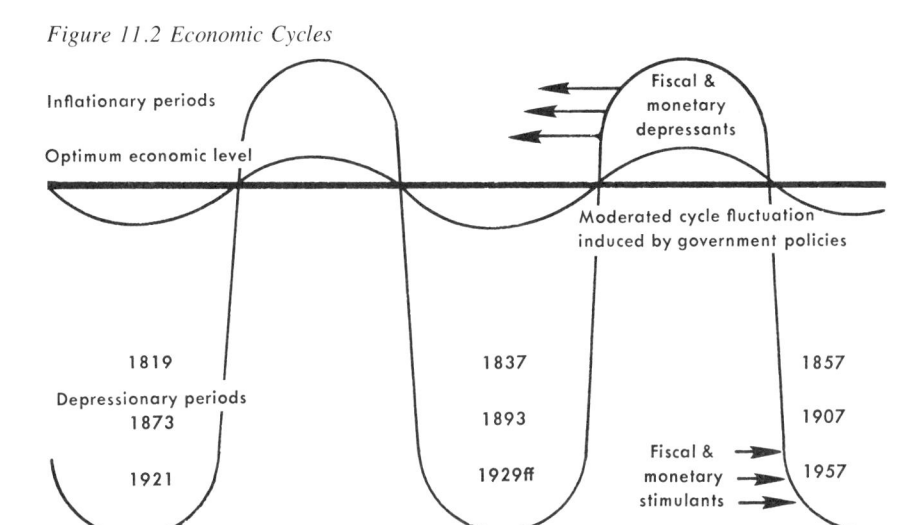

The New Deal type of tinkering with the economy has been practiced by every administration since the Roosevelt Administration in the 1930's and has been legally imposed upon the President since 1946, when recognizing the necessity of economic adjustment following World War II and still remembering the Great Depression, Congress passed the Employment Act of 1946. The act authorized the formation of the Council of Economic Advisers to assist the President in attaining the objectives of the act—full employment and economic stability. The act authorized the use of deficit financing, public works, and those economic controls necessary to maintain full employment, "in a manner calculated to foster and promote free competitive enterprise and the general welfare."

In his final economic report to Congress in January, 1953, President Truman said the Employment Act of 1946 represented the refusal of Americans to accept recurrent depressions as a way of life. Honoring the "New Frontier" campaign pledge to get the country out of the doldrums and get it moving again, President Kennedy proposed an $11 billion federal tax cut to increase private consumption and provide investment incentives. His choice of tax reductions and investment incentives obviated the use of other, more direct controls which were urged upon him, such as reducing the work week, increasing the minimum wage, expansion of credit, higher tariffs to protect American production, and a large public works program. President Johnson was successful in pushing the Kennedy program, which included a tax cut of $11.5 billion, through Congress.

The success of government stimulation of the economy turned into a problem of overheating with the escalation of the war in Vietnam. Economic prosperity brought inflation, which stubbornly resisted governmental efforts to control it.

Restrictive fiscal and monetary policies were applied during the latter part of the Johnson Administration in the form of a tax surcharge, and money and credit were tightened by raising interest rates. The Nixon Administration continued policies to cool down the economy. Federal spending was curtailed in 1969 and again in 1970. The Federal Reserve System maintained a restrictive monetary policy during the same period. These policies had no perceptible effect on inflation; but the flip side of the coin, unemployment, rose significantly during this period.

The sticky problem the Nixon economic policies had to meet was to curb inflation and promote employment at the same time. Because the traditional tools of economic stabilization aggravate one side of the problem if attempts are made to correct the other, the full employment budget of 1972 proposed to grasp both horns of this economic dilemma. It was designed to impose upper limits on outlays, to permit federal tax and spending programs to be planned in an orderly manner consistent with steady growth in the economy, and to "help achieve economic stability by automatically imposing restraint during periods of boom and providing stimulus during periods of slack."

The inflationary problem reached critical proportions during the summer of 1971. President Nixon had announced during the 1968 campaign that he would not resort to "jawboning" (presidential pressure on industry and labor to hold the line on prices and wages), and he resisted an "incomes policy" of wage-price guidelines. But on August 15, 1971, he surprised the nation with an announcement of a wage-price-rent freeze for at least 90 days. He created a Cost of Living Council headed by Secretary of the Treasury John B. Connally to formulate policies which would follow the 90-day freeze. Congress had provided the authority for this action in the Economic Stabilization Act of 1970. Added to this action the President announced a 10 percent import surcharge to promote American industry; freed the dollar from its historic $35-an-ounce gold price; established a "floating" dollar to help reduce foreign pressure on the dollar; ordered a 10 percent cut in foreign economic aid; and submitted a series of job-stimulating legislative proposals to Congress.

Phase II of the Nixon economic controls began in November, 1971, and continued throughout 1972. It set guidelines of 5.5 percent for wage increases and 2.5 percent for price increases. A Pay Board and a Price Commission were created with discretion to allow increases above the wage-price guidelines. The local Internal Revenue Service centers were charged with the responsibility of enforcing these economic policies.

In spite of the continuing inflationary pressures, acknowledged by his budget message to Congress in January, 1973, the President began his second term in office with the announcement on January 11, of Phase III of the Administration's economic policies, which made most of the controls of Phase II voluntary, with a threat that the Cost of Living Council would impose mandatory controls if necessary. Food prices continued to soar; irate housewives organized a meat boycott for April 1–7; President Nixon had to act. On March 29 the President announced on nationwide television: "Meat prices must not go higher"; and he clamped an indefinite ceiling on the retail price of beef, pork, and lamb. Consumer prices increased by 10 percent during Phase III, nearly three times the rate of the pre-Phase I period. Industrial goods on the wholesale market rose 14.8 percent during Phase III, more than three times the pre-Phase I rate. In addition to these rising prices, a falling stock market, a weakening of the dollar abroad, and congressional threats to legislate tougher controls forced the President to reconsider the administration's economic policies under Phase III.

On June 13, 1973, President Nixon announced another price freeze to last for up to sixty days, during which time the controls for Phase IV were to be worked out. Reiterating his distaste for controls, President Nixon said: "The Phase IV that follows the freeze will not be designed to get us permanently into

Cartoon by Arthur B. Poinier. Copyright the *Detroit News*. Used with permission.

Passing Dad on the moving stairs

258 *Public Policies in America*

a controlled economy, and [will be designed] to return us as quickly as possible to the free market system. We are not going to put the American economy in a strait jacket." But with Phase IV some sectors of the nation faced tougher controls than under Phase II—the administration had moved the economy full circle in two years.

President Ford inherited a serious set of economic problems: Inflation was at a record high; unemployment was rapidly approaching depression proportions; and the energy crunch of inadequate domestic supplies and unstable sources and prices of imported oil demanded immediate attention. President Ford's first budget, fiscal year 1976, reflected these problems.

THE BUDGET IN BRIEF

The President's 1976 budget proposed to meet longer-term national needs and the immediate short-run objectives of healthy economic growth without fueling the fire of inflation and to reduce America's dependence on imported oil. Aside from the budget programs to stimulate the economy, the deficits include the

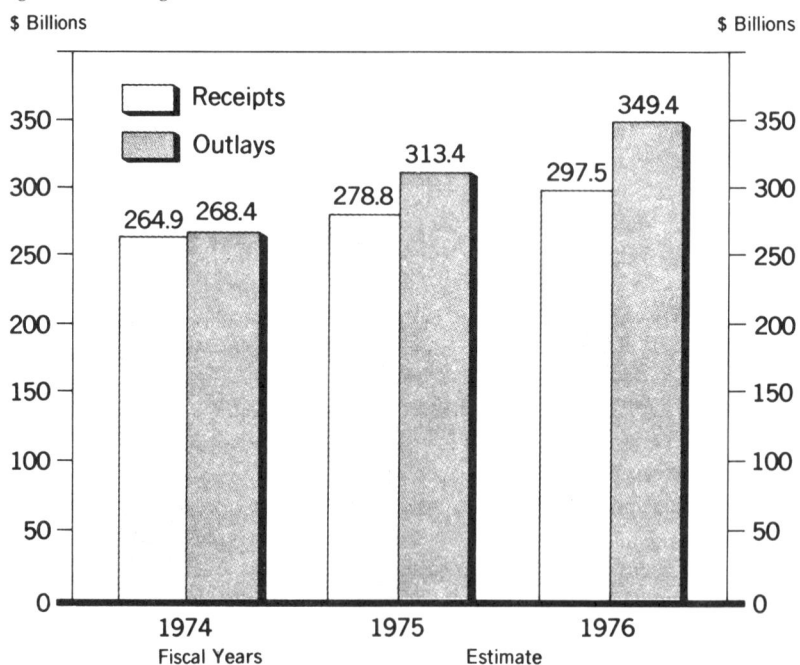

Figure 11.3 Budget Totals Since 1974

Fiscal Year	Receipts ($ Billions)	Outlays ($ Billions)
1974	264.9	268.4
1975	278.8	313.4
1976 (Estimate)	297.5	349.4

SOURCE: Office of Management and Budget, *The U.S. Budget in Brief, Fiscal Year 1976* (Washington, D.C.: U.S. Government Printing Office, 1975).

inevitable result of those aspects of the fiscal system that respond automatically to changes in the economy, such as budget receipts that go down and unemployment benefit payments which go up when the economy is depressed.

The budget proposed outlays of $349.4 billion and anticipated receipts of $298 billion, resulting in a deficit of $51.9 billion. The 1976 budget asked for $385.8 billion in budget authority; that is, new authority to make commitments to spend. Of this amount, $237.8 billion was to be spent in 1976, and $148 billion was to be spent in future years. (See Figures 11.3 and 11.4.)

The federal government relies heavily for its revenues on the personal income tax. This tax is based on ability to pay and provides for progressive or graduated tax-rate increases as income increases. Considering fairness in taxation, the progressive income tax approaches closer than any other tax Adam Smith's canons of taxation which he developed in his book *Wealth of Nations*: (1) taxes should be equitable and based on ability to pay, (2) taxes should not be arbitrary, (3) the payment of taxes should be made as convenient as possible, and (4) the cost of tax collection should be as low as possible. There is little dispute over the fact that the Internal Revenue Service is the most efficient tax collecting agency in America. The income tax also allows flexibility in taxation

Figure 11.4 Relation of Budget Authority to Outlays—1976 Budget
(Figures in brackets represent Federal funds only)

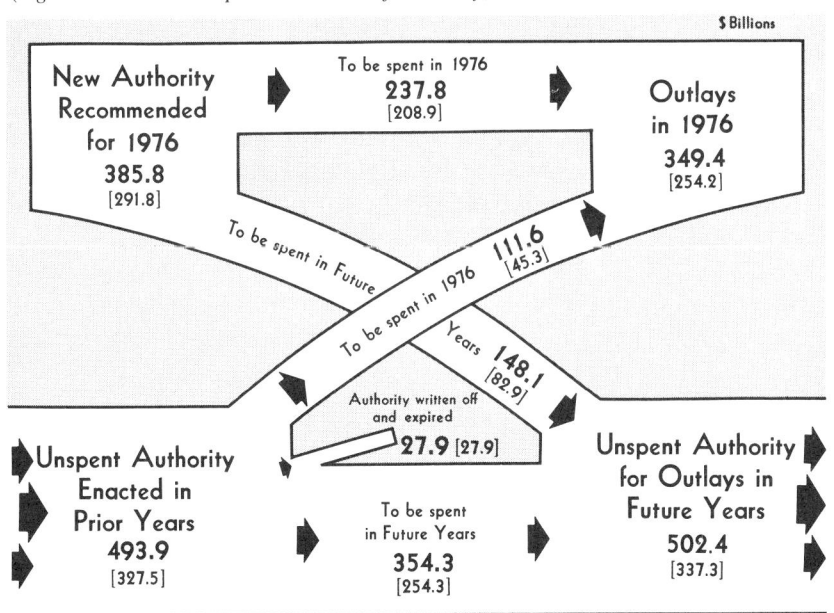

$ Billions

New Authority Recommended for 1976
385.8
[291.8]

To be spent in 1976
237.8
[208.9]

Outlays in 1976
349.4
[254.2]

To be spent in Future Years

To be spent in 1976
111.6
[45.3]

148.1
[82.9]

Authority written off and expired
27.9 [27.9]

Unspent Authority Enacted in Prior Years
493.9
[327.5]

To be spent in Future Years
354.3
[254.3]

Unspent Authority for Outlays in Future Years
502.4
[337.3]

NOTE: The difference between the total budget figures and federal funds shown in brackets consists of trust funds and interfund transactions between fund groups.

SOURCE: Office of Management and Budget, *The U.S. Budget in Brief, Fiscal Year 1976* (Washington, D.C.: U.S. Government Printing Office, 1975).

in providing greater or lesser revenue, as needed, simply by adjusting the tax rates. The income tax, however, does not measure up at all points to its theoretical potential. It is extremely complicated, it offers exemptions and loopholes to the economically powerful; it favors nonwage income and penalizes wage income.

Social insurance taxes and contributions produce the next largest amount of revenue for the federal government. Unlike the progressive income tax, social insurance taxes are regressive in nature, that is, the burden of these taxes falls more heavily upon low-income groups than upon more wealthy taxpayers. Even though the rates are uniform, these taxes take a higher percentage of the total income of low-income persons than of the total income of high-income persons. Regressive taxes are used extensively by state and local governments, which rely heavily on sales and property taxes for their revenues. Sales taxes

Editorial cartoon by Frank Interlandi. Copyright, *Los Angeles Times*. Reprinted with permission.

"Income tax time—when decent Americans turn into common crooks."

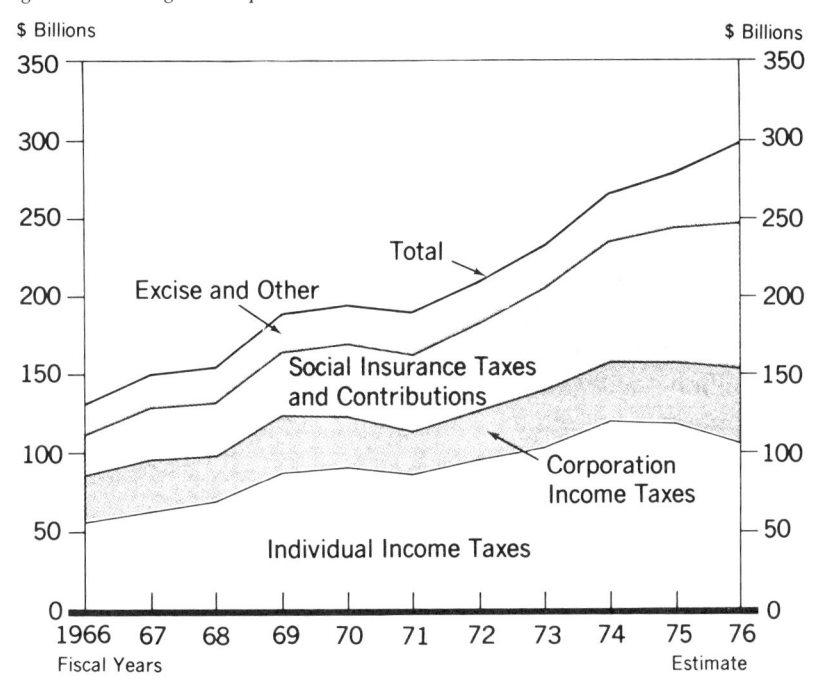

Figure 11.5 Budget Receipts: 1966–1976

SOURCE: Office of Management and Budget, *The U.S. Budget in Brief, Fiscal Year 1976* (Washington D.C.: U.S. Government Printing Office, 1975).

on the necessities of life are usually the most regressive in nature, since a major portion of the expenditures of low-income families is for such commodities.

Individual income tax receipts continue to be the major source of revenue for the national government, even though receipts have been reduced due in part to the tax credits to stimulate the economy, budgeted at $106.3 billion in 1976. Social insurance taxes were estimated to total $91.6 billion in 1976. These taxes include social security and other payroll taxes, unemployment insurance taxes, federal employment retirement payments, and premium payments for supplementary medical insurance. Increased energy tax proposals in the 1976 budget would increase excise taxes sharply, making excise taxes, estate and gift taxes, customs and miscellaneous receipts the next largest bloc of income—$51.9 billion. Corporation taxes, which were the second largest producer of revenue ten years ago, were expected to produce $47.7 billion in 1976. (See Figure 11.5.)

The three largest expenditures anticipated in the 1976 budget are income security, $118.7 billion; national defense, $94 billion; and health, $28 billion. (See Table 11.1) Even though the interest item in the budget appears to be the third largest expenditure at $34.4 billion, a substantial amount of interest out-

Figure 11.6 The Budget Dollar (Fiscal Year 1976 Estimate)

THE BUDGET DOLLAR
Fiscal Year 1976 Estimate

Where it comes from...

- Other 6¢
- Excise Taxes 9¢
- Borrowing 15¢
- Individual Income Taxes 30¢
- Corporation Income Taxes 14¢
- Social Insurance Receipts 13¢ From Employees / 13¢ From Employers

Where it goes...

- Direct Benefit Payments to Individuals 39¢
- National Defense 27¢
- Net Interest 7¢
- Other Federal Operations 11¢
- Other 11¢
- Grants to States and Localities 5¢ For Individuals

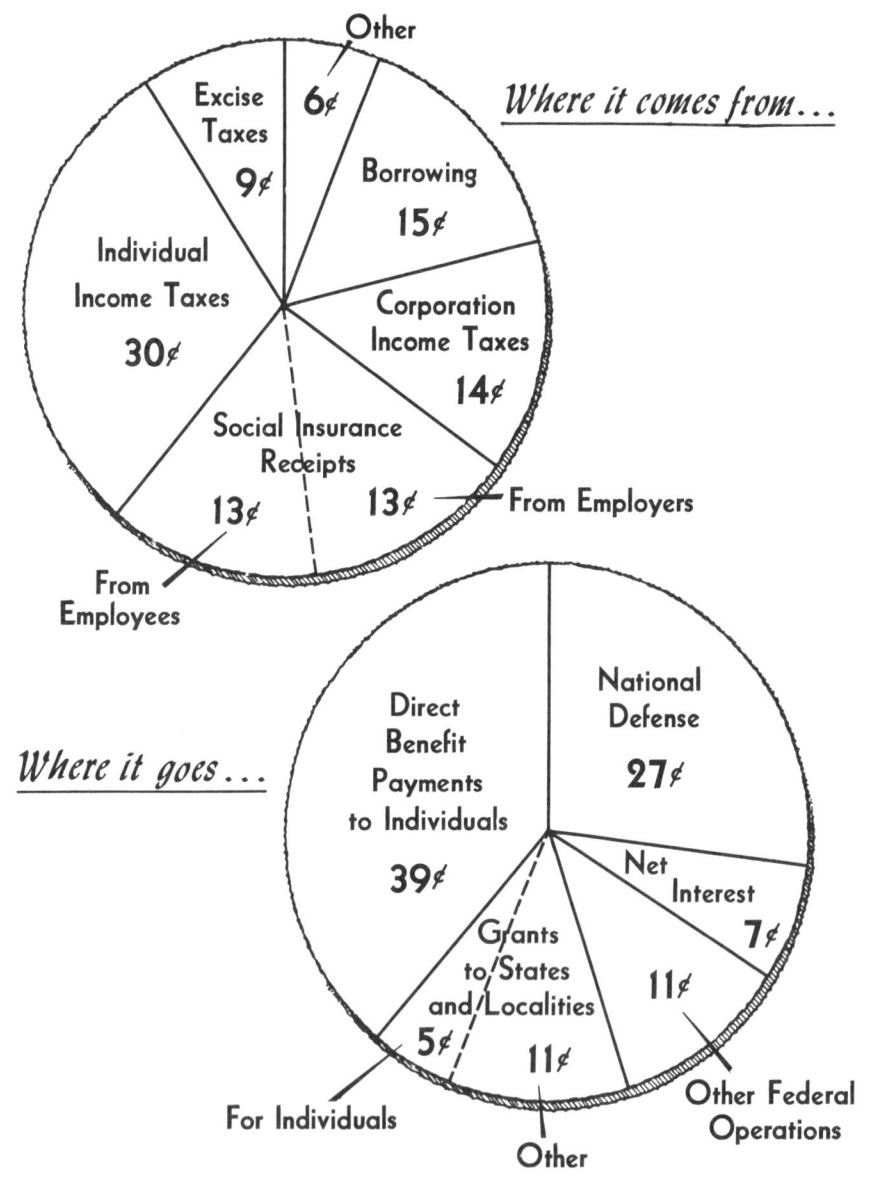

SOURCE: Office of Management and Budget, *The U.S. Budget in Brief, Fiscal Year 1976* (Washington, D.C.: U.S. Government Printing Office, 1975).

lays is paid to trust funds on government securities held by the funds. These payments amount to $8.3 billion, reducing the net interest outlay to $26.1 billion. In addition, $6.1 billion of the interest paid on securities held by the Federal Reserve banks will be returned to the Treasury as miscellaneous receipts, which reduces the amount of interest in 1976 that must be financed from receipts or additional borrowing to $20 billion. Grants-in-aid and general revenue sharing payments to states and local governments account for large outlays by the national government. When these payments are broken out of their functional categories they total 16 percent of the 1976 budget. (See Figure 11.6.)

Defense continues to be a major cost of government, in spite of a greater percentage of the budget dollar going to human resources. The 1976 defense budget was higher than any defense budget during the Vietnam War. Significant public pressure, however, brought about a reordering of American priorities

Cartoon by Bill Crawford. Reprinted by permission of Newspaper Enterprises Association, Inc.

The strongman

Table 11.1 Budget Receipts by Source and Outlays by Function, 1966–76
(In billions of dollars)

Description	1966	1967	1968	1969	1970	1971	1972	1973	1974	1975	1976
					Actual					Estimate	
RECEIPTS BY SOURCE											
Individual income taxes	55.4	61.5	68.7	87.2	90.4	86.2	94.7	103.2	119.0	117.7	106.3
Corporation income taxes	30.1	34.0	28.7	36.7	32.8	26.8	32.2	36.2	38.6	38.5	47.7
Social insurance taxes and contributions	25.6	33.3	34.6	39.9	45.3	48.6	53.9	64.5	76.8	86.2	91.6
Excise taxes	13.1	13.7	14.1	15.2	15.7	16.6	15.5	16.3	16.8	19.9	32.1
Estate and gift taxes	3.1	3.0	3.1	3.5	3.6	3.7	5.4	4.9	5.0	4.8	4.6
Customs duties	1.8	1.9	2.0	2.3	2.4	2.6	3.3	3.2	3.3	3.9	4.3
Miscellaneous receipts	1.9	2.1	2.5	2.9	3.4	3.9	3.6	3.9	5.4	7.7	10.9
Total receipts	**130.9**	**149.6**	**153.7**	**187.8**	**193.7**	**188.4**	**208.6**	**232.2**	**264.9**	**278.8**	**297.5**
OUTLAYS BY FUNCTION											
National defense[1]	55.9	69.1	79.4	80.2	79.3	76.8	77.4	75.1	78.6	85.3	94.0
International affairs	4.6	4.7	4.6	3.8	3.6	3.1	3.7	3.0	3.6	4.9	6.3
General science, space, and technology	6.8	6.3	5.6	5.1	4.6	4.3	4.3	4.2	4.2	4.2	4.6
Natural resources, environment, and energy	3.1	3.4	3.6	3.5	3.6	4.4	5.0	5.5	6.4	9.4	10.0
Agriculture	2.4	3.0	4.5	5.8	5.2	4.3	5.3	4.9	2.2	1.8	1.8
Commerce and transportation	9.0	9.2	10.6	7.1	9.1	10.4	10.6	9.9	13.1	11.8	13.7
Community and regional development	1.5	1.7	2.2	2.5	3.5	4.0	4.7	5.9	4.9	4.9	5.9
Education, manpower, and social services	4.1	6.0	7.0	6.9	7.9	9.0	11.7	11.9	11.6	14.7	14.6
Health	2.6	6.8	9.7	11.8	13.1	14.7	17.5	18.8	22.1	26.5	28.0
Income security	28.9	30.8	33.7	37.3	43.1	55.4	63.9	73.0	84.4	106.7	118.7
Veterans benefits and services	5.9	6.9	6.9	7.6	8.7	9.8	10.7	12.0	13.4	15.5	15.6
Law enforcement and justice	.6	.6	.6	.8	1.0	1.3	1.6	2.1	2.5	3.0	3.3
General government	1.4	1.6	1.7	1.6	1.9	2.2	2.5	2.7	3.3	2.6	3.2
Revenue sharing and general purpose fiscal assistance	.2	.3	.3	.4	.5	.5	.5	7.2	6.7	7.0	7.2
Interest	11.3	12.5	13.8	15.8	18.3	19.6	20.6	22.8	28.1	31.3	34.4
Allowances[2]										.7	8.0
Undistributed offsetting receipts	−3.6	−4.6	−5.5	−5.5	−6.6	−8.4	−8.1	−12.3	−16.7	−16.8	−20.2
Total outlays	**134.7**	**158.3**	**178.8**	**184.5**	**196.6**	**211.4**	**231.9**	**246.5**	**268.4**	**313.4**	**349.4**

[1] Includes civilian and military pay raises for Department of Defense.
[2] Includes energy tax equalization payments, civilian agency pay raises, and contingencies.

SOURCE: Office of Management and Budget, *The U.S. Budget in Brief, Fiscal Year 1976* (Washington, D.C.: U.S. Government Printing Office, 1975).

at the beginning of the 1970's, and in 1971 the amount spent on human resource programs was greater than that spent on defense for the first time in twenty years. (See Figure 11.7.)

The budget reflects changing conditions and felt needs in America and in the world. Budget requests for international affairs for 1976 were double those of 1973. The dramatic increases on the price of oil upset the patterns of international trade and finance, which prompted the budget request for a special financing facility to be used to aid countries suffering from those financial dislocations. The amounts budgeted for lunar space programs were reduced; energy research and development programs were increased. Outlays for environment and natural resources programs reached a high in 1974, and budget requests for 1976 called for a modest cutback, especially in conservation, recreation, and related programs. Farm stabilization programs were reduced four-fold from the high in 1969 in light of the change from farm surpluses to farm shortages. From 1966 to 1976 outlays in transportation have doubled, with the largest increase in the area of mass transit; outlays have more than tripled in the fields of education, community and regional development, and manpower training and social services; and the $28 billion budgeted for health was ten times the amount spent in 1966, reflecting the growth in Medicare and Medicaid payments.

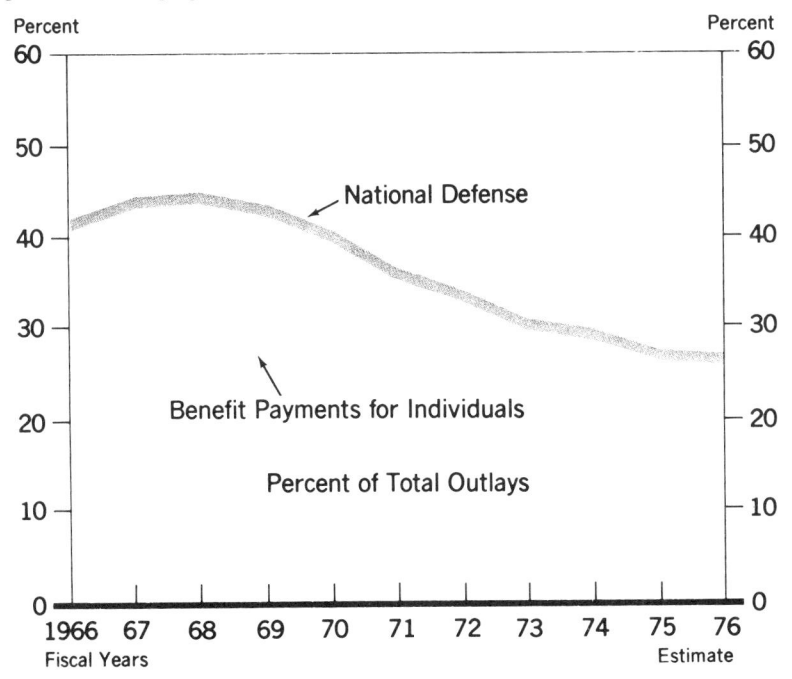

Figure 11.7 Changing Priorities

SOURCE: Office of Management and Budget, *The U.S. Budget in Brief, Fiscal Year 1976* (Washington, D.C.: U.S. Government Printing Office, 1975).

President Ford asked Congress for $16 billion in income tax relief in 1975 and 1976—$12 billion for individuals and $4 billion for businesses—as a temporary stimulant to the economy. The budget also sought to eliminate nonessential spending and curb federal spending initiatives except for energy. Congress responded on March 26, 1975 with a massive $24.8 billion tax-cut bill which President Ford, with some reluctance, signed into law on March 29. President Ford did not like the repeal of the oil depletion allowance tied to this law, nor was he fond of the tax credit for the purchase of new homes. He accepted the more likely deficit figure of $60 billion, but was concerned about the possibility of unleashing the other ravaging monster of the economy—double-digit inflation—if the spending mood in Congress were not controlled. Deficits approaching $100 billion would be unmanageable, he said, and would destroy the balance essential to anti-recession strategy.

CONCLUSION

The federal budget is both an instrument for managing the economy and a blueprint for ambitious government programs. The national government is the voracious beast that it is because of the many services and functions it performs—services and functions demanded by private and public pressure groups. Huge quantities of tax monies must be fed this leviathan to obtain these services. But this is not all. During the decade of the sixties, state and local governments consumed even more of the taxpayer's dollars from a percentage point of view. National governmental expenditures increased 95.8 percent; state governmental expenditures increased 123.2 percent; local governmental expenditures increased 111.5 percent. Excluding foreign and military expenses, which are exclusively the responsibility of the national government but which act for the benefit of all Americans, state and local expenditures exceeded those of the national government by approximately 15 percent. Also approximately 13 percent of the national budget was for aid programs to state and local governments.

Approximately one third of the Gross National Product is accounted for in national, state, and local government expenditures. The government appetite seems insatiable. But the government is like a cow—you have to feed it if you expect to milk it. The American people turn to every level of government and expect innumerable services; and the government therefore has tended to respond in paternalistic ways throughout the entire history of the United States.

12
AMERICA: THE SERVICE STATE

A visitor in the Senate gallery could feel the tense mood Monday afternoon, August 2, 1971, as the clerk called the name of each Senator for his vote. After twenty minutes, the clerk paused, listened briefly to Senator John Tower, R-Texas, and then called the name of Senator Marlow Cook, R-Kentucky. A hushed chamber awaited the senator's response. The vote was tied at forty-eight to forty-eight; the bill in question was $250 million in federal loan guarantees for Lockheed Aircraft Corporation.

Lockheed officials had come to Washington earlier in the summer asking for help to avoid bankruptcy. The Nixon Administration had warned Congress that the economy of the nation would be in peril if Lockheed was allowed to go under. Senator William Proxmire, D-Wisconsin, said bailing out the firm would be a blow against free enterprise. Two months of heated debate had preceded the vote, but now the moment of truth had arrived. The House had passed the bill the Friday before by the narrow margin of 192 to 189.

Senator Cook said, "aye." Vice-President Spiro T. Agnew was in the presiding officer's chair had his tie-breaking vote been needed, which it was not, as three Senators did not vote: Henry Jackson, D-Washington, who gave no reason; Lloyd Bentsen, D-Texas, who disqualified himself because he was a Lockheed director; and Karl Mundt, R-South Dakota, who was ill.

President Nixon was jubilant. He said in a prepared statement:

This action will save tens of thousands of jobs that would otherwise have been eliminated. It will have a major impact on the economy of California, and will contribute greatly to the economic strength of the country as a whole. It will help insure that the nation's largest defense contractor, and its largest airframe manufacturer, will continue serving the nation's needs.

Senator Proxmire, who had accused Lockheed of mismanagement in defense contracting, said: "It's very important that we now watch Lockheed like a hawk." He added further that the administration would require a little watching also: "There will be a big temptation on the part of the administration to keep them afloat by giving them sweetheart contracts."

Government beneficence to business is not new. The first Secretary of the Treasury, Alexander Hamilton, submitted his Report on Manufactures to Congress in 1791, in which he outlined the inducements which the government should employ to promote manufacturing. Foremost among his proposals was a protective tariff to reduce or eliminate competition from foreign manufacturing. Because of the "embarrassments which have obstructed the progress of our external trade," Hamilton said, "the expediency of encouraging manufactures in the United States, which was not long since deemed questionable, appears at this time to be generally admitted."

If not generally admitted, the general practice of American government has been greatly paternalistic over the years. The ebb and flow of this governmental generosity has been felt by different groups, in different degrees, and at different times in our history. A high tide of government gifts to some Americans came in during the post-Civil War period, which Mark Twain dubbed the Gilded Age. Vernon L. Parrington, in his own inimitable way, portrays the period in this selection entitled "The Great Barbecue":

Horace Greeley and Henry Carey were only straws in the wind that during the Gilded Age was blowing the doctrine of paternalism about the land. A Colonel Sellers was to be found at every fireside talking the same blowsy doctrine. Infectious in their optimism, naive in their faith that something would be turned up for them by the government if they made known their wants, they were hoping for dollars to be put in their pockets by a generous administration at Washington. Congress had rich gifts to bestow—in lands, tariffs, subsidies, favors of all sorts; and when influential citizens made their wishes known to the reigning statesmen, the sympathetic politicians were quick to turn the government into the fairy godmother the voters wanted it to be. A huge barbecue was spread to which all presumably were invited. Not quite all, to be sure; inconspicuous persons, those who were at home on the farm or at work in the mills and offices, were overlooked; a good many indeed out of the total number of the American people. But all the important persons, leading bankers and promoters and business men, received invitations. There wasn't room for everybody and these were presumed to represent the whole. It was a splendid feast. If the waiters saw to it that the choicest portions were served to favored guests, they were not unmindful of their numerous homespun constituency and they loudly proclaimed the fine democratic principle that what belongs to the people should be enjoyed by the people—not with petty bureaucratic restrictions, not as a social body, but as individuals, each free citizen using what came to hand for his own private ends, with no questions asked.

It was sound Gilded Age doctrine. To a frontier people what was more democratic than a barbecue, and to a paternalistic age what was more fitting than that the state should provide the beeves for roasting. Let all come and help themselves. As a result the feast was Gargantuan in its rough plenty. The abundance was what was to be expected of a generous people. More food, to be sure, was spoiled than was eaten, and the revelry was a bit unseemly; but it was a fine spree in the name of the people, and the invitations had been written years before by Henry Clay. But unfortunately what was intended to be jovially democratic was marred by displays of plebeian temper. Suspicious commoners with better eyes than manners discovered the favoritism of the waiters and drew attention to the difference between their own meager helpings and the heaped-up plates of more favored guests. It appeared indeed that there was gross discrimination in the service; that the farmers' pickings from the Homestead Act were scanty in comparison with the speculators' pickings from the railway land-grants. The *Credit Mobilier* scandal and the Whisky Ring scandal and divers other scandals came near to breaking up the feast, and the genial host—who was no other than the hero of Appomattox—came in for some sharp criticism. But after the more careless ones who were caught with their fingers where they didn't belong, had been thrust from the table, the eating and drinking went on again till only the great carcasses were left. Then at last came the reckoning. When the bill was sent in to the American people the farmers discovered that they had been put off with the giblets while the capitalists were consuming the turkey. They learned that they were no match at a barbecue for more voracious guests, and as they went home unsatisfied, a sullen anger burned in their hearts that was to express itself in fierce agrarian revolts.[1]

GOVERNMENT AND THE ECONOMIC INTERESTS

The economic goals of the Constitution, which were included to promote the economic growth of America, did not prompt paternalism only during the post-Civil War period when America was undergoing change from a predominantly agricultural to an industrial economy; but they have given rise to government aids to business, industry, and other economic interests throughout the course of American history. Indeed, not only Congress, but state and local units of government also have "rich gifts to bestow"; and the vested interests have not been unwilling to accept these "gifts." As a matter of fact, they have not been reluctant to pressure governments for the economic benefits available whether they are in the form of tariffs or subsidies on the national level, tax advantages on the state level, industrial parks on the local level, or whatever.

The Constitution provides that "Congress shall have power to promote the progress of science and useful arts, by securing for limited times to authors and inventors the exclusive right to their respective writings and discoveries." Under this power, Congress has provided that works such as books, plays, musical compositions, works of art, and photographs be protected by law for a period of twenty-eight years and be renewable for a second similar period. The Copyright Office of the Library of Congress administers this service. New sci-

---

[1] Vernon Louis Parrington, *Main Currents In American Thought,* Vol. 3, pp. 23–24. Copyright, 1930, by Harcourt Brace Jovanovich, Inc., renewed, 1958, by Vernon L. Parrington, Jr., Louise P. Tucker, Elizabeth P. Thomas. Reprinted by permission of the publisher.

entific discoveries and inventions are protected by patent laws (which were revised and codified in 1952), to the exclusive benefit of the inventor for a period of seventeen years. The patent holder can, of course, sell the right to use the invention to others. Because of the pressing problem of pollution, the Johnson Administration had legislation passed which required that pollution-control advances in the automotive field be shared with others in the industry.

Trademarks are authorized by Congress under the commerce power. The Lanham Trade Mark Act of 1964 allows the registration of trademarks which identify a certain product, such as "Coke"; service marks which distinguish a particular service, for example, "Air West" for airline service; collective marks which identify the goods or services of a particular group, such as "Sunkist" in citrus fruits; and certification marks, such as the Good Housekeeping Seal of Approval. Marks of all types are registered with the Patent Office of the Department of Commerce.

The government has promoted uniform standards which are highly beneficial to industrial growth based on mass production. The Bureau of Standards of the Commerce Department has pushed for weights-and-measures uniformity and also for the standardization of nuts, bolts, and so on, such as "national fine" and "national coarse" thread sizes. A uniform and stable money system, which Congress is constitutionally charged to regulate, is a vital aid to the economy.

A catalog of the helps to economic business would include the census and other vital statistics prepared by the Bureau of the Census; weather forecasting provided by the Weather Bureau; loans, guaranteed or direct, through the Federal Housing Administration, the Small Business Administration, and the Export-Import bank; coastal surveys by the Coast and Geodetic Survey; and in an age of wars, defense contracts and direct assistance to defense-related industries. For many of these economic aids, the clientele department is the Department of Commerce.[2]

An indispensable aid to economic activity is the postal system. It is the oldest government agency, antedating even the Constitution. It has undergone sharp criticism over the years because of its deficits and the political spoils role it has played from time to time. The value of a dependable, efficient, and inexpensive postal system is recognized by all Americans; and Congress passed legislation in 1970 converting the Post Office Department into an independent executive agency known as the Postal Service. The new agency went into effect on July 1, 1971.

Transportation in America has been governmentally subsidized from the beginning of the country. Congress has the power to establish post offices and post roads, in addition to its commerce and taxing and spending powers. Under this constitutional authority, the Cumberland Road of early westward-expansion

---

[2] See the *United States Organization Manual* for department and other agency organization charts.

times and the Interstate Freeway system of today were both built to serve the American people, and to serve truck transportation and other economic interests as well. From the digging of the Erie Canal by the State of New York during the infancy of this nation to the contemporary Joint Canadian-American development of the St. Lawrence Seaway—not to mention the direct subsidization of the merchant marine for national security reasons from Jefferson's administration on—maritime interests have had the windfall of government support.

The railroads of America were given help in their beginning with land grants, loans, and outright gifts; they have been supported financially all along the way; and when passenger transportation became a losing undertaking, they unloaded the burden on the government, which established the National Railroad Passenger Corporation to run a nationwide passenger system called Amtrak. The railroads, however, have been regulated "in the public interest" since 1887, when the Interstate Commerce Commission was established by an act of Congress. This regulating was done during a period when the railroads were a virtual transportation monopoly; but now there are competing systems of transportation, all of which are regulated and subsidized.

The newest form of transportation, airlines, has been aided and controlled by government like the rest. Mail contracts; federal funds for airports, landing systems, and the like; and the air controllers and maintenance technicians employed by the Federal Aviation Administration all reduce the costs of air transportation to the private companies.

The Department of Transportation is the primary governmental agency involved in transportation; but a number of regulatory agencies and corporations—such as the Interstate Commerce Commission, the Civil Aeronautics Board, and the Panama Canal Company—also are involved.

GOVERNMENT AND LABOR

The first foothold that organized labor gained in America which was not destroyed by a depression or adverse court action came after the Civil War, at the same time that the large industrial combines developed. The working man learned that he needed the strength of other workers in a union to bargain for employment, wages, working conditions, and other benefits. This was especially true in negotiations with the large industrial concerns which had become corporate-owned, in contrast, say, to negotiations with a private owner of a small firm who had a personal interest in his employees.

Economic combinations were considered conspiracies under the common law. Early in the nineteenth century merchants and businessmen gained the legal right to combine for economic purposes, but unions were considered as illegal conspiracies until the end of the century. In fact, the Sherman Anti-Trust Act of 1890 was probably intended to apply only to the growing business monopolies; but a conservative court applied the law to unions, prosecuting and convicting labor leaders under the act.

The Clayton Act of 1914 exempted labor unions from the Sherman Act's provisions against illegal conspiracies in restraint of trade. The Court ruled, however, that labor unions were exempt from the act only when they were lawfully carrying out their "legitimate objects." Indeed, labor unions were heavily involved in litigation until the Norris-LaGuardia Act of 1932 was passed. It restricted the federal courts in issuing injunctions against the unions and enforcing the provisions of "yellow-dog contracts" (the worker agrees not to join a union before he is hired). Until this legislation was passed, the injunction was used to break strikes, which, of course, weakened the union's bargaining position with management.

The National Labor Relations Act of 1935, commonly called the Wagner Act, brought to labor unions generally what had been gained by the railway unions in the Railway Labor Act of 1926. Employees were given the right to organize free from employer interference, and they were given the right to bargain collectively with employers through their elected representatives. The National Labor Relations Board was established by the act to supervise union elections and to prevent discriminatory hiring or tenure practices on the part of the employers.

The NLRA has sometimes been called a "Magna Charta" for labor, because it brought to labor the government protections labor desired—restricting employers but not applying similar restrictions on the unions themselves. Union power skyrocketed. To many Americans, not involved in labor unions, the act appeared one-sided. Management fought the act, and was able to get it modified in 1947 when Congress passed the Taft-Hartley Act over President Truman's veto.

The two basic provisions of the Wagner Act, the right of unions to organize and bargain collectively, were retained in the new Taft-Hartley Act, but some significant restrictions were imposed on labor: (1) an eighty-day cooling-off period could be invoked by the President if a strike threatened the national health or safety; (2) certain labor practices were made illegal, such as refusing to bargain collectively, discrimination against employees, and certain types of strikes (sympathy strikes, secondary boycotts, and jurisdictional strikes); and (3) the closed shop (a worker must belong to the union to be hired) was prohibited, but union shops (a nonunion worker can be hired, but he must join the union after a specified period of time—usually thirty days) were permitted unless outlawed under Section 14B of the Act.

Section 14B has been fought bitterly by labor. Union strength has been seriously curtailed in a number of states which have taken the option afforded to them by 14B and passed "right-to-work" laws. These laws simply rule out union membership as a condition of employment. Unions claim this allows workers all the benefits of union membership, such as higher wages, better working conditions, and even union arbitration of grievances, without having to pay union dues. Backers of 14B and right-to-work laws maintain that workers should be free to choose whether or not to join a union.

In 1958 the Landrum-Griffin Act was passed. It was aimed at getting rid of boss-rule of some unions and at giving the rank-and-file union member more say in union leadership. Provisions of the act permitted individual grievances of union members to come before a government board to have them aired. It essentially placed the government in the position of a third member in labor-management relations.

Even though the United States has not required compulsory arbitration, the government has intervened in a number of labor disputes during the 1960's. Two federal agencies, the Federal Mediation and Conciliation Service and the National Mediation Board, were created to assist in settling disputes. Additionally, and in some ways more significantly, the President performs a conciliatory role in labor-management disputes. An example of executive influence was the action of President Kennedy and his advisers in the negotiation of a steel contract in 1962. After the administration had insisted on both parties holding the line on wage-and-price demands, Roger M. Blough, the chairman of the board of United States Steel Corporation, announced a price hike. Other steel companies followed suit. Kennedy, and especially his Secretary of Labor, Arthur Goldberg, thought the government had been betrayed. The President turned all of the power of his office to get the price rolled back. The steel companies knuckled under and revoked their announced price increases. (But gradually the price of steel was increased and the consumer ultimately paid for it.)

The government's protection of labor has finally rested on Theodore Roosevelt's "Square Deal" and "New Nationalism" philosophy. He believed that labor, industry, and the consumer should all be given a square deal, and that the government should use its powers to achieve it. Since then we have had the "New Deal" and the "Fair Deal"—and some would add the "raw deal"—attempting to find the proper "balance" in society in which individual opportunities are protected for all. This is difficult. But with the increasing power of both organized labor and the big corporations, it becomes necessary to counter private power with the public power of the state.

THE ABUNDANT LAND

America is a land with rich natural resources for balanced economic growth. The call of free land was the motivation which brought many immigrants to the New World. And expansion across the continent continued to provide abundant land for each succeeding generation for over three centuries. The Jeffersonian agrarian ideas that farming produces a more self-reliant, independent, vigorous, healthier, spiritually stronger people than other occupational pursuits continue to be believed, even though times have changed and those ideas can be contradicted on nearly every point.

Government land policies over the years have promoted agriculture. During the colonial period land was free. The early land policies of the United States in the Old Northwest, which was owned exclusively by the national government, were to survey the area and to sell the land at nominal prices. The Homestead Act of 1862 gave 160 acres of land to any person who would live on and improve the land. The paternalism which Parrington described also applied to farmers.

The national government has encouraged scientific agriculture, beginning in 1839 when an act of Congress provided $1,000 for the collection of seeds and the distribution of information from agriculture investigation and research. In 1862, the Morrill Act established the land-grant colleges with a special emphasis on agriculture. In the same year, the Bureau of Agriculture was created, later changed to the Department of Agriculture. Experiment stations (1887) and county agents (1914) were provided for by acts of Congress to assist the farmer. Today, the Department of Agriculture engages in extensive research to improve farming techniques.

These activities—coupled with the assistance from states, industry, farm implement manufacturers, and farm supply companies—have contributed to a revolution in agriculture which has made the American farmer the best educated, most efficient, and most affluent farmer in the world. Improved agricultural methods have resulted in the ability of the American farmer to produce an ever-increasing amount of food and fibers with less land and labor. Following World War I, the capacity to produce agricultural commodities grew faster than the demand for these commodities, resulting in depressed conditions for farmers. Even during the 1920's, when the economy was booming, agriculture was in a depressed condition; and it had not appreciably changed when America was engulfed by the Great Depression.

The first New Deal program to help the farmer was the Agricultural Adjustment Act of 1933, which attempted to curb production and to bring farm prices of cooperating farmers up to a level equal to their purchasing power during the 1909–14 period (parity period) through a subsidy paid out of a tax imposed on farm commodity processors. This was declared unconstitutional in 1936.

A stopgap measure known as the Soil Conservation Act was then enacted by Congress. It induced farmers to shift from soil-depleting crops to soil-building crops. The farmers who cooperated were given payments out of the general fund. This program was soon followed by the second Agricultural Adjustment Act, passed in 1938. The new act followed the fundamental principles of the first AAA, but used the commerce clause for its authority. Its authors hoped this act would have more chance of being upheld by the Court. By this time, however, the Court had changed—the basic change resulting from changes in personnel, although the Court had also changed its philosophy somewhat.

Agriculture was encouraged during World War II, and an act of 1942 guaranteed supports at ninety percent of parity. After the war the Republican Eightieth Congress adopted a flexible price support for agriculture which paid as low as 60 percent if the crop were abnormally large, but paid up to 90 percent if the crop were below normal. Fixed price supports were reinstated after the election of 1948 and continued until 1954, when Secretary of Agriculture Ezra T. Benson sponsored a new agricultural bill calling for flexible supports on five basic commodities. This was followed in 1956 with the "soil bank," which reduced production by allowing farmers to take part of their land out of production to conserve the soil and water. The cooperating farmers received direct government payments for the land withdrawn.

President Kennedy attempted to embark on a new approach to meet the farm problem by allowing the farm commodity to seek its level on the market, the government then paying the farmer the difference between the lower price and an established "fair price." Congress continued its own program, however, instead of the administration's and allowed the administration only limited authority to set mandatory quotas on wheat production—and this only after a farmer referendum.

The 1960's, however, witnessed a better balance between supply and demand; and the concern over the population explosion caused some to think in terms of farm deficits instead of farm surpluses. Even so, Congress retained commodity supports in the omnibus farm act of 1965. The Agricultural Act of 1970 continued to protect and improve farm income, but to provide more flexibility for farmers to make their own decisions, and to develop greater reliance on the market place and less dependence on the government.

When Congress considered a new farm bill in 1973, it faced a new problem of food shortages and high market prices. In light of this changed condition, Congress revamped the farm program in the Agricultural and Consumer Protection Act of 1973. The new law retained subsidies for wheat, feed grains, and cotton if the market failed to reach a "target price" for each commodity. The initial target price set by the act was $2.05 a bushel for wheat, $1.38 a bushel for corn, and $.38 a pound for cotton. An escalator clause to reflect changing production costs allows an increase in these target prices beginning in 1976.

The 1973 Agricultural Act gave the Department of Agriculture standby authority to pay farmers for retiring land from production, but only if a condition of surpluses returns. One of the scandalous aspects of earlier soil bank programs was the amount paid to some of the large farms. The Washington columnist, Jack Anderson, reported that Senator James O. Eastland of Mississippi received $146,000 for *not* growing cotton; and that James G. Boswell of King County, California, received $4.4 million in soil bank payments in 1970 before Congress put a ceiling on these payments at $55,000. The Agriculture Act of 1973 reduced this subsidy again to $20,000 annual ceiling per farmer who participated in the soil bank program.

The 1973 law set a mandatory milk-price-support rate of 80 percent of parity through March 31, 1975. It extended the Food for Peace program at an annual authorization of $2.5 billion for another four years. It changed the old Rural Electrification Administration into an insured and guaranteed loan program, permitting 2 percent loans for electric and telephone systems in sparsely populated areas. The Rural Environmental Assistance Program (REAP) was reinstated, after the program was terminated by the Administration in December, 1972, emphasizing long-term contracts in dealing with conservation and pollution problems. The administration had also terminated the emergency Farmers Home Administration (FHA) loan program because of its soaring costs provided by generous provisions of acts of Congress in 1970 and 1972. Congress reacted by clearing a bill that was more acceptable to the Administration—one that returned the program to its pre-1970 status, but with interest rates increased from 3 to 5 percent.

GOVERNMENT AND THE ENVIRONMENT

The abundant land of America was initially thought to be inexhaustible. And even at the turn of the twentieth century there were few who were concerned about the preservation of America's precious natural resources. A typical attitude of many of the industrial tycoons at the turn of the century is the reported remark of the president of a large timber company when he was asked what would be left for future generations: "Posterity? What has posterity ever done for me?"

The modern conservation movement had its modest beginning during the administration of Theodore Roosevelt, who desired to be remembered for his conservation work more than for the acquisition of the Panama Canal Zone. Roosevelt appointed Chief Forester Gifford Pinchot to head a National Conservation Commission and to make an inventory of the nation's natural resources and the possibility of their exhaustion. By the end of his administration significant progress had been made toward saving the natural resources from selfish exploitation.

There are many agencies involved in conservation, most of which have been traditionally located in the Department of the Interior. The Department of Agriculture's Soil Conservation and Forest Service are concerned about conservation, as are the Tennessee Valley Authority and other agencies engaged in river development. The Nixon Administration also presented to Congress in 1970 two new agencies: the Environmental Protection Agency and the National Oceanic and Atmospheric Administration.

The EPA was established in December, 1970, with William D. Ruckelshaus as its administrator. Its purpose is to coordinate governmental action to assure the protection of the environment by abating and controlling pollution. The objective is to treat the environment as a single interrelated system and to reinforce efforts among other federal agencies with respect to the impact of their operations on the environment. To meet the engulfing problem of pollution, this agency is expected to coordinate and cooperate with the activities of state and local governments and private groups.

The National Oceanic and Atmospheric Administration (NOAA) was formed on October 3, 1970, within the Commerce Department, charged with conservation and antipollution purposes as follows:

To manage, use, and conserve these animal and mineral resources; monitor and predict the characteristics of the physical environment and the changes of the atmosphere, ocean, sun and solid earth, gravity and geomagnetism, and warn against impending environmental hazards, and ease the human burden of hurricanes, tornadoes, floods, tsunamis, and other destructive natural events.

Editorial cartoon by Lou Grant of the *Oakland Tribune*. Reprinted with permission of Los Angeles Times Syndicate.

"Think of the dough you'll save by firing Smokey the Bear."

278 *Public Policies in America*

The problems of pollution, produced in part by our affluent society, have been developing over a long period of time and have reached emergency proportions in a number of areas. Rachel Carson called attention to the dangers of DDT and other pesticides and herbicides in her book *Silent Spring*. Mayor Carl Stokes of Cleveland told a group of tourists that his city had the only river in the nation that had been legally declared a fire hazard! Not long afterward, the Cuyahoga River caught fire and before the blaze was extinguished, it caused damage amounting to $50,000. Swimming is prohibited in the Potomac River right in the nation's capital because the high level of pollution makes it unsafe.

Tons of pollutants are discharged into the Great Lakes, prompting the establishment of an International Control Commission to combat this problem. Oil spills and leaks, solid wastes and poisons which are discharged into the oceans are making the vast oceans polluted waterways. Another water pollution problem in some bodies of water is thermal pollution. The raising of water tem-

Cartoon by Bill Crawford. Reprinted by permission of Newspapers Enterprises Association, Inc.

"Is there a doctor in the house?"

perature upsets the balance of nature, resulting in plant life growth unsuitable for fish, animals, and human beings in some bodies of water.

The air over America is polluted by millions of tons of waste each year. About half of this pollution comes from automobile emissions. Industrial plants, coal-powered generating plants, smelters, incinerators, and many other pollutant-emitting agents add to the problem. A special air-pollution problem comes from atomic reactors, which contaminate the air with radioactive substances. Air pollution becomes costly and a serious health hazard in certain areas where atmospheric conditions do not permit the pollutants to be blown away.

Noise cannot be overlooked as a pollutant, an expense, and a health hazard. Noise pollution is generated by construction and transportation equipment, motors, engines, and electric or electronic devices. It was reported that a sonic boom caused by a U.S. Navy plane did $250,000 damage to a small Canadian town in ten seconds. Noise pollution is increasing at a rate such that it is projected to double in the decade 1974 to 1984. The EPA estimates that noise subjects about forty million Americans to hearing damage or other physical or mental health hazards, and that up to sixty-four million people live in homes which are affected by aircraft traffic or by construction noise.

A study by the economic unit of *U.S. News and World Report* estimated in 1970 that it would cost $71 billion to clean up America's polluted air, water, and land. It would cost $54 billion to clean up the waterways, $13 billion to fight dirty air, and $4 billion to improve the methods of disposing of solid wastes. On the other hand, this spending would actually save money! The costs of air pollution alone are estimated to reach $13.5 billion a year in property damage from soiling, corrosion, and abrasion of materials. How much more should be added for health care bills? And for farm crops?

President Nixon expressed real concern over the state of the environment when he addressed the American people on January 1, 1970: "The nineteen-seventies absolutely must be the years when America pays its debt to the past by reclaiming the purity of its air, its waters and our living environment. It is literally now or never." He followed this resolve with a message to Congress on February 10 outlining his legislative program. "No longer is it enough to conserve what we have; we must also restore what we have lost," Mr. Nixon said. "We have to go beyond conservation to embrace restoration."

The Congress responded with the Water Quality Improvement Act of 1970, which provided that owners or operators of ships or offshore facilities would be held liable for costs of cleaning up oil spills. Congress also held hearings on phosphates and mercury wastes. It enacted an air pollution bill which set definite deadlines for the production of low-pollution car engines, even though the industry claimed that the deadlines were technologically impossible and the administration felt that they should be set by executive order. Another bill authorized the extension of the solid waste disposal programs. This bill gave greater emphasis than previously to recycling and recovery of materials and energy from solid wastes.

These antipollution efforts, first begun vigorously on a national scale by the Johnson Administration with the passage of the Water Pollution Control Act of 1965, the Solid Waste Disposal Act of the same year, and the Air Quality Act of 1967, were continued with even greater emphasis in 1971, when the new Ninety-second Congress met following the 1970 election. Environment was a major issue in the off-year election. An organization called Environmental Action referred to twelve House members as the "Dirty Dozen" and called for their defeat because of their exceptionally bad records on conservation and other matters. Seven of the twelve were defeated, and six candidates endorsed by the organization won new House seats.

The 1972 session of Congress was the most productive for environmental protection in the nation's history, and set the machinery in motion for further action in 1973 and the years following. Six major measures were passed in the final days of the 1972 session: (1) the Federal Water Pollution Control Act Amendments of 1972 appropriated a whopping $24.7 billion to meet the ambitious goal of eliminating all pollutant discharges into U.S. waters by 1985 and an interim goal of making the waters safe for fish, shellfish, wildlife, and recreation by 1983; (2) a bill designed to protect human health and welfare, the marine environment, and the economic potential of the oceans and coastal waters became law in October, 1972, banning the transportation out to sea or dumping under any circumstances of radiological, chemical, or biological warfare agents or high-level radioactive wastes; (3) the Coastal Zone Management Act established a national program for the management, use, protection, and development of the coastal zones in the national interest, as it was estimated by a Senate committee report that by the year 2000 more than eighty percent of the nation's population will live within fifty miles of the coasts of the Atlantic, Pacific, Gulf of Mexico, or the Great Lakes; (4) the Marine Mammal Protection Act set a permanent moratorium on most killing of sea mammals and import of their products, and it provided for studies to determine sound principles of mammal resource protection and conservation; (5) the Federal Environmental Pesticide Control Act of 1972 required all pesticides to be registered with the EPA, which will regulate their use; (6) the Noise Control Act of 1972—the first comprehensive legislation aimed at reducing noise detrimental to health—which directs the EPA to propose noise emission standards on commercial products, including noise standards for aircraft, but gives the Federal Aviation Administration final authority.

Thus, the pressures of environmentalist groups—such as the Sierra Club, Friends of the Earth, and others—were at first quite successful in Congress. They had some significant initial successes in the courts also; for example, in blocking the Alaskan pipeline and the backing of water from the Glen Canyon Dam into the Rainbow Bridge National Monument. But when environmental policies impinged on economic interests, as they nearly always do, formidable opposition developed. President Nixon felt it necessary to veto the Water Pollution Control Act because of the amount of its appropriation. He called the costs "staggering, budget-wrecking."

The environmentalist gains of 1972 were threatened in 1973 when the summer scarcity of gasoline persuaded many Americans that the energy crisis was real. Congress responded by passing the Alaska Pipeline bill that authorized the construction of the controversial trans-Alaskan oil pipeline to carry crude oil from the rich North Slope fields at Prudhoe Bay. The Emergency Petroleum Act, requiring a mandatory allocation, was put into effect on December 27, 1973, by William E. Simon, the head of the Federal Energy Office. Daylight Saving Time and a mandatory 55 miles per hour speed limit on multiple-lane highways went into effect in January, 1974. The Administration also took action to alter the standards and deadlines established by the EPA because of the energy crisis.

The problem of the environment faces state and local units of government and every American citizen as well as the national government. For example, Governor Calvin L. Rampton explained that the State of Utah faces one of the worst potential air pollution problems of the nation. The valleys in Utah where the majority of the population lives are surrounded by high mountains and subject to temperature inversions. Under these conditions the lack of winds to blow away the pollution would make it difficult to live there if there were as many emissions per square mile as in some of the nation's greater population centers, such as Los Angeles. Identifying Kennecott Copper Corporation and the Geneva plant of U.S. Steel as the state's two major sources of air pollution, he asked: "I've got to keep pressure on them to clean it up, but do I put so much pressure on them that I close them down?"

America cannot afford to shut its economy down; but neither can it allow a further deterioration of its environment. Every American faces this challenge.

CONCLUSION

All levels of government in the American political system participate in the great barbecue served to the American public; but who gets what, when, and how depends to a great extent on the effectiveness of the group applying pressure on the decision makers. The public-be-damned attitude of former years may be gone today, but the profit motive is not. Many concerns spend considerable sums of money on public relations and other activities to gain, directly or indirectly, the paternalistic benefits government has to bestow. The environment, however, belongs to all Americans; and the government can no longer serve any particular interest at the expense of the environment or the public.

13
AMERICA: THE WELFARE STATE

An attractive woman in her late thirties with two young sons walked into the Wicker Park branch of the Cook County Department of Public Aid on a cold January day of 1971. She did not speak English very well, but that was not unusual in her heavily Latino neighborhood on Chicago's North Side. The heat and electricity in her apartment had been turned off three days before. She did not have money to pay the bills. What she wanted was help from welfare; what she got was a number, a seat on the crowded waiting-room bench, then an appointment to come back in a few days to discuss her problems.

The woman did not understand that she was probably lucky, considering the waiting lists for welfare, soon began sobbing, and finally lost her composure completely. She began shouting in Spanish, and when one of her sons tried to restrain her, she bit his hand. Finally she lunged into a hallway and collapsed on the floor.

"Rage, hysteria—and tears—are all staples of the U.S. welfare system," according to *Newsweek*. "In Chicago and in countless other cities around the country, welfare is a maddening mix of compassion and callous bureaucracy, pennypinching and shocking waste—the shame of a nation. And the problem is growing at an alarming rate." [1] National welfare costs nearly doubled during the four years from 1967 to 1971. They jumped a record twenty-seven percent in fiscal year 1971, to $16.3 billion, with 14.3 million Americans receiving welfare in June, 1971.

The commonly expressed stereotype of the person on welfare as a lazy, spineless, freeloader—usually from one of the ethnic groups—is simply invalid. Even though the incidence of poverty falls more heavily on ethnic groups in

---

[1] *Newsweek*, February 8, 1971. The case study is paraphrased from the same issue.

America, it may, from time to time for a variety of reasons, touch the life of any American. An example is that of Jerry Fuller, a middle-class, white Californian who was an electrical engineer for North American Rockwell Corporation. He helped build the command module for the 1969 moon landing, but as contracts for the company declined he was laid off. Fuller spent seven months looking for another engineering position; but all he was able to find was a low-paying, night-shift, clerical job, which was inadequate to cover the medical care for one of his daughters. Welfare was his only recourse, and he turned to it reluctantly.

"I was born at the time of the Depression," he said, "but I never knew anything about it. You really do develop compassion toward people in a situation like this. Maybe you don't really understand how poor people feel and why they can't pull themselves out unless you have been there yourself." His wife added: "I can drop down to a certain level because it is always with the knowledge that I am going to go back up again. But what do people look forward to if they don't believe they are going to rise out of it." [2]

The winter of 1971 found another atypical welfare recipient on the welfare rolls. Lawrence Brooks was a hard-working Maine lobsterman by trade in the summer and a logger in the winter. The demand for his logs fell; his wife became ill; and the bills could not be paid. The pride and rugged independence of this New Englander finally gave way to the need for welfare to carry his family through the cold winter. Brooks is typical of a group of welfare clients who are inadequately trained or otherwise incapable of meeting the demands of a technical and competitive society, or who work in seasonal occupations which produce incomes bordering on poverty.

The largest and fastest growing group on welfare is made up of families with dependent children. Mrs. Ginger Mack, black, in her late thirties, was left with seven children and went on welfare when her husband abandoned her. Born in Alabama, she had hopes of attending college when she came North. Mrs. Mack was forced to turn to welfare to support her family. Living in Chicago, with a welfare allotment in 1971 of $347 a month for everything, she became an expert on the welfare family's budget and on how to stretch the limited dollars. The rent payment and buying food stamps were her first expenditures each month. Even with careful budgeting, she had difficulty meeting her expenses. "I borrow food stamps; I'm always running short," she said. "You can't hardly survive. Everything about welfare is bad. Sure I'd like to get off—everybody wants to get off—but there's nowhere to turn."

Though the Fullers are at the moment without sufficient money to meet their obligations, they are not in poverty the way Ginger Mack and millions of others are. As expressed by Mrs. Fuller, the Fullers have hope that the pendulum will swing back up and they will be able to get out of poverty. But to Mrs. Mack,

---

[2] *Time*, February 8, 1971. The following two cases are also taken from this issue.

and so many like her, "there's nowhere to turn." To the successful over-fifty generation who struggled through the Great Depression, poverty in our affluent society is nearly incomprehensible. Responding to the comment that "I went through the depression and lifted myself out of poverty by my own bootstraps," a young widow who had grown up in a welfare family, married, and was then left with three small dependent children contrasted poverty today to the poverty of the Great Depression: "The poor thirty-five years ago had lots of company. Everybody was in the same deflated boat—but there was hope. Poverty today is not only not having money; it is not being able to look above your shoelaces."

In 1962 Michael Harrington focused attention on America's underclass in his book *The Other America*. The book stimulated President Kennedy to initiate measures which became President Johnson's "war on poverty." It came as a shock to affluent Americans that anyone should launch a war on poverty as a national policy during such prosperous times. It was hard to believe that poverty was as widespread as the Johnson Administration claimed. But the millions of Americans who live in poverty are rarely seen by the majority who live fairly comfortably. Poverty exists in the out-of-the-way places—city slums, withering-away little farming towns, mining ghost-towns—where most Americans rarely venture, or if they do, they seem to have invisible blinders on which screen out the undesirable sights. Many of the poor are old people; many are children; and most of them are unemployable. And, as Harrington puts it, they have no spokesman: "The people of the other America do not, by far and large, belong to unions, to fraternal organizations, or to political parties. They are without lobbies of their own; they put forward no legislative program. As a group, they are atomized. They have no face; they have no program."

Michael Harrington revisited the other America at the end of 1968. He found that the condition he described in his earlier book "is objectively not quite as evil as it was; politically and morally, it is worse than ever. For despite a long, federally induced boom and an 'unconditional' war on poverty, tens of millions of Americans still live in a social underworld and an even larger number are only one recession, one illness, one accident removed from it." [3]

The continuing welfare problem America faces today is due in part to the fact that we have had that one recession, and many people have had that one illness or accident that has thrust them into poverty. Additionally, governmental policies during the first Nixon Administration were willing to "trade off" a little unemployment in an attempt to gain increased price stability. The modest employment gains of the war on poverty were consequently somewhat neutralized by the joblessness that at times reached six percent of the work force and a lingering high rate of inflation.

The war on poverty has won a few rounds, however, as millions of people

[3] "The Other America Revisited," *The Establishment and All That* (Santa Barbara: The Center for the Study of Democratic Institutions, 1970), p. 30.

have crossed the poverty line, about a million a year, since 1946. Citing a 1973 study based on the 1970 census, by Ben Wattenberg and Richard Scammon, the authors of *The Real Majority,* columnist Peter Lisagor said: "A slender majority of black Americans have moved into the lower middle class in the last decade." Partial credit for this improvement must be given to the New Frontier and Great Society programs. The general appraisal of Wattenberg and Scammon is that "the image of the black in America must be changed from an earlier one of an uneducated, unemployed, poverty-stricken slum dweller, to that of an individual earning a living wage at a decent job, with children who stay in school and aspire to still-better wages and still-better jobs, not living in a slum (but still in a ghetto) in a decent if unelaborate dwelling, still economically behind his counterpart but catching up."

Even though some blacks have broken out of poverty and into the lower middle class, the situation is not uniformly good for all blacks. Blacks have not achieved a status comparable to whites, as poverty still afflicts large numbers. Also, poverty is not confined to blacks or other ethnic groups, but afflicts whites as well. There are still millions of Americans who are poor. The antipoverty efforts of the 1960's brought them into visibility, if not out of poverty.

PUBLIC WELFARE

If Americans now are conscious that poverty does exist, they are not convinced that the patchwork of public welfare does or can correct the problem. Indeed, many believe the present welfare system contributes to the continuing cycle of poverty. How did the cycle develop, and, more importantly, where does America go from here?

Background of Welfare

The problem of the poor has always existed. Government programs dealing with the poor began at least as early as 1349 in England during the Black Death, when a law was passed which made it a crime, punishable by branding or mutilation, for any physically fit worker to refuse employment when offered. Later the famous Elizabethan Poor Law, passed in 1601, outlined the relief system used in both England and America for nearly three centuries. Able-bodied adults were put to work; children of the poor became indentured servants; others were placed in almshouses or workhouses.

Private benevolence and religious charity have helped the poor in all periods of time and in all countries. In America, because of our federal system, public assistance was considered to be the responsibility of state and local units of government. Beginning with the Great Depression, though, the states have been unable to meet the welfare demands alone and the national government has lent assistance.

286 *Public Policies in America*

The New Deal

The first national war on poverty of serious proportions was the New Deal during the 1930's. This required a reordering of values which (1) accepted, perhaps grudgingly, the fact that the federal government must attack poverty, which was nationwide; (2) deemphasized the rights of property which characterized America during the "Golden Twenties"; (3) stressed the dignity and worth of every human being; and (4) demanded equal economic opportunity. The challenge of poverty required strategies which would change attitudes and values, improve skills and opportunities of the poor, and alter the political and economic structure to keep the avenues of opportunity open.

There were three major thrusts of the New Deal to overcome the depression. The first was in the area of direct relief. The Works Progress Administration (WPA) and the Civilian Conservation Corps (CCC) were a couple of a number of programs in this area. The WPA offered work to the poor and paid them a modest amount. Many of the make-work projects seemed worthless to the workers and they often stood around, leaned on their shovels, and just put in their time. Though the program became a symbol of indolence promoted by government handouts, the WPA brought food to the hungry and some worth-

Copyright © 1960 by Burr Shafer. Reprinted with permission.

**"This business of taking from the rich and giving
to the poor could easily become a
political theory."**

while public projects—such as irrigation systems, public sanitation projects, and the development of recreational areas—were accomplished. The CCC paid the enlistee a dollar a day and subsistence for a year on a variety of conservation and other worthwhile projects. Flood control measures such as terracing mountains, reforestation projects, and the like were typical undertakings.

The second thrust of the New Deal concerned recovery. The Public Works Administration (PWA) focused on long-range public building projects which would help the poor by promoting jobs. The National Recovery Act (NRA) was an attempt to induce business and industry to establish codes of fair competition, start producing again, and promote economic growth. Farm recovery was to be achieved through the Agricultural Adjustment Act. Many of these recovery programs were declared unconstitutional by the Supreme Court, but President Roosevelt and Congress passed new legislation to achieve the same result—recovery.

The third thrust of the New Deal was in the area of reform. The stock market crash and the bank failures prompted the creation of such agencies as the Securities and Exchange Commission to regulate the sale of stocks and bonds, and reduce the speculative consequences which contributed to "Black Friday" on Wall Street in 1929, and The Federal Deposit Insurance Corporation to protect the person who deposits his money in banks. Other measures regulated the practices of banks to avoid future failures.

The New Deal overturned the Malthusian, Spencerian, Darwinist concepts that government had no business meddling with the economy, that the harsh chips-of-life should be let fall where they may; and replaced them with the Keynesian notion that government has a positive responsibility to promote a stable, productive economy.

Social Security Act of 1935

The heart of the whole New Deal poverty program was the Social Security Act of 1935. This act provided for a twofold program of insurance and public assistance. Insurance programs against the economic hazards of (1) old age, (2) death, (3) disability, and (4) unemployment were (and still are) financed through taxes on the employee, the employer, and the self-employed. The first three goals—old-age, survivor's, and disability insurance (OASDI)—were established on an insurance principle; but today the reserve to pay the beneficiaries is not increasing and the tax income just about covers the outlay in social security. What the social security plan amounts to in this area is a tax on those who are presently working for those who are no longer productive. Social security benefits have been increased periodically, as have the taxes; in 1972, Congress increased the benefits by twenty percent and provided for an automatic increase in benefits whenever the cost of living increased by more than three percent in a calendar year. Benefits and the tax base were again increased in 1973.

Unemployment insurance is financed by a tax which only the employer pays. This is a measure designed to bridge the periods of unemployment and usually only runs for a few weeks. It is a combined federal-state program, hence the base and the tax vary from state to state, as does the amount paid to the unemployed worker and the time of his entitlement.

The Social Security Act of 1935 also established three assistance programs: Old-Age Assistance (OAA), Aid to Families with Dependent Children (AFDC), and Aid to the Blind (AB). In 1950 a fourth assistance program was added: Aid to the Permanently and Totally Disabled (APTD). On January 1, 1974, the Supplemental Security Income program of the national government replaced the state welfare programs for the aged, blind, and disabled.

AFDC

The greatest increase in the number of welfare recipients has been in the number of families with dependent children receiving aid. In 1950, the number of AFDC recipients, largely children and the mothers taking care of them, was 2.2 million, and the cost was $550 million; in 1960 the number had risen to 3.02 million, and the cost to $1.056 billion; in 1970 the number had skyrocketed to 9.5 million and the cost to $4.8 billion. President Ford's budget estimated outlays for 1976 at $4.7 billion. This was based on proposed reforms to improve management and reduce abuses in the AFDC program. The extent of abuse in this program is quite controversial, and studies vary in their estimates. The budget figures estimated that of 3.2 million cases on the rolls in 1974, 9.3 percent were ineligible, 20.6 percent were receiving overpayments, and 8 percent were receiving underpayments. Target limits for agencies administering AFDC were set by the Social Security Administration of no more than 5 percent overpayments and 3 percent ineligibles, otherwise federal money may be withheld.

The typical AFDC recipient stays on the rolls for only twenty-three months, according to the Department of Health, Education, and Welfare (HEW). Moreover these families are not all large. The average is four persons, compared with 4.2 in the general population. The number of illegitimate children in AFDC families is somewhat larger than estimates of all such American children; but figures on illegitimacy among the middle and upper classes—or on their abortions—are not available.

The core of the welfare problem is poor families with small children. Other categories have remained relatively stable and are likely to remain so or decline, such as OAA, which will be reduced in the same proportions as OASDI covers more retiring workers and places a retirement floor under the elderly. It is obvious that rather than treating the symptoms of poverty with various aid programs, the causes of poverty must be attacked.

The War on Poverty

The first major national attack on the roots of poverty came with the passage of the Economic Opportunity Act (EOA) of 1964. The goal of this legislation was the reduction of poverty; the means of trying to achieve it was through training and education; the target was youth. Studies of AFDC families point out that forty percent of the parents of these families were raised in families on public relief; and two-thirds of the families classified as poor are headed by persons with less than an eighth grade education. If the cycle of poverty is to be broken, it follows that training toward productive jobs is essential and employment opportunities must be available.

The Office of Economic Opportunity (OEO), operating on the basis of hard data that demonstrated disadvantaged children become relatively more so under traditional education which is geared to middle-class values and standards, started some ambitious and costly training programs. Project Head Start was begun in the summer of 1965; its objective was to prepare the preschool child from disadvantaged families to meet the competition of school. When it was found that this program needed a follow-up program, Project Head Start Followthrough was added.

Programs were established for teenagers, particularly for those who were neither in school nor working. The Neighborhood Youth Corps helped the youth from poorer families to stay in school through part-time work. Upward Bound gave opportunities to those high school dropouts who had the intellectual potential to go to a college campus for special summer courses to make up their high school deficiencies and to rekindle their enthusiasm to continue their education. Job Corps, about which there was so much public controversy and little real understanding, provided education and training in rural conservation and the trades for young people from the poorest families. The corpsman lived in a center where he learned in a work-training setting.

The EOA provided adult education and help in the Community Action Program (CAP). The philosophy of the CAP program was to help the poor learn how to help themselves. Among the programs under CAP were educational programs for adults; consumer education classes; neighborhood organizations and services for self-help; on-the-job training; and the foster grandparent program, which gave the elderly poor an opportunity to earn money while they taught skills to the youth who were poor.

Another provision of the EOA established the Volunteers in Service to America (VISTA), which was a domestic "peace corps." Volunteers worked in depressed areas to help the poor overcome the conditions of poverty. An interesting irony occurred in VISTA when an Indian volunteer from Idaho was assigned to work with poor blacks in Washington, D.C., while, at the same time, a black from Washington, D.C., was assigned to work with the Ute Indian tribe in Utah.

Paradoxically, while the war on poverty reduced the number of families considered "legally poor," the number of welfare recipients and costs continued to rise. President Lyndon Johnson's domestic war did not end in victory, but neither did it end in defeat. It brought about public discussion of a number of welfare alternatives which, among others, include the controversial guaranteed annual income and negative income tax proposals. The negative income tax would provide tax brackets below the zero-tax line, with the poor receiving payments if below an established poverty line. Most who advocate the negative income tax approach propose modest scales which would encourage privately earned income.

The Nixon "Workfare" Program

When President Nixon proposed the Family Assistance Plan (FAP) in August, 1969, he did not propose to improve the existing system; he proposed to replace it. In addition to the revolutionary proposal of a guaranteed annual income to every American family—working or nonworking—the FAP proposed to transfer welfare from the states to the national government. Welfare had become a national scandal; it was also a national problem, suggesting a national solution.

Daniel Patrick Moynihan, Nixon's principal designer of the FAP, contended there is a connection between wealth and poverty: "As we have rushed ahead toward more efficient systems of production, we have been pretty careless about the people who got left behind in the process." He also concluded the problem is national in scope: "Most of the problem of dependency in America today is the by-product of a defunct system of Southern agriculture. It has been a kind of fly-now, pay-later arrangement, only the bills come due not in Mississippi but in Chicago. A lot of persons in Chicago ask, reasonably enough, in what way they are responsible and why they should pay."

President Nixon's State of the Union address, in January, 1971, urged Congress to make the unfinished business of the Ninety-first Congress the first priority business of the Ninety-second Congress, among which, he said, "the most important is welfare reform." The President continued:

The present welfare system has become a monstrous, consuming outrage—an outrage against the community, against the taxpayer, and particularly against the children it is supposed to help.

We may honestly disagree, as we do, on what to do about it. But we can all agree that we must meet the challenge, not by pouring more money into a bad program, but by abolishing the present welfare system and adopting a new one.

So let us place a floor under the income of every family with children in America—and without those demeaning, soul-stifling affronts to human dignity that so blight the lives of welfare children today. But let us also establish an effective work requirement.

The Family Assistance Plan, according to the President's budget message, would remove the principal evils of the existing system by setting national eligibility standards; balancing strong training and work requirements with equally strong training and work incentives; giving financial relief to the states; and establishing a federal floor under benefit payments for *all* families with children, including for the first time, those with working fathers. It contained the following provisions:

I. Eligibility: Those families whose income is less than $500 per year for each of the first two members of the family, $300 per year for each additional member, and whose resources are less than $1,500 per year. (For a family of four the income floor would be $1,600.)
 II. Exclusions from Income:
     1. The first $720 per year of family earnings plus one half of the remainder.
     2. Income of a child or for child maintenance while training for employment.
     3. Home Produce.
     4. One half of all unearned effects.
III. Exclusions from Resources: Home, household goods, personal effects.
 IV. Basic Federal Payment: $1,600 per year.
     Family earnings beyond $720 would reduce the federal payment 50¢ for each dollar earned until the family's income reached $3,920, when benefits would cease. (The family works itself out of poverty.)

Congressman Wilbur Mills of the House Ways and Means Committee reported out a comprehensive welfare reform measure patterned after the Nixon proposal in a major amendment to the Social Security Act (HR 1). The Family Assistance Plan provision of the bill increased the income floor to $2,400 for a family of four with no outside income. The House passed the bill on June 22, 1971, but a deeply divided Senate killed welfare reform in October, 1972, passing instead three test programs. In addition to the administration's FAP, the Senate Finance Committee's plan (which made families headed by able-bodied adults ineligible for welfare and the adults were required to take federally guaranteed jobs), and a more liberal plan guaranteeing $2,600 to a family of four were to be tested for two to four years at a cost of $400 million each year.

Even though welfare reform was one of President Nixon's six major goals during his last two years of his first term in office, after the 1972 election he dropped the FAP and concluded that the welfare mess was a result of running down the "work ethic." He recommended that the poor pull themselves up by their bootstraps. "The average American is just like the child in the family," he said in an interview on the eve of the election with the *Washington Star-News*. "You give him some responsibility and he is going to amount to something. He is going to do something. If, on the other hand, you make him completely dependent and pamper him and cater to him too much, you are going to make him soft, spoiled and eventually a very weak individual."

PUBLIC HEALTH SERVICES

In 1798, Congress established hospitals for merchant seamen, which began a national public health role. Today, the Public Health Service (PHS) not only provides health and hospital services for merchant seamen; but similar services are provided for American Indians, war veterans, active military personnel, congressmen and other civilian public employees in certain circumstances. Over thirty million Americans are so served.

Immigration prompted the Public Health Service to concern itself with communicable diseases. Today, through the National Institutes of Health, the PHS is supporting medical research to find cures for or to prevent the major health hazards: heart disease, cancer, stroke, and other diseases. President Nixon's budget for fiscal 1972 called for $1.355 billion for biomedical research, including $100 million to launch an intensive campaign to find a cure for cancer. The President said: "The time has come in America when the same kind of concentrated effort that split the atom and took man to the moon should be turned toward conquering this dread disease. Let us make a total national commitment to achieve this goal. America has long been the wealthiest nation in the world. Now is the time we became the healthiest nation in the world." The 1974 budget called for a sharp increase of $4 billion over the 1973 amount to a total of $21.7 billion for health programs—with significant increases in funds for cancer and heart disease research, expanded funding of vital health manpower programs, and increased financial support for health services.

To protect the consumer, Congress in the early 1900's passed the Pure Food and Drug Act and the Meat Inspection Act. These acts have been strengthened as new threats to the health of the American public have arisen. The Food and Drug Administration (FDA), a division of the Department of Health, Education, and Welfare, investigates the effects of certain drugs and certifies them for use only after exhaustive testing. When thalidomide, a sedative given to pregnant mothers in Europe, caused the birth of deformed babies, American mothers were spared this tragedy because the FDA had not certified the drug for use in America. The FDA attempts to protect the consumer from contaminated, adulterated, or otherwise harmful foods and drugs. National health agencies cooperate with state and local agencies which have similar agencies and responsibilities.

The federal government has subsidized heavily the training of health personnel over the years. During wartime, the need for medical personnel prompted the national government to help the medical schools and the medical students financially in order to obtain their skills. The federal government also has been active in promoting medical education and services in the postwar period. Under the 1946 Hill-Burton Act, the federal government granted over $5 billion during a twenty-year period toward hospital construction. In 1963, Congress passed the Health Professions Educational Assistance Act, authorizing grants to build medical and dental schools and providing loans to medical and dental students. In 1964, Congress passed the Nurse Training Act to assist the nursing profession in similar ways. And in 1965, scholarships for needy students in health fields were set up by Congress. President Nixon continued national support for medical training; his 1972 budget request called for a $89 million increase, to a level of $577 million, for health manpower programs. This support was sharply increased again in the 1974 budget.

Following his election in 1948, President Truman proposed a national health-insurance program to be financed through a payroll tax; but the idea was branded as "socialized medicine" by the powerful American Medical Association. The AMA hired a leading public relations firm and pumped millions of dollars into its campaign against the program. Although the AMA successfully blocked any legislation throughout the 1950's, the arguments that the poor—especially among the chronically ill senior citizens—could not afford private medical insurance nor pay costly medical bills brought forth a compromise measure in the form of the Kerr-Mills Act of 1960. This act provided some help to the poor through federal grants-in-aid.

In 1965, President Johnson delivered a special message to Congress on health. He noted that four out of five persons sixty-five or older have chronic diseases that require hospitalization or other services which the retired person cannot afford. He urged Congress to extend the social security system to cover basic health services for the elderly. Congress complied with the President's request and passed the Health Insurance for the Aged Act, popularly known as Medicare.

Medicare covers hospitalization and nursing home care for specified periods of time, and home visits by nurses or other health workers after release from the hospital. These services are financed by a payroll tax on the employee and employer which is included in the social security tax. The tax rate is scheduled to increase as the demand increases.

Another insurance feature under the act covers doctors' bills. This plan is voluntary and is financed by a modest deduction from the senior citizen's monthly social security check, if so requested, and is matched by the federal government.

Most states have adopted Medicaid programs similar to the national Medicare program; but they are designed primarily to assist the AFDC families, the blind, and the disabled. These state programs to help the poor were induced by the Medicare act, which provides federal funds for such programs.

These combined programs have prompted some to agitate for comprehensive health insurance for all Americans regardless of age. Senator Edward Kennedy and Representative Martha Griffiths have introduced a bill in Congress which would extend Medicare coverage to all Americans. Estimates of costs are around $70 to $80 billion a year. The Nixon Administration has proposed a combined public and private health insurance package which is much more modest, but which would extend health coverage. This is to fulfill the President's proposal for "a program to insure that no American family will be prevented from obtaining basic medical care by inability to pay." A variety of differing health insurance programs, including the AMA's "medicredit" plan, have been proposed also.

PUBLIC EDUCATION

Education has been an important value of the American democratic spirit. Beginning as early as 1647, when Massachusetts passed a public education act, the belief in education for all, to be paid for out of tax monies, has been fundamentally accepted by the American people. Long before European nations adopted public school systems, the United States had them on both the elementary and secondary levels. Currently the United States is moving into mass education on the college level.

Americans have generally thought that public education should be the responsibility of state and local governments, and for 170 years the national government did not play a major role in education. The national government, however, has been actively interested in education and has promoted it ever since the Northwest Ordinance of 1785, which set aside section sixteen of each township for public school purposes. The tempo of federal grants-in-aid to education has gradually increased over the years; but a sense of urgency with respect to the need for quality education and for more federal aid programs was thrust into the American mind with the Russian launch of its first sputnik. With sputnik, the resistance toward federal aid from "states' righters" and the Catholic-Protestant school-aid hassle began to melt away.

Americans clamored for an increased emphasis on science in the schools in the belief that America was technologically behind the Russians. Congress responded with the National Defense Education Act (1958), which provided assistance to the public schools in the areas of science, mathematics, and foreign languages. Grants were made to improve laboratories and instructional aids. Subsequently other courses were included in this federal aid; and, since 1963, grants and loans have been authorized for the construction of classroom buildings on both public and private college campuses.

In 1965, Congress was able to pass the Elementary and Secondary Education Act, a major breakthrough, which appropriated more than $1 billion for textbooks, library materials, and other instructional aids to be used by public and private school pupils. The funds were designed to improve the quality of education in deprived areas, but all school systems have profited by the act. The act specifically prohibits any control of the curriculum, which had worried some who believed that federal aid to education meant thought-control by "big brother."

Higher education has been promoted since World War II through the G.I. Bill of Rights, which included benefits to veterans who attended college or vocational schools, or participated in on-the-job training. Although other measures have benefited higher education, another significant act in 1965 was the Higher Education Act. This act concentrated its efforts in support of needy students by allocating substantial funds for undergraduate scholarships. In 1970, President Nixon proposed that no qualified student should be barred from going to college for lack of money. The President's budget request for 1974 placed the highest priority in higher education to achieving equal access to postsecondary education. His objective was to provide every eligible student needing financial aid with a grant of up to $1,400 for the 1974–75 school year.

HOUSING AND URBAN RENEWAL

The creation of the Department of Health, Education, and Welfare in 1953 was an indication that social welfare was a national problem. Likewise, the creation of the Department of Housing and Urban Development (HUD) points to the urban problems prompted in part by industrialization. These urban problems appear to transcend the capacities of the states and local governments to solve them.

The national government began to help its people gain adequate housing in the Great Depression with the passage of the act creating the Federal Housing Administration (FHA), which insures private housing loans, amounting recently to $7 to $8 billion annually. The Veterans Administration has helped veterans through direct and insured loans since World War II. The Farmers Home Administration also makes direct loans for housing.

The federal government recently embarked on a new approach as an alternative to public housing projects. In 1966, Congress authorized a pilot "rent-subsidy" program. Through this program the federal government pays the difference between the normal rent and one-fourth of the renter's income. A parallel program was established for building new housing units in the Housing and Urban Development Act of 1968. Of the projected twenty-six million units to be built in the 1970's, six million are to be subsidized housing for low-income families. George Romney initiated Operation Breakthrough while he was Secretary of HUD, which was designed to meet this monumental housing objective through new methods of mass production, such as the modular home. While the Ninety-second Congress failed to pass an omnibus housing bill which would have consolidated the federal mortgage insurance program and created a system of block grants to states and localities for urban development, it did pass legislation extending the authority of the Federal Housing Administration and appropriated $150 million for public housing. President Nixon's budget for 1974 called for support for over 2.5 million subsidized housing units; but his overall objective was to insure the private market's ability to meet the nation's housing needs, and to help state and local governments solve their own development problems.

The federal government has made direct grants to cities recently, especially for urban renewal projects. The cities, which were once the centers of culture and beauty, are rapidly becoming tax-supported "concentration camps" for the poor and the disadvantaged. America has the resources and the technical capabilities to restore the cities, but does it have the judgment and will to do so?

CONCLUSION

It is obvious that social welfare measures have been part of the American political system from the beginning of the nation. There has been a rapid acceleration of these welfare measures, however, since World War II; but these have come into "full bloom" one or two generations later than similar measures in Europe—with the exception of public education, an area in which America has been committed to an educational philosophy that the children of all Americans, whether they are rich or poor, should have educational opportunities. America has devoted a much smaller percentage of its gross national revenues to social welfare measures than have European countries. This has been consistent with traditional ideological beliefs about free enterprise and capitalism, but it has been at the expense of human dignity among some classes of Americans.

In response to a question about whether America was becoming a welfare state or not, Jack Anderson, the Washington columnist, said: "Yes we have a welfare state—but the welfare goes to the rich." He explained this by saying that there are twenty-five million poor people in America, "over half have never received a penny of taxpayers' money." He maintained that more tax dollars go to twenty-five thousand millionaires in America than to the twenty-five million poor. On balance, American paternalism may have been niggardly on some social welfare needs over the years, where it has been generous to the politically powerful; but the focus of American priorities is presently shifting to domestic needs and social values.

14
AMERICA: WAR AND PEACE

On Tuesday morning, October 16, 1962, shortly after 9:00, President Kennedy called his brother Bobby, who was the Attorney General, and asked him to come to the White House, saying only that America was facing great trouble. At the White House, Robert Kennedy was informed that the intelligence community had become convinced that Russia was placing missiles and atomic weapons in Cuba.

At 11:45 that same morning, a formal presentation was made by the Central Intelligence Agency (CIA) to a number of high officials of the government. Photographs were displayed which showed, according to the experts, a missile base being constructed in a field near San Cristobal, Cuba. Robert Kennedy admitted that he had to take their word for it, for what he saw appeared like a clearing of a field for a basement of a house. A later picture looked like a football field to the President.[1]

Stunned surprise was the reaction of those at the meeting. The Soviets had denied that the buildup of military equipment in Cuba included any offensive ground-to-ground missiles as recently as just a few weeks before. The group was made up of the top officials of the government concerned with foreign policy: key military, intelligence, and diplomatic officers and the President and his close advisers. The group, which was later to be called the "Ex Comm" (the Executive Committee of the National Security Council), included Secretary of State Dean Rusk; Secretary of Defense Robert McNamara; Director of the Central Intelligence Agency John McCone; Secretary of the Treasury Douglas Dillon; President Kennedy's adviser on national security affairs.

---

[1] Robert F. Kennedy, *Thirteen Days* (New York: Norton, 1971), is the primary source of data for this case study on decision making in the Cuban missile crisis.

McGeorge Bundy; Presidential Counsel Ted Sorensen; Under Secretary of State George Ball; Deputy Under Secretary of State U. Alexis Johnson; General Maxwell Taylor, Chairman of the Joint Chiefs of Staff; Edward Martin, Assistant Secretary of State for Latin America; originally, Chip Bohlen, who, after the first day, left to become Ambassador to France and was succeeded by Llewellyn Thompson as the adviser on Russian affairs; Roswell Gilpatric, Deputy Secretary of Defense; Paul Nitze, Assistant Secretary of Defense; and, intermittently at various meetings, Vice-President Lyndon B. Johnson; Adlai Stevenson, Ambassador to the United Nations; Ken O'Donnell, Special Assistant to the President; and Don Wilson, who was Deputy Director of the United States Information Agency.

For thirteen days this group met, talked, argued, and fought together and ultimately made recommendations from which the President selected his course of action. They met in secret. At times the President did not meet with them for two reasons: (1) even strong, intelligent, courageous, and patriotic men will be inclined to tell the President what they think he wants to hear; and (2) the President kept campaign and other types of appointments, including one with the Soviet Foreign Minister, Andrei Gromyko, to keep the Russians unsuspecting and from taking the initiative in the crisis.

During the afternoon and evening of the first day of the crisis, the idea of a quarantine or blockade began to be discussed. Secretary of Defense McNamara, by Wednesday, became the blockade's strongest advocate. He argued that it was limited pressure, which could be increased as the circumstances warranted. He reinforced his position by reporting that a surprise air strike against the missile bases alone, a "surgical strike" as it was called, was militarily impractical according to the Joint Chiefs of Staff, who believed at the time that any such military action would have to include all military installations in Cuba, eventually leading to an invasion. Perhaps this action would come, "but let's not start with that course," McNamara said. He wanted to avoid, if possible, that kind of confrontation with Cuba, and of necessity with the Soviet Union.

Those who argued for the military strike instead of a blockade pointed out that a blockade would not in fact remove the missiles and would not even stop the work from going ahead on the missile sites themselves. Their most forceful argument was that a blockade around Cuba would invite the Russians to do the same to Berlin. If the United States demanded the removal of missiles from Cuba as the price for lifting the blockade, the Soviets would demand the removal of missiles surrounding the Soviet Union. The members of the Joint Chiefs of Staff were unanimous in calling for immediate military action. When the President questioned what the Russian response might be, General Curtis LeMay, Air Force Chief of Staff, assured him there would be no reaction. President Kennedy was skeptical. "They can't, after all their statements, permit us to take out their missiles, kill a lot of Russians, and then do nothing. If they don't take action in Cuba, they certainly will in Berlin.''

Later, outlines of definite plans were written. For the group that advocated the blockade, it was an outline of the legal basis for the proposed action, an agenda for a meeting of the Organization of American States, recommendations for the role of the United Nations, the military procedures for stopping ships, and, finally, the circumstances under which military force might be used. For the group that advocated immediate military action, it was an outline of the areas to be attacked, a defense of this action in the United Nations, suggestions as to how to obtain support from Latin American countries, and a proposed communication to Khrushchev to convince him of the inadvisability of moving militarily against the United States in the Caribbean, Berlin, or elsewhere in the world.

On Saturday, "Ex Comm" was ready to present the respective plans to the President. Secretary McNamara presented the arguments for the blockade; others presented the arguments for the military attack. One member of the JCS argued that nuclear weapons could be used, on the basis that Cuba and Russia would use nuclear weapons in an attack. Robert Kennedy was concerned about the ethical questions involved as he listened to those who wanted a military solution. "I now know how Tojo felt when he was planning Pearl Harbor," he scribbled on a note to the President. "I thought, as I listened, of the many times that I had heard the military take positions which, if wrong, had the advantage that no one would be around at the end to know."

The President made his decision that afternoon in favor of the blockade. There was one final meeting the next morning, with General Walter C. Sweeney, Jr., Commander-in-Chief of the Tactical Air Command, who told the President that even a major surprise air attack could not guarantee the destruction of all the missile sites and nuclear weapons in Cuba. That ended the small, lingering doubt that remained in the President's mind.

During this same period, military preparations went forward. Missile crews were placed on maximum alert. Troops were moved into Florida and the southeastern part of the United States. The base at Guantanamo Bay was strengthened. The Navy deployed one hundred eighty ships into the Caribbean. The Strategic Air Command was dispersed to civilian landing fields around the country, to lessen its vulnerability in case of attack. The B-52 bomber force was ordered into the air fully loaded with atomic weapons. As one came down to land, another immediately took its place in the air.

Preparations were now made. It was time to bring others into the action and inform Khrushchev of the policy position of the United States. A speech was scheduled for Monday evening, October 22. Prior to the speech, the President met first with his Cabinet and then with leaders of Congress—neither group had been included in the decision making. A meeting of the Organization of American States was called for Tuesday morning, and other diplomatic measures were taken.

The diplomatic effort was of great significance. By making this effort the United States was able to establish a firm legal foundation for the course of action chosen under the OAS Charter; and America's position around the world was greatly strengthened when the OAS unanimously supported the recommendation for a quarantine. Thus the Soviet Union and Cuba faced the united action of the whole Western Hemisphere. Further, with the support of detailed photographs, former Secretary of State Dean Acheson was able to convince French President Charles de Gaulle of the correctness of the response and later to reassure German Chancellor Konrad Adenauer. Harold Macmillan, the Prime Minister of Great Britain, made it clear the United States would have his country's support. General de Gaulle said, "it is exactly what I would have done," adding that it was not necessary to see the photographs, as "a great government such as yours does not act without evidence." The Soviet Union was therefore prevented from separating the United States from Europe.

The President composed a letter to Khrushchev, asking him to observe the quarantine legally established by a vote of the OAS, making it clear that the United States did not wish to fire on any ships of the Soviet Union. He concluded: "I am concerned that we both show prudence and do nothing to allow events to make the situation more difficult to control than it is."

On October 26, the first vessel was stopped and boarded. It was the *Marucla,* an American-built Liberty ship, Panamanian-owned, registered from Lebanon, and bound for Cuba under a Soviet charter from the Baltic port of Riga. The *Marucla* had been carefully and personally selected by President Kennedy to be the first ship stopped and boarded. He was demonstrating to Khrushchev that the United States was determined to enforce the quarantine; but it was important that the ship stopped did not represent a direct affront to the Soviets, requiring a response from them. This particular boarding operation gave the Soviets more time, but simultaneously demonstrated that the United States meant business. The vessel was found to contain no weapons and was allowed to sail on.

On the following Friday, Khrushchev's answer came. He proposed the following: no more weapons would be sent to Cuba and those within Cuba were to be withdrawn or destroyed; the United States was to reciprocate by withdrawing the blockade and by also agreeing not to invade Cuba. This message brought a slight feeling of optimism. The feeling was strengthened by the fact that John Scali, an able and experienced reporter for the American Broadcasting Company, had been approached by an important official of the Soviet Embassy with a proposal that the Soviet Union would remove the missiles under United Nations supervision and inspection if the United States would lift the blockade and give a pledge not to invade Cuba as its part of the understanding. Scali was asked to transmit this message to the United States government, which he did immediately.

On Saturday morning, October 27, a new letter arrived from Khrushchev to President Kennedy. It was obviously no longer Mr. Khrushchev personally who was writing, but the Foreign Office of the Kremlin. The letter was quite different from the letter received twelve hours before. "We will remove our missiles from Cuba, you will remove yours from Turkey. . . . The Soviet Union will pledge not to invade or interfere with the internal affairs of Turkey; the U.S. to make the same pledge regarding Cuba."

Robert Kennedy suggested that the United States ignore the latest Khrushchev letter and respond to his earlier letter's proposal, as refined in the offer made to John Scali. Robert Kennedy and Theodore Sorensen composed a response; the President refined it, had it typed, and signed it. It accepted Khrushchev's "offer."

On Sunday morning, the thirteenth day of the crisis, Attorney General Kennedy met with Ambassador Anatol Dobrynin. Khrushchev had agreed to dismantle and withdraw the missiles under adequate supervision and inspection. The world breathed easier! Most agreed the President had acted wisely. The President instructed all involved that "no interview should be given, no statement made, which would claim any kind of victory." Bobby concluded: "If it was a triumph—it was a triumph for the next generation and not for any particular government or people."

In April, 1970, another fateful decision was before the President of the United States. This time it was Richard M. Nixon who finally had to make the choice.

President Nixon had been the Vice-President when the United States became involved in Southeast Asia. When the former French colony of Indochina was broken up and Vietnam divided at the 17th parallel, the Eisenhower Administration supported South Vietnam with economic aid, then technical assistance, and finally military advisers. American assistance, however, was countered by Russian and Chinese assistance to the North Vietnamese.

President John F. Kennedy brought about greater involvement in Vietnam, committing some ground forces to the conflict. President Lyndon B. Johnson escalated the conflict into a major military operation involving the Army, Navy, and the Air Force. After three years of increasing military involvement, the "Americanization" of the war had not brought victory in Vietnam, but it had caused frustration and conflict at home. President Johnson read the resentment correctly and, influenced by this, along with other reasons, chose not to run for reelection.

During the campaign of 1968, Mr. Nixon promised the American voters that he had a plan to end the war in Vietnam. After the election, months passed and protests grew before the new President announced his policy of "Vietnamization," which was a gradual shifting of the burden of the ground war back to the Vietnamese, while at the same time bringing American fighting men home.

In spite of the presence of over a half-million ground forces, periods of intensive bombing of North Vietnam and parts of the Ho Chi-Minh Trail, and naval action in the Gulf of Tonkin and elsewhere, the war was fought on a limited-war basis. Throughout the conflict certain military actions were prohibited. The military chafed under these "political" restrictions, claiming that they prevented a military victory. Many civilians back home held similar views. But, with the policy of Vietnamization and the phased withdrawal of American forces, the President had ruled out a military victory.

The success of the President's policy was threatened, however, by continued buildup of communist forces in neutral Cambodia, which the United States' secret bombings and clandestine military activities had not checked. The fateful decision that faced the President in 1970 was whether or not he should openly invade Cambodia to destroy the pro-communist sanctuaries to give the South Vietnamese a better chance of successfully fighting the communists as the Americans continued to withdraw.

The President met with the National Security Council (NSC) in an announced session on April 22, 1970. He met secretly with that body on April 26. He also met with an informal body known as the Special Action Group (SAG), composed of the President's chief adviser on national security affairs, the undersecretaries of State and Defense, the Chairman of the Joint Chiefs of Staff, and the Director of the CIA. Judging from newspaper columnists' accounts of these events, it would appear that SAG was relied on more than NSC.

SAG met several times to assess the possible reactions of Russia, China, and North Vietnam to an American invasion of Cambodia. The President spent several days studying the data and position papers prepared for him. On Thursday night, April 30, he appeared on nationwide television and announced that he was sending American forces into Cambodia. The address was a detailed explanation of why this action was in the American interest: it would protect the American forces in their withdrawal from Vietnam from attack from these sanctuaries; it would save American lives in the long run; and it would uphold the honor of the United States.

A storm of protest broke across the nation. Editorials in some of America's major newspapers criticized the President for expanding the war in Southeast Asia. Television news commentators were especially harsh, questioning the President's credibility on the grounds that this action was in conflict with his professed program of withdrawal. Members of Congress from both parties rebuked the President for not having consulted Congress before he committed the troops. The stock market declined sharply, demonstrations occurred in the capitals of friendly nations, and students across the nation reacted angrily to the news.

What do these two case studies tell us about American foreign policy today?

First, major foreign policies decided by similar methods may result in quite different reactions, suggesting either differences in personal qualities of the Presidents responsible for the decisions, or different substantive natures of the decisions. Second, major policy discussions involve high-level committees, in which although the President is a participant and presumably amenable to suggestions, the final decision, and responsibility for it, rests with the President. Third, foreign policy goals must be clearly articulated by the policy makers, and clearly understood by the press and the public, which, if the policies are reasonable, may prompt more general acceptance and less criticism. Fourth, the traditional beliefs about the checks and balances between Congress and the President in foreign affairs must be revised. Fifth, there are major components of foreign policy formulation and administration today—diplomatic, military, and intelligence—which require unity of action for success. Sixth, other government functions, such as economic policies, figure importantly in foreign affairs, and must be harmonized with the major components. Seventh, the only person or agency capable of bringing unity to the foreign policy function among the decision makers, the administrators, and the public is the President of the United States.

PRESIDENTIAL STYLE AND DECISION MAKING

The Kennedy Cuban missile decision and the Nixon Cambodian decision followed similar patterns. The President, as the Commander-in-Chief, was central to the whole decision-making process. The formal agency which Congress provided in 1947 to assist the President in problems of this type, the National Security Council, was used by both Presidents, but probably was not as heavily relied upon as was the "inner circle" of public and private persons whose judgment each President trusted. Those brought into the discussions were the President's choice and his alone. Free discussion of the different personal positions was permitted, but the final decision was the President's. Congress remained ignorant of the discussions and was informed of the decisions only hours before the public announcements.

Some of the sharpest criticism of both decisions came from congressional leaders. In the Kennedy decision, the criticism was that the President should have taken stronger, more militant action; in the Nixon decision the criticism turned more on the point that Congress was not consulted before the decision was made, even though the decision to invade Cambodia was thought to be a mistake by many in Congress.

The public applauded Kennedy for his decision; the public was divided over Nixon's decision, a sizable number being highly vocal in opposition. Allies of the United States agreed with the Kennedy decision; they were visibly concerned over the Nixon policy.

What makes the difference? Is it charisma? Is it credibility? Is it competence or capability? These may be partial explanations, but the real reasons appear more fundamental, involving the nature of the two decisions and the mood of the nation. Since World War II, Congress and the American people expect the President to take positive action in nuclear crises; but Congress and the public have demonstrated their unwillingness to allow the President an absolute control of foreign affairs in more limited, nonnuclear crises.

Before President Ford's administration was a year old, it faced the problem of the collapse of Vietnam following the major offensive of the North Vietnamese, begun March 5, 1975, in the Central Highlands; and the probable defeat of the Lon Nol government of Cambodia by the Khmer Rouge insurgents. President Ford's request for emergency funds to further assist the Thieu regime was refused by Congress. Cambodia surrendered on April 17, and Vietnam followed on April 30. The continuance of the American presence in Southeast Asia was not considered by Congress to be among the vital interests of the United States. The mood of America supported the action of Congress. The leaders in Congress, however, are the first to admit that the power of the President in foreign affairs must not be destroyed. They simply want to play a policy formulating role on those levels of decision making which do not demand immediate action of the President.

The Administration's feeling of defeat in Southeast Asia was turned to one of victory in May with the recovery of the Mayaguez, a merchant vessel captured by the Khmer Rouge Cambodians, and its crew. In this odd, but popular venture, conspicuous efforts were made by administrative officials to prove that President Ford, not Kissinger, was calling the signals—an attempt to recover the initiative in foreign policy formulation for the President and the executive branch.

FOREIGN POLICY GOALS

Another aspect of the conflict over the Cambodian invasion is in regard to foreign policy goals. When confusion seems to exist in foreign policy goals, there is always more criticism of even reasonable objectives than when the goals seem clear. The Cuban missile crisis did not offer the confusion in foreign policy goals that the Cambodian invasion did, which was one more element introduced into an already confused perception of American objectives in Southeast Asia.

Another case in point is the Bay of Pigs invasion of Cuba, attempted in the first months of the Kennedy Administration, which ended in a fiasco. Here the decision makers were divided as to their tactics, if not their objectives; and the attempt of the administration to straddle the idealistic-realistic positions resulted in failure and public disdain for the undertaking. When the CIA, the Army, the Air Force, and others involved were blaming each other for the failure, Kennedy said, "I am responsible"—illustrating the ultimate responsibility of the President and the necessity of his giving clear and certain direction in foreign policy.

The goal seemed quite clear during World War II, and the criticism as a result was minimal. Peacetime or cold war policies are not nearly as clearly perceived as wartime policies, as evidenced by the isolation-intervention conflicts preceding the war and the cold war confusions which existed in the immediate postwar period. This confusion was reduced as America settled into the "containment" policy suggested by George F. Kennan while he was director of the Policy Planning Staff of the Department of State after World War II.

NEW CHECKS AND BALANCES

The original checks and balances of shared responsibility in foreign affairs between the President and Congress have given way in the missile age to a sharp diminution of congressional powers and augmentation of presidential powers. Many policy decisions in foreign and military affairs are made by the President with little direct input from Congress. Congressional influence beyond that which can be generated in committee hearings, debates on the floor of Congress, press releases, and vocal protests is minimal. There are checks on the President, however, within the executive apparatus.

Those who helped to make the momentous decisions in both crises cited above were all appointive or co-optive; that is, private citizens or congressmen who may be invited to participate if the President so desires. Those who are normally involved are the President's own appointees, such as department heads, White House aides, and others whose governmental responsibilities make their presence vital to the policy decision. Richard E. Neustadt and Graham T. Allison in the Afterword of *Thirteen Days* suggest that this method of decision making begins to form a new checks-and-balances system: "As this implies, they [decision-making participants] are by no means 'mere' subordinates. The President is no freer than he would have been with Congress to ignore them. But neither are they colleagues in the sense of sharing either his legitimacy or accountability. Nowadays those rest with him alone."

Several men had to be involved in these policy decisions, as they were responsible for the possible actions to be followed, such as the secretaries of State and Defense, the Director of the CIA, the Chairman of the Joint Chiefs of Staff, and the White House Assistant for National Security Affairs. One or more of these men were responsible for the collection of data which brought knowledge of the problem, or were needed to consider the feasibility of various alternative courses of action, or would be responsible for implementing the policy decisions.

Neustadt and Allison suggest that there were men, somewhat distinct from the others, who influenced the final decision in the Cuban missile crisis but who also constituted a check on the President: "The President's men: his brother and campaign manager, the Attorney General, and his Special Counsel, Theodore Sorensen." Sorensen was one of the closest personal advisers of Kennedy from the time he joined the Senator in 1953. He offered the President more than just speeches as he, along with Robert Kennedy, helped the President assess the full responsibilities of his office.

Another group of men Kennedy relied on were drawn from private as well as public life. They were included because the President valued their judgment. An example or two will suffice: Dean Acheson and Robert Lovett were called in; both had served as former secretaries of State and Defense respectively under President Truman. Adlai Stevenson was called in because of a variety of valuable talents and experiences going beyond his official position of Ambassador to the United Nations. Douglas Dillon's inclusion was as much for his role as Eisenhower's former Undersecretary of State as for his official position of Secretary of the Treasury in the Kennedy cabinet.

The importance of these individuals in a President's foreign policy is twofold. They assist in the formulation of the President's policy; and, in doing so, they constitute a modern-day system of checks and balances. The deliberations of the total group refine the issues involved and influence the President's choice of action.[2] General foreign policy decisions of the President and many lower-level decisions are influenced, of course, by the executive agencies charged with foreign policy formulation and administration.

CONTEMPORARY FOREIGN POLICY

There are many agencies involved in present-day foreign policy formulation and administration. Virtually every department of government, as well as certain offices or assistants in the Executive Office of the President, are involved. The Department of Health, Education and Welfare, for example, works closely with the World Health Organization (WHO); the Department of Labor interacts with the International Labor Organization (ILO). Both of these departments are consulted on foreign policies that relate to their areas of responsibility. During the first term and early part of the second term of the Nixon Administration, it was obvious that the Assistant to the President on National Security Affairs, Dr. Henry Kissinger, and his staff played a most significant role in foreign policy formulation and negotiation—overshadowing the Secretary of State and the Secretary of Defense. This conflict was resolved by the appointment of Dr.

[2] In the wake of Watergate, Congress would prefer to return to the more traditional role of checks and balances, in which Congress shares in the foreign policy decisions. In the confirmation hearings of Henry Kissinger as Secretary of State, for example, Kissinger promised a close working relationship with the Senate Foreign Relations Committee.

Kissinger as Secretary of State. There are three main agencies involved in the nuts-and-bolts, daily operations of contemporary foreign policy: the Department of State, which handles diplomatic affairs; the Department of Defense, which is responsible for all military services; and the Central Intelligence Agency, which is the hub of the American intelligence community. The first two departments were created by the first Congress of the United States; the CIA is a post-World War II addition.

American Diplomacy

American diplomacy began before the nation was born, when the Continental Congress appointed a secret committee of correspondence in the fall of 1775 to make contacts with foreign powers and to gain aid and support for America against England. The name of this committee has changed over the years and the volume of work has increased tremendously, but its fundamental purpose—to serve the nation in its foreign relations—has remained the same.

The President is the Chief Diplomat and stands at the center of a worldwide network of embassies, special missions, and other foreign service posts abroad which represent the United States throughout the world. He has special assistants in the White House Office to advise and assist him in the final decisions that he must make. The Department of State is also responsible for foreign policy formulation, and for the day-to-day work of diplomacy.

The Department of State is headed by a secretary who is next to the President as the highest-ranking executive officer in the national government. The Secretary of State is responsible for the administration of this vast department, which gathers information from all over the world and represents American interests abroad through its diplomatic missions.

The diplomatic missions in foreign countries are headed by ambassadors or ministers, who are made responsible for the many different activities of America in these countries. The ambassadors are appointed by the President, and in times past these appointments were "political plums" to faithful partisans. While this continues to be so for many of the more pleasant posts in Europe and Latin America, an increasing number of ambassadors are appointed on the basis of capability, with approximately forty-five percent currently drawn from the career service. This change of appointment policy was encouraged by the Rogers Act of 1924, which also altered the traditional separation of political and economic functions handled by diplomatic and consular officers respectively, and brought the handling of political and economic affairs into closer harmony. The diplomatic personnel are located in the capital of the country to handle political, economic, and commercial affairs; and the consuls are located in the major cities of the country to promote trade, assist Americans with their almost endless variety of problems, and to perform certain notarial, citizenship, and immigration tasks,—such as renewing U.S. passports and issuing visas for prospective visitors or immigrants to the United States.

In addition to having direct responsibility for the many aid programs, which are administered through the Agency for International Development (AID) and the Peace Corps, the Secretary of State works closely with the United States Information Agency (USIA) and the many departments and agencies which have international involvement, such as the Treasury Department with its interests in the international monetary problems, and the Department of Agriculture with its disposal of farm commodities abroad. Close cooperation with the military, in today's complex and troubled world, is obviously a necessity.

The Military

The most striking feature of the American military is its nonmilitary base. At the head of the military is a civilian, the President, who is responsible to the people of America. Article II, Section 2, of the Constitution states: "The President shall be Commander-in-Chief of the Army and Navy of the United States, and the Militia of the several States, when called into the actual service of the United States." Even though the military has grown in power throughout the years, this concept has not changed and America is not threatened by military dictatorship.

From the Minute Man to the G.I. Joe to the Vietnam Grunt, Americans have relied on the civilian who becomes a soldier during the emergency and then returns to civilian life. Only after the many years of an unpopular war in Vietnam have the American people seriously considered the idea of an all-volunteer army. The strength of the armed services still rests, and will continue to do so, on the concept of the citizen soldier and civilian supremacy, instead of on professional soldiers and a military high command.

America was born as a result of revolution, and has experienced only short periods of peace between the nine major wars of its history. Yet, traditionally, the most basic principle of U.S. foreign policy was a desire to be isolated from the conflicts of Europe. The military was the defensive arm of this policy; and when the nation went to war, its military machine was expanded with civilian soldiers, to be contracted again when the war was over. Then the isolationist philosophy returned; America resumed peacetime activities and a weak defense posture.

At the close of World War II, the United States entered the atomic age and officially ended the isolationist policies of previous periods, as evidenced by its sponsorship of the United Nations. America was thrust into the position of a world leader and in the process became a world policeman, using its technological and military capabilities as an "umbrella" to protect its allies. After an initial reduction of forces resulting from the traditional cry, "bring our boys home," the United States maintained bases and large numbers of military men throughout the world.

One of the most significant developments of this new period of worldwide, military involvement was the reorganization of the military establishment by the National Defense Act of 1947. A new superdepartment was created, called the Department of Defense, headed by a civilian secretary. The departments of the Army and the Navy, and a third department created out of the old Army Air Corps called the Air Force, were placed under the Department of Defense. Each of the three major armed services is headed by a military officer and over him is a civilian secretary.

The National Defense Act provided for interservice coordination by creating the Joint Chiefs of Staff, which is comprised of the highest ranking officers of each of the major services and the Commandant of the Marine Corps. The act also created the National Security Council to assist the President in international emergencies, and the Central Intelligence Agency.

Since 1947, the defense establishment has grown in size, prominence, and power. The Cold War has perpetuated the military presence. Military hardware has become increasingly more expensive as the two major world powers have

Cartoon by Bill Crawford. Reprinted by permission of Newspaper Enterprises Association, Inc.

"Wow! Our own little peace dividend!"

fought for military superiority. Like a voracious beast, the military has devoured a disproportionate amount of the national budget since World War II. Even President Eisenhower, a former general, was concerned about the costs of defense. At the time he took office, one bomber cost the equivalent of twenty schools and two hospitals. "Humanity," Eisenhower lamented, "is hanging from a cross of iron." In his farewell speech, he warned the American people about the power of the military-industrial complex. He believed that too much power in the hands of this combine could upset the civilian controls over military matters.

The concept of America as world policeman, denying as it has the civilian orientation of its defense tradition, may be changing; but the neoisolationist position demanded by some of the anti-military-establishment spokesmen does not face up to world realities. What seems to be suggested for the immediate future is for the United States to continue its leadership role as a responsible partner in world affairs, working for world peace, while maintaining only the defense posture necessary for national security.

Intelligence

One of the necessary ingredients of national security and effective foreign policy is an accurate, effective intelligence agency. This was no more effectively demonstrated than in the crucial Cuban missile crisis. After military intelligence had displayed its elaborate charts to Ex Comm and the President, suggesting that American missile power would not have a superiority in a showdown with Russia, a man from the CIA brought in a single piece of paper, which revealed that the Soviet arsenal was in fact much weaker than had been feared. John Kennedy then knew he had the muscle to twist Khrushchev's arm in the confrontation that lay ahead. The source of the information was Oleg Penkovskiy, a colonel in Soviet military intelligence who had been passing military intelligence to the West for some time, only to be caught a month after the Cuban missile crisis and executed.[3]

The "cloak and dagger" days of espionage which characterized the intelligence function of yesteryears is rapidly being replaced by technological methods using computers, reconnaissance planes, satellites, and other sophisticated technical devices. The modern-day spy is most often an academic type who can fill the niche required of him in a huge intelligence conglomerate involving a number of government agencies, 200,000 employees, and a large budget, which is disguised under other budgetary designations.

Intelligence activities are not rooted deeply in U.S. government history. Among intelligence agencies, military intelligence has had the longest history, but many agencies have their own intelligence arms, which prompted the attempt to bring them under control with the creation of the Central Intelligence Agency in 1947.

[3] See *Newsweek,* November 22, 1971, pp. 28–40.

The CIA is the central agency among the many involved in intelligence, and its director heads the entire intelligence community. The agency has four sections: Intelligence, which is involved in the collection and sifting of foreign intelligence, its overseas operations usually attached to the embassy in each country; science and technology, which is involved in the collection of data from U-2 or SR-71 flights, spy satellites, and a variety of "eavesdropping" equipment monitoring the sensitive areas of the world; Support, which is involved in logistics and communications, and so on; and Plans, which is the section involved in a variety of clandestine activities throughout the world.

Within the Defense Department are two major intelligence agencies: the National Security Agency, which takes on the cryptological functions of making and breaking codes, accomplished today through a complex computer system; and the Defense Intelligence Agency, which is designed to coordinate all military intelligence. The Army, Navy, and Air Force, however, each has its separate intelligence arm.

In addition there are intelligence activities conducted by the Bureau of Intelligence and Research of the Department of State, the Federal Bureau of Investigation, the Atomic Energy Commission, and the Treasury Department.

Prompted by a number of newspaper allegations that the CIA had been involved in a variety of illegal and improper activities, the Senate acted to restore confidence in federal intelligence and law enforcing agencies. On January 27, 1975, the Senate created an eleven-member select committee to investigate the CIA, FBI, and other such agencies to determine if they had engaged in "illegal, improper or unethical activities"—the first congressional probe of the post-World War II intelligence community.

THE PRESIDENT AND FOREIGN POLICY

Considering the many departments and agencies involved in current foreign policy, the complexities and troubles facing the nations of the world, the missile age of possible nuclear holocaust, the "brush fires" which keep breaking out around the globe, the international economic problems, the agricultural surpluses, and deficiencies of different nations, the industrial "giants" and the "have-not" nations—and the list could go on—the responsibility for the coordination of American foreign policy and the direction of the international destiny of this nation in the years ahead is an awesome task. This responsibility rests upon the shoulders of the President. He cannot do this coordinating alone, however. The President's assistants in the White House Office, especially those in the foreign policy areas, serve the President in the performance of the many activities incident to his immediate office. These assistants are personal aides and assist the President in such matters as he may direct. It is in reality, then, the "Office of the President," with the President at its apex, rather than the man himself, which assumes the responsibility for coordinating American foreign policy.

Of necessity many aspects of diplomatic, military, and intelligence functions in foreign policy must be kept secret. There is little question that in a nuclear crisis, the President and a small circle of advisers must come to decisions which may hold mankind at the edge of oblivion. There may be other decisions which are of vital importance to national security and America's well-being, but these are of less than emergency proportions. The wise President will carefully assess his powers, using the unlimited authority conferred upon him when necessary, but sharing decisions with Congress and informing the public on matters which are proper subjects for wide-based democratic action.

APPENDIX

THE DECLARATION OF INDEPENDENCE *

In Congress, July 4, 1776. A Declaration by the Representatives of the United States of America, in General Congress Assembled.
When in the Course of human Events, it becomes necessary for one People to dissolve the Political Bands which have connected them with another, and to assume among the Powers of the Earth, the separate and equal Station to which the Laws of Nature and of Nature's God entitle them, a decent Respect to the Opinions of Mankind requires that they should declare the causes which impel them to the Separation.

We hold these Truths to be self-evident, that all Men are created equal, that they are endowed by their Creator with certain unalienable Rights, that among these are Life, Liberty, and the Pursuit of Happiness—That to secure these Rights, Governments are instituted among Men, deriving their just Powers from the Consent of the Governed, that whenever any Form of Government becomes destructive of these Ends, it is the Right of the People to alter or to abolish it, and to institute new Government, laying its Foundation on such Principles, and organizing its Powers in such Form, as to them shall seem most likely to effect their Safety and Happiness. Prudence, indeed, will dictate that Governments long established should not be changed for light and transient Causes; and accordingly all Experience hath shewn, that Mankind are more disposed to suffer, while Evils are sufferable, than to right themselves by abolishing the Forms to which they are accustomed. But when a long Train of Abuses and Usurpations, pursuing invariably the same Object, evinces a Design to reduce them under absolute Despotism, it is their Right, it is their Duty, to throw off such Government, and to provide new Guards for their future Security. Such has been the patient Sufferance of these Colonies; and such is now the Necessity which constrains them to alter their former Systems of Government. The History of the present King of Great-Britain is a History of repeated Injuries and Usurpations, all having in direct Object the Establishment of an absolute Tyranny over these States. To prove this, let Facts be submitted to a candid World.

He has refused his Assent to Laws, the most wholesome and necessary for the public Good.

He has forbidden his Governors to pass Laws of immediate and pressing Importance, unless suspended in their Operation till his Assent should be obtained; and when so suspended, he has utterly neglected to attend to them.

He has refused to pass other Laws for the Accommodation of large Districts

SOURCE: House Document No. 92-328, United States Government Printing Office.

of People, unless those People would relinquish the Right of Representation in the Legislature, a Right inestimable to them, and formidable to Tyrants only.

He has called together Legislative Bodies at Places unusual, uncomfortable, and distant from the Depository of their public Records, for the sole Purpose of fatiguing them into Compliance with his Measures.

He has dissolved Representative Houses repeatedly, for opposing with manly Firmness his Invasions on the Rights of the People.

He has refused for a long Time, after such Dissolutions, to cause others to be elected; whereby the Legislative Powers, incapable of Annihilation, have returned to the People at large for their exercise; the State remaining in the mean time exposed to all the Dangers of Invasion from without, and Convulsions within.

He has endeavoured to prevent the Population of these States; for that Purpose obstructing the Laws for Naturalization of Foreigners; refusing to pass others to encourage their Migrations hither, and raising the Conditions of new Appropriations of Lands.

He has obstructed the Administration of Justice, by refusing his Assent to Laws for establishing Judiciary Powers.

He has made Judges dependent on his Will alone, for the Tenure of their Offices, and the Amount and Payment of their Salaries.

He has erected a Multitude of new Offices, and sent hither Swarms of Officers to harrass our People, and eat out their Substance.

He has kept among us, in Times of Peace, Standing Armies, without the consent of our Legislatures.

He has affected to render the Military independent of and superior to the Civil Power.

He has combined with others to subject us to a Jurisdiction foreign to our Constitution, and unacknowledged by our Laws; giving his Assent to their Acts of pretended Legislation:

For quartering large Bodies of Armed Troops among us:

For protecting them, by a mock Trial, from Punishment for any Murders which they should commit on the Inhabitants of these States:

For cutting off our Trade with all Parts of the World:

For imposing Taxes on us without our Consent:

For depriving us, in many Cases, of the Benefits of Trial by Jury:

For transporting us beyond Seas to be tried for pretended Offences:

For abolishing the free System of English Laws in a neighbouring Province, establishing therein an arbitrary Government, and enlarging its Boundaries, so as to render it at once an Example and fit Instrument for introducing the same absolute Rule into these Colonies:

For taking away our Charters, abolishing our most valuable Laws, and altering fundamentally the Forms of our Governments:

For suspending our own Legislatures, and declaring themselves invested with Power to legislate for us in all Cases whatsoever.

He has abdicated Government here, by declaring us out of his Protection and waging War against us.

He has plundered our Seas, ravaged our Coasts, burnt our Towns, and destroyed the Lives of our People.

He is, at this Time, transporting large Armies of foreign Mercenaries to compleat the Works of Death, Desolation, and Tyranny, already begun with circumstances of Cruelty and Perfidy, scarcely paralleled in the most barbarous Ages, and totally unworthy the Head of a civilized Nation.

He has constrained our fellow Citizens taken Captive on the high Seas to bear Arms against their Country, to become the Executioners of their Friends and Brethren, or to fall themselves by their Hands.

He has excited domestic Insurrections amongst us, and has endeavoured to bring on the Inhabitants of our Frontiers, the merciless Indian Savages, whose known Rule of Warfare, is an undistinguished Destruction, of all Ages, Sexes and Conditions.

In every stage of these Oppressions we have Petitioned for Redress in the most humble Terms: Our repeated Petitions have been answered only by repeated Injury. A Prince, whose Character is thus marked by every act which may define a Tyrant, is unfit to be the Ruler of a free People.

Nor have we been wanting in Attentions to our British Brethren. We have warned them from Time to Time of Attempts by their Legislature to extend an unwarrantable Jurisdiction over us. We have reminded them of the Circumstances of our Emigration and Settlement here. We have appealed to their native Justice and Magnanimity, and we have conjured them by the Ties of our common Kindred to disavow these Usurpations, which, would inevitably interrupt our Connections and Correspondence. They too have been deaf to the Voice of Justice and of Consanguinity. We must, therefore, acquiesce in the Necessity, which denounces our Separation, and hold them, as we hold the rest of Mankind, Enemies in War, in Peace, Friends.

We, therefore, the Representatives of the UNITED STATES OF AMERICA, in GENERAL CONGRESS, Assembled, appealing to the Supreme Judge of the World for the Rectitude of our Intentions, do, in the Name, and by Authority of the good People of these Colonies, solemnly Publish and Declare, That these United Colonies are, and of Right ought to be, FREE AND INDEPENDENT STATES; and they are absolved from all Allegiance to the British Crown, and that all political Connection between them and the State of Great-Britain, is and ought to be totally dissolved; and that as FREE AND INDEPENDENT STATES, they have full Power to levy War, conclude Peace, contract Alliances, establish Commerce, and to do all other Acts and Things which INDEPENDENT STATES may of right do. And for the support of this Declaration, with a firm Reliance on the Protection of divine Providence, we mutually pledge to each other our Lives, our Fortunes, and our sacred Honor.

ARTICLES OF CONFEDERATION *

To all to whom these Presents shall come, we the under signed Delegates of the States affixed to our Names, send greeting.

Whereas the Delegates of the United States of America, in Congress assembled, did, on the 15th day of November, in the Year of our Lord One thousand Seven Hundred and Seventy seven, and in the Second Year of the Independence of America, agree to certain articles of Confederation and perpetual Union between the States of Newhampshire, Massachusetts-bay, Rhodeisland and Providence Plantations, Connecticut, New-York, New-Jersey, Pennsylvania, Delaware, Maryland, Virginia, North-Carolina, South-Carolina and Georgia in the words following, viz. "Articles of Confederation and perpetual Union between the states of Newhampshire, Massachusetts-bay, Rhodeisland and Providence Plantations, Connecticut, New-York, New-Jersey, Pennsylvania, Delaware, Maryland, Virginia, North-Carolina, South-Carolina and Georgia.

Article I. The Stile of this confederacy shall be "the United States of America."

Article II. Each state retains its sovereignty, freedom, and independence, and every Power, Jurisdiction and right, which is not by this confederation expressly delegated to the United States, in Congress assembled.

Article III. The said states hereby severally enter into a firm league of friendship with each other, for their common defence, the security of their Liberties, and their mutual and general welfare, binding themselves to assist each other, against all force offered to, or attacks made upon them, or any of them, on account of religion, sovereignty, trade, or any other pretence whatsoever.

Article IV. The better to secure and perpetuate mutual friendship and intercourse among the people of the different states in this union, the free inhabitants of each of these states, paupers, vagabonds and fugitives from justice excepted, shall be entitled to all privileges and immunities of free citizens in the several states; and the people of each state shall have free ingress and regress to and from any other state, and shall enjoy therein all the privileges of trade and commerce, subject to the same duties, impositions and restrictions as the inhabitants thereof respectively, provided that such restriction shall not extend so far as to prevent the removal of property imported into any state, to any other state, of which the Owner is an inhabitant; provided also that no imposition, duties or restruction shall be laid by any state, on the property of the united states, or either of them.

* SOURCE: *Journals of the Continental Congress, 1774–1789* (Washington, D.C.: United States Government Printing Office) XIX (1912), 214–22.

If any Person guilty of, or charged with treason, felony, or other high misdemeanor in any state, shall flee from Justice, and be found in any of the united states, he shall, upon demand of the Governor or executive power, of the state from which he fled, be delivered up and removed to the state having jurisdiction of his offence.

Full faith and credit shall be given in each of these states to the records, acts and judicial proceedings of the courts and magistrates of every other state.

Article V. For the more convenient management of the general interests of the united states, delegates shall be annually appointed in such manner as the legislature of each state shall direct, to meet in Congress on the first Monday in November, in every year, with a power reserved to each state, to recal its delegates, or any of them, at any time within the year, and to send others in their stead, for the remainder of the Year.

No state shall be represented in Congress by less than two, nor by more than seven Members; and no person shall be capable of being a delegate for more than three years in any term of six years; nor shall any person, being a delegate, be capable of holding any office under the united states, for which he, or another for his benefit receives any salary, fees or emolument of any kind.

Each state shall maintain its own delegates in a meeting of the states, and while they act as members of the committee of the states.

In determining questions in the united states in Congress assembled, each state shall have one vote.

Freedom of speech and debate in Congress shall not be impeached or questioned in any Court, or place out of Congress, and the members of congress shall be protected in their persons from arrests and imprisonments, during the time of their going to and from, and attendence on congress, except for treason, felony, or breach of the peace.

Article VI. No state, without the Consent of the united states in congress assembled, shall send any embassy to, or receive any embassy from, or enter into any conference, agreement, alliance or treaty with any King prince or state; nor shall any person holding any office of profit or trust under the united states, or any of them, accept of any present, emolument, office or title of any kind whatever from any king, prince or foreign state; nor shall the united states in congress assembled, or any of them, grant any title of nobility.

No two or more states shall enter into any treaty, confederation or alliance whatever between them, without the consent of the united states in congress assembled, specifying accurately the purposes for which the same is to be entered into, and how long it shall continue.

No state shall lay any imposts or duties, which may interfere with any stipulations in treaties, entered into by the united states in congress assembled, with any king, prince or state, in pursuance of any treaties already proposed by congress, to the courts of France and Spain.

No vessels of war shall be kept up in time of peace by any state, except such number only, as shall be deemed necessary by the united states in congress assembled, for the defence of such state, or its trade; nor shall any body of forces be kept up by any state, in time of peace, except such number only, as in the judgment of the united states, in congress assembled, shall be deemed requisite to garrison the forts necessary for the defence of such state; but every state shall always keep up a well regulated and disciplined militia, sufficiently armed and accoutred, and shall provide and constantly have ready use, in public stores, a due number of field pieces and tents, and a proper quantity of arms, ammunition and camp equipage.

No state shall engage in any war without the consent of the united states in congress assembled, unless such state be actually invaded by enemies, or shall have received certain advice of a resolution being formed by some nation of Indians to invade such state, and the danger is so imminent as not to admit of a delay till the united states in congress assembled can be consulted: nor shall any state grant commissions to any ships or vessels of war, nor letters of marque or reprisal, except it be after a declaration of war by the united states in congress assembled, and then only against the kingdom or state and the subjects thereof, against which war has been so declared, and under such regulations as shall be established by the united states in congress assembled, unless such state be infested by pirates, in which case vessels of war may be fitted out for that occasion, and kept so long as the danger shall continue, or until the united states in congress assembled, shall determine otherwise.

Article VII. When land-forces are raised by any state for the common defence, all officers of or under the rank of colonel, shall be appointed by the legislature of each state respectively, by whom such forces shall be raised, or in such manner as such state shall direct, and all vacancies shall be filled up by the State which first made the appointment.

Article VIII. All charges of war, and all other expences that shall be incurred for the common defence or general welfare, and allowed by the united states in congress assembled, shall be defrayed out of a common treasury, which shall be supplied by the several states in proportion to the value of all land within each state, granted to or surveyed for any Person, as such land and the buildings and improvements thereon shall be estimated according to such mode as the united states in congress assembled, shall from time to time direct and appoint. The taxes for paying that proportion shall be laid and levied by the authority and direction of the legislatures of the several states within the time agreed upon by the united states in congress assembled.

Article IX. The united states in congress assembled, shall have the sole and exclusive right and power of determining on peace and war, except in the cases mentioned in the sixth article—of sending and receiving ambassadors—entering into treaties and alliances, provided that no treaty of commerce shall be made whereby the legislative power of the respective states shall be restrained from imposing such imposts and duties on foreigners, as their own people are subjected to, or from prohibiting the exportation or importation of any species of goods or commodities whatsoever—of establishing rules for deciding in all cases, what captures on land or water shall be legal, and in what manner prizes taken by land or naval forces in the service of the united states shall be divided or appropriated—of granting letters of marque and reprisal in times of peace—appointing courts for the trial of piracies and felonies committed on the high seas and establishing courts for receiving and determining finally appeals in all cases of captures, provided that no member of congress shall be appointed a judge of any of the said courts.

The united states in congress assembled shall also be the last resort on appeal in all disputes and differences now subsisting or that hereafter may arise between two or more states concerning boundary, jurisdiction or any other cause whatever; which authority shall always be exercised in the manner following. Whenever the legislative or executive authority or lawful agent of any state in controversy with another shall present a petition to congress stating the matter in question and praying for a hearing, notice thereof shall be given by order of congress to the legislative or executive authority of the other state in controversy, and a day assigned for the appearance of the parties by their lawful agents, who shall then be directed to appoint by joint consent, commissioners or judges to constitute a court for hearing and determining the matter in question: but if they cannot agree, congress shall name three persons out of each of the united states, and from the list of such persons each party shall alternately strike out one, the petitioners beginning, until the number shall be reduced to thirteen; and from that number not less than seven, nor more than nine names as congress shall direct, shall in the presence of congress be drawn out by lot, and the persons whose names shall be so drawn or any five of them, shall be commissioners or judges, to hear and finally determine the controversy, so always as a major part of the judges who shall hear the cause shall agree in the determination: and if either party shall neglect to attend at the day appointed, without showing reasons, which congress shall judge sufficient, or being present shall refuse to strike, the congress shall proceed to nominate three persons out of each state, and the secretary of congress shall strike in behalf of such party absent or refusing; and the judgment and sentence of the court to be appointed, in the manner before prescribed, shall be final and conclusive; and if any of the parties shall refuse to submit to the authority of such court, or to appear or defend their claim or cause, the court shall nevertheless proceed to pronounce sentence, or judgment, which shall in like manner be final and decisive, the judgment or sentence and other proceedings being in either case transmitted to congress, and lodged among the acts of congress for the security of the parties concerned: provided that every commissioner, before he sits in judgment, shall take an oath to be administred by one of the judges of the supreme or superior court of the state, where the cause shall be tried, ''well and truly to hear and determine the matter in question, according to the best of his judgment, without favour, affection or hope of reward:" provided also, that no state shall be deprived of territory for the benefit of the united states.

All controversies concerning the private right of soil claimed under different grants of two or more states, whose jurisdictions as they may respect such lands, and the states which passed such grants are adjusted, the said grants or either of them being at the same time claimed to have originated antecedent to such settlement of jurisdiction, shall on the petition of either party to the congress of the united states, be finally determined as near as may be in the same manner as is before prescribed for deciding disputes respecting territorial jurisdiction between different states.

The united states in congress assembled shall also have the sole and exclusive right and power of regulating the alloy and value of coin struck by their own authority, or by that of the respective states—fixing the standard of weights and measures throughout the united states—regulating the trade and managing all affairs with the Indians, not members of any of the states, provided that the legislative right of any state within its own limits be not infringed or violated—establishing or regulating post-offices from one state to another, throughout all the united states, and exacting such postage on the papers passing thro' the same as may be requisite to defray the expences of the said office—appointing all officers of the land forces, in the service of the united states, excepting regimental officers—appointing all the officers of the naval forces, and commissioning all officers whatever in the service of the united states—making rules for the government and regulation of the said land and naval forces, and directing their operations.

The united states in congress assembled shall have authority to appoint a committee, to sit in the recess of congress, to be denominated "A Committee of the States," and to consist of one delegate from each state; and to appoint such other committees and civil officers as may be necessary for managing the general affairs of the united states under their direction—to appoint one of their number to preside, provided that no person be allowed to serve in the office of president more than one year in any term of three years; to ascertain the necessary sums of Money to be raised for the service of the united states, and to appropriate and apply the same for defraying the public expences—to borrow money, or emit bills on the credit of the united states, transmitting every half year to the respective states an account of the sums of money so borrowed or emitted,—to build and equip a navy—to agree upon the number of land forces, and to make requisitions from each state for its quota, in proportion to the number of white inhabitants in such state; which requisition shall be binding, and thereupon the legislature of each state shall appoint the regimental officers, raise the men and cloath, arm and equip them in a soldier like manner, at the expence of the united states; and the officers and men so cloathed, armed and equipped shall march to the place appointed, and within the time agreed on by the united states in congress assembled: But if the united states in congress assembled shall, on consideration of circumstances judge proper that any state should not raise men, or should raise a smaller number than its quota, and that any other state should raise a greater number of men than the quota thereof, such extra number shall be raised, officered, cloathed, armed and equipped in the same manner as the quota of such state, unless the legislature of such state shall judge that such extra number cannot be safely spared out of the same, in which case they shall raise officer, cloath, arm and equip as many of such extra number as they judge can be safely spared. And the officers and men so cloathed, armed and equipped, shall march to the place appointed, and within the time agreed on by the united states in congress assembled.

The united states in congress assembled shall never engage in a war, nor grant letters of marque and reprisal in time of peace, nor enter into any treaties or alliances, nor coin money, nor regulate the value thereof, nor ascertain the sums and expences necessary for the defence and welfare of the united states, or any of them, nor emit bills, nor borrow money on the credit of the united states, nor appropriate money, nor agree upon the number of vessels of war, to be built or purchased, or the number of land or sea forces to be raised, nor appoint a commander in chief of the army or navy, unless nine states assent to the same: nor shall a question on any other point, except for adjourning from day to day be determined, unless by the votes of a majority of the united states in congress assembled.

The congress of the united states shall have power to adjourn to any time within the year, and to any place within the united states, so that no period of adjournment be for a longer duration than the space of six Months, and shall publish the Journal of their proceedings monthly, except such parts thereof relating to treaties, alliances or military operations, as in their judgment require secrecy; and the yeas and nays of the delegates of each state on any question shall be entered on the Journal, when it is desired by any delegate; and the delegates of a state, or any of them, at his or their request shall be furnished with a transcript of the said Journal, except such parts as are above excepted, to lay before the legislatures of the several states.

Article X. The committee of the states, or any nine of them, shall be authorized to execute, in the recess of congress, such of the powers of congress as the united states in congress assembled, by the consent of nine states, shall from time to time think expedient to vest them with; provided that no power be delegated to the said committee, for the exercise of which, by the articles of confederation, the voice of nine states in the congress of the united states assembled is requisite.

Article XI. Canada acceding to this confederation, and joining in the measures of the united states, shall be admitted into, and entitled to all the advantages of this union: but no other colony shall be admitted into the same, unless such admission be agreed to by nine states.

Article XII. All bills of credit emitted, monies borrowed and debts contracted by, or under the authority of congress, before the assembling of the united states, in pursuance of the present confederation, shall be deemed and considered as a charge against the united states, for payment and satisfaction whereof the said united states, and the public faith are hereby solemnly pledged.

Article XIII. Every state shall abide by the determinations of the united states in congress assembled, on all questions which by this confederation are submitted to them. And the Articles of this confederation shall be inviolably observed by every state, and the union shall be perpetual; nor shall any alteration at any time hereafter be made in any of them; unless such alteration be agreed to in a congress of the united states, and be afterwards confirmed by the legislatures of every state.

And Whereas it hath pleased the Great Governor of the World to incline the hearts of the legislatures we respectively represent in congress, to approve of, and to authorize us to ratify the said articles of confederation and perpetual union. Know Ye that we the undersigned delegates, by virtue of the power and authority to us given for that purpose, do by these presents, in the name and in behalf of our respective constituents, fully and entirely ratify and confirm each and every of the said articles of confederation and perpetual union, and all and singular the matters and things therein contained: And we do further solemnly plight and engage the faith of our respective constituents, that they shall abide by the determinations of the united states in congress assembled, on all questions, which by the said confederation are submitted to them. And that the articles thereof shall be inviolably observed by the states we respectively represent, and that the union shall be perpetual. In Witness whereof we have hereunto set our hands in Congress. Done at Philadelphia in the state of Pennsylvania the ninth day of July, in the Year of our Lord one Thousand seven Hundred and Seventy-eight, and in the third year of the independence of America. [Ratification completed March 1, 1781]

THE CONSTITUTION OF THE UNITED STATES OF AMERICA *

We, the People of the United States, in order to form a more perfect union, establish justice, insure domestic tranquility, provide for the common defence, promote the general welfare, and secure the blessings of liberty to ourselves and our posterity, do ordain and establish this Constitution for the United States of America.

ARTICLE I

Sect. 1. ALL legislative powers herein granted shall be vested in a Congress of the United States, which shall consist of a Senate and House of Representatives.

Sect. 2. The House of Representatives shall be composed of members chosen every second year by the people of the several states, and the electors in each state shall have the qualifications requisite for electors of the most numerous branch of the state legislature.

No person shall be a representative who shall not have attained to the age of twenty-five years, and been seven years a citizen of the United States, and who shall not, when elected, be an inhabitant of that state in which he shall be chosen.

[1] [Representatives and direct taxes shall be apportioned among the several states which may be included within this Union, according to their respective numbers, which shall be determined by adding to the whole number of free persons, including those bound to service for a term of years, and excluding Indians not taxed, three-fifths of all other persons.] The actual enumeration shall be made within three years after the first meeting of the Congress of the United States, and within every subsequent term of ten years, in such manner as they shall by law direct. The number of representatives shall not exceed one for every thirty thousand, but each state shall have at least one representative; and until such enumeration shall be made, the state of New-Hampshire shall be entitled to chuse three, Massachusetts eight, Rhode-Island and Providence Plantations one, Connecticut five, New-York six, New-Jersey four, Pennsylvania eight, Delaware one, Maryland six, Virginia ten, North-Carolina five, South-Carolina five, and Georgia three.

---

* SOURCE: House Document No. 92-328, United States Government Printing Office.

[1] The part enclosed by brackets was changed by section 2 of Amendment XIV.

When vacancies happen in the representation from any state, the Executive authority thereof shall issue writs of election to fill such vacancies.

The House of Representatives shall chuse their Speaker and other officers; and shall have the sole power of impeachment.

Sect. 3. The Senate of the United States shall be composed of two senators from each state, [2][chosen by the legislature thereof,] for six years; and each senator shall have one vote.

Immediately after they shall be assembled in consequence of the first election, they shall be divided as equally as may be into three classes. The seats of the senators of the first class shall be vacated at the expiration of the second year, of the second class at the expiration of the fourth year, and of the third class at the expiration of the sixth year, so that one-third may be chosen every second year; [3][and if vacancies happen by resignation, or otherwise, during the recess of the Legislature of any state, the Executive thereof may make temporary appointments until the next meeting of the Legislature, which shall then fill such vacancies.]

No person shall be a senator who shall not have attained to the age of thirty years, and been nine years a citizen of the United States, and who shall not, when elected, be an inhabitant of that state for which he shall be chosen.

The Vice-President of the United States shall be President of the senate, but shall have no vote, unless they be equally divided.

The Senate shall chuse their other officers, and also a President pro tempore, in the absence of the Vice-President, or when he shall exercise the office of President of the United States.

The Senate shall have the sole power to try all impeachments. When sitting for that purpose, they shall be on oath or affirmation. When the President of the United States is tried, the Chief Justice shall preside: And no person shall be convicted without the concurrence of two-thirds of the members present.

Judgment in cases of impeachment shall not extend further than to removal from office, and disqualification to hold and enjoy any office of honor, trust or profit under the United States; but the party convicted shall nevertheless be liable and subject to indictment, trial, judgment and punishment, according to law.

Sect. 4. The times, places and manner of holding elections for senators and representatives, shall be prescribed in each state by the legislature thereof; but the Congress may at any time by law make or alter such regulations, except as to the places of chusing Senators.

The Congress shall assemble at least once in every year, and such meeting shall [4][be on the first Monday in December,] unless they shall by law appoint a different day.

---

[2] The clause enclosed by brackets was changed by clause 1 of Amendment XVII.

[3] The part enclosed by brackets was changed by clause 2 of Amendment XVII.

[4] The clause enclosed by brackets was changed by section 2 of Amendment XX.

Sect. 5. Each house shall be the judge of the elections, returns and qualifications of its own members, and a majority of each shall constitute a quorum to do business; but a smaller number may adjourn from day to day, and may be authorized to compel the attendance of absent members, in such manner, and under such penalties as each house may provide.

Each house may determine the rules of its proceedings, punish its members for disorderly behaviour, and, with the concurrence of two-thirds, expel a member.

Each house shall keep a journal of its proceedings, and from time to time publish the same, excepting such parts as may in their judgment require secrecy; and the yeas and nays of the members of either house on any question shall, at the desire of one-fifth of those present, be entered on the journal.

Neither house, during the session of Congress, shall, without the consent of the other, adjourn for more than three days, nor to any other place than that in which the two houses shall be sitting.

Sect. 6. The senators and representatives shall receive a compensation for their services, to be ascertained by law, and paid out of the treasury of the United States. They shall in all cases, except treason, felony and breach of the peace, be privileged from arrest during their attendance at the session of their respective houses, and in going to and returning from the same; and for any speech or debate in either house, they shall not be questioned in any other place.

No senator or representative shall, during the time for which he was elected, be appointed to any civil office under the authority of the United States, which shall have been created, or the emoluments whereof shall have been encreased during such time; and no person holding any office under the United States, shall be a member of either house during his continuance in office.

Sect. 7. All bills for raising revenue shall originate in the house of representatives; but the senate may propose or concur with amendments as on other bills.

Every bill which shall have passed the house of representatives and the senate, shall, before it become a law, be presented to the president of the United States; if he approve he shall sign it, but if not he shall return it, with his objections to that house in which it shall have originated, who shall enter the objections at large on their journal, and proceed to reconsider it. If after such reconsideration two-thirds of that house shall agree to pass the bill, it shall be sent, together with the objections, to the other house, by which it shall likewise be reconsidered, and if approved by two-thirds of that house, it shall become a law. But in all such cases the votes of both houses shall be determined by yeas and nays, and the names of the persons voting for and against the bill shall be entered on the journal of each house respectively. If any bill shall not be returned by the President within ten days (Sundays excepted) after it shall have been presented to him, the same shall be a law, in like manner as if he had signed it, unless the Congress by their adjournment prevent its return, in which case it shall not be a law.

Every order, resolution, or vote to which the concurrence of the Senate and House of Representatives may be necessary (except on a question of adjournment) shall be presented to the President of the United States; and before the same shall take effect, shall be approved by him, or, being disapproved by him, shall be repassed by two-thirds of the Senate and House of Representatives, according to the rules and limitations prescribed in the case of a bill.

Sect. 8. The Congress shall have power

To lay and collect taxes, duties, imposts and excises, to pay the debts and provide for the common defence and general welfare of the United States; but all duties, imposts and excises shall be uniform throughout the United States;

To borrow money on the credit of the United States;

To regulate commerce with foreign nations, and among the several states, and with the Indian tribes;

To establish an uniform rule of naturalization, and uniform laws on the subject of bankruptcies throughout the United States;

To coin money, regulate the value thereof, and of foreign coin, and fix the standard of weights and measures;

To provide for the punishment of counterfeiting the securities and current coin of the United States;

To establish post offices and post roads;

To promote the progress of science and useful arts, by securing for limited times to authors and inventors the exclusive right to their respective writings and discoveries;

To constitute tribunals inferior to the supreme court;

To define and punish piracies and felonies committed on the high seas, and offences against the law of nations;

To declare war, grant letters of marque and reprisal, and make rules concerning captures on land and water;

To raise and support armies, but no appropriation of money to that use shall be for a longer term than two years;

To provide and maintain a navy;

To make rules for the government and regulation of the land and naval forces;

To provide for calling forth the militia to execute the laws of the union, suppress insurrections and repel invasions;

To provide for organizing, arming, and disciplining, the militia, and for governing such part of them as may be employed in the service of the United States, reserving to the States respectively, the appointment of the officers, and the authority of training the militia according to the discipline prescribed by Congress;

To exercise exclusive legislation in all cases whatsoever, over such district (not exceeding ten miles square) as may, be cession of particular States, and the acceptance of Congress, become the seat of the government of the United States, and to exercise like authority over all places purchased by the consent of the legislature of the state in which the same shall be, for the erection of forts, magazines, arsenals, dock-yards, and other needful buildings;—And

To make all laws which shall be necessary and proper for carrying into execution the foregoing powers, and all other powers vested by this constitution in the government of the United States, or in any department or officer thereof.

Sect. 9. The migration or importation of such persons as any of the states now existing shall think proper to admit, shall not be prohibited by the Congress prior to the year one thousand eight hundred and eight, but a tax or duty may be imposed on such importation, not exceeding ten dollars for each person.

The privilege of the writ of habeas corpus shall not be suspended, unless when in cases of rebellion or invasion the public safety may require it.

No bill of attainder or ex post facto law shall be passed.

No capitation, or other direct, tax shall be laid, unless in proportion to the census or enumeration herein before directed to be taken.[5]

No tax or duty shall be laid on articles exported from any state. No preference shall be given by any regulation of commerce or revenue to the ports of one state over those of another: nor shall vessels bound to, or from, one state, be obliged to enter, clear, or pay duties in another.

No money shall be drawn from the treasury, but in consequence of appropriations made by law; and a regular statement and account of the receipts and expenditures of all public money shall be published from time to time.

No title of nobility shall be granted by the United States:—And no person holding any office of profit or trust under them, shall, without the consent of the Congress, accept of any present, emolument, office, or title, of any kind whatever, from any king, prince, or foreign state.

Sect. 10. No state shall enter into any treaty, alliance, or confederation; grant letters of marque and reprisal; coin money; emit bills of credit; make any thing but gold and silver coin a tender in payment of debts; pass any bill of attainder, ex post facto law, or law impairing the obligation of contracts, or grant any title of nobility.

No state shall, without the consent of the Congress, lay any imposts or duties on imports or exports, except what may be absolutely necessary for executing its inspection laws; and the net produce of all duties and imposts, laid by any state on imports or exports, shall be for the use of the Treasury of the United States; and all such laws shall be subject to the revision and controul of the Congress. No state shall, without the consent of Congress, lay any duty of tonnage, keep troops, or ships of war in time of peace, enter into any agreement or

---

[5] See also Amendment XVI.

compact with another state, or with a foreign power, or engage in war, unless actually invaded, or in such imminent danger as will not admit of delay.

I I

Sect. 1. The executive power shall be vested in a president of the United States of America. He shall hold his office during the term of four years, and, together with the vice-president, chosen for the same term, be elected as follows.

Each state shall appoint, in such manner as the legislature thereof may direct, a number of electors, equal to the whole number of senators and representatives to which the state may be entitled in the Congress: but no senator or representative, or person holding an office of trust or profit under the United States, shall be appointed an elector.

[6][The electors shall meet in their respective states, and vote by ballot for two persons, of whom one at least shall not be an inhabitant of the same state with themselves. And they shall make a list of all the persons voted for, and of the number of votes for each; which list they shall sign and certify, and transmit sealed to the seat of the government of the United States, directed to the president of the senate. The president of the senate shall, in the presence of the senate and house of representatives, open all the certificates, and the votes shall then be counted. The person having the greatest number of votes shall be the president, if such number be a majority of the whole number of electors appointed; and if there be more than one who have such majority, and have an equal number of votes, then the house of representatives shall immediately chuse by ballot one of them for president; and if no person have a majority, then from the five highest on the list the said house shall in like manner chuse the president. But in chusing the president, the votes shall be taken by states, the representation from each state having one vote; a quorum for this purpose shall consist of a member or members from two-thirds of the states, and a majority of all the states shall be necessary to a choice. In every case, after the choice of the president, the person having the greatest number of votes of the electors shall be the vice-president. But if there should remain two or more who have equal votes, the senate shall chuse from them by ballot the vice-president.]

The Congress may determine the time of chusing the electors, and the day on which they shall give their votes; which day shall be the same throughout the United States.

No person except a natural born citizen, or a citizen of the United States, at the time of the adoption of this constitution, shall be eligible to the office of president; neither shall any person be eligible to that office who shall not have

---

[6] This paragraph has been superseded by Amendment XII.

attained to the age of thirty-five years, and been fourteen years a resident within the United States.

[7]In case of the removal of the president from office, or of his death, resignation, or inability to discharge the powers and duties of the said office, the same shall devolve on the vice-president, and the Congress may by law provide for the case of removal, death, resignation or inability, both of the president and vice-president, declaring what officer shall then act as president, and such officer shall act accordingly, until the disability be removed, or a president shall be elected.

The president shall, at stated times, receive for his services, a compensation, which shall neither be encreased nor diminished during the period for which he shall have been elected, and he shall not receive within that period any other emolument from the United States, or any of them.

Before he enter on the execution of his office, he shall take the following oath or affirmation:

"I do solemnly swear (or affirm) that I will faithfully execute the office of president of the United States, and will to the best of my ability, preserve, protect and defend the constitution of the United States."

Sect. 2. The president shall be commander in chief of the army and navy of the United States, and of the militia of the several States, when called into the actual service of the United States; he may require the opinion, in writing, of the principal officer in each of the executive departments, upon any subject relating to the duties of their respective offices, and he shall have power to grant reprieves and pardons for offences against the United States, except in cases of impeachment.

He shall have power, by and with the advice and consent of the senate, to make treaties, provided two-thirds of the senators present concur; and he shall nominate, and by and with the advice and consent of the senate, shall appoint ambassadors, other public ministers and consuls, judges of the supreme court, and all other officers of the United States, whose appointments are not herein otherwise provided for, and which shall be established by law. But the Congress may by law vest the appointment of such inferior officers, as they think proper, in the president alone, in the courts of law, or in the heads of departments.

The president shall have power to fill up all vacancies that may happen during the recess of the senate, by granting commissions which shall expire at the end of their next session.

Sect. 3. He shall from time to time give to the Congress information of the state of the union, and recommend to their consideration such measures as he shall judge necessary and expedient; he may, on extraordinary occasions, convene both houses, or either of them, and in case of disagreement between them,

---

[7] This clause has been affected by Amendment XXV.

with respect to the time of adjournment, he may adjourn them to such time as he shall think proper; he shall receive ambassadors and other public ministers; he shall take care that the laws be faithfully executed, and shall commission all the officers of the United States.

Sect. 4. The president, vice-president and all civil officers of the United States, shall be removed from office on impeachment for, and conviction of, treason, bribery, or other high crimes and misdemeanors.

I I I

Sect. 1. The judicial power of the United States, shall be vested in one supreme court, and in such inferior courts as the Congress may from time to time ordain and establish. The judges, both of the supreme and inferior courts, shall hold their offices during good behaviour, and shall, at stated times, receive for their services, a compensation, which shall not be diminished during their continuance in office.

Sect. 2. The judicial power shall extend to all cases, in law and equity, arising under this constitution, the laws of the United States, and treaties made, or which shall be made, under their authority; to all cases affecting ambassadors, other public ministers and consuls; to all cases of admiralty and maritime jurisdiction; to controversies to which the United States shall be a party; to controversies between two or more States, between a state and citizens of another state,[8] between citizens of different States, between citizens of the same state claiming lands under grants of different States, and between a state, or the citizens thereof, and foreign States, citizens or subjects.

In all cases affecting ambassadors, other public ministers and consuls, and those in which a state shall be party, the supreme court shall have original jurisdiction. In all the other cases before mentioned, the supreme court shall have appellate jurisdiction, both as to law and fact, with such exceptions, and under such regulations as the Congress shall make.

The trial of all crimes, except in cases of impeachment, shall be by jury; and such trial shall be held in the state where the said crimes shall have been committed; but when not committed within any state, the trial shall be at such place or places as the Congress may by law have directed.

Sect. 3. Treason against the United States, shall consist only in levying war against them, or in adhering to their enemies, giving them aid and comfort. No person shall be convicted of treason unless on the testimony of two witnesses to the same overt act, or on confession in open court.

The Congress shall have power to declare the punishment of treason, but no attainder of treason shall work corruption of blood, or forfeiture except during the life of the person attainted.

---

[8] This clause has been affected by Amendment XI.

I V

Sect. 1. Full faith and credit shall be given in each state to the public acts, records, and judicial proceedings of every other state. And the Congress may by general laws prescribe the manner in which such acts, records and proceedings shall be proved, and the effect thereof.

Sect. 2. The citizens of each state shall be entitled to all privileges and immunities of citizens in the several states.

A person charged in any state with treason, felony, or other crime, who shall flee from justice, and be found in another state, shall, on demand of the executive authority of the state from which he fled, be delivered up, to be removed to the state having jurisdiction of the crime.

[9][No person held to service or labour in one state, under the laws thereof, escaping into another, shall, in consequence of any law or regulation therein, be discharged from such service or labour, but shall be delivered up on claim of the party to whom such service or labour may be due.]

Sect. 3. New states may be admitted by the Congress into this union; but no new state shall be formed or erected within the jurisdiction of any other state; nor any state be formed by the junction of two or more states, or parts of states, without the consent of the legislatures of the states concerned as well as of the Congress.

The Congress shall have power to dispose of and make all needful rules and regulations respecting the territory or other property belonging to the United States; and nothing in this Constitution shall be so construed as to prejudice any claims of the United States, or of any particular state.

Sect. 4. The United States shall guarantee to every state in this union a Republican form of government, and shall protect each of them against invasion; and on application of the legislature, or of the executive (when the legislature cannot be convened) against domestic violence.

V

The Congress, whenever two-thirds of both houses shall deem it necessary, shall propose amendments to this constitution, or, on the application of the legislatures of two-thirds of the several states, shall call a convention for proposing amendments, which, in either case, shall be valid to all intents and purposes, as part of this constitution, when ratified by the legislatures of three-fourths of the several states, or by conventions in three-fourths thereof, as the one or the other mode of ratification may be proposed by the Congress; Provided, that no amendment which may be made prior to the year one thousand eight hundred and eight shall in any manner affect the first and fourth clauses in

---

[9] This paragraph has been superseded by Amendment XIII.

the ninth section of the first article; and that no state, without its consent, shall be deprived of its equal suffrage in the senate.

V I

All debts contracted and engagements entered into, before the adoption of this Constitution, shall be as valid against the United States under this Constitution, as under the confederation.

This constitution, and the laws of the United States which shall be made in pursuance thereof; and all treaties made, or which shall be made, under the authority of the United States, shall be the supreme law of the land; and the judges in every state shall be bound thereby, any thing in the constitution or laws of any state to the contrary notwithstanding.

The senators and representatives beforementioned, and the members of the several state legislatures, and all executive and judicial officers, both of the United States and of the several States, shall be bound by oath or affirmation, to support this constitution; but no religious test shall ever be required as a qualification to any office or public trust under the United States.

V I I

The ratification of the conventions of nine States, shall be sufficient for the establishment of this constitution between the States so ratifying the same.

Done in Convention, by the unanimous consent of the States present, the seventeenth day of September, in the year of our Lord one thousand seven hundred and eighty-seven, and of the Independence of the United States of America the twelfth. In witness whereof we have hereunto subscribed our Names.

AMENDMENTS

Articles in addition to, and Amendment of the Constitution of the United States of America, proposed by Congress, and ratified by the Legislatures of the several States, pursuant to the Fifth Article of the original Constitution.

ARTICLE I

Congress shall make no law respecting an establishment of religion, or prohibiting the free exercise thereof; or abridging the freedom of speech, or of the press; or the right of the people peaceably to assemble, and to petition the Government for a redress of grievances.

ARTICLE II

A well regulated Militia, being necessary to the security of a free State, the right of the people to keep and bear Arms, shall not be infringed.

ARTICLE III

No Soldier shall, in time of peace be quartered in any house, without the consent of the Owner, nor in time of war, but in a manner to be prescribed by law.

ARTICLE IV

The right of the people to be secure in their persons, houses, papers, and effects, against unreasonable searches and seizures, shall not be violated, and no Warrants shall issue, but upon probable cause, supported by Oath or affirmation, and particularly describing the place to be searched, and the persons or things to be seized.

ARTICLE V

No person shall be held to answer for a capital, or otherwise infamous crime, unless on a presentment or indictment of a Grand Jury, except in cases arising in the land or naval forces, or in the Militia, when in actual service in time of War or public danger; nor shall any person be subject for the same offence to be twice put in jeopardy of life or limb; nor shall be compelled in any criminal case to be a witness against himself, nor be deprived of life, liberty, or property, without due process of law; nor shall private property be taken for public use, without just compensation.

ARTICLE VI

In all criminal prosecutions, the accused shall enjoy the right to a speedy and public trial, by an impartial jury of the State and district wherein the crime shall have been committed, which district shall have been previously ascertained by law, and to be informed of the nature and cause of the accusation; to be confronted with the witnesses against him; to have compulsory process for obtaining witnesses in his favor, and to have the Assistance of Counsel for his defence.

ARTICLE VII

In Suits at common law, where the value in controversy shall exceed twenty dollars, the right of trial by jury shall be preserved, and no fact tried by a jury, shall be otherwise re-examined in any Court of the United States, than according to the rules of the common law.

ARTICLE VIII

Excessive bail shall not be required, nor excessive fines imposed, nor cruel and unusual punishments inflicted.

ARTICLE IX

The enumeration in the Constitution, of certain rights, shall not be construed to deny or disparage others retained by the people.

ARTICLE X

The powers not delegated to the United States by the Constitution, nor prohibited by it to the States, are reserved to the States respectively, or to the people. [The first ten Amendments were adopted in 1791.]

ARTICLE XI

The Judicial power of the United States shall not be construed to extend to any suit in law or equity, commenced or prosecuted against one of the United States by Citizens of another State, or by Citizens or Subjects of any Foreign State. [Adopted 1798.]

ARTICLE XII

The Electors shall meet in their respective states, and vote by ballot for President and Vice-President, one of whom, at least, shall not be an inhabitant of the same state with themselves; they shall name in their ballots the person voted for as President, and in distinct ballots the person voted for as Vice-President, and they shall make distinct lists of all persons voted for as President, and of all persons voted for as Vice-President, and of the number of votes for each, which lists they shall sign and certify, and transmit sealed to the seat of the government of the United States, directed to the President of the Senate;—The President of the Senate shall, in the presence of the Senate and House of Representatives, open all the certificates and the votes shall then be counted;—The person having the greatest number of votes for President, shall be the President, if such number be a majority of the whole number of Electors appointed; and if no person have such majority, then from the persons having the highest numbers not exceeding three on the list of those voted for as President, the House of Representatives shall choose immediately, by ballot, the President. But in choosing the President, the votes shall be taken by states, the representation from each state having one vote; a quorum for this purpose shall consist of a member or members from two-thirds of the states, and a majority of all the states shall be necessary to a choice. [10][And if the House of Representatives shall not choose a President whenever the right of choice shall devolve upon them, before the fourth day of March next following, then the Vice-President shall act as President, as in the case of the death or other constitutional disability of the President.]—The person having the greatest number of votes as Vice-President, shall be the Vice-President, if such number be a majority of the whole number of Electors appointed, and if no person have a majority, then from the two highest numbers on the list, the Senate shall choose the Vice-President; a quorum for the purpose shall consist of two-thirds of the whole number of Senators, and a majority of the whole number shall be necessary to a choice. But no person constitutionally ineligible to the office of President shall be eligible to that of Vice-President of the United States. [Adopted 1804.]

ARTICLE XIII

Section 1. Neither slavery nor involuntary servitude, except as a punishment for crime whereof the party shall have been duly convicted, shall exist within the United States, or any place subject to their jurisdiction.
Section 2. Congress shall have power to enforce this article by appropriate legislation. [Adopted 1865.]

ARTICLE XIV

Section 1. All persons born or naturalized in the United States, and subject to the jurisdiction thereof, are citizens of the United States and of the State wherein they reside. No State shall make or enforce any law which shall abridge the privileges or immunities of citizens of the United States; nor shall any State deprive any person of life, liberty, or property, without due process of law; nor deny to any person within its jurisdiction the equal protection of the laws.
Section 2. Representatives shall be apportioned among the several States according to their respective numbers, counting the whole number of persons in each State, excluding Indians not taxed. But when the right to vote at any election for the choice of electors for President and Vice President of the United States, Representatives in Congress, the Executive and Judicial officers of a State, or the members of the Legislature thereof, is denied to any of the male inhabitants of such State, being twenty-one years of age, and citizens of the United States, or in any way abridged, except for participation in rebellion, or other crime, the basis of representation therein shall be reduced in the proportion which the number of such male citizens shall bear to the whole number of male citizens twenty-one years of age in such State.

---

[10] The part enclosed by brackets has been superseded by section 3 of Amendment XX.

Section 3. No person shall be a Senator or Representative in Congress, or elector of President and Vice President, or hold any office, civil or military, under the United States, or under any State, who, having previously taken an oath, as a member of Congress, or as an officer of the United States, or as a member of any State legislature, or as an executive or judicial officer of any State, to support the Constitution of the United States, shall have engaged in insurrection or rebellion against the same, or given aid or comfort to the enemies thereof. But Congress may by a vote of two-thirds of each House, remove such disability.

Section 4. The validity of the public debt of the United States, authorized by law, including debts incurred for payment of pensions and bounties for services in suppressing insurrection or rebellion, shall not be questioned. But neither the United States nor any State shall assume or pay any debt or obligation incurred in aid of insurrection or rebellion against the United States, or any claim for the loss or emancipation of any slave; but all such debts, obligations and claims shall be held illegal and void.

Section 5. The Congress shall have power to enforce, by appropriate legislation, the provisions of this article. [Adopted 1868.]

ARTICLE XV

Section 1. The right of citizens of the United States to vote shall not be denied or abridged by the United States or by any State on account of race, color, or previous condition of servitude.

Section 2. The Congress shall have power to enforce this article by appropriate legislation. [Adopted 1870.]

ARTICLE XVI

The Congress shall have power to lay and collect taxes on incomes, from whatever source derived, without apportionment among the several States, and without regard to any census or enumeration. [Adopted 1913.]

ARTICLE XVII

The Senate of the United States shall be composed of two Senators from each State, elected by the people thereof, for six years; and each Senator shall have one vote. The electors in each State shall have the qualifications requisite for electors of the most numerous branch of the State legislatures.

When vacancies happen in the representation of any State in the Senate, the executive authority of such State shall issue writs of election to fill such vacancies: *Provided,* That the legislature of any State may empower the executive thereof to make temporary appointments until the people fill the vacancies by election as the legislature may direct.

This amendment shall not be so construed as to affect the election or term of any Senator chosen before it becomes valid as part of the Constitution. [Adopted 1913.]

ARTICLE XVIII [11]

[Section 1. After one year from the ratification of this article the manufacture, sale, or transportation of intoxicating liquors within, the importation thereof into, or the exportation thereof from the United States and all territory subject to the jurisdiction thereof for beverage purposes is hereby prohibited.

[Sec. 2. The Congress and the several States shall have concurrent power to enforce this article by appropriate legislation.

[Sec. 3. This article shall be inoperative unless it shall have been ratified as an amendment to the Constitution by the legislatures of the several States, as provided in the Constitution, within seven years from the date of the submission hereof to the States by the Congress.] [Adopted 1919.]

ARTICLE XIX

The right of citizens of the United States to vote shall not be denied or abridged by the United States or by any State on account of sex.

Congress shall have power to enforce this article by appropriate legislation. [Adopted 1920.]

ARTICLE XX

Section 1. The terms of the President and Vice President shall end at noon on the 20th day of January, and the terms of Senators and Representatives at noon on the 3d day of January, of the years in which such terms would have ended if this article had not been ratified; and the terms of their successors shall then begin.

Sec. 2. The Congress shall assemble at least once in every year, and such meeting shall begin at noon on the 3d day of January, unless they shall by law appoint a different day.

Sec. 3. If, at the time fixed for the beginning of the term of the President, the President elect shall have died, the Vice President elect shall become President. If a President shall not have been chosen before the time fixed for the

---

[11] Repeal of the 18th Amendment on December 5, 1933, was proclaimed by the President in his proclamation of that date, when the ratification of the 21st Amendment was certified by the Acting Secretary of State.

beginning of his term, or if the President elect shall have failed to qualify, then the Vice President elect shall act as President until a President shall have qualified; and the Congress may by law provide for the case wherein neither a President elect nor a Vice President elect shall have qualified, declaring who shall then act as President, or the manner in which one who is to act shall be selected, and such person shall act accordingly until a President or Vice President shall have qualified.

Sec. 4. The Congress may by law provide for the case of the death of any of the persons from whom the House of Representatives may choose a President whenever the right of choice shall have devolved upon them, and for the case of the death of any of the persons from whom the Senate may choose a Vice President whenever the right of choice shall have devolved upon them.

Sec. 5. Sections 1 and 2 shall take effect on the 15th day of October following the ratification of this article.

Sec. 6. This article shall be inoperative unless it shall have been ratified as an amendment to the Constitution by the legislatures of three-fourths of the several States within seven years from the date of its submission. [Adopted 1933.]

ARTICLE XXI

Section 1. The eighteenth article of amendment to the Constitution of the United States is hereby repealed.

Sec. 2. The transportation or importation into any State, Territory, or possession of the United States for delivery or use therein of intoxicating liquors, in violation of the laws thereof, is hereby prohibited.

Sec. 3. This article shall be inoperative unless it shall have been ratified as an amendment to the Constitution by conventions in the several States, as provided in the Constitution, within seven years from the date of the submission hereof to the States by the Congress. [Adopted 1933.]

ARTICLE XXII

Section 1. No person shall be elected to the office of the President more than twice, and no person who has held the office of President, or acted as President, for more than two years of a term to which some other person was elected President shall be elected to the office of the President more than once. But this Article shall not apply to any person holding the office of President when this Article was proposed by the Congress, and shall not prevent any person who may be holding the office of President, or acting as President, during the term within which this Article becomes operative from holding the office of President or acting as President during the remainder of such term.

Sec. 2. This article shall be inoperative unless it shall have been ratified as an amendment to the Constitution by the legislatures of three-fourths of the several States within seven years from the date of its submission to the States by the Congress. [Adopted 1951.]

ARTICLE XXIII

Section 1. The District constituting the seat of Government of the United States shall appoint in such manner as the Congress may direct:

A number of electors of President and Vice President equal to the whole number of Senators and Representatives in Congress to which the District would be entitled if it were a State, but in no event more than the least populous State; they shall be in addition to those appointed by the States, but they shall be considered, for the purposes of the election of President and Vice President, to be electors appointed by a State; and they shall meet in the District and perform such duties as provided by the twelfth article of amendment.

Section 2. The Congress shall have power to enforce this article by appropriate legislation. [Adopted 1961.]

ARTICLE XXIV

Section 1. The right of citizens of the United States to vote in any primary or other election for President or Vice President, for electors for President or Vice President, or for Senator or Representative in Congress, shall not be denied or abridged by the United States or any State by reason of failure to pay any poll tax or other tax.

Section 2. The Congress shall have power to enforce this article by appropriate legislation. [Adopted 1964.]

ARTICLE XXV

Section 1. In case of the removal of the President from office or of his death or resignation, the Vice President shall become President.

Sec. 2. Whenever there is a vacancy in the office of the Vice President, the President shall nominate a Vice President who shall take office upon confirmation by a majority vote of both Houses of Congress.

Sec. 3. Whenever the President transmits to the President pro tempore of the Senate and the Speaker of the House of Representatives his written declaration that he is unable to discharge the powers and duties of his office, and until he transmits to them a written declaration to the contrary, such powers and duties shall be discharged by the Vice President as Acting President.

Sec. 4. Whenever the Vice President and a majority of either the principal officers of the executive departments or of such other body as Congress may by law provide, transmit to the President pro tempore of the Senate and the Speaker of the House of Representatives their written declaration that the President is unable to discharge the powers and duties of his office, the Vice President shall immediately assume the powers and duties of the office as Acting President.

Thereafter, when the President transmits to the President pro tempore of the Senate and the Speaker of the House of Representatives his written declaration that no inability exists, he shall resume the powers and duties of his office unless the Vice President and a majority of either the principal officers of the executive department or of such other body as Congress may by law provide, transmit within four days to the President pro tempore of the Senate and the Speaker of the House of Representatives their written declaration that the President is unable to discharge the powers and duties of his office. Thereupon Congress shall decide the issue, assembling within forty-eight hours for that purpose if not in session. If the Congress, within twenty-one days after receipt of the latter written declaration, or, if Congress is not in session, within twenty-one days after Congress is required to assemble, determines by two-thirds vote of both Houses that the President is unable to discharge the powers and duties of his office, the Vice President shall continue to discharge the same as Acting President; otherwise, the President shall resume the powers and duties of his office. [Adopted 1967.]

ARTICLE XXVI

Sec. 1. The right of citizens of the United States, who are eighteen years of age or older, to vote shall not be denied or abridged by the United States or by any State on account of age.

Sec. 2. The Congress shall have power to enforce this article by appropriate legislation. [Adopted 1971.]

ARTICLE XXVII [12]

Section 1. Equality of rights under the law shall not be denied or abridged by the United States or by any State on account of sex.

Section 2. The Congress shall have the power to enforce, by appropriate legislation, the provisions of this article.

Section 3. This amendment shall take effect two years after the date of ratification.

---

[12] Proposed to the states in 1972. At the beginning of 1974, thirty states had ratified the proposed equal rights amendment to the Constitution, including Nebraska, which later voted to rescind its ratification. In twelve states during 1973, the equal rights amendment was defeated in a floor vote in one of the houses of the legislature. These states are Alabama, Florida, Illinois, Indiana, Maine, Missouri, Nevada, North Carolina, North Dakota, Oklahoma, South Carolina, and Utah. In Arkansas, the Amendment was itself amended on the floor of the senate, in effect, defeating it for the purpose of ratification.

INDEX

Abington School District v. *Schempp* (1963), 55
Abortion, 76
Acheson, Dean, 300, 306
Adams, Abigail, 122
Adams, John, 4, 35, 122
Adams, John Quincy, 126
Adams, Samuel, 15, 123
Adams, Sherman, 185
Adenauer, Konrad, 300
Adler, Norman, 83
Advertising, 104-105
Age, political socialization and, 93-94
Agency for International Development (AID), 308
Agnew, Spiro T., 84, 102, 188, 267
Agricultural Act of 1970, 275
Agricultural Act of 1973, 275-276
Agricultural Adjustment Act of 1933, 274, 287
Agricultural Adjustment Act of 1938, 274
Agricultural and Consumer Protection Act of 1973, 275
Agriculture, 274-275
Agriculture, Department of, 109, 152, 184, 274, 275, 276, 308
Aid to the Blind (AB), 288
Aid to Families with Dependent Children (AFDC), 288
Aid to the Permanently and Totally Disabled (APTD), 288
Air Quality Act of 1967, 280
Alaska pipeline, 281
Albany Plan of Union, 3
Albert, Carl, 193, 204
Alberts v. *California* (1957), 52

Alexander v. *Holmes* (1969), 60
Alexander v. *Louisiana* (1972), 73
Alien Registration Act of 1940, *see* Smith Act
Alien and Sedition Acts, 60
Allen, William, 101
Alliance for Labor Action, 109
Allison, Graham T., 305
American Bar Association (ABA), 110, 111
American Civil Liberties Union, 111
American Commonwealth, The (Bryce), 98
American Farm Bureau Federation, 109-110
American Federation of Labor-Congress of Industrial Organizations (AFL-CIO), 109
American Independent Party, 126
American Legion, 111
American Medical Association (AMA), 110-111, 112, 113, 153, 293, 294
American Petroleum Institute, 107
Amish, 57
Annapolis Convention, 4
Anderson, Clinton, 102
Anderson, Jack, 275, 296
Anthony, Susan B., 141
Anti-bigamy Act of 1862, 56
Anti-Federalists, 14-17
Anti-Masonic Party, 126
Anti-Saloon League, 113
Apodaca v. *Oregon* (1972), 73
Argersinger v. *Hamlin* (1972), 71, 243
Arizona v. *California* (1963), 243
Arnall, Ellis, 136
Articles of Confederation, 3-4, 8-9, 12, 169, 316-322
Ash, Roy L., 184

342 Index

Atomic Energy Commission, 311
Attorney General of the United States, 225-226
Avery v. *Midland County* (1968), 28

Bad tendency doctrine, 50
Baker v. *Carr* (1962), 27
Baldwin v. *New York* (1971), 73
Ball, George, 298
Ballots, 156-157
Bank of the United States, 36
Banzhaf, John, 104-105, 113
Bay of Pigs invasion, 304
Bayh, Birch, 102
Beard, Charles A., 6
Benson, Ezra T., 275
Bentley, Arthur F., 106-107
Benton v. *Maryland* (1969), 70
Bentsen, Lloyd, 102, 267
Betts v. *Brady* (1942), 46, 71
Bicameralism, 33
Bill of Rights, 21, 30, 46, 47, 57, 68-69
Bills, *see* Legislative process
Bills of attainder, 15, 47
Bivens v. *Six Unknown Named Agents* (1971), 70
Black, Hugo L., 27, 45-46, 48, 49, 55, 243
Black Caucus, 93, 141
Black Codes, 139
Blackmun, Harry A., 74
Blacks, 47
 poverty and, 285
 segregation, 58-59
 voting, 93, 139
Blanc, Bertrand de, 74
Block grants, 41
Blough, Roger M., 273
Board of Education v. *Allen* (1968), 56
Boggs, Hale, 193, 196
Bohlen, Chip, 298
Bolling, Richard, 203
Boorstin, Daniel J., 20
Bosses, 123
Boswell, James G., 275
Bradley, Joseph P., 58
Brandeis, Louis, 49
Brandenburg v. *Ohio* (1969), 51
Branzburg v. *Hayes* (1972), 52
Brennan, William J., 53, 73, 74, 241
British constitution, 22, 23, 32
Brooks, Lawrence, 283
Brown, H. Rap, 93
Brown v. *Board of Education* (1954), 59-60, 63
Bryce, James, 98
Buchanan, James, 189
Budget, 249-266
 in brief, 258-266

 budgeting and accounting process, 252-253
 economy and, 254-258
 full employment principle, 250, 254, 256
Budget and Accounting Act of 1921, 217, 251, 252
Bundy, McGeorge, 170, 298
Burger, Warren E., 53, 57, 60, 61, 68, 70, 74, 75, 143-144, 246
Burke, Edmund, 120, 205
Burleson, Albert S., 180
Burnham, Walter Dean, 119, 127
Burns, James MacGregor, 189-190
Burns v. *Fortson* (1973), 76
Burr, Aaron, 22
Burton, Laurence, 152
Busing, 61
Butz, Earl L., 184
Byrd, Robert C., 55, 203

Cabinet, 181, 183-185
Calhoun, John C., 213
Cambodia, 176, 302, 303-304
Campaign committees, 130
Campaigns
 corruption, 155-156
 costs, 151-155
 presidential, 161-162
 strategies, 150-151
Candidate campaign committees, 131-132
Cannon, Howard, 151
Cannon, Joseph, 197
Capital punishment, 74
Carolyn Bradley v. *State Board of Education of Virginia* (1973), 62
Carpetbaggers, 139
Carson, Rachel, 278
Caucus, 146
Censorship, 84, 87
Census, Bureau of the, 270
Central Intelligence Agency (CIA), 178, 186, 296, 307, 309, 311
Certification, 233
Certiorari, writ of, 45, 70, 71, 233
Checks and balances, 32-34
Chimel v. *California* (1969), 69
Chisholm, Shirley, 93
Church, Frank, 176
Church, political socialization and, 83-84
Churchill, Winston, 175
Circuit courts, 21
City committees, 131
Civil actions, 237-238
Civil Aeronautics Board, 271
Civil liberties, 46-47
Civil rights, 47, 57-68
Civil Rights Act of 1866, 66, 139

Civil Rights Act of 1875, 58
Civil Rights Act of 1957, 63-64, 140
Civil Rights Act of 1960, 64, 140
Civil Rights Act of 1964, 65
Civil Rights Act of 1968, 65, 66
Civil Rights Cases (1883), 58
Civil Rights Commission, 64
Civil War, 89
Civilian Conservation Corps (CCC), 286, 287
Clark, Tom, 55, 65, 69
Class status, political socialization and, 89-91
Clayton Act of 1914, 272
Clear and present danger, 49-51
Cleveland, Grover, 124, 155, 163
Clinton, George, 14
Closed primary, 147
Cloture, 212, 214-215
Coast and Geodetic Survey, 270
Coastal Zone Management Act of 1972, 280
Colegrove, Kenneth, 27
Colegrove v. *Green* (1946), 27
Colorado River Compact, 38
Commager, Henry Steele, 20
Commerce, 22-23
Commerce, Department of, 270
Committee on the Conduct of the War, 22
Committee for Economic Development, 108, 109
Committee of Public Education v. *Nyquist* (1973), 56
Committee to Re-elect the President, 132, 154
Common Cause, 101, 105, 154, 200
Communications Act of 1934, 154
Communist Party, 50
Community Action Program (CAP), 289
Concurrent resolutions, 209
Congress of the United States, 31, 66, 192-193, 196-220
  committee system, 198-201
  courts, creation of, 230-231
  deliberative function, 213-215
  economic powers, 250-251, 253-254
  education legislation, 294-295
  environmental legislation, 279-281
  foreign policy, 178, 302-305, 311, 312
  health legislation, 292-294
  legislative oversight, 216-219
  legislative process, 207-212
  norms and power in, 201-204
  party leadership, 197-198
  powers of, 11, 23-24, 33-34
  representative function, 204-207
  revenue-sharing legislation, 42, 43
  seniority system, 192, 199-202
  Supreme Court and, 242-244
  voting age, 137, 138
  war-making powers, 176-177

welfare legislation, 287, 290
See also House of Representatives; Senate
Congressional Record, 213
Connally, John B., 102, 256
Constitution, British, 22, 23, 32
Constitution of the United States, 323-340
  amendment procedure, 21
  basic principles, 25-44
  British constitution, compared to, 22, 23
  checks and balances, 32-34
  contract clause, 24
  double jeopardy clause, 47, 70, 74
  draft, 11-12
  due process clause, 57, 71, 74
  economic goals, 22-24, 269
  Electoral College, 163
  full faith and credit clause, 37
  interstate rendition, 38
  judicial process, 230-231
  limited government, 30
  necessary and proper clause, 15
  political goals, 25
  popular sovereignty, 29
  Preamble, 25, 29
  Presidency, 168-169, 172, 175
  privileges and immunities clause, 37-38
  ratification, 13-17
  representation, 26-29
  separation of powers, 31-32
  signing, 13
  social goals, 24-25
  supremacy clause, 5, 12, 15, 22, 36
  See also Bill of Rights; specific amendments
Constitutional Convention, 4-13
Constitutional courts, 230-231
Constitutionalism, 30
Containment policy, 305
Contract clause, 24
Convention-primary systems, 147-148
Cook, Marlow, 267
Cooper, John Sherman, 102, 176
Cooperative federalism, 39
Corporation income taxes, 261
Corporations, 153, 154
Corwin, Edward S., 168, 178
Cost of Living Council, 256
Council of Economic Advisers (CEA), 187, 255
Council on Environmental Quality (CEQ), 187
Council on International Economic Policy, 188
Counsel, right to, 48, 70-72, 243
County committees, 131
Court of Claims, 230, 231
Court of Customs and Patent Appeals, 230, 231
Court of Military Appeals, 231
Court system
  federal, *see* Federal court system
  functions of, 241-245

Court system (*continued*)
 procedure in, 236-241
 reform in, 245-246
 state, *see* State court system
Courts of appeal
 federal, 233
 state, 235
Crime, 227-230
Criminal actions, 238-239
Cruel and unusual punishment, 48, 73-74
Cuban missile crisis, 170, 297-301, 304, 306
Customs Court, 230, 231

Davis v. *Beason* (1890), 56
De facto segregation, 62
De Gaulle, Charles, 300
De jure segregation, 62
Dean, Suzanne, 116, 117
Death penalty, 74
Debs, Eugene V., 49
Declaration of Independence, 3, 24, 46, 313-315
Declaration of the Rights of Women, 141
Defense, Department of, 181, 307, 309, 311
Defense spending, 261, 263
Democratic National Convention (1968), 80, 134
Democratic National Convention (1972), 159
Democratic Party, 89-91, 93-97, 110, 118-119, 123-125, 152-154, 158-159
Dennis v. *United States* (1951), 50
Dickinson, John, 5, 8
Dillon, Douglas, 297, 306
Diplomacy, 307-308
Direct primary, 146-147
Dirksen, Everett, 28
Discrimination, 47, 58
District of Columbia, 143
District courts, 21, 233-234
Divorce decrees, 37
Dobrynin, Anatol, 301
Dodson, Dan, 225
Doe v. *Bolton* (1973), 76
Domestic Council, 186-187
Double jeopardy clause, 47, 70, 74
Douglas, Paul, 214
Douglas, William O., 27, 50, 62, 65, 71, 73, 74
Due process of law clause, 57, 71, 74
Duncan v. *Louisiana* (1968), 76
Dunn v. *Blumstein* (1972), 74, 143

Eagleton, Thomas, 129
Eastland, James O., 275
Easton, David, 81
Economic Interpretation of the Constitution of the United States, An (Beard), 6
Economic Opportunity Act of 1964, 289

Economic Stabilization Act of 1970, 256
Economy
 budget and, 254-258
 Constitution and, 22-24
Education, 40, 294-295
 busing, 61-62
 desegregation, 59-62
 prayer and Bible reading decisions, 55
 school aid programs, 55-56
 unequal wealth distribution, 62-63
Eisenhower, Dwight D., 76, 137, 172, 175, 177, 188, 189, 190
 Cabinet and, 181
 on military-industrial complex, 104, 310
 1952 election, 96, 125, 160
 1956 election, 96, 97, 125
 personal advisers, 185
 on Presidency, 167
Elections, 148-157
 ballots, casting and counting, 156-157
 campaign corruption, 155-156
 campaign costs, 151-155
 campaigns, strategies of, 150-151
 candidates, characteristics of, 148-149
 candidates, motives of, 149-150
 nominating process, 145-148, 157-161
 presidential, *see* Presidential elections
Electoral College, 11, 162-164
Elementary and Secondary Education Act of 1965, 55, 294
Ellsworth, Oliver, 5
Emancipation Proclamation, 139
Emergency Petroleum Act, 281
Employment Act of 1946, 255
Energy crisis, 281
Engel v. *Vitale* (1962), 55
Environment, 276-281
Environmental Protection Agency, 276, 280, 281
Equal Educational Opportunities Act, 61
Equal protection clause, 27
Equal Rights Amendment, 67-68
Equality, principles of, 24
Erlenborn, John, 200
Ervin, Sam J., Jr., 19-20, 202-203
Escobedo v. *Illinois* (1964), 72
Espionage Act of 1917, 49
Ethnic factors, political socialization and, 91, 93
Evansville-Vanderburgh Airport Authority District v. *Delta Air Lines* (1972), 243
Everson v. *Board of Education* (1947), 54
Ex parte McCardle (1868), 219
Ex post facto laws, 15, 47
Excise taxes, 261
Exclusionary rule, 69-70
Executive Branch, 181-189
 Cabinet, 181, 183-185

Executive Office of the President, 172, 183, 185-188, 266
reorganization of, 181, 183-185
Executive Office of the President, 172, 183, 185-188, 266
Executive privilege, 20, 185, 203, 217-218
Export-Import Bank, 270

Fair Campaign Practices Committee, 156
Family, political socialization and, 81
Family Assistance Plan (FAP), 290-291
Farm groups, 109-110
Farmers Home Administration (FHA), 276, 295
Faubus v. *Aaron* (1959), 60
Federal Aviation Administration, 271, 280
Federal Bureau of Investigation (FBI), 72, 224, 227, 311
Federal Communications Commission (FCC), 104
Federal Corrupt Practices Act of 1925, 105, 152, 154
Federal court system, 230-234
  constitutional courts, 230-231
  courts of appeal, 233
  district courts, 233-234
  legislative courts, 231
  Supreme Court, *see* Supreme Court of the United States
Federal debt, 265
Federal Deposit Insurance Corporation, 287
Federal Election Campaign Act of 1971, 154, 155
Federal Election Campaign Act of 1973, 155
Federal Environmental Pesticide Control Act of 1972, 280
Federal government
  economic interests and, 269-271
  education, 294-295
  environment and, 276-281
  health services, 292-294
  housing, 295-296
  labor and, 271-273
  land policies, 273-275
  urban renewal, 296
  welfare system, *see* Welfare system
Federal grant programs, 40
Federal Housing Administration (FHA), 270, 295, 296
Federal Mediation and Conciliation Service, 273
Federal Regulation of Lobbying Act of 1946, 114-115
Federal Reserve System, 254, 256, 265
Federal Water Pollution Control Act Amendment of 1972, 280, 281
Federalism, 35-44
Federalist Papers (Hamilton, Madison, and Jay), 17, 25, 26, 30, 31, 34, 35, 36, 103

Federalists, 14-17, 122, 123
Fifteenth Amendment, 24, 48, 65-66, 93, 139, 149
Fifth Amendment, 48, 65, 68-69, 70, 74
Filibuster, 212, 214, 215
First Amendment, 47, 54
Fiske, John, 4
Food and Drug Administration (FDA), 292
Food for Peace program, 276
Ford, Gerald R., 189
Foreign Agents Registration law of 1938, 114
Foreign policy, 25, 177-178, 297-312
  Cambodian decision, 176, 302, 303-304
  checks and balances, 305-306
  contemporary, 306-311
  Cuban missile crisis, 170, 297-301, 304, 306
  goals, 304-305
  President and, 303-306, 311-312
Founding Fathers, 5-6
Fourteenth Amendment, 24, 27, 30, 47, 57, 58-60, 65, 68, 69, 71, 73, 74, 93, 143, 243
Fourth Amendment, 47, 68-69
Francis, Willie, 74
Frankfurter, Felix, 68
Franklin, Benjamin, 3, 6, 10, 13, 25-26
Free exercise of religion, 56-57
Freedom of the press, 16, 47, 48, 51-52
Freedom of religion, 16, 47, 54
Freedom of speech, 47, 48-51
Fulbright, J. William, 213
Full faith and credit clause, 37
Fuller, Jerry, 283
Funds, presidential impoundment of, 202, 216, 217, 243
Furman v. *Georgia* (1972), 74, 241

Gardner, John, 101, 105
Garwin, Richard L., 87
General Accounting Office (GAO), 153, 252, 253
Gerry, Elbridge, 5, 12, 13, 14
G.I. Bill of Rights, 295
Gideon, Clarence Earl, 45-46
Gideon v. *Wainright* (1963), 46, 71, 72, 242, 243
Gideon's Trumpet (Lewis), 45
Gilpatric, Roswell, 298
Ginzburg, Ralph, 53
Gitlow v. *New York* (1925), 47, 49
Goldberg, Arthur, 273
Goldwater, Barry, 96, 97, 98, 156, 160, 161
Grandfather clauses, 140
Grange, The, 109, 110
Grants-in-aid, 40, 41
Gray, L. Patrick, III, 217
Gray v. *Sanders* (1963), 27

Great Compromise, 10
Great Depression, 40, 89, 124
Great Game of Politics, The (Kent), 123
Green v. County Board of New Kent County (1968), 60
Greenstein, Fred, 81
Griffin v. County School Board of Prince Edward County (1964), 60
Griffiths, Martha, 294
Grodzins, Morton, 39
Gromyko, Andrei, 298
Guaranteed annual income, 290
Guinn v. United States (1915), 140
Gustafson v. Florida, 70

Habeas corpus, writ of, 15, 24, 47, 57, 70, 242
Habeas Corpus Act of 1867, 219
Haldeman, H. R., 184
Hamilton, Alexander, 4-6, 9, 10, 13, 17, 23-25, 34, 36, 122, 245, 268
Harlan, John M., 51, 58, 244
Harrington, Charles, 83
Harrington, Michael, 284
Harris, Fred, 199
Harrison, Benjamin, 163
Harrison, William Henry, 124
Harvey, Paul, 116
Hatch Act of 1939, 152
Hatch Act of 1940, 152
Hayes, Rutherford B., 145
Hays, Wayne, 193
Head Start, 289
Health, Education, and Welfare, Department of, 295, 306
Health Insurance for the Aged Act, *see* Medicare
Health Professions Educational Assistance Act of 1963, 293
Health services, 263, 292-294
Heart of Atlanta Motel v. United States (1964), 65
Hébert, F. Edwart, 207
Heller, Walter, 41
Helms, Richard, 311
Henderson v. United States (1950), 59
Henry, Patrick, 16
Hess, Robert D., 81, 82
Higher Education Act Amendment of 1972, 219
Hill-Burton Act of 1946, 293
Hinckley, Barbara, 199
Hollander, Neil, 84
Holmes, Oliver Wendell, 49, 244
Holtzmann, Abraham, 106
Homestead Act of 1862, 274
Hoover, Herbert, 55
Hopkins, Harry, 185
Horton, Frank, 200
House, Edward Mandell, 185

House of Commons, 32
House of Lords, 32
House of Representatives, 11, 196
  Appropriations Committee, 198, 200-201, 253
  Armed Services Committee, 198
  impeachment powers, 216
  officers of, 197-198
  Public Works Committee, 198
  Rules Committee, 198
  Ways and Means Committee, 198, 202, 253
  See also Congress of the United States
Housing, 59, 66, 295-296
Housing and Urban Development, Department of, 184, 295
Housing and Urban Development Act of 1968, 295
Humphrey, Hubert H., 80, 102, 159, 162, 163
Humphrey's Executor v. United States (1935), 175
Hyman, Herbert, 81
Hymel, Gary, 196

Illinois Apportionment Act of 1901, 27
Immigrants, 91
Impeachment, 216
In re Gault (1967), 236
Income security, 263
Income tax, 259-260, 261
Independent voters, 95, 119
Inflation, 254-256
Intelligence, 310-311
Interest groups, 100-115, 120
  business and industrial, 107-109
  farm, 109-110
  ingredients of success, 113-114
  labor organizations, 109
  lobbying, 112, 114-115
  professions, 110-111
Interior, Department of the, 184, 276
Internal Revenue Service (IRS), 155, 259
International Labor Organization (ILO), 306
Interposition, doctrine of, 60
Interstate Commerce Act, 59
Interstate Commerce Commission (ICC), 271
Interstate rendition, 38
Isolationism, 308
Item veto, 179

Jackson, Andrew, 126, 189, 217
Jackson, Henry, 102, 267
Jackson, Robert H., 37
Jackson, William, 6
Jacobellis v. Ohio (1964), 52
Javits, Jacob, 120
Jay, John, 17, 25

Jefferson, Thomas, 4, 5, 16, 17, 21, 22, 35, 54, 60, 76, 122, 123, 168, 189, 215, 217, 244
Jeffersonian Republicans, 122, 123, 125
Jehovah's Witnesses, 57
Jensen, Merrill, 3, 14, 15
Jews, 91, 93
Jim Crow laws, 58
Job Corps, 289
Johnson, Andrew, 139, 216
Johnson, Lyndon B., 137-138, 177, 180, 190, 298
  Cabinet and, 181
  domestic policies, 40, 140-141, 179, 255, 284, 290, 293
  foreign policy, 97, 175, 176, 301
  personal advisers, 185
Johnson, U. Alexis, 298
Johnson, William, 76
Johnson v. Louisiana (1972), 73
Johnson v. New Jersey (1966), 72
Johnson v. Zerbst (1938), 71
Joint Chiefs of Staff, 309
Joint resolutions, 209
Jones v. Mayer Co. (1969), 66
Judicial process, 221-227
  corrections, 226-227
  law enforcement agencies, 223-225
  prosecutors, 225-226
  See also Court system
Judicial review, principle of, 22, 31, 34-35, 242-244
Judiciary Act of 1789, 21, 35
Judiciary Act of 1801, 35
Jury trial, right to, 24, 48, 73
Justice, Department of, 51, 224, 226, 234
Juvenile justice, 236

Katzenbach v. McClung (1964), 65
Kefauver, Estes, 159, 161
Kennan, George F., 305
Kennedy, Edward M., 203, 293-294
Kennedy, John F., 76, 137, 149, 161, 180, 188, 189, 190, 255
  Cabinet and, 181
  campaign strategy, 162
  Cuban missile crisis, 170, 297-301, 303-304, 306, 310
  domestic policies, 40, 60, 140, 179, 255, 274, 275, 284
  1960 election, 91, 145, 159
  on Presidency, 167-168
Kennedy, Robert F., 297, 299, 301, 306
Kent, Frank, 123
Kentucky resolution, 60
Kerr-Mills Act of 1960, 293
Key, V. O., 98
Keyes v. School District No. 1 (1973), 62

Khrushchev, Nikita, 168, 299-301
King, Martin Luther, 140
Kirkpatrick v. Preisler (1969), 28
Kissinger, Henry A., 184, 185, 186, 306-307
Knowles, John, 111
Koenig, Louis W., 189

Labor organizations, 109
Labor unions, 153, 154, 271-273
Laird, Melvin R., 101, 185
Landrum-Griffin Act of 1958, 273
Lanham Trade Mark Act of 1964, 270
Lansing, John, 9
Law enforcement agencies, 223-225
League of Women Voters, 111
Lee, Richard Henry, 14, 15-16
Legislative courts, 231
Legislative oversight, 215-219
Legislative process, 207-212
  bills, sources and introduction of, 208-209
  committee action, 209-211
  conference action, 212
  floor action, 211-212
  presidential action, 212
Legislative Reorganization Act of 1970, 200
LeMay, Curtis, 298
Lemon v. Kurtzman (1971), 56
Letters from the Federal Farmer (Lee), 15
Leuba, Clarence, 79
Levy, Leonard W., 12
Lewis, Anthony, 45
Limited government, 30
Lincoln, Abraham, 22, 30, 168, 175, 176, 189, 217
Lippmann, Walter, 85-86
Lisagor, Peter, 285
Literacy tests, 139, 140
Litt, Edgar, 82
Little Rock, Arkansas, 60
Lobby Registration Act of 1927, 114
Lobbying, 112, 114-115
Locke, John, 29
Lodge, Henry Cabot, 148
Log rolling, 201
Los Angeles Times, 102
Louisiana ex rel. Francis v. Resweber (1947), 74
Lovett, Robert, 306
Lynn, James T., 184

MacArthur, Douglas, 87, 176
McCollum v. Board of Education (1948), 55
McCone, John, 297
McCormack, John, 192-193
McCulloch v. Maryland (1819), 36, 66
McFall, John, 203
McGovern, George, 93, 96, 97, 118-120, 159

McGovern Commission, 159
McKeiver v. *Pennsylvania* (1971), 236
Macmillan, Harold, 300
McNamara, Robert, 297-299
Mack, Ginger, 283
Mack, Richard A., 175
Madison, James, 4-7, 9-11, 13, 16, 17, 26, 30-32, 35, 36, 60, 76, 103, 122, 169, 189
Mahan v. *Howell* (1973), 28
Mahon, George, 204, 258
Mahon Amendment, 204, 219
Malloy v. *Hogan* (1964), 70, 72
Manual of Parliamentary Procedure (Jefferson), 215
Mapp, Dollree, 221-222
Mapp v. *Ohio* (1961), 69, 70, 222, 242
Marbury, William, 35
Marbury v. *Madison* (1803), 22, 35, 242
Marine Mammal Protection Act of 1972, 280
Marshall, John, 16, 21, 22, 24, 35, 36, 66
Marshall, Thurgood, 63, 73, 74
Marston v. *Lewis* (1973), 75, 144
Martin, Edward, 298
Martin, Luther, 5
Mason, George, 5, 12, 13, 14, 16
Massiah v. *United States* (1964), 72
Meat Inspection Act, 292
Media, political socialization and, 84-86
Medicaid, 293
Medicare, 293-294
Memoirs v. *Massachusetts* (1966), 52, 53
Meredith, James, 54, 60
Merhige, Robert, Jr., 62
Michels, Robert, 121
Military, 308-310
Military-industrial complex, 104, 310
Mill, John Stuart, 48-49
Miller v. *California* (1973), 53
Mills, Wilbur, 42, 201, 202, 204, 215, 291
Miranda v. *Arizona* (1966), 242
Missouri ex rel. Gaines v. *Canada* (1938), 59
Mitchell, John, 60
Mitchell v. *United States* (1941), 59
Montesquieu, Charles de Secondat, 20, 31
Montgomery, Alabama, 140
Morgan v. *Virginia* (1946), 59
Morgenthau, Hans J., 20
Mormons, 56
Morrill Act of 1862, 274
Morris, Gouverneur, 5, 11, 12, 13, 169
Morse, Wayne, 214
Morton v. *Wilderness Society* (1973), 76
Moss, Frank E., 151, 152
Moyers, Bill, 185
Moynihan, Daniel Patrick, 290
Multiparty political systems, 126-127
Mundt, Karl, 267
Murphy, Frank, 27

Muskie, Edmund S., 202, 213-214
Myers v. *United States* (1926), 175

Nader, Ralph, 104
"Nader's Raiders," 104, 200
National Aeronautics and Space Council, 188
National Association for the Advancement of Colored People (NAACP), 60, 111
National Association of Manufacturers, 108
National chairman, 129-130
National committee, 129-130
National Council of Churches, 111
National Defense Act of 1947, 309
National Defense Education Act of 1958, 294
National Education Association, 110, 111, 113, 114
National Farmers' Union, 109, 110
National Labor Relations Act of 1935, *see* Wagner Act
National Labor Relations Board, 272
National Mediation Board, 273
National Oceanic and Atmospheric Administration (NOAA), 276, 277
National Recovery Act (NRA), 287
National Security Council (NSC), 186, 302, 303, 309
Necessary and proper clause, 15
Negative income tax, 290
Neighborhood Youth Corps, 289
Neustadt, Richard E., 174, 180, 305
New Deal, 40, 91, 98, 170, 179, 243, 244, 286-287
New Jersey Plan, 8-9, 12
New York Times, 51, 87
New York Times Co. v. *United States* (1971), 51
Newman, Jon, 149
Nineteenth Amendment, 24, 142
Nitze, Paul, 298
Nixon, Richard M., 75, 86, 87, 98, 179, 190, 267, 311
  Cabinet and, 181
  economic policy, 249-251, 253-254, 256-258, 265
  education and, 295
  environmental policy, 279
  executive privilege and, 20, 218
  executive reorganization, 181, 183-185
  Family Assistance Plan, 290-291
  foreign policy, 170, 175, 176, 301-304
  funds, impoundment of, 215, 217, 243
  health care, 292, 293
  housing, 296
  1960 election, 145, 161, 162
  1968 election, 93, 97, 125, 162, 163-164
  1972 election, 118-119, 125, 152, 153, 162
  personal advisers, 185
  revenue sharing, 41-43

southern strategy, 60, 141
SST and, 100-102
as Vice-President, 188
Watergate affair, 18, 20
Noise Control Act of 1972, 280
Nominating convention, 146
Nominating process, 145-148, 157-161
Nonvoters, 145
Norris-LaGuardia Act of 1932, 272
Nurse Training Act of 1964, 293

O'Brien, David Paul, 53
O'Brien v. *Brown* (1972), 239
Obscenity, 52-53
O'Donnell, Ken, 298
Office of Consumer Affairs, 188
Office of Economic Opportunity, 40, 188, 266, 289
Office of Emergency Preparedness, 188
Office of Intergovernmental Relations, 188
Office of Management and Budget (OMB), 187, 252, 253
Office of Science and Technology, 188
Office of Telecommunications, 188
O'Hara, James, 193
Old-Age, Surviver's, and Disability Insurance (OASDI), 287
Old-Age Assistance (OAA), 288
Omnibus Crime Control and Safe Streets Act of 1968, 72
On Liberty (Mill), 48-49
One man, one vote rule, 27-28
One-party political systems, 126
Open primary, 147
Operation Breakthrough, 295
Organization of American States, 299-300
Organized crime, 229
Other America, The (Harrington), 284

Paris Adult Theater v. *Slaton* (1973), 53
Parochaid, 56
Parole, 227
Parrington, Vernon L., 268-269, 274
Parsons, Talcott, 79
Participation 70, 116-118
Participation 72, 118
Patent laws, 270
Patent Office, 230, 270
Paternalism, 268, 269, 274, 296
Paterson, William, 5, 8
Patronage, 95-96
Patton v. *United States* (1930), 73
Peace Corps, 308
Penkovskiy, Oleg, 310
Pennsylvania Gazette, 14
Pennsylvania Herald, 169

Pentagon, 178
Pentagon Papers, 51, 87
People's Republic of China, 178
Peters v. *Kiff* (1972), 73
Philips, Channing E., 93
Pinchot, Gifford, 276
Pinckney, Charles, 8
Plessy v. *Ferguson* (1896), 58
Plunkitt, George Washington, 123, 144
Poage, W. R., 203
Pocket veto, 179, 212
Police, 224-225
Political information and propaganda, political socialization and, 86-88
Political participation, 94-99
Political parties, 116-135
  birth of, 122
  criticisms of, 134-135
  development of, 22
  formal organization, 129-131
  functions of, 132-134
  informal organization, 131-132
  multiparty systems, 126-127
  nominating process, 146-148, 157-161
  one-party systems, 126
  organization, need for, 128-129
  structure of, 128-132
  third parties, 126, 148, 163
  two-party systems, 122-128
  See also names of parties
Political Parties (Michels), 121
Political socialization, 80-94
  age, 93-94
  agents of, 80-88
  aggregate socializing agents, 88-89
  church and, 83-84
  class status and, 89-91
  factors in, 89-94
  family and, 81
  political information and propaganda and, 86-88
  religion and ethnic factors, 91, 93
  residence and, 91
  school and, 81-83
Politics the American Way (Ribicoff and Newman), 149
Polk, James, 169
Pollock v. *Farmers' Loan and Trust Co.* (1895), 219
Pollution, 278-281
Popular sovereignty, 29
Populists, 126
Port of New York Authority, 38
Postal system, 270
Poverty, 40, 282-285, 289-290
Powell, Lewis F., 62, 74, 75
Powell, William A., 152-153
Powell v. *Alabama* (1932), 69, 71

Powell v. *Texas* (1968), 74
Preamble to the Constitution of the United States, 25, 29
President of the United States, 167-191
 as Chief Diplomat, 177-178, 307
 as Chief Executive, 32, 172, 174-175
 as Chief Legislator, 33, 178-180, 208, 212
 as Chief of Party, 180
 as Chief of State, 171-172
 as Commander-in-Chief, 33, 175-177, 308
 Congress and, 33-34, 217-220
 economic staff, 249-253
 foreign policy, 303-306, 311-312
 growth of office, 169
 personality and style, 189-191
 See also Executive Branch; Presidential elections
Presidential elections, 31, 157-164
 campaign, 161-162
 Electoral College, 11, 162-164
 1946, 96
 1952, 96, 125
 1960, 91, 145
 1964, 93, 96, 97
 1968, 93, 97, 98, 125, 163-164
 1972, 93, 96, 97, 118-119, 125, 127
 nomination, 157-161
Presidential Power (Neustadt), 174
President's Commission on Law Enforcement and Administration of Justice, 225, 227
Press, freedom of the, 16, 47, 48, 51-52
Pressure groups, *see* Interest groups
Primaries, 146-147, 159
Prisons, 227, 246
Privileges and immunities clause, 37-38
Probation, 226-227
Procedural rights, 48, 68-74
Process of Government, The (Bentley), 106-107
Progressive Party, 126
Prosecutors, 225-226
Proxmire, William, 100-102, 201-202, 267, 268
Public Health Service (PHS), 292-294
Public opinion, 98, 138
Public Works Administration (PWA), 287
Punishment, cruel and unusual, 48, 73-74
Pure Food and Drug Act, 292

Railroads, 271
Railway Labor Act of 1926, 272
Rampton, Calvin L., 281
Randolph, Edmund, 7, 12, 13
Randolph, Jennings, 137
Real Majority, The (Wattenberg and Scammon), 285
Reapportionment, 27-28
Reed v. *Reed* (1971), 68
Rehnquist, William H., 28, 70, 74, 75, 76

Religion
 establishment of, 54-56
 free exercise of, 56-57
 freedom of, 16, 47, 54
 political socialization and, 91, 93
Reorganization Acts, 218
Representation, 10, 26-29, 204-207
Republican government, 26-29
Republican Party, 89-91, 94-97, 112, 119, 123-125, 152-154, 158-159
Residence, political socialization and, 91
Residency requirements, 76, 143-144
Revenue sharing, 41-43, 250, 266
Reynolds v. *Sims* (1964), 28
Reynolds v. *United States* (1879), 56
Ribicoff, Abraham, 149
Rice v. *Rice* (1949), 37
Robinson v. *California* (1962), 74
Roe v. *Wade* (1973), 76
Rogers, Will, 85
Rogers, William P., 217-218
Rogers Act of 1924, 307
Romney, George, 160, 177, 295
Roosevelt, Franklin D., 168, 169, 189
 Cabinet and, 181
 domestic policies, 40, 91, 170, 179, 244, 287
 personal advisers, 185
 on Presidency, 172, 174, 180-181
Roosevelt, Theodore
 Cabinet and, 181
 conservation work, 276
 legislative programs, 179, 273
 on Presidency, 189
Rossiter, Clinton, 171
Roth v. *United States* (1957), 52, 53
Ruckelshaus, William D., 203, 276
Rural Electrification Administration, 276
Rural Environmental Assistance Program (REAP), 276
Rusk, Dean, 297
Rutledge, John, 5

Sales taxes, 260
San Antonio Independent School District v. *Rodriguez* (1973), 62-63, 76
Scalawags, 139
Scales v. *United States* (1961), 51
Scali, John, 300-301
Scammon, Richard, 285
Schenck v. *United States* (1919), 49
School, political socialization and, 81-83
School desegregation, 59-62
Scottsboro Cases, 71
Scranton, William, 160
Searches and seizures, unreasonable, 16, 47, 69-70
Second Continental Congress, 3

Secret Service, 224
Securities and Exchange Commission, 287
Segregation, 58-59
Self-incrimination, immunity from, 47, 70
Selma, Alabama, 140
Senate, 11, 196
  appointment confirmation, 217
  Appropriations Committee, 198
  Civil Service Committee, 198
  deliberation in, 214-215
  Finance Committee, 198
  Foreign Relations Committee, 198
  Judiciary Committee, 198
  officers of, 198
  See also Congress of the United States
Seniority system, 192, 199-202
Separate but equal doctrine, 58-59
Separation of powers, principle of, 18, 20, 22, 31-34
Shays, Daniel, 4, 16
Shelley v. *Kraemer* (1948), 59
Sherman, Roger, 5, 8
Sherman Anti-Trust Act of 1890, 271-272
Sherrill, Robert, 200, 214
Shriver, Sargent, 129
Shultz, George P., 184
Silent Spring (Carson), 278
Simon, William E., 281
Simple resolutions, 209
Sirica, John J., 19
Sisk, Bernie, 193
Sixteenth Amendment, 219
Sixth Amendment, 47-48, 69, 71-72
Slavery, 8, 10
Small Business Administration, 270
Smith, Adam, 259
Smith, Howard, 199
Smith, J. Allen, 6
Smith, Margaret Chase, 101, 102
Smith Act, 50, 51
Smith v. *Allwright* (1944), 140
Social insurance taxes, 250, 261
Social Security Act of 1935, 98, 287
Socialization, 79-80
Soft veto, 179
Soil Conservation Act, 274
Solid Waste Disposal Act of 1965, 280
Sorensen, Theodore, 298, 301, 306
SOUP (Students Opposed to Unfair Practices), 105
South Carolina v. *Katzenbach* (1966), 65, 141
Southern strategy, 60, 141
Special Action Group (SAG), 302
Special Action Office for Drug Abuse Prevention, 188
Special Representative for Trade Negotiations, 188

Speech, freedom of, 47, 48-51
Spellman, Francis, 55
Spirit of American Government (Smith), 6
Spirit of the Laws (Montesquieu), 20
Standard Oil of California, 107, 112
Standards, Bureau of, 270
Stanley v. *Georgia* (1969), 53
Stanton, Elizabeth Cady, 141
State, Department of, 172, 178, 181, 307, 311
State central committees, 130, 159
State conventions, 159
State court system, 234-236
  courts of appeal, 235
  supreme courts, 235-236
  trial courts, 234-235
State legislatures, 220
Stevenson, Adlai, 159, 161, 298, 306
Stewart, Potter, 51, 52, 62, 66, 73, 74, 75
Stokes, Carl, 278
Stone, Harlan F., 244
Story, Joseph, 76
Strauder v. *West Virginia* (1880), 73
Strauss, Robert S., 129
Street v. *New York* (1969), 53, 54
Student political activity, 116-118
Student Transportation Moratorium Act, 61
Substantive rights, 48
Suffrage
  black, 139-141
  universal, struggle for, 138-143
  women's, 141-143
  See also Voting
Supersonic transport plane (SST), 87, 100-103
Supremacy clause, 5, 12, 15, 22, 26
Supreme Court of the United States, 231-232
  abortion cases, 76
  apportionment cases, 27-28
  bad tendency doctrine, 50
  busing, 61-62
  capital punishment, 74
  civil rights acts, support of, 65-66
  clear and present danger doctrine, 49
  congressional oversight, 219
  counsel, right to, 45-46, 71-72, 243
  cruel and unusual punishment, 73-74
  divorce decrees, 37
  double jeopardy, 70
  interstate rendition, 38
  judicial review, 35, 242-244
  jury procedure, 72-73
  juvenile justice, 236
  obscenity, 52-53
  powers, 22, 33, 34
  presidential appointment powers, 75
  press, freedom of the, 51-52
  procedure, 239-241
  religion, establishment of, 56-57

Supreme Court of the United States (cont.)
  religion, free exercise of, 56-57
  residency requirements, 75, 143
  school desegregation, 59-62
  searches and seizures, 69-70, 222
  self-incrimination, immunity from, 70
  separate but equal doctrine, 58-59
  speech, freedom of, 49-51
  symbolic speech, 53-54
  terms, 239
  voting age, 138
  voting rights, 140, 141
Supreme courts, state, 235-236
Survey Research Center of the University of Michigan, 91, 94
Sutherland, Edwin H., 229
Sutherland, George, 71
Swann v. Charlotte-Mecklenburg Board of Education (1971), 61, 219
Sweeney, Walter C., Jr., 299
Symbolic speech, 53-54

Taft, Robert A., 160
Taft, William Howard, 189
Taft-Hartley Act of 1947, 109, 152, 172
Talmadge, Eugene, 136
Tariffs, 23
Taxation, 11, 259-261
Taylor, Maxwell, 298
Taylor, Zachary, 124
Tea Pot Dome scandal, 180
Television, 84-86, 170
Tennessee Valley Authority, 276
Terminiello v. Chicago (1949), 49-50
Third parties, 126, 148, 163
Thirteen Days (Neustadt and Allison), 305
Thirteenth Amendment, 24, 48, 66, 93, 139
Thompson, Llewellyn, 298
Thurmond, James Strom, 120
Tilden, Samuel J., 145
Tinker v. Des Moines School District (1969), 54
Torney, Judith V., 82
Toward a More Responsible Two-Party System (Committee on Political Parties), 135
Tower, John, 267
Trade associations, 107
Trademarks, 270
Transportation, 58, 59, 270-271
Transportation, Department of, 184, 271
Treasury, Department of the, 172, 224, 311
Trial courts, 234-235
Trop v. Dulles (1958), 74
Truman, David, 103, 107, 120
Truman, Harry S., 87, 159, 161, 169-170, 176, 188, 243, 272
  Cabinet and, 181
  domestic policies, 63, 179, 293
  foreign policy, 175, 176
  on Presidency, 172, 174
Tweed Ring, 123
Twenty-fifth Amendment, 181, 188
Twenty-first Amendment, 21
Twenty-sixth Amendment, 24, 136-138
Twenty-third Amendment, 143
Two-party political system, 122-128

Udall, Morris, 192-193, 196, 207
Udall, Stewart, 192
Unemployment, 256
Uniform Crime Reports for the United States (FBI), 227
Union of Soviet Socialist Republics, 178
United States Chamber of Commerce, 108
United States Information Agency (USIA), 308
United States Steel, 112
United States v. Curtiss-Wright Export Corporation (1936), 178
United States v. O'Brien (1968), 53
United States v. Robinson, 70
Unsafe at Any Speed (Nader), 104
Upward Bound, 289
Urban renewal, 296

Vandenberg, Arthur, 137
Veterans Administration, 295
Veto, 179, 212
Viavant, William, 117
Vice-President, 188-189, 198
Vietnam War, 97, 98, 175-176, 255, 301-302
Virginia Plan, 7-9, 12
Virginia resolution, 60
Virginia v. Rives (1880), 73
Volunteers in Service to America (VISTA), 289-290
Voting
  age, 136-138, 144
  apathy, 118
  nonvoters, 145
  registration, 144
  residency requirements, 143-144
  state restrictions on, 143-144
  See also Suffrage
Voting machines, 156-157
Voting Rights Act of 1965, 65, 140-141

Wage-price-rent freeze, 256-258
Wagner Act, 109, 272-273
Wald, Patricia M., 225
Wallace, George, 93, 163-164
War, Department of, 172
War on Poverty, 40, 284-285, 289-290
Warren, Earl, 53, 59, 66, 72, 76
Washington, George, 4-7, 16, 17, 168, 175, 189, 217

Washington Post, 51, 215
Water Pollution Control Act of 1965, 280
Water Quality Improvement Act of 1970, 279
Watergate affair, 18-20, 155, 156, 180, 203
Watergate Committee, 19, 153
Wattenberg, Ben, 285
Wealth of Nations (Smith), 259
Weather Bureau, 270
Webster, Daniel, 213
Weeks v. *United States* (1914), 69
Weinberger, Caspar W., 184
Welfare system, 282-292
  AFDC, 288
  background of, 285
  education, 294-295
  Family Assistance Plan, 290-292
  health services, 292-294
  housing and urban renewal, 295-296
  myths surrounding, 288
  New Deal programs, 286-287
  Social Security Act of 1935, 287-288
  war on poverty, 289-290
Wesberry v. *Sanders* (1964), 28
West Virginia Board of Education v. *Barnette* (1943), 57
Western Oil and Gas Association, 107
Westwood, Jean, 129
Whigs, 124
White, Byron, 51-53, 66, 73-76
White House Office, 185-186

White primary laws, 140
White supremacy, 58
White-collar crime, 229
Whitney, Eli, 100
Whitten, Jamie, 203
Wide-open primary, 147
Williams v. *Florida* (1971), 73
Wilson, Don, 298
Wilson, James, 5, 8, 13, 169
Wilson, T.A., 101
Wilson, Woodrow, 124, 141, 169, 178, 189, 197, 198
  Cabinet and, 181
  legislative programs, 179
  personal advisers, 185
Wilson-Gorman Tariff Act of 1894, 219
Wisconsin v. *Yoder* (1972), 57
Wolf v. *Colorado* (1949), 69
Women's Liberation Movement, 67
Women's suffrage, 141-143
Works Progress Administration (WPA), 286-287
World Health Organization (WHO), 306

Yates v. *United States* (1957), 51
Young, Stephen M., 206
Youngstown Sheet and Tube Co. v. *Sawyer* (1952), 243

Zorach v. *Clauson* (1952), 55

ADDENDUM

Budget (1976), 258–266
Budget and Impoundment Act of 1974, 253
Cambodia, 304
Congressional Budget Office (CBO), 253
Ford, Gerald R., 189
Khmer Rouge, 304
Lon Nol, 304
Mayaguez, 304
Rockefeller, Nelson, 189
Southeast Asia, 304
Supplemental Security Income program, 288
U.S. v. *Nixon*, 189
Vietnam, 304